PENTATEUCH, HEXATEUCH, OR ENNEATEUCH?

Society of Biblical Literature

Ancient Israel and Its Literature

Steven L. McKenzie, General Editor

Number 8

PENTATEUCH, HEXATEUCH, OR ENNEATEUCH?
Identifying Literary Works in Genesis through Kings

PENTATEUCH, HEXATEUCH, OR ENNEATEUCH?

Identifying Literary Works in Genesis through Kings

edited by

Thomas B. Dozeman
Thomas Römer
Konrad Schmid

Society of Biblical Literature
Atlanta

PENTATEUCH, HEXATEUCH, OR ENNEATEUCH?
Identifying Literary Works in Genesis through Kings

Library of Congress Cataloging-in-Publication Data

Pentateuch, Hexateuch, or Enneateuch : identifying literary works in Genesis through Kings / edited by Thomas Dozeman, Thomas Römer, and Konrad Schmid.
    p. cm. — (Society of Biblical Literature : ancient Israel and its literature ; v. 8)
    Includes bibliographical references and index.
    ISBN 978-1-58983-542-9 (paper binding : alk. paper) — ISBN 978-1-58983-543-6 (electronic format)
    1. Bible. O.T. Pentateuch—Criticism, interpretation, etc. 2. Bible. O.T. Former Prophets—Criticism, interpretation, etc. I. Dozeman, Thomas B. II. Römer, Thomas, 1955- III. Schmid, Konrad, 1965- IV. Society of Biblical Literature. V. Title. VI. Series.
    BS1225.52.P465 2011
    222'.06—dc22

                                                                    2011008513

Typeset by Upper Case Textual Services
www.uppercasetext.com

Contents

METHODOLOGICAL STUDIES

CASE STUDIES

ABBREVIATIONS

AASF	Annales Academiae scientiarum fennicae
AB	Anchor Bible
ABD	*Anchor Bible Dictionary.* Ed. D. N. Freedman. 6 vols. New York: Doubleday, 1992
ABR	*Australian Biblical Review*
ABRL	Anchor Bible Reference Library
AOAT	Alter Orient und Altes Testament
ATANT	Abhandlungen zur Theologie des Alten und Neuen Testaments
ATD	Das Alte Testament Deutsch
ATJ	*Ashland Theological Journal*
BBB	Bonner biblische Beiträge
BBET	Beiträge zur biblischen Exegese und Theologie
BEATAJ	Beiträge zur Erforschung des Alten Testaments und des antiken Judentum
BETL	Bibliotheca ephemeridum theologicarum lovaniensium
Bib	*Biblica*
BIOSCS	*Bulletin of the International Organization for Septuagint and Cognate Studies*
BJS	Brown Judaic Studies
BKAT	Biblischer Kommentar. Altes Testament. Edited by M. Noth and H. W. Wolff
BN	*Biblische Notizen*
BWAT	Beiträge zur Wissenschaft vom Alten Testament
BWANT	Beiträge zur Wissenschaft vom Alten und Neuen Testament
BZABR	Beihefte der Zeitschrift für altorientalische und biblische Rechtgeschichte
BZAW	Beihefte zur Zeitschrift für die alttestamentliche Wissenschaft
CBET	Contributions to Biblical Exegesis and Theology
CBQ	*Catholic Biblical Quarterly*
ConBOT	Coniectanea biblica: Old Testament Series

DDD	*Dictionary of Deities and Demons in the Bible.* Edited by K. van der Toorn, B. Becking, and P. W. van der Horst. Leiden: Brill, 1995
DJD	Discoveries in the Judaean Desert
DSD	*Dead Sea Discoveries*
EdF	Erträge der Forschung
ErIsr	*Eretz-Israel*
ETL	*Ephemerides theologicae lovanienses*
ETR	*Etudes théologiques et religieuses*
EvQ	*Evangelical Quarterly*
EvT	*Evangelische Theologie*
FAT	Forschungen zum Alten Testament
FB	Forschung zur Bibel
FOTL	Forms of the Old Testament Literature
FRLANT	Forschungen zur Religion und Literatur des Alten und Neuen Testaments
GAT	Grundrisse zum Alten Testament
HAR	*Hebrew Annual Review*
HAT	Handbuch zum Alten Testament
HCOT	Historical Commentary on the Old Testament
HKAT	Handkommentar zum Alten Testament
HSM	Harvard Semitic Monographs
HSS	Harvard Semitic Studies
HTKAT	Herders theologischer Kommentar zum Alten Testament
HTR	*Harvard Theological Review*
HUCA	*Hebrew Union College Annual*
IBS	*Irish Biblical Studies*
ICC	International Critical Commentary
IDB	*The Interpreter's Dictionary of the Bible.* Edited by G. A. Buttrick. 4 vols. Nashville, 1962
Int	*Interpretation*
JBL	*Journal of Biblical Literature*
JBTh	Jahrbuch für Biblische Theologie
JETS	*Journal of the Evangelical Theological Society*
JJS	*Journal of Jewish Studies*
JRH	*Journal of Religious History*
JSOT	*Journal for the Study of the Old Testament*
JSOTSup	Journal for the Study of the Old Testament Supplement Series
JTS	*Journal of Theological Studies*

KAI	*Kanaanäische und aramäische Inschriften.* H. Donner and W. Röllig. 3 vols. 2d ed. Wiesbaden: Harrassowitz, 1966–1969; 5th ed (vol. 1), 2002
KAT	Kommentar zum Alten Testament
KHC	Kurzer Hand-Commentar zum Alten Testament
LHB	Library of Hebrew Bible
MdB	Le Monde de la Bible
NICOT	New International Commentary on the Old Testament
OBO	Orbis biblicus et orientalis
OBT	Overtures to Biblical Theology
Or	*Orientalia* (NS)
OTL	Old Testament Library
OTS	Old Testament Studies
OtSt	Oudtestamentische Studiën
RB	*Revue biblique*
RelSRev	*Religious Studies Review*
RevQ	*Revue de Qumrân*
SAA	State Archives of Assyria
SBAB	Stuttgarter biblische Aufsatzbände
SBLDS	Society of Biblical Literature Dissertation Series
SBLMS	Society of Biblical Literature Monograph Series
SBLSCS	Society of Biblical Literature Septuagint and Cognate Studies
SBLSS	Society of Biblical Literature Semeia Studies
SBLSymS	Society of Biblical Literature Symposium Series
SBLWAW	Society of Biblical Literature Writings from the Ancient World
SBS	Stuttgarter Bibelstudien
SBT	Studies in Biblical Theology
SFSHJ	South Florida Studies in the History of Judaism
SJOT	*Scandinavian Journal of the Old Testament*
SOTSMS	Society for Old Testament Studies Monograph Series
STDJ	Studies on the Texts of the Desert of Judah
TB	Theologische Bücherei: Neudrucke und Berichte aus dem 20. Jahrhundert
TCS	Texts from Cuneiform Sources
ThW	Theologische Wissenschaft
TRu	*Theologische Rundshau*
TSK	*Theologische Studien und Kritiken*
UF	*Ugarit-Forschungen*
VAB	Vorderasiatische Bibliothek
VF	*Verkündigung und Forschung*

VT	*Vetus Testamentum*
VTSup	Supplements to Vetus Testamentum
WBC	Word Biblical Commentary
WdF	Wege der Forschung
WMANT	Wissenschaftliche Monographien zum Alten und Neuen Testament
WUNT	Wissenschaftliche Untersuchungen zum Neuen Testament
ZA	*Zeitschrift für Assyriologie*
ZABR	*Zeitschrift für altorientalische und biblische Rechtgeschichte*
ZAH	*Zeitschrift für Althebräistik*
ZAW	*Zeitschrift für die alttestamentliche Wissenschaft*
ZBK	Zürcher Bibelkommentare
ZTK	*Zeitschrift für Theologie und Kirche*

INTRODUCTION

The identification of literary works in the Pentateuch and the Former Prophets is a hallmark of the modern historical-critical interpretation of the Hebrew Bible. B. de Spinoza rejected the Mosaic authorship of the Pentateuch in part through his identification of a literary Enneateuch, which he suspected was written by Ezra.[1] The identification of a Hexateuch by source critics provided the literary context for identifying the authors of the separate documents, J, E, and P, who were thought to tell a narrative in which the promise of the land at the beginning of the story was fulfilled by the conquest of the land in Joshua. In the same way, the separation of the books from Genesis through Kings into a Tetrateuch (Genesis–Numbers) and a Deuteronomistic History (Deuteronomy–Kings) supported Martin Noth's detection of the exilic Deuteronomistic historian.[2] In each case, the identification of literary works was linked to theories about the literary history of the Pentateuch and the Former Prophets.

The breakdown of both source criticism and the tradition-historical approach of Martin Noth in more recent interpretations of the Pentateuch and the Former Prophets has forced scholars to reevaluate the criteria for identifying literary works in the formation of the Hebrew Bible. The emergence of redaction criticism has intensified the problem of defining the boundaries of literary works, since this model of composition attributes a more formative role to editors, now seen as the authors of literary works, than is the case in either source criticism, where the focus is on the source documents J, E, and P, or in tradition history, where the Tetrateuch and the Deuteronomistic History are identified as separate "blocks," themselves in turn constructed of formerly oral or written thematic units. The most recent redaction-critical contributions concerning the composition of the Pentateuch and the Former Prophets demonstrate that it is no longer possible to interpret these bodies

---

1. Benedict de Spinoza, *A Theologico-Political Treatise and, A Political Treatise* (trans. R. H. M. Elwes; New York: Dover, 1951), 7 et passim.

2. Martin Noth, *The Deuteronomistic History* (trans. J. Doull et al.; JSOTSup 15; Sheffield: University of Sheffield Press, 1981; 2d ed., 1991); trans. of *Überlieferungsgeschichtliche Studien: Die sammelnden und bearbeitenden Geschichtswerke im Alten Testament* (Halle: Niemeyer Verlag, 1943; repr. Darmstadt: Wissenschaftliche Buchgesellschaft, 1967); ibid., *Josua* (HAT 7; Tübingen: J. C. B. Mohr [Paul Siebeck], 1971).

of literature as though they were separate and independent literary works. At the same time, these studies also raise new problems in determining what criteria are important for identifying a literary work in the composition of the Pentateuch and the Former Prophets. When, for example, is a redaction part of a larger programmatic composition and when is it simply an isolated addition; how does a redactional composition influence the identification of more traditional sources; how does the emergence of separate books relate to larger redactional compositions? Are we able to detect literary strategies that indicate the beginnings and endings of formerly "independent" literary works within Genesis–Kings? And, finally, if we read Genesis–Kings as a unified literary Enneateuch, does 2 Kgs 25 present an adequate ending? The canonical shape of the Hebrew Bible suggests that this is not the case.

The present volume is intended to explore anew the composition history of the Pentateuch and the Former Prophets without either presupposing the classical theories of the sources—"JEDP" and the Deuteronomistic History, "DtrH"—or excluding them. The nature of the volume is therefore exploratory and open-ended. The papers are the fruit of a two-year consultation, in 2007–8, between the Pentateuch Section and the Deuteronomistic History Section of the Society of Biblical Literature, during which members from each group shared research on the central question of how to identify literary works in the Pentateuch and the Former Prophets. We have organized the articles into two sections. The first comprises a series of essays on the broad methodological problems of identifying literary works in the Pentateuch and the Former Prophets. The second section is made up of case studies, in which authors explore a variety of different literary relationships between the Pentateuch and the Former Prophets.

THE METHODOLOGICAL STUDIES

The discussion of the appropriate methodology for identifying literary works in Genesis through Kings is wide-ranging and open-ended. The articles gathered in this section explore a variety of methodologies, while often concluding their essays with probing question that invite further research. Konrad Schmid reviews the history of scholarship that has led to the dominant view of the late twentieth century that the Tetrateuch/Pentateuch is a distinct literary work from the Deuteronomistic History. The essays of Thomas Römer and Erhard Blum explore in different ways the problem of how interpreters determine what compositional and literary features provide evidence for identifying a literary work. David Carr broadens the lens by suggesting a more empirical comparison of Chronicles and Samuel–Kings as a springboard to evaluating the relationship between the Pentateuch and the

Former Prophets throughout their history of composition. These essays on methodology can be summarized in the following manner.

Konrad Schmid, in "The Emergence and Disappearance of the Separation between the Pentateuch and the Deuteronomistic History in Biblical Studies," analyzes the history of research that has resulted in the scholarly separation of the Pentateuch (in fact, the Tetrateuch) from the Deuteronomistic History, in the interpretation of Genesis through Kings. He reviews, in particular, the pivotal research of Martin Noth, who advanced two related arguments that have influenced the identification of literary works in contemporary scholarship: namely, the absence of the traditional sources J, E, and P in the book of Joshua, on the one hand; and the lack of Deuteronomistic editing in the Tetrateuch, on the other. The result has been the clear literary separation of the Tetrateuch from the Deuteronomistic History. This strict separation was further strengthened by the scholarly compromise between Gerhard von Rad and Martin Noth that allowed the model of the Hexateuch and the model of the Deuteronomistic History to coexist throughout the twentieth century, even though the two models were not really compatible with one another. Finally, Schmid traces the breakdown of both theories in current research, which has led to proposals of new literary works that combine the Pentateuch and the Former Prophets in a variety of different ways within the larger literary framework of the Enneateuch.

Thomas Römer, in "How Many Books (*teuchs*): Pentateuch, Hexateuch, Deuteronomistic History, or Enneateuch?" notes the recent shift in scholarly interest from recovering the oldest literary sources in the Pentateuch and Former Prophets to identifying the latest redactions that have shaped that literature. He notes that the change in focus is accompanied by an interest in the question of how major literary works were formed and whether they may be identified. Römer explores the past and present arguments for the existence of the Hexateuch, the Deuteronomistic History, and the Enneateuch, noting how the explanations for different literary works are tied to distinct models of the formation of the Hebrew Bible. After taking the reader through a range of recent proposals on the identification of the Pentateuch, Hexateuch or Enneateuch, Römer concludes by exploring three important questions for recognizing literary works in the Pentateuch and Former Prophets: First, what are the criteria for identifying the beginnings and endings of literary works? Second, how were scrolls produced and stored in the Second Temple period, and what insight does this provide towards identifying literary works? And, third, how can a researcher control the methodology of redaction criticism in order to distinguish comprehensive editorial revisions that are related to the formation of literary works from more limited additions to specific texts?

Erhard Blum, in "Pentateuch–Hexateuch–Enneateuch? Or: How Can One Recognize a Literary Work in the Hebrew Bible?" begins his article with the truism that "in order to understand a text, one must know where it begins and ends." The remainder of the article, however, illustrates just how difficult it is to identify beginnings and endings of literary works in the Pentateuch and Former Prophets, and how the answers to these questions depend on many factors beyond the text itself. Blum explores a variety of literary and thematic links that connect the books of Genesis through Kings, while also distinguishing the Pentateuch as the Torah of Moses. He concludes that this simultaneity of independence and continuity is, in fact, an essential structural element of the written canon. This variety of literary relationships between books gives rise to a methodological problem, noted also by Römer: How is the interpreter able to determine when inner-canonical links represent merely *intertextual* repetition of motifs between books, and when they indicate more programmatic *intratextual* redaction, wherein the compositional repetitions are intended to create a literary work? Blum applies the distinction between inter- and intratextual repetitions to the recent studies by E. Aurelius and R. Kratz, before going on to explore the function of the internal (*autoreferenza*) references to the "Torah" within the Pentateuch as an indicator of a literary work.

David M. Carr, in "'Empirical' Comparison and the Analysis of the Relationship of the Pentateuch and the Former Prophets," moves the methodological problem of recognizing literary works in the Pentateuch and the Former Prophets in a different direction. Rather than exploring the internal literary relationships between the Pentateuch and the Former Prophets, which is the focus of the studies by Blum and Römer, he compares the overlapping historical narratives in Samuel–Kings and Chronicles for clues that may provide insight into the relationship between the Pentateuch and the Former Prophets. Building on the research of Jeffrey Tigay, Carr defines this approach as "empirical," which he characterizes as a sustained focus on the comparison of documents from the ancient Near East, in order to understand the growth of texts. The empirical comparison yields insights concerning three factors in the growth of texts that may assist in interpreting the relationship of the Pentateuch and the Former Prophets: first, an oral-written dynamic in transmission; second, a trend toward expansion and harmonization in the transmission of tradition; and, third, at least in the sections where Chronicles and Samuel–Kings overlap, indications that the author of Chronicles was likely using an earlier form of Samuel–Kings. When these insights are applied to a study of the relationship between the Pentateuch and the Former Prophets, Carr suggests that they may also "provide additional evidence of authorial work that binds the Torah to the Former Prophets, 'harmonizing' the one with the other in ways consonant with modes used in many other examples of documented growth of ancient tradition."

The Case Studies

The broader methodological essays are complemented by case studies, in which authors explore the literary relationship between the Pentateuch and the Former Prophets though the interpretation of specific texts. The essays are wide-ranging and explorative in nature. The topics include: the P source and supports for the identification of a literary Hexateuch; the emergence of the nine books of the Enneateuch from more comprehensive redactions; the function of Gen 2–4 and 2 Kgs 24–25 as a framing device in the creation of an Enneateuch; the literary relationship between the story of the golden calf of Exod 32 and the calves of Jeroboam in 1 Kgs 12; the relationship between the sequence of intercessions by Moses in Exod 32–34 and the enneateuchal literature; the distinct literary function of Joshua in the MT and the LXX canons; the question of the literary connections between the story of the Egyptian bondage in Exod 1–15 and that of the forced labor of Solomon in 1 Kgs 1–12; and the arguments against the Deuteronomistic History hypothesis that emerge from the interpretation of the judgment speeches in 1 and 2 Kings.

Suzanne Boorer, in "The Envisioning of the Land in the Priestly Material: Fulfilled Promise or Future Hope?" addresses the long-debated issue of whether there is Priestly material in the book of Joshua; and, if so, whether it represents a literary source or a redaction. Boorer reviews past arguments in favor of interpreting the Priestly source as ending in Joshua, so as to create a literary Hexateuch. She focuses in particular on the most debated texts, which include Josh 4:19; 5:10–12; 14:1–2*; 18:1; and 19:51. Boorer argues that, although there is some similarity in style, these texts contrast with the Priestly source in Genesis–Numbers. She concludes from this that the P source lacks the theme of the fulfillment of the promise of the land and, instead, pictures its future realization. According to Boorer, "it might be imagined that later redactors are responsible for the P-like texts in Joshua, perhaps in an attempt to align the return to the land in postexilic times with Pg's vision and perhaps in this way at some stage to represent an attempt to formulate a Hexateuch."

Christoph Levin, in "On the Cohesion and Separation of Books within the Enneateuch," begins his essay by noting the literary problem that confronts any reading of the Enneateuch, which is that "the great biblical work contained in the books of Genesis to Kings constitutes a continuous unit"; and yet, it is "obvious that the Enneateuch is a collection, which brings together diverse material." How does the interpreter account for these two literary facts in evaluating the coherent story of creation to exile and the present division of the nine individual books of the Enneateuch? The question is complicated by the limited size of ancient scrolls, which could not possibly accommodate the whole text of Genesis to 2 Kings. Levin's essay explores a process of growth by which the early redactional versions of the tradition, such as the exilic Yahwist narrative, or the Deuteronomistic History, were separated secondarily into distinct scrolls or books as the tradition grew. Levin evaluates the diverse criteria by which the original redactions were broken into separate scrolls by interpreting the caesurae between Samuel and Kings, Judges and Samuel, Joshua and Judges, Deuteronomy and Joshua, Genesis and Exodus, Exodus and Leviticus, Leviticus and Numbers, and finally Numbers and Deuteronomy. He concludes that the narrative coherence of the material is based on the unity of the first redactions and that the fact that the Enneateuch was separated into nine books was due to the technical requirement of the scrolls. This hypothesis leaves no room for an original Hexateuch, a work comprising Exodus to Joshua, a narrative consisting of Deuteronomy and Joshua, or a Deuteronomistic History composed only of the books of Samuel and Kings.

Cynthia Edenburg, in "From Eden to Babylon: Reading Gen 2–4 as a Paradigmatic Narrative," begins with a careful literary comparison of the stories of Eden and Cain. She finds that the stories exhibit the same structure and similar language, which leads her to the conclusion that together the stories deal with two different types of tests, the failure of which leads in each case to exile and alienation. Edenburg proposes that "the purpose of the two stories is to establish an exemplar for the pattern carried out in the rest of the biblical narrative," for which the thematic *inclusio* is the description of the Babylonian conquest and exile in 2 Kgs 24:1–25:21. This *inclusio* that thus brackets the "Primary History" raises the methodological question of how to determine whether the repetition "signifies that Genesis to Kings were conceived as a compositional unit or Enneateuch?" Edenburg seeks an answer to the question by reviewing research on the production of scrolls; the concept of the "book" in the ancient world; recent theories on the independent composition of the primeval history; and the "block" paradigm for understanding the composition of the Pentateuch.

Michael Konkel, in "Exod 32–34 and the Quest for an Enneateuch," explores whether literary connections between Exod 32–34 and Genesis through 2 Kings support the identification of an Enneateuch. Konkel focuses on three intercessions of Moses in Exodus 32–34: (1) at the summit of Mount Sinai during the worship of the golden calf (Exod 32:11–13); (2) at the base of the mountain after the destruction of the golden calf and the tablets (Exod 32:31–32); and (3) after the extended dialogue between Moses and the Deity in Exod 33 (Exod 34:8–9). Konkel explores the innerbiblical ties between these three texts and Genesis through 2 Kings from two methodological perspectives. First, he investigates the innerbiblical links through the synchronic study of a range of specific texts (e.g., Exod 32:2, 8, 10, 12, 13, 26–29; 33:1–13, 4–6, 8–9) that indicate literary connections throughout Genesis–2 Kings (e.g., Gen 6:7–8; 12:2, 7; 13:14–17; 17; 22:17; Deut 33:8–11; 34:4; Judg 2:1–5; and

1 Kgs 12:28; 2 Kgs 23:26; 24:3–4). Second, he applies a diachronic analysis to four texts (Exod 32:7–14; 32:26–29; 33:1–11; 34:8–10) that are often attributed to a late Deuteronomistic redaction. Konkel concludes that the texts represent the work of a single author, who is combining both Priestly and Deuteronomistic material. Such an identification of authorship could support the view that the redactor is working within the literary framework of the Enneateuch, but Konkel concludes that no such literary work can be identified. Instead, the intertextual references between Exod 32–34 and Kings actually support the notion of the separation of the Pentateuch from the Former Prophets.

Thomas Dozeman, in "The Book of Joshua as an Intertext in the MT and the LXX Canons," begins his study by noting the pivotal role of the book of Joshua for identifying literary works, because of its central location as an intertext between the Pentateuch and the Former Prophets. A. Kuenen and J. Wellhausen located the conclusion of the pentateuchal narrative in Joshua's fulfillment of the promise of land, thus conceptualizing the Hexateuch; while Martin Noth detached the composition of Joshua from these sources, proposing instead the existence of two distinct literary works: the Tetrateuch and the Deuteronomistic History. The ambiguity over the appropriate context for interpreting Joshua, illustrated by Wellhausen and Noth, intensified with the emergence of redaction criticism, according to Dozeman; this resulted in part from divergent views concerning the final form of Joshua, which in turn influenced the understanding of the redactor's literary horizon as the basis for identifying the larger literary work. Dozeman notes that the problem of determining the final form of Joshua is compounded by the significantly different versions of the book in the MT and the LXX canons, where Joshua is also related differently to the Pentateuch and the Former Prophets. The study underscores that the redaction-critical approach must determine which final form of Joshua will be the starting point for interpreting the composition of the book, since this decision will influence the identification of the literary works—Pentateuch, Hexateuch, Enneateuch, or Deuteronomistic History.

Christoph Berner, in "The Egyptian Bondage and Solomon's Forced Labor: Literary Connections Between Exod 1–15 and 1 Kgs 1–12?" examines the parallel motifs and similar narrative traits in the story of the exodus and that of the forced labor of Solomon, which led to the revolt of Jeroboam. Do these correspondences denote an original literary Enneateuch, or are the parallels simply later literary allusions to the Exodus in the story of Solomon? Berner concludes that the literary evidence for both motifs is more complex than is widely held, and that a unified picture of the Egyptian bondage and of Solomon's forced labor does not exist. Instead, both texts exhibit a complex literary development, in which both stories developed independently. Berner therefore concludes that "there is not one single instance in which it could be demonstrated that one of the passages in Exodus and 1 Kings pertaining to the topic of servitude was composed in light of an enneateuchal intertext."

Felipe Blanco Wißmann, in "'He Did What was Right': Criteria of Judgment and Deuteronomism in the Books of Kings," examines the judgment texts in the books of Kings—texts in which prophets, kings, or the Deity are presented as evaluating the actions of rulers. The speeches in these texts are intended to provide interpretations of the narrative, according to Wissmann, and thus express the authors' or redactors' views of history and theology, termed "historiosophy," which provides a means for interpreting the literary origin and history of composition of the books of Kings. A comparison of the judgment speeches to nonbiblical texts suggests that the earliest forms of the speeches come from the Neo-Assyrian period, when Judean scribes used elements of Assyrian royal ideology to create the *Urdeuteronomium*, which was intended to function in a "subversive manner." A more detailed interpretation of central features of the judgment speeches—including the motifs of doing right or evil in the eyes of Yнwн, the fathers, the high place, foreign gods, the sin of Jeroboam, or the law—indicates that the judgment formulas in Kings do not derive from Deuteronomy and that Deuteronomy was not part of the same literary entity as Kings; thus, this analysis calls into question the Deuteronomistic History hypothesis. Blanco Wissmann concludes, instead, that "the literary context of the books of Kings within the history of biblical theology should be the place that it acquired already in the Jewish canonical tradition of the Tanakh: among the prophets."

This overview already indicates the diversity of approaches represented here; it is our hope that the essays in this volume will provide a resource for further research on the important and central question of how we identify literary works in the composition of the Pentateuch and the Former Prophets. While this volume does not argue for one specific model in order to explain the formation of Genesis–Kings, it nevertheless points out that the traditional delimitations or identifications of "J," "E," "D," and "P," and the strict separation between Tetrateuch and Deuteronomistic History, can no longer be taken for granted. The traditional divisions may be supported to some extent by further research, but there may also emerge a clear need to abandon at least some of these assumptions to gain a plausible image of the literary growth of Genesis–Kings.

Thomas B. Dozeman
Thomas Römer
Konrad Schmid

METHODOLOGICAL STUDIES

THE EMERGENCE AND DISAPPEARANCE OF THE SEPARATION BETWEEN THE PENTATEUCH AND THE DEUTERONOMISTIC HISTORY IN BIBLICAL STUDIES

Konrad Schmid

The aim of this article is to review the history of scholarship that led to the separation of the Pentateuch from the Deuteronomistic History in biblical studies. While the material presented here is not necessarily new, it may be helpful to provide a close reading of the main arguments in the history of scholarship and to highlight the inner dynamics of the debate. In the twentieth century one person in particular has enduringly influenced the literary evaluation of the relationship between the Pentateuch and the Deuteronomistic History—Martin Noth. When Noth died in 1968, Rudolf Smend wrote in his obituary: "In a broader sense, most present day Old Testament scholars are, to some extent, his students."[1] Smend is probably correct in this conclusion. It is, however, another question, whether these scholars were right to follow in Noth's path.

The fact that the quasi-canonical status of Noth's theory of the Deuteronomistic History continues in Old Testament scholarship into the present can be demonstrated by looking at recent introductions to the Old Testament. For example, in John J. Collins's, *Introduction to the Hebrew Bible*,[2] four main headings organize the Old Testament canon:

> Part One: The Torah/Pentateuch
> Part Two: The Deuteronomistic History
> Part Three: Prophecy
> Part Four: The Writings

---

1. Rudolf Smend, "Nachruf auf Martin Noth," in Noth, *Gesammelte Studien zum Alten Testament 2* (TB 39; Munich: Kaiser, 1969), 114: "In einem weiteren Sinn sind heute die meisten Alttestamentler ein wenig seine Schüler." All translations mine unless otherwise indicated.

2. Collins, *Introduction to the Hebrew Bible* (Minneapolis: Fortress, 2004), v–vi.

There is one major difference between the Jewish biblical canon and the structure of this introduction: the books Joshua through Kings are not called the "Former Prophets," according to their canonical designation, but "The Deuteronomistic History"—an indication that the influence of Martin Noth's thesis on contemporary biblical scholarship is so strong that his description of the Former Prophets has come to function as a deuterocanonical term for the same text block.

The four-part organization of the Hebrew Bible in Collins' introduction gives the impression that the Pentateuch must be read as a body of literature distinct from the Deuteronomistic History, in much the same way that it would be distinguished from the Prophets or the Writings. This approach to the Hebrew canon has hermeneutical implications. For example, Collins is especially skeptical of Erhard Blum's thesis of a D-composition in the Pentateuch, because the mention of several sanctuaries in Genesis apparently contradicts the Deuteronomistic ideal of a single central sanctuary in Jerusalem; this point is also stressed by Christoph Levin.[3] Collins concludes: "It is surely more plausible that the pentateuchal narrative was already established and authoritative before Deuteronomy was added."[4] My aim is not to pursue this literary argument any further. It is rather to demonstrate that the strict separation between the Pentateuch and the Deuteronomistic History began with Martin Noth and continues to exert a broad influence upon contemporary biblical interpretation.

How is this immense influence of Martin Noth's theory to be explained? Before Noth, in the nineteenth and early twentieth centuries, many scholars reckoned that the pentateuchal sources J, E, and P extended into Joshua, Judges, Samuel and even Kings.[5] For example, Carl Cornill, Karl Budde,

---

3. Christoph Levin, *Der Jahwist* (FRLANT 157; Göttingen: Vandenhoeck & Ruprecht, 1993), 430–35.

4. Collins, *Introduction to the Hebrew Bible*, 63.

5. See Carl H. Cornill, "Ein elohistischer Bericht über die Entstehung des israelitischen Königthums in I Samuelis 1–15 aufgezeigt," *Zeitschrift für kirchliche Wissenschaft und kirchliches Leben* 6 (1885): 113–41; idem, "Noch einmal Sauls Königswahl und Verwerfung," *ZAW* 10 (1890): 96–109; idem, "Zur Quellenkritik der Bücher Samuelis," *Königsberger Studien* 1 (1887): 25–89; Karl Budde, *Das Buch der Richter* (KHC 7; Freiburg: Mohr, 1897), xii–xv; idem, *Die Bücher Richter und Samuel: Ihre Quellen und ihr Aufbau* (Giessen: Ricker, 1890), 165–66, 268–69; idem, *Die Bücher Samuel*, (KHC 8; Tübingen: Mohr, 1902), xii–xxi; idem, *Geschichte der althebräischen Litteratur: Apokryphen und Pseudepigraphen von Alfred Bertholet* (Leipzig: Amelangs, 1909), 57–59; Immanuel Benzinger, *Jahvist und Elohist in den Königsbüchern* (BWAT 2; Berlin: Kohlhammer, 1921); idem, *Die Bücher der Könige* (KHC 9; Freiburg: Mohr, 1899); Willy Staerk, *Die Entstehung des Alten Testaments* (Sammlung Göschen 272; Leipzig: Göschen, 1905), 11–16; Rudolf Smend, Sr., "JE in den geschichtlichen Büchern des AT," *ZAW* 39 (1921): 181–217; Gustav Hölscher, "Das Buch der Könige, seine Quellen und seine Redaktion," in *Eucharistérion:*

Immanuel Benzinger, Willy Staerk, Rudolf Smend, Sr., and Cuthbert A. Simpson all reached this conclusion. J, E, and P were also clearly present at several points in the book of Joshua for Julius Wellhausen.[6] What, then, gave the force to Noth's arguments that allowed him to challenge this broad consensus *successfully* and to propose a *strict* division between the Pentateuch and the Deuteronomistic History?

Noth's argument for the literary identification of the Deuteronomistic History was twofold. First, he explained in his 1938 commentary on Joshua that the book of Joshua must be interpreted *without relying on the Documentary Hypothesis* and without presupposing that the traditional sources J, E, and P continue into Joshua.[7] Strictly speaking, this idea was original not with Noth, but rather with his "Doktorvater" Albrecht Alt, as Noth indicates himself in the preface to this commentary:[8]

> Daß es möglich ist, auf diesem Forschungsgebiet heute weiterzukommen, als es früheren Auslegungen desselben Buches gelingen konnte, beruht in erster Linie auf den dem Josua-Buche gewidmeten, mannigfachen und grundlegenden Arbeiten von Albrecht Alt, mit dem ich auch persönlich viele die Auslegung dieses Buches betreffende Fragen besprechen konnte.[9]

> The fact that it is possible for scholarly interpretations of the book of Joshua to be more successful today than was the case earlier should be credited

---

Studien zur Religion und Literatur des Alten und Neuen Testaments (ed. H. Schmidt; FRLANT 19; Göttingen: Vandenhoeck & Ruprecht, 1923), 158–213; idem, *Geschichtsschreibung in Israel: Untersuchungen zum Jahvisten und Elohisten* (Lund: Gleerup, 1952); idem, *Geschichte der israelitischen und jüdischen Religion* (Giessen: Töpelmann, 1922), 135 n. 1; Otto Eißfeldt, *Die Quellen des Richterbuches in synoptischer Anordnung ins Deutsche übertragen samt einer in Einleitung und Noten gegebenen Begründung* (Leipzig: Hinrichs, 1925); idem, *Einleitung in das Alte Testament, unter Einschluß der Apokryphen und Pseudepigraphen sowie der apokryphen und pseudepigraphenartigen Qumran-Schriften: Entstehungsgeschichte des Alten Testaments* (3d ed.; Neue theologische Grundrisse; Tübingen: Mohr, 1964), 178–79, 771; Cuthbert A. Simpson, *Composition of the Book of Judges* (Oxford: Blackwell, 1957). See the overviews provided by Hölscher, *Geschichtsschreibung,* 7–19; Ernst Jenni, "Zwei Jahrzehnte Forschung an den Büchern Josua bis Könige," *TRu* 27 (1961): 1–32, 97–146; Georg Fohrer, *Einleitung in das Alte Testament* (10th ed.; Heidelberg: Quelle & Meyer, 1965), 212–57. An early critical assessment of this assumption is provided by Rudolf Kittel, "Die pentateuchischen Urkunden in den Büchern Richter und Samuel," *TSK* 65 (1892): 44–71.

6. Julius Wellhausen, *Die Composition des Hexateuch und der historischen Bücher des Alten Testaments* (3d ed.; Berlin: Reimer, 1899), 116–34.

7. Martin Noth, *Das Buch Josua* (HAT 1/7; Tübingen: Mohr Siebeck, 1938), vii–viii.

8. On Alt see especially Rudolf Smend, *Deutsche Alttestamentler in drei Jahrhunderten* (Göttingen: Vandenhoeck & Ruprecht, 1989), 182–207.

9. Noth, *Josua,* v.

foremost to the numerous and ground-breaking works of Albrecht Alt, with whom I was able to discuss many questions concerning the exegesis of this book [sc. Joshua].

Noth relied in particular on a 1936 article by Alt entitled, "Josua."[10] In this work, Alt determined Joshua 1–11 to be:

> eine Reihe von Erzählungen, deren jede ihren Daseinsgrund in sich selbst hat und darum auch dann ihren Sinn nicht verliert, sondern nur noch deutlicher offenbart, wenn man sie aus der uns vorliegenden Verknüpfung mit den anderen herauslöst.[11]

> a series of tales that existed on their own and which do not lose their meaning when they are detached one from another. Rather, they become much clearer when encountered individually.

Noth's second argument was that no Deuteronomistic editorial activity had taken place in Genesis through Numbers. This argument goes beyond Alt's influence. Alt never mentions J, E, or P anywhere in his article. Alt himself had something of a forerunner in Hugo Gressmann, who had proposed a similar approach to Joshua in his 1914 commentary on Joshua in the series *Schriften des Alten Testaments*.[12] Noth explained the book of Joshua on the foundation laid by Gressmann and Alt. He found that different individual traditions in the book were combined by a so-called "collector" (*Sammler*)[13] whom he identified with neither J nor E.[14] This was a new idea that went against the position well established since de Wette. Noth stated:

> Now the view that Dtr. started with the book of Genesis is obviously mistaken, for it is generally recognised that there is no sign of "Deuteronomistic editing" in Genesis–Numbers.[15]

---

10. Albrecht Alt, "Josua," in *Werden und Wesen des Alten Testaments* (eds. P. Volz et al.; BZAW 66; Berlin: Töpelmann, 1936), 13–29.

11. Noth, *Josua*, 14.

12. *Die Anfänge Israels (von 2. Mosis bis Richter und Ruth)* (Schriften des Alten Testaments 1/2; Göttingen: Vandenhoeck & Ruprecht, 1914).

13. Noth, *Josua*, ix–xiii.

14. Noth, *Josua*, xiii. Alt points to the similar stance of Hugo Gressmann in his 1914 commentary on Joshua (*Die Anfänge Israels*). Gressmann characterizes the book of Joshua as a "Sammlung von Sagen" (14), but he still recognizes the continuation of the pentateuchal sources throughout Joshua.

15. Martin Noth, *The Deuteronomistic History* (trans. J. Doull et al.; JSOTSup 15; Sheffield: University of Sheffield Press, 1981), 12–13 (Original text: "In den Büchern Gen.–Num. fehlt jede Spur einer 'deuteronomistischen Redaktion,' wie allgemein anerkannt ist"; Martin Noth, *Überlieferungsgeschichtliche Studien: Die sammelnden und bearbeitenden Geschichtswerke im Alten Testament* [Halle: Niemeyer, 1943; 2d repr. ed, 1957; 3d repr. ed.: Darmstadt: Wissenschaftliche Buchgesellschaft, 1967], 13).

> Given that the books Genesis–Numbers show no signs of such an adapta-
> tion by Dtr. and that these books, therefore, look completely different from
> Joshua–Kings, we can only conclude that the books Genesis–Numbers, or at
> any rate the form of these books that antedated the Priestly work, were no
> part of Dtr's work.[16]

Noth, however, also qualified his second argument that Genesis through
Numbers lack all forms of Deuteronomistic reworking, adding in a footnote:

> Quite rightly, no one has yet, as far as I know, interpreted the occasional
> passages where the old text is augmented in Deuteronomistic style, e.g. Ex.
> 23:20ff. and Ex. 34:10ff., as sign of a thorough "redaction."[17]

With his notion that Genesis through Numbers is completely non-Deuter-
onomistic and that Joshua through Kings has nothing to do with the sources
of the Pentateuch, Noth set the stage for the subsequent interpretation of
Genesis through Kings in the second half of the twentieth century. Noth was
certainly *the* pivotal figure for what might be called "the separation model,"
which assumes a huge gap between the Pentateuch and the Deuteronomistic
History; but he would not have been so successful without the help of others.

To exaggerate for a moment, please forgive me if I describe the "separation
model" as a success only because of an explicit, but misguided, compromise
between Martin Noth and Gerhard von Rad. To be sure, Martin Noth and
Gerhard von Rad were among the most talented and gifted scholars of their
time, but it was precisely their high reputation that allowed them to establish together—though ironically also to a certain extent *against* each other—a
redactional model for the Enneateuch (Genesis–Kings) that was mainly based
on a gentleman's agreement rather than on good arguments. What supports
this conclusion?

The foundations of the scholarly compromise between Noth and von Rad
were laid in 1938. This was the publication year, not only of Martin Noth's
commentary on Joshua, but also of Gerhard von Rad's study on the form-critical problem of the Hexateuch.[18] These studies, however, came to *contradictory*

---

16. Noth, *Deuteronomistic History*, 13. Original text: "… daß die Bücher Gen.–Num.
bzw. deren alter, vorpriesterschriftlicher Bestand, nicht mit zu dem Werke von Dtr gehört
haben"; Noth, *Überlieferungsgeschichtliche Studien*, 13.

17. Noth, *Deuteronomistic History*, 103–4 n. 2; original text: "Daß es einzelne Stellen
gibt, an denen der alte Text im deuteronomistischen Stile erweitert worden ist, wie etwa
Ex. 23,20ff. und Ex. 34,10ff., hat mit Recht meines Wissens noch niemand für ein Merkmal
einer durchgehenden 'Redaktion' erhalten"; Noth, *Überlieferungsgeschichtliche Studien*,
103 n. 1.

18. Gerhard von Rad, "Das formgeschichtliche Problem des Hexateuchs (1938)," in
idem, *Gesammelte Studien zum Alten Testament* (TB 8; Munich: Kaiser, 1958), 9–86.
English translation: "The Form-Critical Problem of the Hexateuch," in *The Problem of the*

results. Von Rad proposed an original narrative arc spanning the entire Hexateuch, while Noth denied the presence of the pentateuchal sources in Joshua. Nevertheless, Noth and von Rad ironically succeeded in proposing a harmonizing compromise for Old Testament scholarship that became the standard model.

Von Rad's contribution to the compromise was the hypothesis of an earlier form of the Hexateuch. He concluded that 1) an older hexateuchal narrative had once continued into the book of Joshua; however, 2) this earlier text form was no longer extant in Joshua, because it had been replaced when the hexateuchal narrative was combined with the Deuteronomistic History. The omission of the original hexateuchal sources from Joshua was von Rad's tribute to Noth; and it gave rise to the very well-known standard model of the compositional history of Genesis–Kings as promulgated in the second half of the twentieth century. Recent scholarship, however, has shown that this compromise can no longer be maintained, because it leads to major problems that can no longer be overlooked. This model must come to terms with an immense loss of text. It presupposes that the Yahwist's and Elohist's accounts of the conquest of the land were lost when their works were combined with the Deuteronomistic History.[19] This is not only quite inelegant, but also highly improbable. Why should the redactors of the Old Testament invest so much energy combining and conflating older texts such as in Genesis 6–9 or Exodus 13–14 when they could just leave out large sections? Yet von Rad gave in to Noth's exclusion of the book of Joshua from the Documentary Hypothesis and thus to the destruction of the Hexateuch theory: a Hexateuch without an account of the conquest of the land is no longer a Hexateuch. Von Rad illustrates his compromise with Noth in his *Old Testament Theology*:

> Because of the thesis of Noth, who completely denies the occurrence of the sources J, E, and P in the Book of Joshua, the literary analysis of this book has again become uncertain. ... So until there is further clarification on this question, we do not take the picture given in the source documents as our starting point, but confine ourselves to drawing upon the older and later literary parts which make it up.[20]

Hexateuch and Other Essays (trans. E. W. Trueman Dicken; Edinburgh: Oliver & Boyd, 1966; reprinted: London: SCM Press, 1984), 1–78.

19. Martin Noth, *A History of Pentateuchal Traditions* (trans. B. W. Anderson; Scholars Press Reprint 5; Atlanta: Scholars Press, 1981), 20; trans. of *Überlieferungsgeschichte des Pentateuch* (2d ed.; Stuttgart: Kohlhammer, 1948); idem, *Überlieferungsgeschichtliche Studien: Die sammelnden und bearbeitenden Geschichtswerke im Alten Testament* (Tübingen: Niemeyer, 1957), 211.

20. Gerhard von Rad, *The Theology of Israel's Historical Traditions* (vol. 1 of *Old Testament Theology*; trans. D. Stalker; New York: Harper, 1962), 298 n. 4. See already von Rad, "Hexateuch oder Pentateuch?" *VF* (1947–48, appearing 1949–50): 52–56.

Noth also compromised his hypothesis of the Deuteronomistic History to incorporate von Rad's research on the Hexateuch. In particular Noth accepted von Rad's model of the very old and stable blueprint of the Hexateuch in the short historical creedal texts. At the beginning of his *A History of Pentateuchal Traditions* from 1948, he maintained:

> This basic form [sc. of the Pentateuch] did not finally emerge as the later consequence of a substantive combination and arrangement of *individual* traditions and individual complexes of traditions. Rather, this form was already given in the beginning of the history of traditions in a small series of themes essential for the faith of the Israelite tribes. ... This has been clearly shown by Gerhard von Rad in his important study on the "Hexateuch."[21]

This conclusion is rather surprising since Noth had developed a completely different approach to the composition of the Pentateuch in this book. He proposed a composition that developed from several independent traditions—what he calls "major themes": "Guidance out of Egypt," "Guidance into the Arable Land," "Promise to the Patriarchs," and so on. But, a peaceful man himself, Noth accepted von Rad's theory of an older Hexateuch; and therefore, he assumed that the "major themes" of the Pentateuch existed independently only in the realm of its probable oral prehistory in premonarchic times. It is almost tragic to read passages like the following from Noth's commentary on the book of Numbers:

> If we were to take the book of Numbers on its own, then we would think not so much of "continuing sources" as of an unsystematic collection of innumerable pieces of very varied content, age and character ("Fragment Hypothesis"). ... It is, therefore, justifiable to approach the book of Numbers with the results of Pentateuchal analysis elsewhere and to expect the continuing Pentateuchal "sources" here, too, even if, as we have said, the situation in Numbers, of itself does not exactly lead us to these results.[22]

If not for the compromise with von Rad, Noth probably would have advanced an approach to the composition of the Pentateuch more similar to the one he proposed for the book of Joshua or the Deuteronomistic History as a whole,

---

21. Noth, *A History of Pentateuchal Traditions*, 2. For a recent treatment see Jan Christian Gertz, "Die Stellung des kleinen geschichtlichen Credos in der Redaktionsgeschichte von Deuteronomium und Pentateuch," in *Liebe und Gebot: Studien zum Deuteronomium* (ed. R. Kratz and H. Spieckermann; FRLANT 190; Göttingen: Vandenhoeck & Ruprecht, 2000), 30–45.

22. Martin Noth, *Numbers: A Commentary* (trans. J. Martin; OTL; London: SCM, 1968 [German original: *Das vierte Buch Mose: Numeri* (ATD 7; Göttingen: Vandenhoeck & Ruprecht, 1966)]), 4–5.

than to the source model. Then he might even have felt compelled to include the entirety of Genesis through Kings as a single literary work. But there was the compromise to be agreed upon, and in the aftermath of Martin Noth and Gerhard von Rad, Old Testament scholarship chose to remain in its golden cage for about half a century.

It is fair to say that the separation between the Pentateuch and the Deuteronomistic History has started to disappear in current scholarship. Evidence of the problems in the Noth–von Rad separation model began to appear in the 1970s. First, books by John Van Seters,[23] Hans Heinrich Schmid,[24] and Rolf Rendtorff,[25] all from the mid-seventies, in various ways suggested a much closer relationship between the Deuteronomistic History and the Pentateuch than that proposed by the Noth–von Rad compromise. Van Seters and Schmid dated the Yahwist very close to the Deuteronomist and also detected some theological affinities between the two. This position was in fact a return to Wellhausen, who had already found the Jehovist (that is, the combined JE) and the Deuteronomist to be kindred spirits ("*Geistesverwandtschaft*"). Wellhausen himself even wavered on the issue of whether the "D" texts in the Pentateuch (which he acknowledged, unlike Noth) should be attributed to the "Jehovist" (JE), who himself was something like a "Deuteronomist"; or whether he should conclude that there had also been a "D" redaction of the Pentateuch.

> Dessen [sc. des Jehowisten] Geistesverwandtschaft mit dem Deuteronomium tritt wiederum auffallend hervor—wenn nicht ausser ihm noch ein Deuteronomist anzunehmen ist.[26]

> Again, his strikingly kindred spirit with Deuteronomy appears—unless one should assume that there was another additional Deuteronomist besides him.

Somewhat differently from Van Seters and Schmid, Rendtorff argued for a compositional model for the Pentateuch similar to that proposed by Martin Noth for the Deuteronomistic History. Noth himself might have considered such a model if he had applied his own methodology more carefully. Rend-

---

23. John Van Seters, *Abraham in History and Tradition* (New Haven: Yale University Press, 1975).

24. Hans Heinrich Schmid, *Der sogenannte Jahwist: Beobachtungen und Fragen zur Pentateuchforschung* (Zurich: Theologischer Verlag, 1976).

25. Rolf Rendtorff, *The Problem of the Process of Transmission in the Pentateuch* (trans. J. J. Scullion; JSOTSup 89; Sheffield: Sheffield Academic Press, 1990); trans. of *Das überlieferungsgeschichtliche Problem des Pentateuch* (BZAW 147; Berlin: de Gruyter, 1977).

26. Wellhausen, *Composition*, 94 n. 1.

torff theorized that there were major text blocks not only in Deuteronomy through Kings, but also in Genesis through Deuteronomy, that had subsequently been linked together in a Deuteronomistic redactional layer. So, the history and the method of composition of the Pentateuch and the Deuteronomistic History were understood to be closer to each other than was the case in the Noth–von Rad compromise.

Subsequent interpreters continued to move away from the synthesis established by Martin Noth and Gerhard von Rad. One example was Rudolf Smend's introduction to the Old Testament, published in 1978.[27] This work remained strongly influenced by the compromise of Noth and von Rad, while also differentiating Noth's Dtr into DtrH, DtrP, and DtrN. Smend sympathized with the notion that DtrN could be present in Deuteronomy through Kings, as well as in pentateuchal texts like Exod 23:20–33; 34:11–16, or Num 33:50–55.[28] Hans-Christoph Schmitt also provided an important contribution in the 1980s and 1990s among German speaking scholars, which continued to move interpreters away from the Noth–von Rad compromise by advocating an integrative perspective on Genesis through Kings.[29] He reckons with a late Deuteronomistic redaction in Genesis through Kings, which represents a mediating perspective between Priestly and Deuteronomistic theology.

Erhard Blum provided a significant breakthrough beyond the Noth–von Rad compromise in 1984, with his book on the composition of the ancestors' story in Genesis 12–50, and again in his 1990 companion volume on Exodus through Numbers and Deuteronomy.[30] He extended and elabo-

---

27. *Die Entstehung des Alten Testaments* (ThW 1; Stuttgart: Kohlhammer, 1978).

28. Smend, *Die Entstehung des Alten Testaments*, 115.

29. Hans-Christoph Schmitt, "Die Suche nach der Identität des Jahweglaubens im nachexilischen Israel," in *Theologie in Prophetie und Pentateuch: Gesammelte Schriften* (BZAW 310; Berlin: de Gruyter, 2001), 255–76; idem, "Das spätdeuteronomistische Geschichtswerk Gen I–2Regum XXV und seine theologische Intention," in *Theologie in Prophetie und Pentateuch*, 277–94; idem, "Die Josephsgeschichte und das Deuteronomistische Geschichtswerk. Genesis 38 und 48–50," in *Theologie in Prophetie und Pentateuch*, 295–308; idem, "Die Erzählung vom Goldenen Kalb Ex. 32* und das Deuteronomistische Geschichtswerk," in *Theologie in Prophetie und Pentateuch*, 311–25; idem, "Das sogenannte jahwistische Privilegrecht in Ex 34,10–28 als Komposition der spätdeuteronomistischen Endredaktion des Pentateuch," in *Abschied vom Jahwisten: Die Komposition des Hexateuch in der jüngsten Diskussion* (ed. J. C. Gertz, K. Schmid, and M. Witte; BZAW 315; Berlin: de Gruyter, 2002), 157–71; idem, "Dtn 34 als Verbindungsstück zwischen Tetrateuch und Deuteronomistischen Geschichtswerk," in *Das Deuteronomium zwischen Pentateuch und Deuteronomistischem Geschichtswerk* (ed. E. Otto and R. Achenbach; FRLANT 206; Göttingen: Vandenhoeck & Ruprecht, 2004), 180–92; idem, *Arbeitsbuch zum Alten Testament: Grundzüge der Geschichte Israels und der alttestamentlichen Schriften* (Uni-Taschenbücher 2146; Göttingen: Vandenhoeck & Ruprecht, 2005), 242–48.

30. Erhard Blum, *Die Komposition der Vätergeschichte* (WMANT 57; Neukirchen-

rated Rendtorff's view from 1977 that the Pentateuch is basically shaped by Deuteronomistic and Priestly compositional layers. With regard to the Deuteronomistic texts in the Pentateuch, he developed the notion that they were composed within a literary horizon that overarches both the Pentateuch and the Deuteronomistic History.

> Vielmehr hatte sich bei Dtn 31,14f.23; 34,10 ergeben, … dass diese KD-Komponenten als unselbständige Ergänzungen in einen vorgegebenen Zusammenhang eingebettet sind, näherhin in den Zusammenhang des "deuteronomistischen Geschichtswerks" (im Sinne von M. Noth).[31]

> It is apparent in Deut 31:14f.23; 34:10, … that these KD-elements are embedded as additions dependent on a larger given textual entity, namely the so-called "Deuteronomistic History" (in the sense of M. Noth).

A closer analysis reveals that Blum actually reckons with two Deuteronomists. The first is the Deuteronomist who corresponds with Noth's hypothesis. This author, however, plays a minor role in Blum's research, so minor, in fact, that he is discussed, astonishingly, in only one small footnote in the two large books on the Pentateuch:

> Die verzweigte Diskussion über eine eventuelle interne Redaktionsgeschichte des "DtrG" kann und braucht hier nicht aufgenommen zu werden. … Schließlich gelangen auch die diversen post-Nothschen Schichten- und Blockmodelle irgendwann zu einer Größe, die mehr oder weniger mit Noths Geschichtswerk übereinstimmt. Von dieser ist hier die Rede.[32]

> The complex discussion about the possible internal redaction history of the "Deuteronomistic History" cannot and need not be brought up here. … Eventually all the different post-Nothian layers or block models end up with an entity more or less identical to Noth's [Deuteronomistic] history. This is what I mean here.

There is also a second Deuteronomist, who incorporated the traditions from Genesis, or rather—as Blum corrected himself in 2002—from Exodus to Numbers, into a work reaching from Exodus to Kings. Blum writes of this author:

Vluyn: Neukirchener, 1984); idem, *Studien zur Komposition des Pentateuch* (BZAW 189; Berlin: de Gruyter, 1990).

31. Blum, *Pentateuch*, 109.

32. Ibid, 109 n. 35.

Damit legt sich eine Neubegrenzung der—vorpriesterlichen—"D-Kom-
position" nahe: Ihr Handlungs- und Darstellungsraum deckt sich mit der
Geschichte Moses zwischen Ex 1 und Dtn 34.[33]

Therefore, we should reckon with a new framework of the pre-Priestly
"D-composition." Its narration coincides with the Moses story running
from Exod 1 to Deut 34.

The influential nature of Blum's position, especially as expressed in the
extended version from 1990, can be seen by the fact that most English-speak-
ing introductions to the Old Testament assume a D and a P layer throughout
the Pentateuch, as seen most clearly in Joseph Blenkinsopp's introduction
into the Pentateuch.[34] As an expression of this overarching D-perspective
on Genesis to Kings, it has become more customary to speak of the so-
called "Primary History," a term previously introduced to Old Testament
scholarship by David Noel Freedman in 1962.[35] This perspective could not

---

33. Erhard Blum, "Die literarische Verbindung von Erzvätern und Exodus: Ein
Gespräch mit neueren Endredaktionshypothesen," in Gertz, Schmid, and Witte, *Abschied
vom Jahwisten*, 119–56 (at n. 165).

34. *The Pentateuch: An Introduction to the First Five Books of the Bible* (New York:
Doubleday, 2000).

35. Cf. David N. Freedman, "The Law and the Prophets," in *Congress Volume Bonn,
1962* (ed. G. W. Anderson et al.; VTSup 9; Leiden: Brill, 1963), 250–65, especially 251, 254,
257; David N. Freedman and Jeffrey C. Geoghegan, "Martin Noth: Retrospect and Prospect," in *The History of Israel's Traditions: The Heritage of Martin Noth* (ed. S. L. McKenzie
and M. P. Graham; JSOTSup 182; Sheffield: Sheffield Academic Press, 1994), 129–52, especially 129; Sara Mandell and David N. Freedman, *The Relationship between Herodotus'
History and Primary History* (SFSHJ 60; Atlanta: Scholars Press, 1993), ix (see also 85);
Paul J. Kissling, *Reliable Characters in the Primary History: Profiles of Moses, Joshua,
Elijah and Elisha* (JSOTSup 224; Sheffield: Sheffield Academic Press, 1996); Ehud Ben Zvi,
"Looking at the Primary (Hi)story and the Prophetic Books as Literary/Theological Units
Within the Frame of the Early Second Temple: Some Considerations," *SJOT* 12 (1998):
26–43 (see 26: Primary "Historical Narrative"); Sara Mandell, "Primary History as a Social
Construct of a Privileged Class," in *Concepts of Class in Ancient Israel* (ed. M. R. Sneed;
Atlanta: Scholars Press, 1999), 21–35; Anthony Abela, "Is Genesis the Introduction of the
Primary History?" in *Studies in the Book of Genesis: Literature, Redaction and History* (ed.
A. Wénin; BETL 155; Leuven: Leuven University Press, 2001), 397–406; A. Graeme Auld,
"Counting Sheep, Sins and Sour Grapes: The Primacy of the Primary History?" in *Sense
and Sensitivity: Essays on Reading the Bible in Memory of Robert Carroll* (ed. A. Hunter
and P. R. Davies; JSOTSup 348; Sheffield: Sheffield Academic Press, 2002), 63–72; David
N. Freedman and Brian Kelly, "Who Redacted the Primary History?" in *Sefer Moshe: The
Moshe Weinfeld Jubilee Volume: Studies in the Bible and the Ancient Near East, Qumran,
and Post-Biblical Judaism* (ed. C. Cohen, A. Hurvitz, and S. M. Paul; Winona Lake: Eisenbrauns, 2004), 39–47; Jan-Wim Wesselius, "The Functions of Lists in Primary History," in
"Basel und Bibel": Collected Communications to the XVIIth Congress of the International

be further removed from Noth's classical stance, *which denied the presence of any genuine D-texts in Genesis through Numbers.* The separation of the Pentateuch into D and P layers has much more to do with the influence of Rendtorff and Blum than with Noth.

The most recent scholarship on the composition of the Pentateuch and the Former Prophets begins from the aforementioned self-correction of Blum, namely that the literary stratum of KD is best restricted to Exodus through Deuteronomy, and therefore does not include Genesis. Blum based this conclusion on two main observations. First, it is quite obvious that the "Deuteronomistic" idiom can be found more clearly in Exodus and Numbers than in Genesis. Second, at least among German-speaking scholars, there is a growing sympathy for the theory proposed first by Albert de Pury and Thomas Römer that Genesis and Exodus were not found together in a single literary work before the composition of the Priestly Code.

The discussion of these points is now documented in two volumes, *Abschied vom Jahwisten* and *A Farewell to the Yahwist?*[36] It is helpful to note that the English title is followed by a question mark, in order to indicate that the concept of a "farewell to the Yahwist" is more controversial in American biblical scholarship than in its European counterpart. In the wake of the literary separation of Genesis, on the one hand, and Exodus through Kings, on the other, it has become necessary to seek new solutions to replace Martin Noth's previous hypothesis of the "Deuteronomistic History."

The growing research on the literary development of the Pentateuch and the Former Prophets as an Enneateuch has most recently been gathered in a 2006 volume entitled *The Deuteronomistic Histories.*[37] It is not possible to summarize this publication, since the different contributions do not propose a new consensus. But this much can be seen: there seems to be some sympathy for speaking of "Deuteronomistic Histories" in the plural instead of in the singular. Some of the contributors are ready to recognize an old or

---

Organization for the Study of the Old Testament, 2001 (ed. M. Augustin and H. M. Niemann; BEATAJ 51; Frankfurt: Lang, 2004), 83–89; idem, *The Origin of the History of Israel: Herodotus's Histories as Blueprint for the First Books of the Bible* (JSOTSup 345; Sheffield: Sheffield Academic Press, 2002).

36. Jan Christian Gertz, Konrad Schmid, and Markus Witte, eds., *Abschied vom Jahwisten: Die Komposition des Hexateuch in der jüngsten Diskussion* (BZAW 315; Berlin: de Gruyter, 2002); Thomas B. Dozeman and Konrad Schmid, eds., *A Farewell to the Yahwist? The Composition of the Pentateuch in Recent European Interpretation* (SBLSymS 34; Atlanta: Society of Biblical Literature, 2006).

37. Markus Witte, Konrad Schmid, Doris Prechel, and Jan Christian Gertz, eds., *Die deuteronomistischen Geschichtswerke: Redaktions- und religionsgeschichtliche Perspektiven zur "Deuteronomismus"-Diskussion in Tora und Vorderen Propheten* (BZAW 365; Berlin: de Gruyter, 2006).

original "Deuteronomistic History," located in the books of Samuel and Kings, and to identify subsequent editions of later "Deuteronomistic Histories." Examples of the different renditions of "Deuteronomistic Histories" include a version that may have extended from Exodus through Kings. Such a version of the "Deuteronomistic History" may eventually also have included Genesis, when the Moses story in Exodus–Joshua was later combined with the story of the ancestors in Genesis 12–50. The research on the "Deuteronomistic Histories" is ongoing and open to revision. Yet the hypothesis of multiple "Deuteronomistic Histories" reaches back to the famous double theme of the "Deuteronomistic History" identified by Frank Moore Cross. He, too, argued that the literary themes of the dynastic promise to David (2 Sam 7) and the sin of Jeroboam (1 Kgs 12) only extend through the books of Samuel to Kings, creating an early "Deuteronomistic History." This early Deuteronomistic History is not present in Deuteronomy, Joshua, or Judges.[38] The same process of composition could account for much larger blocks of literature in the Enneateuch. The late Deuteronomistic reception of the sin of Jeroboam in Exodus 32 could point to a "Deuteronomistic History" that starts in Exodus rather than in Deuteronomy. And finally, there are also Deuteronomistic texts in Genesis that exhibit distinctive features, such as Abraham's obedience to the Torah. This distinctive theme may point to a still later stage of Deuteronomistic reflection and composition, as Erik Aurelius has proposed.[39]

The reexamination of the Noth–von Rad compromise approach to the composition of the Pentateuch and the Former Prophets extends beyond the newer attempts to differentiate Deuteronomistic layers in Genesis through Kings. It also requires a reevaluation of Priestly texts in Genesis through Kings. In the framework of the traditional Documentary Hypothesis, P was something like a proto-Pentateuch, beginning in Genesis 1 and ending in Deuteronomy 34. Today, there is a growing awareness 1) that P probably did not cover the full range of the Pentateuch;[40] and 2) that there are redactional texts in Joshua through Kings that are clearly inspired by P but not neces-

---

38. Frank Moore Cross, "The Themes of the Book of Kings and the Structure of the Deuteronomistic History," in idem, *Canaanite Myth and Hebrew Epic: Essays in the History of Religion of Israel* (Cambridge, Mass.: Harvard University Press, 1973), 274–89.

39. Erik Aurelius, *Zukunft jenseits des Gerichts: Eine redaktionsgeschichtliche Studie zum Enneateuch* (BZAW 319; Berlin: de Gruyter, 2003).

40. See Lothar Perlitt, "Priesterschrift im Deuteronomium?" *ZAW* 100 Supplement (1988): 65–88; Thomas Pola, *Die ursprüngliche Priesterschrift: Beobachtungen zur Literarkritik und Traditionsgeschichte von Pg* (WMANT 70; Neukirchen-Vluyn: Neukirchener, 1995); Eckart Otto, "Forschungen zur Priesterschrift," *TRu* 62 (1997): 1–50.

sarily part of a Priestly composition,[41] e.g., in Joshua 13–21[42] or in 1 Kings 8. So, not only the D texts, but also the P texts are relevant for any critical evaluation of the literary entanglement of the Pentateuch and the Deuteronomistic History. What emerges throughout the range of current approaches to the Pentateuch and the Former Prophets is the disappearance of the "separation model" to configure the relationship between the Pentateuch and the Deuteronomistic History. We probably also will have to overcome the conceptual separation between the historical and the prophetic books (the Latter Prophets), because Genesis through Kings is a theologically open-ended unit: it ends with the loss of the land, leaving the question of Israel's future unanswered. Readers are apparently supposed to read on, but this is another chapter.

---

41. See Eep Talstra, *Solomon's Prayer: Synchrony and Diachrony in the Composition of I Kings 8, 14–61* (CBET 3; Kampen: Kok Pharos, 1993).

42. Enzo Cortese, *Josua 13–21: Ein priesterschriftlicher Abschnitt im Deuteronomistischen Geschichtswerk* (OBO 94; Fribourg: Universitätsverlag, 1990).

How Many Books (*TEUCHS*):

Pentateuch, Hexateuch, Deuteronomistic History, or Enneateuch?

Thomas Römer

1. Introduction: A New Interest in the "Latest Redactors"

"The older the better." This adage applies to the mainstream of historical and critical research on the Hebrew Bible from its very beginnings in the nineteenth century. Pentateuchal research in the time of the classical Documentary Hypothesis as elaborated by Wellhausen and others was mainly interested in the oldest source, the so-called Yahwist; many works on the Former Prophets or the Historical Books were eager to recover the oldest sources, putting aside the passages stemming from later redactors that obstructed the way to the "original and historical account." Most commentaries and monographs on the Latter Prophets were interested in reconstructing the *ipsissima verba*, the authentic oracles of the Prophets, which were apparently more "valuable" than the later additions. We will not analyze here the reasons for this fascination with the oldest parts of the Bible, which may well be a heritage of romanticism, or may betray the quite naïve assumption that the oldest text of the Bible could prove the historicity of the related events. Suffice it to say that the quest for the oldest sources did not generate a real interest in the questions of how the major literary works of the Bible came into being, and of their meaning or intention. Challenged by more synchronically oriented methods, such as narratology, innerbiblical exegesis, and others, diachronically oriented exegesis has become interested in the question of the formation of the biblical books or literary works. This is particularly apparent in research on the Prophets, where the interest has shifted from the prophet to the book, with a growing scepticism concerning the possibility of reconstructing the "historical" prophets. Research on the Pentateuch and the Former Prophets has become more and more interested in the question of the latest redactions that shaped the Pentateuch and the other major literary productions. But here the question arises: what other literary works do we have in the Torah and the Nebiim?

If one starts reading the Hebrew Bible, one may of course consider that the death of Moses reported in Deut 34 represents a major conclusion, and that this is the idea of the editors of the Torah. Others may determine that this episode is not a very fitting conclusion, since God's promise of the land, which is repeated throughout all books of the Torah, has not been fulfilled. Therefore one should add to the main account the book of Joshua, where the conquest of the land is narrated. In this perspective, the Pentateuch is replaced by the idea of an original Hexateuch. One may also suggest that there is a major narrative that runs from Gen 1 to 2 Kgs 25; these books can be read, as Joseph Blenkinsopp puts it, as "a consecutive history from creation to exile."[1] In the first book of the Latter Prophets, the chronological framework is no longer respected, since Isa 1:1 brings us back into the time of the two kingdoms of Israel and Judah. Therefore some scholars posit the existence, at some stage of the formation of the biblical books, of an "Enneateuch" or a "Primary History,"[2] running from the book of Genesis to the books of Kings, from Paradise lost to the loss of Jerusalem.[3] And there is yet another possible major literary unit. If one looks at the openings of the books that constitute the Pentateuch, one realizes that Exodus, Leviticus and Numbers are closely related to the foregoing book by a consecutive waw: *wĕ'elleh šĕmôt; wayyiqrā', wayyĕdabbēr*, whereas the book of Deuteronomy opens in an "absolute" way: *'ēlleh haddĕbārîm*. This may suggest that the book of Deuteronomy should be understood as a new beginning of a work that runs until the end of Kings. In Moses' final discourse, he announces the possibility of the loss of the land and the exile, and that is what happens in the last chapters of Kings. This entity of Deuteronomy–Kings is the so-called "Deuteronomistic History," as invented or discovered by Martin Noth.[4]

---

1. Joseph Blenkinsopp, *The Pentateuch: An Introduction to the First Five Books of the Bible* (ABRL; New York: Doubleday, 1992), 34. This idea can already be found in Benedict de Spinoza, *A Theologico-Political Treatise and, A Political Treatise* (trans. R. H. M. Elwes; New York: Dover, 1951), 128, "all these books … were all written by a single author, who wished to relate the antiquities of the Jews from their first beginning down to the first destruction of the city."

2. David N. Freedman, "Pentateuch," *IDB* 3:711–27, p. 713.

3. Bernard Gosse, "L' inclusion de l'ensemble Genèse–II Rois, entre la perte du jardin d'Eden et celle de Jérusalem," *ZAW* 114 (2002): 189–211.

4. Martin Noth, *The Deuteronomistic History* (trans. J. Doull et al.; JSOTSup 15; Sheffield: Sheffield Academic Press, 1981; 2d ed., 1991); trans. of *Überlieferungsgeschichtliche Studien: Die sammelnden und bearbeitenden Geschichtswerke im Alten Testament*

Of all these units—Pentateuch, Hexateuch, Deuteronomistic History, Primary History—only the Pentateuch is a canonical reality. One could argue that the Enneateuch covers roughly the two first parts of the canon of the Septuagint: the Law and the Historical Books; one should not forget, however, that the second part of the Greek canon[5] does not end with the fall of Jerusalem and the exile, but continues with the books of Ezra and Nehemiah to the reconstruction of the temple, and with the Maccabees into the Roman period. Should we then reject all these *teuchs* and other Deuteronomistic Histories and restrict ourselves to Torah and Nebiim? This solution does not take into account a number of scholarly observations that had led to the idea of the different literary units that I mentioned. Let us therefore examine briefly the arguments for the existence (or non-existence) of the Hexateuch, the Deuteronomistic History, and the Enneateuch. The various possibilities for explaining the different literary units may make one think of a puzzle; these various options are in fact related to different models for the formation of the two first parts of the Hebrew Bible and also to various theological options for understanding Israel's earliest history.[6]

2. From a Deuteronomistic History to the Enneateuch—and Then to the Pentateuch?

When Noth invented (or discovered) the Deuteronomistic History, he encountered a literary problem, since the remaining Tetrateuch (the books of Genesis to Numbers) had then no fitting conclusion. He therefore postulated that the end of the older sources (the Yahwist and the Elohist) had been lost when the pentateuchal documents were combined with the Deuteronomistic History. After European and some American scholarship said "farewell" to the traditional Documentary Hypothesis,[7] new solutions were put forward that resolved Noth's problem differently.

(Halle: Niemeyer, 1943; 2d repr. ed., 1957; 3d repr. ed.: Darmstadt: Wissenschaftliche Buchgesellschaft, 1967).

5. I cannot discuss here the question of whether the Greek canon is originally a Jewish construction or a Christian invention; see on this recently Jean-Daniel Kaestli, "La formation et la structure du canon biblique: Que peut apporter l'étude de la Septante?" in *The Canon of Scripture in Jewish and Christian Tradition—Le canon des Écritures dans les traditions juive et chrétienne* (ed. P. S. Alexander and J.-D. Kaestli; Publications de l'institut romand des sciences bibliques 4; Prahins: Zèbre, 2007), 99–113.

6. See especially Suzanne Boorer, "The Importance of a Diachronic Approach: the Case of Genesis–Kings," *CBQ* 51 (1989): 195–208, who shows that we can discern very different approaches to the theme of the land.

7. For an overview of the pentateuchal debate see David M. Carr, "Controversy and

John Van Seters considers the Yahwist to be a post-Deuteronomistic author who wrote the pre-Priestly traditions of Genesis, Exodus and Numbers as a "prologue" to the Deuteronomistic History—which means that he envisions, in fact, an Enneateuch.[8] P, according to Van Seters, is a redactor who adds his texts to that of the Yahwist, but whose work is also perceptible in the beginning of the book of Judges and even in 1 Kgs 8. But who is then responsible for the Pentateuch? Van Seters does not—if I understand him correctly—provide a clear answer. In his "social science commentary" on the Pentateuch, Van Seters claims that there is no clear evidence for a Pentateuch before the first century c.e., and that "the unity implied in ... the Pentateuch is not a literary one, but a theological one."[9] The idea of a D-composition and a P-composition (in Genesis/Exodus–Numbers/Deuteronomy), as advocated by E. Blum, R. Albertz, J. Blenkinsopp, and others,[10] comes close to Van Seters's J and P in that these "compositions" also presuppose the Deuteronomistic History and were created in order to supplement the work of the Deuteronomists in Deuteronomy to Kings.[11] But this model offers a quite clear theory about the rise of the Pentateuch, which is seen as a compromise between the Deu-

---

Convergence in Recent Studies of the Formation of the Pentateuch," *RelSRev* 23 (1997): 22–31; Thomas B. Dozeman and Konrad Schmid, eds., *A Farewell to the Yahwist? The Composition of the Pentateuch in Recent European Interpretation* (SBLSymS 34; Atlanta: Society of Biblical Literature, 2006).

8. See especially John Van Seters, *In Search of History: History in the Ancient World and the Origin of Biblical History* (New Haven: Yale University Press, 1983); idem, *Prologue to History: The Yahwist as Historian in Genesis* (Zurich: Theologischer Verlag, 1992); idem, *The Life of Moses: The Yahwist as Historian in Exodus–Numbers* (Louisville: Westminster; and Kampen: Kok Pharos, 1994).

9. John Van Seters, *The Pentateuch: A Social Science Commentary* (Trajectories; Sheffield: Sheffield Academic Press, 1999), 17.

10. Erhard Blum, *Studien zur Komposition des Pentateuch* (BZAW 189; Berlin: de Gruyter, 1990); Rainer Albertz, *A History of Israelite Religion in the Old Testament Period: Volume 2: From the Exile to the Maccabees* (trans. J. Bowden; London: SCM Press, 1992); trans. of *Religionsgeschichte Israels in alttestamentlicher Zeit 2* (ATD Ergänzungsreihe Band 8/2; Göttingen: Vandenhoeck & Ruprecht, 1992); Joseph Blenkinsopp, "Deuteronomic Contribution to the Narrative in Genesis–Numbers: A Test Case" in *Those Elusive Deuteronomists: The Phenomenon of Pan-Deuteronomism* (ed. L. S. Schearing and S. L. McKenzie; JSOTSup 268; Sheffield: Sheffield Academic Press, 1999), 84–115; William Johnstone, "Recounting the Tetrateuch," in *Covenant As Context: Essays in Honour of E. W. Nicholson* (ed. A. D. H. Mayes and R. B. Salters; Oxford: Oxford University Press, 2003), 209–34.

11. Recently, as a result of the debate about the link between the patriarchs and the Exodus, Blum has modified his model; he now concludes that the D-composition did not include the Genesis traditions. See Erhard Blum, "The Literary Connection Between the Books of Genesis and Exodus and the End of the Book of Joshua," in Dozeman and Schmid, *A Farewell to the Yahwist?* 89–106.

teronomistic and Priestly groups in the middle of the Persian period in order to provide an identity to rising Judaism.[12] Cutting off the books of Joshua to Kings reflects the desire both to accept the loss of political autonomy and also to provide a document acceptable to Jews and Samaritans. According to this model, the Pentateuch results from a political and theological will to relegate the books relating the conquest and the history of the monarchy to a "secondary status." But how should one then explain the fact that starting with the book of Genesis we find passages that apparently make more or only sense in the context of a Hexateuch?

3. HEXATEUCH OR PENTATEUCH?

The idea that there was an original Hexateuch and not a Pentateuch is as old as the Documentary Hypothesis. It arose because of the idea that the book of Joshua is the fitting conclusion to the narration that starts with the promise of the land in the book of Genesis, so that the end of J and E (and also P) should be preserved in Joshua.[13] The assumption of an "old" Yahwistic Hexateuch (covering the stories from the origins to the entry into the land) seems nowadays very difficult to maintain,[14] since the texts in Genesis through Joshua that try to "create" a Hexateuch are apparently late insertions, as for instance Gen 50:25 and Exod 13:19, which deal with the transportation of Joseph's bones from Egypt to Israel. These verses do not make much sense in the context of the Pentateuch, but do serve as preparation for Joshua 24. Joshua 24:32 is thus the end of a narrative trajectory that starts in Gen 50:25 (or even in 33:19).[15] Exodus 16:35, which relates the beginning of God's gift

---

12. Whether this compromise was fostered by the Persian imperial authorization is a matter of debate; see the different opinions in James W. Watts, ed., *Persia and Torah: The Theory of the Imperial Authorization of the Pentateuch* (SBLSymS 17; Atlanta: Society of Biblical Literature, 2001).

13. This idea was made popular by Julius Wellhausen, *Die Composition des Hexateuchs und der historischen Bücher des Alten Testaments* (Berlin: Reimer, 1899; repr. Berlin: de Gruyter, 1963).

14. Recent attempts to reconstruct an "old" predeuteronomistic Hexateuch can be found in Erich Zenger, ed., *Einleitung in das Alte Testament* (5th ed.; Studienbücher Theologie 1/1; Stuttgart: Kohlhammer, 2004), 100–106; or Reinhard G. Kratz, *The Composition of the Narrative Books of the Old Testament* (trans. J. Bowden; London: T&T Clark; New York: Continuum, 2005), 216; trans. of *Die Komposition der erzählenden Bücher des Alten Testaments: Grundwissen der Bibelkritik* (Uni-Taschenbücher 2157; Göttingen: Vandenhoeck & Ruprecht, 2000), 221.

15. In fact, the explicit suggestion that Joseph was buried in Shechem might even bring us back to the beginning of the Joseph story; as noted by the great medieval Jewish commentator, Rashi (Rabbi Solomon son of Isaac, 1040–1105), "They [Joseph's brothers]

of manna, opens a period that ends only after the entry in the land, as stated in Josh 5:12: "The manna ceased the day they ate the produce of the land." The introduction and praise of the figure of Caleb in Num 13–14 only makes sense together with Josh 14:13–15, where he receives the territory of Hebron.

The most decisive argument for the existence of a Hexateuch is Josh 24. This final discourse is clearly later than Joshua's last words in chapter 23,[16] which stem from Deuteronomistic redactors. Joshua 24, already described by Gerhard von Rad as the summary of a Hexateuch,[17] recapitulates all major events from the days of the patriarchs to the conquest of the land. And Joshua introduces his speech by the prophetic formula: "Thus says Yнwн, the God of Israel" (v. 2), and appears to be here a "prophet like Moses" (Deut 18:15). At the end of the speech, he becomes even more comparable to Moses; he concludes a covenant, gives the people statutes and ordinances, and writes all "these words" in the book of the law of God (sēper tôrat 'ĕlōhîm) (vv. 25–26). The expression haddĕbārîm hā'ēlleh, may refer back to the beginning of the book of Deuteronomy, 'ēlleh haddĕbārîm (according to Seidel's law, which denotes an inverted or chiastic citation) and may be understood as an attempt to present the book of Joshua as inseparably linked to Deuteronomy. One way or another, the author of Josh 24, who is writing in the Persian period, wants to create a Hexateuch,[18] and this attempt is prepared for by several texts in the Pentateuch.

Therefore, E. Otto, R. Achenbach, and others are right in distinguishing within the Torah a "hexateuchal redaction" and a "pentateuchal redaction."[19]

---

stole him from Shechem (see Gen 37: 13), and they [Joshua's generation] returned him to Shechem." Rashi ad Josh 24 (translated by M. Brettler). For this theme see also Markus Witte, "Die Gebeine Josefs," in Auf dem Weg zur Endgestalt von Genesis bis II Regum (ed. M. Beck and U. Schorn; BZAW 370; Berlin: de Gruyter, 2006), 139–56, who argues that these very late texts reflect the transport of Alexander's corpse.

16. Joshua 24 presupposes Deuteronomistic and Priestly terminology and texts. M. Anbar has convincingly demonstrated that Josh 24 is a very late text, and this idea is shared by a growing number of scholars: see Moshé Anbar, Josué et l'alliance de Sichem (Josué 24:1–28) (BBET 25; Frankfurt: Lang, 1992).

17. Gerhard von Rad, "The Form-Critical Problem of the Hexateuch," in idem, The Problem of the Hexateuch and Other Essays (trans. E. W. Trueman Dicken; Edinburgh: Oliver & Boyd; 1966; repr. London: SCM Press, 1984), 1–78. German original: "Das formgeschichtliche Problem des Hexateuchs (1938)," in idem, Gesammelte Studien zum Alten Testament (TB 8; Munich: Kaiser, 1958), 9–86.

18. Thomas C. Römer and Marc Z. Brettler, "Deuteronomy 34 and the Case for a Persian Hexateuch," JBL 119 (2000): 401–19.

19. Eckart Otto, Das Deuteronomium im Pentateuch und Hexateuch: Studien zur Literaturgeschichte von Pentateuch und Hexateuch im Lichte des Deuteronomiumrahmens (FAT 30; Tübingen: Mohr Siebeck, 2000); idem, "The Pentateuch in Synchronical and Diachronical Perspectives: Protorabbinical Scribal Erudition Mediating Between

According to this model, an important number of texts that were formerly considered "Yahwistic" and "Deuteronomistic" are now attributed to the hexateuchal or pentateuchal redactors; but it is not always clear which stylistic or other reasons allow for those attributions. According to Otto and Achenbach, both groups of redactors belong to the priestly class of the Zadokites. But they do not say why these two groups should have had competing ideas about the extent of the scriptural foundations of developing Judaism. Is it in any case plausible that the redactors of the Pentateuch all stem from the same priestly faction, given the fact that Judeans as well as Samaritans adopted the Torah, and that it contains both Priestly and non-Priestly (Deuteronomistic and other) texts? One should rather think of both sets of redactors as mixed social groups. As Otto has rightly observed, the two options betray quite different ideas about what should be cardinal to Judaism: for the Hexateuch the main theme is the land, whereas for the Pentateuch Israel's identity is founded in the Torah mediated by Moses. This makes it quite understandable that the idea of a Hexateuch was rejected in favor of the Torah.

The last words of Deuteronomy, which quite obviously belong to the redactors of the Pentateuch, assert that "never again has a prophet arisen in Israel like Moses, whom YHWH knew face to face" (Deut 34:10)—thereby establishing an important hiatus between the activity of Moses and the story told in the succeeding books. Joshua 24 tries to present Joshua as a prophet and a "second Moses," whereas Deut 34:10–12 states that Moses and Joshua cannot be put on the same level. Contrary to Deut 34:8–9, which highlights Joshua as Moses' successor, vv. 10–12 insist on the coherence of the Pentateuch as a theological but also a literary unit. The same is true for the last redactions in vv. 1–7* of the same chapter. John Van Seters has argued that, "the Pentateuch does not have a final 'form' because the division at the end of Deuteronomy was not based upon literary considerations. Unless one can convincingly demonstrate such a design by careful literary analysis, the concept of a Pentateuch remains problematic for any literary analysis of the Hebrew Bible."[20]

To be sure, the Pentateuch is a theological construct. But there are also clear indicators of a "pentateuchal redaction," as Konrad Schmid and others

---

Deuteronomy and the Priestly Code," in *Das Deuteronomium zwischen Pentateuch und Deuteronomistischem Geschichtswerk* (ed. E. Otto and R. Achenbach; FRLANT 206; Göttingen: Vandenhoeck & Ruprecht, 2004), 14–35; Reinhard Achenbach, *Die Vollendung der Tora: Studien zur Redaktionsgeschichte des Numeribuches im Kontext von Hexateuch und Pentateuch* (BZABR 3; Wiesbaden: Harrassowitz, 2003); idem, "Pentateuch, Hexateuch und Enneateuch: Eine Verhältnisbestimmung," *ZABR* 11 (2005): 122–54.

20. Van Seters, *Pentateuch*, 17.

have demonstrated.[21] The promise to the patriarchs, which is expressed by the verb *nišba'* (Deut 34:4), contains a formulation that is a quote of Gen 12:7. The whole Torah is framed by the promise of the land, but the *nišba'*-formula, linked to the patriarchs, runs through the whole Pentateuch, thereby fostering its coherence.[22] Interestingly, this formula does not occur in the Former Prophets, which clearly favors the attribution of these texts to a pentateuchal redaction. Moses' death at 120 years (Deut 34:7) is a reference to Gen 6:3, which creates an *inclusio* with the Primary History and underlines the idea that Moses' death has nothing to do with a divine sanction, but results from God's decision to limit the age of mankind to 120 years. Finally, the idea that Moses stands above all other prophets and mediators, as expressed in Deut 34:10, also occurs in Exod 33:11 and Num 12:8, which therefore may also stem from a pentateuchal redaction.

Joshua 24 and Deut 34, as well as the texts that are related to these chapters, provide in my view good evidence for the attempt to create a "real" Hexateuch and, probably in reaction to this attempt, a "real" Pentateuch; that is to say, a scroll or a collection of scrolls that were kept separately from others. But if one tends to give credence to this hypothesis, as I am inclined to do, two further questions arise: from which earlier literary unit did the redactors separate the first books in order to constitute a Hexa- or a Pentateuch? And should one understand Deut 34 and Josh 24 as absolute endings, or as literary devices whose function is to subdivide a larger literary unit. This brings us to the question of the Enneateuch, or "Primary History."

4. From an Enneateuch to the Pentateuch?

The idea that the books of Genesis to Kings constitute the Bible's first story is quite common, especially in synchronic readings such as the work of Danna Fewell and David Gunn; they claim that this "Primary History" ten-

---

21. See for instance Konrad Schmid, "Der Pentateuchredaktor: Beobachtungen zum theologischen Profil des Toraschlusses in Dtn 34," in *Les dernières rédactions du Pentateuque, de l'Hexateuque et de l'Ennéateuque* (ed. T. Römer and K. Schmid; BETL 203; Leuven: Leuven University Press and Peeters, 2007), 183–97; Schmid takes up observations made by Felix García López, "Deut 34, Dtr History and the Pentateuch," in *Studies in Deuteronomy: In Honour of C. J. Labuschagne on the Occasion of his 65th Birthday* (ed. F. García Martínez et al.; VTSup 53; Leiden: Brill, 1994), 47–61; Thomas Römer, *Israels Väter: Untersuchungen zur Väterthematik im Deuteronomium und in der deuteronomistischen Tradition* (OBO 99; Fribourg: Universitätsverlag; Göttingen: Vandenhoeck & Ruprecht, 1990), 554–68 and others.

22. Genesis 50:24; Exod 31:13; 33:1; (see also Lev 26:42); Num 32:11; and seven times in Deuteronomy.

tatively dated from the end of the Babylonian or the beginning of the Persian period and is "placed first in the Bible (whether the Jewish or the Christian scriptures)."[23] That means that this epic story is earlier than its canonical subdivision, an opinion shared by a number of scholars working with historical-critical methods. In 1975, Clements suggested that the Former Prophets should be seen together with the Pentateuch as constituting the first corpus of Scripture in nascent Judaism.[24] Thomas Dozeman, in a recent article and in this volume, analyzes Exodus 32 and claims that this text was written for an Enneateuch, since it merges Deut 9:7–10.11 and 1 Kgs 12:26–32 into one story. This Enneateuch existed as a Deuteronomistic and pre-Priestly composition.[25] This idea comes close to the concept of a great "Deuteronomistic History," composed during the Babylonian Exile, and running from Gen 2:4b through 2 Kgs 25, as advocated by Weimar and Zenger.[26]

H.-Chr. Schmitt also thinks that the Enneateuch came before the Pentateuch. According to him one can recover in Genesis–Kings the hand of a late Deuteronomistic redactor who combines a Tetrateuch, into which the Priestly texts have already been integrated, and the Deuteronomistic History (as formulated by Noth), in order to create a "late Deuteronomistic History" (*spätdeuteronomistisches Geschichtswerk*). The evidence for such a work can be found, according to Schmitt, especially in late redactional texts emphasizing the theme of the faith (the root *'-m-n, hip'il,* as in Gen 15:6; Exod 14:31; 19.9; Num 14:11; 20:11; running until 2 Kgs 17:14), as well as the necessity of "listening to the voice of YHWH" (*šāmar bĕqôl Yhwh*).[27] Konrad Schmid is also sympathetic to the idea of an Enneateuch, but he is more sceptical about the idea that such an Enneateuch ever existed without the Latter Prophets. Schmid distinguishes an earlier, pre-Priestly Enneateuch running from

---

23. Danna Nolan Fewell and David M. Gunn, *Gender, Power, and Promise: The Subject of the Bible's First Story* (Nashville: Abingdon, 1993), 12. This assumption is not totally correct: in the Christian Bibles (and in the LXX) Ruth comes between Judges and Samuel and Kings is followed by Chronicles, Ezra, Nehemiah and Esther.

24. Ronald E. Clements, *Prophecy and Tradition* (Growing Points in Theology; Oxford: Blackwell, 1975), 55.

25. Thomas B. Dozeman, "The Composition of Ex 32 within the Context of the Enneateuch," in Beck and Schorn, *Auf dem Weg zur Endgestalt*, 175–89, pp. 188–89.

26. See for instance Erich Zenger, "Theorien über die Entstehung des Pentateuch im Wandel der Forschung," in idem, *Einleitung*, 74–123.

27. Hans-Christoph Schmitt, "Das spätdeuteronomistische Geschichtswerk Gen i–2 Regum xxv und seine theologische Intention," in *Congress Volume Cambridge 1995* (ed. J. A. Emerton; VTSup 66; Leiden: Brill, 1997), 261–79; repr. in *Theologie in Prophetie und Pentateuch: Gesammelte Aufsätze* (ed. U. Schorn and M. Büttner; BZAW 310; Berlin: de Gruyter, 2001), 277–94; idem, *Arbeitsbuch zum Alten Testament* (Uni-Taschenbücher 2146; Göttingen: Vandenhoeck & Ruprecht, 2005), 242–46.

Exod 3 through 2 Kgs 25:21, since he agrees with others that the literary link between the patriarchs and the exodus was first created by the Priestly writer. For Schmid then, the idea of an Enneateuch covering Genesis through Kings must therefore be a post-Priestly construction.[28] Finally, we should also mention the work of Erik Aurelius, who claims that the Enneateuch took form "in reverse" (first Samuel–Kings, then the literarily "earlier" books), an idea that is also expressed by Graeme Auld.[29] In the beginning there was a first exilic edition of Samuel–Kings—the only books that we may, according to Aurelius, label "Deuteronomistic History." Several redactors expanded these books and at a later stage integrated the Mosaic and patriarchal traditions, thus creating an Enneateuch. This Enneateuch is "framed," in a way, by Exod 19:3b–8 and 2 Kgs 18:12; which are, with the exception of Judg 2:20, the only texts in the Hebrew Bible wherein the exhortations to listen to YHWH's voice and to keep his covenant are combined.[30]

If there was an original Enneateuch with canonical status in Persian period Judaism, as argued by Schmitt and also Chapman,[31] for what reasons was this Enneateuch then shortened to a Pentateuch? Schmitt simply argues that the concept of a Pentateuch arose only in the Hellenistic period because of the late Deuteronomistic idea that Moses was the only mediator of the Law.[32] For the advocates of an Enneateuch, texts like Deut 34 or Josh 24 are not considered to be conclusions. Schmitt explains the end of Deuteronomy not as a conclusion but as a transition;[33] but does a verse like "never again has a prophet arisen in Israel like Moses" (Deut 34:10), really sound like a tran-

---

28. Konrad Schmid, *Erzväter und Exodus: Untersuchungen zur doppelten Begründung der Ursprünge Israels innerhalb der Geschichtsbücher des Alten Testaments* (WMANT 81; Neukirchen-Vluyn: Neukirchener, 1999); ET: *Genesis and the Moses Story* (Siphrut 3; Winona Lake: Eisenbrauns, 2010); idem, "The So-Called Yahwist and the Literary Gap Between Genesis and Exodus," in Dozeman and Schmid, *A Farewell to the Yahwist?* 29–50. A similar model can be found in the work of Kratz, *Composition*.

29. A. Graeme Auld, "The Deuteronomists and the Former Prophets, or What Makes the Former Prophets Deuteronomistic?" in Schearing and McKenzie, *Those Elusive Deuteronomists*, 116–26 repr. in idem, *Samuel at the Threshold* (SOTSMS; Burlington, Vt.: Ashgate, 2004), 185–91.

30. Erik Aurelius, *Zukunft jenseits des Gerichts: Eine redaktionsgeschichtliche Studie zum Enneateuch* (BZAW 319; Berlin: de Gruyter, 2003).

31. Stephen B. Chapman, "How the Biblical Canon Began: Working Models and Open Questions," in *Homer, the Bible and Beyond: Literary and Religious Canons in the Ancient World* (ed. M. Finkelberg and G. G. Stroumsa; Jerusalem Studies in Religion and Culture 2; Leiden: Brill, 2003), 29–51.

32. Schmitt, *Arbeitsbuch*, 243.

33. Hans-Christoph Schmitt, "Dtn 34 als Verbindungsstück zwischen Tetrateuch und Deuteronomistischem Geschichtswerk," in Otto and Achenbach, *Das Deuteronomium zwischen Pentateuch und Deuteronomistischem Geschichtswerk*, 181–92.

sition? And what about Josh 24? According to Aurelius the author of these
texts wants to counterbalance the Deuteronomistic insistence on the Sinaitic
covenant by creating a covenant in the land. For Konrad Schmid, Josh 24 was
conceived as a hinge to the following story in order to create two major parts
of the Primary History: the time of salvation (from the origins to the conquest) and the time of decline and judgment (from the Judges to the end of
the monarchy). Schmid highlights especially Joshua's claim: "You cannot serve
YHWH, for he is a holy God, he is a jealous God, he will not forgive your trans-
gressions and your sins ..." (vv. 19–20), which indeed prepares the reader or
the listener for the following story of divine judgment. Schmid also points to
Judg 6:7–10 and 10:6–16, where the people are accused of worshipping other
gods, transgressing Joshua's exhortation and fulfilling his prediction about
Israel's incapacity to serve YHWH. There is certainly a link between these three
texts. But Josh 24:19–20 is clearly an insertion, which interrupts the narrative logic of 24:18 (the people's commitment) and 24:22 (Joshua's ratifying of
the commitment) and contradicts the whole point of the dialogue between
Joshua and the Israelites.[34] Judges 6:7–10 and 10:6–16 are also late interpola-
tions, which recall the style and the theology of the Chronicles; Josh 6:7–10 is
absent from a fragment of a scroll of Joshua found in Qumran.[35] This means
that these texts were only added after the idea of a Hexateuch was rejected, in
order to integrate the scroll of Joshua definitively into the Former Prophets as
the opening of *this* collection.

4.1. Enneateuch or Pentateuch and the First Part of the Prophets?

Do the books of Kings have a fitting conclusion? The question of the meaning of 2 Kgs 25:27–30 is still heavily debated and has been understood in very
different ways: as a sign of messianic hope;[36] as a quite defeatist "no future"
statement;[37] as an indication that the Deuteronomist was an archivist of

---

34. V. 21 is clearly a *Wiederaufnahme* according to Seidel's law. For v. 19–21 as insertion see also Aurelius, *Zukunft*, 175; Thomas Römer, "Das doppelte Ende des Josuabuches:
Einige Anmerkungen zur aktuellen Diskussion um 'deuteronomistisches Geschichtswerk'
und 'Hexateuch,'" *ZAW* 118 (2006): 523–48, esp. 539.
35. See Blum, "Literary Connection," in Dozeman and Schmid, *A Farewell to the Yahwist?* 103–4; Römer, "Ende," 546–47.
36. Gerhard von Rad, "Die deuteronomistische Geschichtstheologie in den Königsbüchern," in idem, *Gesammelte Studien*, 189–204; repr. from *Deuteronomium-Studien*
(FRLANT 40; Göttingen: Vandenhoek & Ruprecht, 1947), 52–64; Jon D. Levenson, "The
Last Four Verses in Kings," *JBL* 103 (1984): 353–61, Juha Pakkala, "Zedekiah's Fate and the
Dynastic Succession," *JBL* 125 (2006): 443–52.
37. This was Noth's idea.

a sort;[38] or as a paradigm for the transformation of exile into Diaspora.[39] In a way the answer depends on the literary context in which one reads the ending of Kings. If one takes 2 Kgs 25:27–30 to be the conclusion of an Enneateuch, one may find in these last verses an echo of the ending of the book of Genesis, since the transformation of Jehoiachin's status reminds the reader of Joseph's career in Genesis 37–50.[40] But whereas Genesis 50 ends with the death of Joseph (and the following book relates the exodus from Egypt), the last words of 2 Kgs 25:27–30 are "all the days of his life." This may be understood as a differentiation between the Egyptian and the Babylonian Diaspora:[41] the Jews of the Babylonian Diaspora may accept life outside the land for many generations. In this perspective the end of Kings could be read as an aetiology of exile and Diaspora. One may also observe a parallel between the ending of Deuteronomy and the ending of Kings, since both end outside the land.

Nevertheless, there is no canonical evidence for an Enneateuch, so that one may ask if one should read 2 Kgs 25:27–30 or, as argued by E. A. Knauf,[42] the whole book of Kings, as a transition to the following prophetic books. In the context of the Nebiim, the book of Kings relates of course the decline and the fall of the Israelite and Judean monarchy, but in so doing it functions as an introduction to the prophetic oracles of judgment and salvation of the prophetic books. One may observe that the book of Kings contains a number of cross-references to the following books of Isaiah and Jeremiah: 2 Kgs 18–20 (Isaiah's meeting with King Hezekiah) has a parallel in Isa 36–39; 2 Kgs 22–23 (Josiah's reform) is echoed in Jehoiachim's "counter reform" (Jer 36); and 2 Kgs 25 has a parallel in Jer 52. These parallels indicate that there was a will to unite all these books into one collection. One may even observe a number of cross-references between the end of Kings and the opening of the book of Isaiah.[43] Isaiah 1:7: "Your country lies desolate, your cities are burned with

---

38. Serge Frolov, "Evil-Merodach and the Deuteronomists: The Sociohistorical Setting of Dtr in the Light of 2 Kgs 25,27–30," *Bib* 88 (2007): 174–90

39. Jeremy Schipper, "'Significant Resonances' With Mephiboshet in 2 Kings 25:27–30: A Response to Donald F. Murray," *JBL* 124 (2005): 521–29; Ronald E. Clements, "A Royal Privilege: Dining in the Presence of the Great King," in *Reflection and Refraction* (ed. R. Rezetko, T. H. Lim, and W. B. Aucker; VTSup 113; Leiden: Brill, 2007), 49–66.

40. Thomas Römer, "Transformations in Deuteronomistic and Biblical Historiography: On 'Book-Finding' and Other Literary Strategies," *ZAW* 109 (1997): 1–11.

41. There is no doubt that the Babylonian Diaspora thought of the Egyptian Jews, especially those of Elephantine, in a quite negative way (Jer 44).

42. Ernst Axel Knauf, "1–2 Rois," in *Introduction à l'Ancien Testament* (ed. T. Römer, J.-D. Macchi, and C. Nihan; MdB 49; Geneva: Labor et Fides, 2004; 2009 2nd. ed.), 384–93.

43. Konrad Schmid, "Buchtechnische und sachliche Prolegomena zur Enneateuchfrage," in Beck and Schorn, *Auf dem Weg zur Endgestalt*, 1–14, 10–12.

fire" can be read as taking up the destruction of Judah and Jerusalem (see especially 2 Kgs 25:9 where the destruction is described as burning). Isa 1:8–9: "Daughter Zion is left like a booth in a vineyard. ... YHWH Sabaoth has left some survivors. ..." reminds the reader of 2 Kgs 25:12, where it is said that the Babylonians had left some people in the land to be vinedressers and tillers of the soil. So Isaiah alludes to the judgment related in Kings in order to introduce a collection of oracles of doom, which are followed by oracles of salvation and restoration. These give the explicit reasons for the failure of the monarchies in Israel and Judah, but they also show that judgment is not YHWH's last word, that there is hope for a future and a gathering from all the nations. The link between the Former and the Latter Prophets may therefore be stronger than is commonly acknowledged. But how is one able to explain this link from a historical perspective?

5. FROM DEUTERONOMISTIC AND PRIESTLY LIBRARIES TO PENTATEUCH AND THE PROPHETS

For the advocates of an Enneateuch, the book of Deuteronomy presents a problem because Moses' reenactment of the Law is located apart from the Sinai revelation. Paolo Sacchi, who thinks that the Pentateuch is the "wrong problematic" and that one should speak of an Enneateuch, wants to cut Deuteronomy off from the Primary History; Konrad Schmid also thinks of Deuteronomy as a possibly very late insertion into the narrative running from Exodus through Kings.[44] But where had this scroll of Deuteronomy been preserved before it was integrated into a larger unit? The literary history of Deuteronomy may suggest that it was first conceived as an independent scroll during the seventh century B.C.E.; but when revised and supplemented during the Babylonian era, it was clearly linked to the books of Joshua–Kings, much more than to the Tetrateuch.[45] Suffice it here to list the following examples:[46] Deuteronomy 6:5 has only one exact parallel in the Hebrew Bible—2 Kgs 23:25, the characterization of King Josiah. The "law of the king" in Deut 17:14–20 prepares for the various Deuteronomistic stories about the rise of kingship in 1 Sam 8–12, as well as the stories about Solomon's

44. Paolo Sacchi, "Le Pentateuque, le Deutéronomiste et Spinoza," in *Congress Volume Paris 1992* (ed. J. A. Emerton; Leiden: Brill, 1995), 276–88, 286; Schmid, *Erzväter*, 164.

45. I have tried to argue for this view of the Deuteronomistic History in Thomas Römer, *The So-Called Deuteronomistic History: A Sociological, Historical and Literary Introduction* (London: T&T Clark and New York: Continuum, 2005; 2d ed., 2007).

46. Thomas Römer, "The Form-Critical Problem of the So-Called Deuteronomistic History," in *The Changing Face of Form Criticism for the Twenty-First Century* (ed. M. A. Sweeney and E. Ben Zvi; Grand Rapids: Eerdmans, 2003), 240–52.

decline in 1 Kgs 9–11*, and also the end of the book of Kings (the descent to
Egypt). There is also evidence on the level of vocabulary that Deuteronomy–
Kings was edited in the same redactional context: the frequent mention of
the "other gods" (ʾĕlōhîm ʾăḥērîm) is a standard expression in the books of
Deuteronomy–Kings, but is attested only two or three times in Exodus; the
same may be said of the root š-m-d (to destroy), which is frequently attested
in Deuteronomy and the Prophets, but rare in the Tetrateuch. One may
also mention the expression "to do what is evil in the eyes of YHWH," which
occurs often in all books from Deuteronomy–Kings (28 times), but only once
before (in Num 32:13). The root k-ʿ-s (hipʿil, "to offend") is attested in Deuteronomy and the Prophets, but not in the Tetrateuch.

These multiple links, to which others could be added, support the idea
of a "Deuteronomistic Library" (not necessarily a "Deuteronomistic History," written on one scroll). This library probably also contained an older
story of Moses, which may be recovered in the book of Exodus, but also some
prophetic scrolls edited by the same Deuteronomistic group. The book of
Jeremiah certainly underwent Deuteronomistic editing,[47] and this may also
be the case for the so-called "Book of the Four," even if the Deuteronomistic
character of Micah or Zephaniah is matter of debate.[48] If the idea that the
Deuteronomistic Library contained some prophetic scrolls is acceptable, it
would explain why the so-called Deuteronomistic History, without the book
of Deuteronomy, became part of the Nebiim. This would also perhaps explain
the "nonmention" of "Deuteronomistic" prophets like Jeremiah or Hosea in
the Deuteronomistic History, because their books were kept together with the
Deuteronomistic History.[49] We would then have two "libraries" containing
scrolls that were used to construct the Pentateuch and later on the Prophets:
the Deuteronomistic one, and the Priestly one.

As Christophe Nihan has shown, the original P document probably ended
in Lev 16. It was supplemented by the "Holiness School," which added Lev
17–26, and which probably already had the intention to combine the Priestly

47. Rainer Albertz, *Israel in Exile: The History and Literature of the Sixth Cen-
tury B.C.E* (trans. D. Green; Studies in Biblical Literature 3; Atlanta: Society of Biblical
Literature, 2003); German original: *Der Exilszeit* (Biblische Enzyklopädie 7; Stuttgart:
Kohlhammer, 2001), distinguishes three Deuteronomistic editions of Jeremiah.

48. For a Deuteronomistic "Book of the Four" see James D. Nogalski, *Literary Precursors to the Book of the Twelve* (BZAW 217; Berlin: de Gruyter, 1993); for a more cautious
position see Rainer Albertz, "Exile as Purification: Reconstructing the 'Book of the Four,'"
in *Thematic Threads of the Book of the Twelve* (ed. P. L. Reddit and A. Schart; BZAW 325;
Berlin: de Gruyter, 2003), 232–51.

49. Clements, *Tradition*, 47–48.

texts with the book of Deuteronomy.[50] The removal of Deuteronomy from the Deuteronomistic Library is due to the fact that the coherence of the Torah as a compromise or consensus between the Priestly and the lay party was found in the figure of Moses. When Deuteronomy became the conclusion of the Torah, it acquired a new status: it was now considered to provide an explanation for the Sinai revelation.[51] The origin of the Pentateuch was, according to this model, the partition of Deuteronomy from the following books.

If one follows this model, the idea of an original Enneateuch should be rejected. But this does not mean that efforts were not made by the guardians of the Pentateuch and those of the first collection of the Nebiim to strengthen the links between both collections: the introduction to the exodus story in Exod 1:6–8[52] is written in analogy to Judg 2:6–10; and during the second century B.C.E., there was an attempt to introduce in Genesis–Kings a chronology that is related to the dedication of the temple in 164 B.C.E.; but which is, with the exception of 1 Kgs 6:1, apparently limited to the Pentateuch.[53] There might have been a conception of reading Genesis–Kings as an "epic story," but not of making this story into a canonical unit, since it did not really end with Kings, but was followed by the Latter Prophets.

6. Instead of a Conclusion: Some Open Questions

6.1. How Do We Define Literary Introductions, Conclusions and Transitions?

As we have already seen, only two books in the Pentateuch have an "absolute" beginning: Gen 1:1 and Deut 1:1–5. In the Former Prophets only 1 Sam 1:1 looks like the beginning of a new story. Joshua 1:1 and Judg 1:1 feature similar literary constructions, but are closely related to the foregoing book by the first words "after the death of Moses" (Josh 1:1) and "after the death of Joshua" (Judg 1:1). If one accepts this line of argument,[54] then we would

---

50. Christophe Nihan, *From Priestly Torah to Pentateuch: A Study in the Composition of the Book of Leviticus* (FAT II/25; Tübingen: Mohr Siebeck, 2007).

51. For the question of the function of Deuteronomy in the Pentateuch see Otto, "The Pentateuch in Synchronical and Diachronical Perspectives," 14–35.

52. According to Christoph Levin, *Der Jahwist* (FRLANT 157; Göttingen: Vandenhoeck & Ruprecht, 1993), 315, Exod 1:1–7 was written later than the pentateuchal redaction.

53. See especially Jeremy Hughes, *Secrets of the Times: Myth and History in Biblical Chronology* (JSOTSup 66; Sheffield: Sheffield Academic Press, 1990), who also addresses the difficult problem of the differences between MT, LXX and Sam. Apparently MT depends on a Priestly chronology which tried to situate the dedication of the temple in the year 4000 and the Exodus in 2666 (see ibid., 43–45).

54. Which is not really formalistic, but based on the formulation of the opening;

have, on the level of introductions, evidence for a Pentateuch (if Deut 34 is an ending) or an Enneateuch; for a Deuteronomistic History (Deuteronomy–Kings); and maybe for a story about the monarchy in Samuel–Kings.

The question of conclusions seems even more complicated. Deuteronomy 34 is without a doubt a conclusion, at least on the canonical level, since this is the last chapter of the Torah as it stands. But some authors have challenged the idea that this chapter had always functioned in this fashion. Chapman, following Schmitt, thinks that Moses' description as the greatest of all prophets serves to correlate the Torah with the Prophets.[55] But this correlation could also function as a qualitative distinction; which would still speak in favor of conceiving Deut 34 as a conclusion, but as the conclusion of a literary work that indicates the existence of other literary collections. The case of Josh 24 and 2 Kgs 25 is still more difficult, since we have no canonical evidence for an independent Hexateuch or Deuteronomistic History. But even if Josh 24 does not conclude a Hexateuch, as I have argued, it is at least conceived as a conclusion to the book of Joshua: it clearly interrupts the Deuteronomistic transition, in which Josh 23 was followed directly by Judg 2:6. The function of 2 Kgs 25:27–30 depends on whether these verses are considered to be the conclusion of the "exilic" version of the Deuteronomistic History, or whether they were a later addition. If this history ended with 2 Kgs 25:21 ("Judah was exiled from its land") or with 2 Kgs 25:26 ("all the people … went to Egypt") as is sometimes argued, then 2 Kgs 25:27–30 could encompass an Enneateuch, but an Enneateuch which was probably already followed by some Prophetic scrolls.

6.2. How Many Scrolls for the "Larger Literary Units"?

When scholars speak about a Pentateuch, Hexateuch, Deuteronomistic History or Enneateuch, they most often think of one scroll comprising the whole;[56] especially for the Pentateuch it is commonly accepted that its separation in five scrolls only occurred at a very late stage of its formation. But if one perceives the different Torah references to the patriarchs as belonging to a pentateuchal redaction, it is of interest that these passages occur in all five books; so that one may then ask whether the pentateuchal redactors are not presupposing a collection of several scrolls, which they try to bind together more closely. The length of the five books of the Torah also speaks against the

---

for a formalistic approach see Wolfgang Schneider, "Und es begab sich …: Anfänge von Erzählungen im Biblischen Hebräisch," *BN* 70 (1993): 62–87.

55. Chapman, "How the Biblical Canon Began," 41.

56. Schmid, "Prolegomena," 5–7, for instance, tries to show that one scroll containing the whole Enneateuch is materially possible.

idea of a quite mechanical division for strictly practical reasons. It is immediately clear that each book of the Torah has its own profile. This is especially the case for Genesis and Deuteronomy, whereas Exodus and Leviticus are more closely connected.[57]

If one thinks more about scrolls as being kept together in vessels made of clay, the question of the larger literary units becomes a bit less exclusive. If there was, for instance, a Deuteronomistic Library with different scrolls including some prophetic ones, one can easily understand that these scrolls were not necessarily revised altogether at the same time or by the same person. It is also understandable that it would have been easy to transfer Deuteronomy and Joshua into another vessel in which priests and Deuteronomists collected the scrolls of the future Torah.

6.3. Intertextuality and Comprehensive Redactions

Finally I would like to address a methodological issue: How can we distinguish comprehensive redactional activity from restricted additions that are limited to one or two passages, or from cases of intertextuality, which do not necessarily imply redactional activities. One may, for instance, observe that the story of Jephthah sacrificing his daughter has many parallels with the Aqedah story in Gen 22, but this does not mean that the author of Judg 11 wrote his story in the context of an Enneateuch. Does the obvious relation between Exod 32 and 1 Kgs 12 support the idea of an Enneateuch? One could also argue that Exod 32 was written (or revised) in order to integrate "Jeroboam's sin" into the Torah, maintaining that the former Deuteronomistic History had become "secondary" after the publication of the Pentateuch and the separation of Deuteronomy from the following books. In order to discern comprehensive redactions, several stylistic and thematic observations should coalesce. We have seen that Schmitt emphasizes a "faith-redaction" whose horizon would be the Enneateuch; if, however, one examines the passages he quotes, they are all limited, with one exception (2 Kgs 17:14), to the books of (Genesis,) Exodus, Numbers and Deuteronomy.[58] Is that enough evidence? Otto has observed that it is quite easy to distinguish several themes or motifs that bind together Genesis–Deuteronomy or Joshua;[59] I would add Deuteronomy–Kings as well, but it seems difficult to me to find evidence of

---

57. See on this also Blenkinsopp, *Pentateuch*, 45.

58. Quite on the same theological level are Exod 4:1–9; 14:31; 19:9; Num 14:11; Deut 1:31; 9:32; and 1 Kgs 17:14 (the case of Gen 15:1 is difficult to decide); the other occurrences of the root refer to very different meanings.

59. Otto, *Deuteronomium*, 219: "If one wants to claim a literary unit that includes after Joshua 24 the rest of the Former Prophets, one should explain why such chains (like

an Enneateuch redaction. Priestly passages occur in 1 Kgs 6–8, but this is not enough to posit a thoroughgoing Priestly redaction of the Enneateuch.[60] On the redactional level, there is almost no evidence for an Enneateuch.

Should we then be happy with Torah and Nebiim and give up the idea of other larger literary units? This option does not take into account that Torah and Nebiim both have forerunners that did not totally disappear after the publication of the Torah. The so-called "historical Psalms" and other historical summaries refer to a Pentateuch (Ps 95), a Hexateuch (Ps 105; Ps 114), maybe even a Tetrateuch (Ps 136),[61] or an Enneateuch (Jer 32; Pss 78, 80, 106).[62] As in any library, it would have been possible to take out or to combine all or only part of the scrolls of the Persian period temple library. And it was also possible to focus on different scrolls depending of the context in which they were used, edited and finally read.

Gen 50:25f.–Exod 13:19–Josh 24:32) do not extend further then Joshua 24" (my translation).

   60. See for these the interesting explanations of Reinhard Achenbach, "Der Pentateuch, seine theokratischen Bearbeitungen und Josua–2 Könige," in Römer and Schmid. *Les dernières rédactions*, 225–53.

   61. It is also possible that Psalm 136 has in mind a Hexateuch, or even a "Heptateuch," including Judges.

   62. This listing is a bit arbitrary because these texts do not cover all traditions of the larger units they are referring to; for some Psalms it is difficult to decide which "great story" they are summarizing.

Pentateuch–Hexateuch–Enneateuch?

Or: How Can One Recognize a Literary Work in the Hebrew Bible?*

Erhard Blum

In order to understand a text, one should know where it begins and ends. In the study of the Old Testament this question is often tied to the issue of which texts actually are intended to be read as literary units. The answer quite often is anything but clear. Without exaggerating one can say that the most essential disputes among Old Testament scholars are over the definitions of their texts. To put it somewhat pointedly, these disputes are over which interpretations deal with real literary works, and which deal with literary units that exist only in the exegetical imagination. Given the large number of competing suggestions, the conclusion seems inevitable that the latter group predominates in numbers.

The particular problematic of the biblical texts can be illuminated by a comparison with epigraphic sources. In cases where the original layout of an epigraphic source can be restored, the interpreter has a reliable perspective on what belongs to this "text."[1] Looking for an analogy in the Old Testament, one could refer to the traditional book units. Regarding the texts under discussion here, the first corpus to be considered a literary unit might be the πεντάτευχος βίβλος, the Pentateuch. Nevertheless, Old Testament scholarship, at least in its early period, almost unanimously agreed that the book of Joshua should be added. The reason is that it is only in Joshua that the Israelites reach the goal of their journey out of Egypt. The solemn land promises to Abraham, Isaac,

* I would like to thank David M. Carr and Thomas B. Dozeman for preparing the translation of this essay into English, and Peter Altmann for his assistance in this task.

4. Even a very fragmentary inscription such as the so-called Balaam inscription from Tell Deir Alla (Combination 1) is already clearly defined—in any case in its beginning—through its layout, with a frame and a reddish written "heading."

and Jacob are fulfilled only with the conquest. In this extent a great narrative arc stretches from at least Abraham to the death of Joshua. Therefore, scholars often referred to the "Hexateuch" rather than to the "Pentateuch." Accordingly, interpreters sought and found the pentateuchal sources throughout this Hexateuch—predominately the two preexilic sources, the Yahwist (J) and the Elohist (E), joined together by the Yehovist (JE), and the exilic/postexilic Priestly source (P); while Deuteronomy existed separately.[2]

Why, however, should one stop at the end of Joshua? The narrative line of the history of Israel continues further in a seamless manner up to the loss of the land at the end of the book of Kings. From this larger perspective, the historical narrative from Genesis to 2 Kings presents—as M. Weippert puts it—a double etiology "of the possession and of the loss of the land."[3] As such, the Enneateuch was itself considered a composition and was often analyzed source-critically through the identification of pentateuchal sources in the Former Prophets,[4] or by postulating a great "History" from Genesis through 2 Kings.[5]

The temporary end of the Enneateuch and the Hexateuch came about with the influential new analysis of the so-called historical books by M. Noth. On the one hand, he contested the existence of pentateuchal sources in the book of Joshua. On the other hand, he discovered a great compositional connection that extended from Deuteronomy to the books of Kings, his "Deu-

---

2. Suffice it to refer to Julius Wellhausen (*Die Composition des Hexateuchs und der historischen Bücher des Alten Testaments* [3d ed.; Berlin: Reimer, 1899], original 1866); for a source-critical hypothesis involving three preexilic sources see Otto Eißfeldt, *Hexateuch-Synopse: Die Erzählung der fünf Bücher Mose und des Buches Josua mit dem Anfange des Richterbuches in ihre vier Quellen zerlegt und in deutscher Übersetzung dargeboten samt einer in Einleitung und Anmerkungen gegebenen Begründung* (Leipzig: Hinrichs, 1922).

3. Manfred Weippert, "Fragen des israelitischen Geschichtsbewusstseins," *VT* 23 (1973): 415–42, esp. 441.

4. See, for example, Carl H. Cornill, "Zur Quellenkritik der Bücher Samuelis," *Königsberger Studien* 1 (1887): 25–59, who argued for the presence of "E" in Sam; Karl Budde, *Die Bücher Richter und Samuel: Ihre Quellen und ihr Aufbau* (Gießen: Ricker, 1890); Gustav Hölscher, *Geschichtsschreibung in Israel: Untersuchungen zum Jahwisten und Elohisten* (Skrifter utgivna av [K.] Humanistika Vetenskapssamfundet i Lund 50; Lund: Gleerup, 1952); and the representation by Otto Eißfeldt, *The Old Testament: An Introduction* (trans. P. R. Ackroyd; New York: Harper & Row, 1965), §37.

5. See Carl H. Cornill (*Einleitung in das Alte Testament* [3d and 4th eds.; Grundriss der Theologischen Wissenschaft 2/1; Freiburg: Mohr (Siebeck), 1896], §19: "Das exilische Geschichtswerk des Volkes Israel"), who describes an exilic historical work, to which belongs the Hexateuch without P, plus the Dtr adaptation of Judg, Sam, and Kgs; so also Ernst Sellin, *Einleitung in das Alte Testament* (5th ed.; Evang.-Theologische Bibliothek; Leipzig: Quelle & Meyer, 1929), 80–81, the section entitled, "Anhang: Das deuteron. Geschichtswerk aus dem babylonischen Exil."

teronomistic History" (DtrG), which was written after the fall of the kings of Judah as a negative evaluation of Israel's history in the land.[6] Along with this discovery, Noth dissolved the Pentateuch, for only a Tetrateuch remained next to the DtrG. The Pentateuch came into being only secondarily from the interweaving of JE and P and their further combination with the book of Deuteronomy from the DtrG.[7] As a consequence, almost a whole generation of European OT scholars considered the main literary-historical problems of the Pentateuch and of the historical books of the Old Testament to have been solved.[8]

The destabilization of this fundamental consensus began in the 1970s with the renewed discussion of the question of Pentateuch or "Tetrateuch." The result was, at least in research within the European continent, that the classical pentateuchal sources J and E were barely employed.[9] Along with this, the dating of the non-Priestly texts to the early or middle period of the Judean monarchy was mostly given up. Over against this sea change, Noth's DtrG retained the function of the fixed point against which the coordination of the pentateuchal models was to be adjusted. Given, however, the recapitulation of materials from the exodus-Moses tradition within the beginning of Deuteronomy, the question has been inevitable, whether the increasingly later dating of the non-Priestly Tetrateuch does not in fact collide with the DtrG hypothesis. On these and other grounds almost anything appears to be imaginable, including discourse on the "Pentateuch," and/or the "Hexateuch," and/or the "Enneateuch," and/or the "Deuteronomistic History" in various forms. The entire range of possibilities is presently open for consideration, in determining the literary-historical priority of one hypothesis over another.

So much for a rough sketch of the state of the research to which this study is linked. I will proceed in three parts: in the first part of this discussion, I will call to mind some elementary indicators of divisions of books or literary works in the Pentateuch and the Former Prophets; in the second part I will discuss two recent hypotheses about the Hexateuch and the Enneateuch; and in the third part I will offer proposals of my own.

---

6. Martin Noth, *Überlieferungsgeschichtliche Studien: Die sammelnden und bearbeitenden Geschichtswerke im Alten Testament* (Halle: Niemeyer Verlag, 1943; 2d repr. ed., 1957; 3d repr. ed.: Darmstadt: Wissenschaftliche Buchgesellschaft, 1967); trans. as *The Deuteronomistic History* (trans. J. Doull et al.; JSOTSup 15; Sheffield: Sheffield Academic Press, 1981; 2d ed., 1991).

7. Ibid., 206ff., 211ff.

8. Even Gerhard von Rad, who always spoke of a "Hexateuch" in referring to the conception of salvation history, apparently avoided a controversial discussion over the literary-historical question.

9. Compare the representation and discussion by Erich Zenger, *Einleitung in das Alte Testament* (5th ed.; Stuttgart: Kohlhammer, 2004), Section C.2–6.

1

A continuous reading or even a quick overview of Genesis through 2 Kings, with a focus on the transitions between the books, is enough to see fundamental grounds for a textual continuum extending from Genesis to the end of the books of Kings:

(1) The first indication is formal. The books represent a continuous and consecutive narrative. Even speeches, songs, or prescriptive texts (both cultic and legal/ethical regulations) all remain embedded in the large narrative framework.

(2) Within this larger narrative there is a basic coherence of plot with regard to time, space, and characters: The timeline progresses to its end in a linear fashion, without breaks. The primeval beginning, with the creation that inaugurates human history, leads to the history focused on Israel's origin, which continues on into the history of Israel in the land until its loss—in just the sense of a double etiology of land possession and land lost suggested by Weippert. The narrative continuity remains even in the critical transitional seams between Deuteronomy and Joshua, between Joshua and Judges, and between Judges and the time of the kings, the last period, which begins in the middle of the first book of Samuel.

(3) Finally there are broader lines of composition. K. Schmid, for example, notes the chronological indicators in the Pentateuch and Joshua through Kings, which in the Masoretic Text relate the exodus and the initial building of Solomon's temple and extend further to the rededication of the temple by the Maccabees in 164 b.c.e.[10] Still other far-reaching literary structures also force themselves upon the reader, such as the correspondence between Israel's original sin with Aaron's golden calf in Exod 32 and the original sin of the northern kingdom with the calves of Jeroboam I in 1 Kgs 12. It is not surprising that such correspondences and literary relationships are often evaluated diachronically as compositional features. Thus, Schmid, for example, concludes: "Genesis-2 Kings is ... to be considered as a redactional unity."[11]

---

10. Konrad Schmid, *Erzväter und Exodus: Untersuchungen zur doppelten Begründung der Ursprünge Israels innerhalb der Geschichtsbücher des Alten Testaments* (WMANT 81; Neukirchen-Vluyn: Neukirchener, 1999), 19–22.

11. Ibid., 26. A corresponding tendency to speak of the "great DtrG" from Gen to 2 Kgs, now detached from the classical source hypothesis, had been current already for some time; compare the literature in Erhard Blum, *Studien zur Komposition des Pentateuch* (BZAW 189; Berlin: de Gruyter, 1990), 208–10. See in particular the various writings of Hans-Christoph Schmitt (especially "Das spätdeuteronomistische Geschichtswerk Genesis i–2 Reg xxv und seine theologische Intention," in *Congress Volume Cambridge 1995* [ed. J. A. Emerton; VTSup 66; Leiden: Brill, 1997], 261–79); in English language literature the topic is covered under the term, "primary history."

Is this, however, actually the case? This is exactly the question, or one of the questions, that is under debate here.

There is, in my opinion, above all a need to avoid some methodical simplifications. I will exemplify this point with two trivial, but seemingly opposite data.

First, let us consider the macro-structure of the Hebrew canon: The most significant break in the canon does not lie between the books of Kings and Isaiah but between Deuteronomy and Joshua, that is between the "Torah" and the "Prophets/Nebiim," which begin with Joshua and end with Malachi. This canonical structure, as is well known, is evident in the liturgical use of the Torah and the Prophets in the synagogue. This division did not arise only in the rabbinic Jewish reception of the text, but goes back at least to the Hellenistic period. Evidence for this structure includes the references to the "Law and the Prophets" in the New Testament; the formulation of "the book of Moses and the books of the prophets" in 4QMMT^d; the prologue to Ben Sira;[12] and also the Samaritan canon and the beginnings of the LXX with the translation of the Pentateuch.

Of fundamental significance, furthermore, is the designation of the Pentateuch as "the book of the Torah of Moses," which assigns it to a particular genre. This assignment implies a specific character of the corpus in terms of pragmatics; that is, the genre determines how the addressees are to receive the text. For the first tradents, the Pentateuch was distinguished in this respect from the historical books of the "Former Prophets" in a fundamental way. As a consequence, the literary-historical question of the priority of a narrative work that extends from Genesis through Kings, or of the Pentateuch as Torah depends basically on the history of the genre "book of the Torah." I will return to this topic later.

No less fundamental than the division between the Pentateuch and the Former Prophets is the fact that the independence of the canonical Pentateuch on the one hand and its narrative continuation into Joshua, etc., on the other hand were never understood as contradictory: Any reader of the Torah cannot help but anticipate the continuation of the history of the Pentateuch in the Former Prophets, while the reverse is also true! Moreover, the simultaneity of independence and continuity seems to be an essential structure of a written canon, in which each instance of innercanonical intertextuality also represents a kind of "intratextuality."[13] It is no wonder, therefore, that this

---

12. Sirach, Prologue, 1: "Many great teachings have been given to us through the Law and the Prophets and others that follow them."

13. Actually, the distinction between "intertextual" correlations, i.e., references between literarily independent works, and "intratextual" references, i.e., interrelations

intertextuality is *inter alia* evident in such phases of the formation of tradition, which extend into the textual history of the Hebrew Bible.

A clear example is 1 Sam 2:22b*b* in the MT, in which the sanctuary at Shiloh is identified with the Priestly tent of meeting of the exodus. In this case the author takes up Exod 38:8 and creates a correspondence to the Priestly notices in the book of Joshua (Josh 18:1, 8–10; 19:51; 21:2; 22:9, 12). It would be a mistake, however, to interpret such an element as an indication of a Priestly redaction of the books of Samuel. The evidence is provided by the older LXX tradition, where 1 Sam 2:22b*b* is missing, and this is confirmed by the Hebrew witness of 4QSam[a].[14] What we have here is an isolated insertion that is intended to indicate the continuity of the Mosaic tent of meeting into the time of the judges and beyond.[15]

Joshua 20 provides another example, in which the literary-historical analysis results in a Priestly-modeled report on asylum and a harmonizing supplementation with a mixture of Priestly and Deuteronomistic elements. The evidence suggests that the author who supplemented the account already had the completed Pentateuch before him. Most of the secondary elements, in fact, are absent in the LXX.[16]

Finally, perhaps the clearest example is offered by K. Schmid, in his exposition of the chronological system in the Pentateuch and the Former Prophets: If it is true that the original chronology extended to the rededication of the temple by Judas Maccabee, then its final form goes back to a redactional revision that was carried out on the longstanding independent and normative Mosaic Torah, and at the same time—since nothing else is possible—built on the chronological data in Judges to Kings.

There are more examples like these. They demonstrate a simple, but often overlooked, fact: Not every literary connection, nor every parallel or cross-reference, no matter how uncontroversial, is evidence for a compositional connection within a single work. Such literary features, though intentional, might function as instances of intertextual linking. Even interventions by one and the same person in separate texts do not prove *per se* a "redactional unity." Even more, especially in canonical or protocanonical collections one must reckon with a tendency in which different books in the course of their ongoing use are related and harmonized with each other.

---

between different parts of the same work, if applied to Gen–2 Kgs, helps to reveal the maze of diachronic and synchronic difficulties confronting biblical exegesis.

14. For discussion see Emanuel Tov, *Textual Criticism of the Hebrew Bible* (2d ed.; Minneapolis: Fortress, 1992), 342–43.

15. The report of the sanctification of the temple by Solomon in 1 Kgs 8:1–11 exhibits analogous retouchings, which were, for the most part, probably still absent in the LXX *Vorlage*.

16. A full exegetical discussion cannot be undertaken here. For a persuasive analysis of the fundamental issues see Alexander Rofé, "Joshua 20: Historico-Literary Criticism Illustrated," in *Empirical Models for Biblical Criticism* (ed. J. H. Tigay; Philadelphia: University of Pennsylvania Press, 1985), 131–47.

In terms of the question of the subtitle of this study, how one can recognize a literary work in the Hebrew Bible, two alternatives stand out so far: Either one may rely on clear external data of the reception history, which limits one to the closing phases of the formation of the canon; or one may enter into the question of the composition history of the Old Testament, in which case one is left with often multivalent internal indicators, and with the question of how to distinguish intratextual connections from intertextual references. The search for additional indicators naturally arises; we will return to this in section 3.

2

Before continuing, the problematic just outlined shall be defined more clearly in light of recent analyses in the realm of the Enneateuch. To this end, I will limit myself to two significant approaches that are presented in current monographs on this theme.

E. Aurelius offers a new hypothesis concerning the Enneateuch in his monograph, *Zukunft jenseits des Gerichts*, which departs from earlier source-critical models. His approach starts rather from the present pentateuchal debate and some fundamental revisions of Noth's Deuteronomistic History hypothesis. He develops a detailed stratigraphy and pedigree of programmatic Deuteronomistic texts in the Former Prophets, as well as in the Pentateuch and the book of Jeremiah. Through this analysis he describes inter alia a Deuteronomistic redaction of the Enneateuch, which is dependent on two anchor texts, namely the prologue to the Sinai pericope in Exod 19:3b–8 and 2 Kgs 18:12, one of the Deuteronomistic epilogues to the history of the northern kingdom.[17]

Exod 19:3–8

19:3 Then Moses went up to God;
    And YHWH called to him from the mountain, saying,
        "Thus you shall say to the house of Jacob, and tell the Israelites:
19:4 'You have seen what I did to the Egyptians,
    and how I bore you on eagles' wings
        and brought you to myself.
19:5 Now therefore,
    if you obey my voice and keep my covenant (*berit*),
        you shall be my treasured possession out of all the peoples;
            for the whole earth is mine.
19:6 You shall be for me a kingdom of priests and a holy nation.'

---

17. Erik Aurelius, *Zukunft jenseits des Gerichts: Eine redaktionsgeschichtliche Studie zum Enneateuch* (BZAW 319; Berlin: de Gruyter, 2003), 95–110, 208–216

These are the words that you shall speak to the Israelites."
19:7 So Moses came, summoned the elders of the people, and set before
them all these words that Yʜwʜ had commanded him.
19:8 The people all answered as one and spoke:
"Everything that Yʜwʜ has spoken, we will do."

2 Kgs 18:11–12

18:11 The king of Assyria carried the Israelites away to Assyria …
18:12 because they did not obey the voice of Yʜwʜ their God but trans-
gressed his covenant—all that Moses the servant of Yʜwʜ had commanded;
they neither listened nor obeyed.

The parallels between the two passages are in fact manifold: the combination
of keeping or breaking the covenant (*berit*) and of "hearing or not hearing
the voice (of God)," as well as the formulation, "all that he has commanded,"
and the "doing" of God's will. Yet the redaction-historical significance of
these parallels requires critical examination. Indeed a quick check in the
concordance shows that these phrases and expressions are common in Deuteronomistic and post-Deuteronomistic texts. This applies to the phrase, "to
listen to the voice,"[18] which occurs over sixty times in the Old Testament in
reference to the voice of Yʜwʜ;[19] but also the phrase, "to disobey the covenant," which is found in diverse Deuteronomistic documents (conceived in
the widest possible sense).[20] Both phrases occur next to each other in Judg
2:20. The frequent formal reference to "all that he has commanded" is also
not very indicative in terms of tradition history;[21] in addition, the phrase is
referring to different matters in Exod 19:7 and 2 Kgs 18:12. In Exod 19 it indicates a conditioned promise given by Yʜwʜ; while in 2 Kgs 18 it refers to
"all that Moses the servant of Yʜwʜ had commanded." Given that there is
so little precise agreement between the texts, it is difficult to decide whether
this is an intentional literary connection or a simple coincidence, as such
repetitions are inevitable and expected in the quite limited repertoire of this
theological language.

---

18. The Hebrew is predominantly שמע בקול, and less frequently with the preposition
ל (see Exod 4:1, 8, 9).

19. In both Deuteronomistic and post-Deuteronomistic literature. The phrase is per
se, of course, not restricted to theological use, but appears also as an unspecific idiom—
(more than 30 times in the OT). Aurelius, nevertheless, uses it as the thread of Ariadne
for his reconstruction of a literary-historical pedigree; compare the overview in *Zukunft*,
208–211. See also n. 37.

20. Deut 17:2; 29:11; Josh 7:11, 15; 23:16; Judg 2:20; 2 Kgs 18:12; Jer 14:18; Hos 8:1b.

21. (…) אשר צוה (…) כל. There are over 60 instances of this phrase in the Hebrew
Bible, in theological contexts that include Deuteronomistic, Priestly, and other traditions.

At first sight one might think that a further particularly striking connection[22] might be decisive in such a case: The sequence of "to hear" and "to do" occurs in both 2 Kgs 18:12 and Exod 24:3–8, which is the report of the carrying out of the directives from Exod 19:3–8. In Exod 24, the verb "to do" takes the primary position in a striking manner: "we will do it and we will hear it (be obedient) (24:7)." In corroboration of this evidence, one might adduce the argument that intertextual connections are frequently found in chiastic form.[23] Yet even this congruence does not itself support an original *inclusio* between 2 Kgs 18:12 and the Sinai pericope: (1) the combination of the words, "to hear" and "to do" appears to be idiomatic;[24] (2) it is Deut 5:27 that provides the closest parallel to Exod 24:7, especially if one takes in account the resemblances between the two contexts in terms of language and narrative plot.[25] The above-mentioned resemblance is diachronically due to a reciprocal relationship between Deut 5 and the pre-Priestly Sinai pericope, which was further developed later on, with particular adjustments, as is partially evident in the textual history.[26] Thus ונשמעה in Exod 20:19a (MT) is not attested in the pre-Hexaplaric Septuagint.[27] In an analogous way, one might view ונשמע in Exod 24:7 as a scribal gloss supplemented from Deut 5:27, which would explain not only its logically odd position,[28] but also the difference from Exod 19:8 and 24:3. The supposed connection of the passage to 2 Kgs 18:12 proves to be accidental on the basis of the genesis of the present wording of Exod 24:7.

The proposed relationship between Exod 19:3b–8 and 2 Kgs 18:12 presents a similar case. Aurelius concludes that the two passages "come from the

---

22. As far as I can see, however, Aurelius does not refer to this possibility.

23. Compare Meir Weiss, *The Bible From Within: The Method of Total Interpretation* (Jerusalem: The Hebrew University Magnes Press, 1984 [Hebr., 1962]), 96–97, 116–17; Raphael Weiss, "Chiasm in the Bible" in idem, *Studies in the Text and Language of the Bible* (Jerusalem: The Hebrew University Magnes Press, 1981), 259–73 (Hebrew; first published in 1962). R. Weiss refers to A. Ibn Ezra, who occasionally noted that in the Hebrew Bible textual elements frequently are taken up in retrograde, i.e., in a chiastic structure (see his Commentary to Exod 17:7 et passim).

24. Compare, in addition to Exod 24:7: Deut 5:27; 2 Kgs 18:12; also (relating to different connections of content) Jer 35:10; 1 Kgs 8:32, 43; 1 Kgs 20:25; and Deut 30:12.

25. The (pre-Priestly) KD-context in the former Sinai pericope unfolds the paradigmatic primeval events of revelation 'retold' in Deut 5 (the people hear the Decalogue as direct address by God, they fall back in fear and ask Moses for mediation, promising to do all the words of God) in Exod 20–24: proclamation of the Decalogue, fear of God, and Moses' commission for mediation in chap. 20, its carrying out in chap. 20–24*, and Israel's exemplary self-commitment in 24:3, 7.

26. First, Deut 5 was designed on the pre-KD context of Exod 19–24 (without 20:19–21a, 22*, *inter alia*); later on, there was an elaboration of Exod 19–24*, oriented on the conception of the Deuteronomic representation (note the resumptive repetition of 20:18 [end] in v. 21a); compare Blum, *Studien*, 93–96

27. Conversely, the Septuagint (or its *Vorlage*) also expanded Exod 19:8 and 24:3 to "we will do and hear."

28. Rabbinic interpretation did not miss the logical peculiarity, which has given rise to rich Midrashim. See Benno Jacob, *The Second Book of the Bible: Exodus* (trans. W. Jacob; Hoboken: Ktav, 1992 [original 1943]).

same hand, thus from a redactor who focuses on the account from Exodus through 2 Kings and has worked on the beginning and the end of that account."[29] This far-reaching thesis is unlikely if only for the reason that one would have to assume that the author who made the insertion in 2 Kgs 18 had forgotten the program expressed in Exod 19:3b–8: In Exod 19 the keeping of the *berit* is bound with the promise of divine immediacy, presence among Israel as a holy people of priests. The promised singular status of the people is realized primordially and paradigmatically in Exod 24:3–8, 9–11 on the basis of the mere assent to the wish to do the divine will. This realization of divine immediacy culminates in the vision of God seen by the representatives of the people. It is then immediately lost with the sin of the golden calf (Exod 32).[30] There is no trace whatsoever of this exceptional (broken) majestic relationship between YHWH and Israel to be found in 2 Kgs 18.

With regard to Exod 19:5–6, Aurelius shares the view that the offer to Israel to be a ממלכת כהנים concerns the condition of the entire people, and accordingly is not to be understood as an intermediation with an Aaronide concept of Israel's constitution.[31] He also concedes the conceptual relationship of Exod 19:3–8 to the narrated events in Exod 24:3–8, as a secondary interpretation of 24:3–8.[32] His diachronic discussion is confined, however, to the blood rite executed on the people (24:8), even though this is only one element in a cluster of actions that represent in narrative form the unique and at the same time ephemeral nearness of God to Israel—a divine immediacy which will be broken with the subsequent sin of the golden calf (compare Exod 32 with the appointment of a priesthood). In addition, it must be said that the intention of this narrative theology is distorted, if one measures the ritual of 24:3–8 against Aaronide-priestly standards.[33] For the concept of a general priesthood of all Israelites implies the abolition of the *institution* of priesthood! At the same time no constellation applicable to the world of the addressee is described here, nor can the narrative be read metaphorically. Rather it is a primordially realized constellation that represents a constitution of Israel as it was actually intended: as a manifestation of God's immediate nearness! The ritual context in Exod 24 is a singular

---

29. Aurelius, *Zukunft*, 208.

30. For discussion of these compositional contexts see Blum, *Studien*, 51–65.

31. Aurelius, *Zukunft*, 146–150. For discussion of both questions see already Erhard Blum, "Esra, die Mosetora und die persische Politik," in *Religion und Religionskontakte im Zeitalter der Achämeniden* (ed. R. G. Kratz; Veröffentlichungen der Wissenschaftlichen Gesellschaft für Theologie 22; Gütersloh: Gütersloher Verlagshaus, 2002), 231–56, esp. 236–38.

32. Ibid., 162.

33. Aurelius (*Zukunft*, 161) refers to Walter Groß, *Zukunft für Israel: Alttestamentliche Bundeskonzepte und die aktuelle Debatte um den Neuen Bund* (SBS 176; Stuttgart: Katholisches Bibelwerk, 1998), 14–19. (Groß refers here to a particular reception of my interpretation of Exod 19–24 by E. Otto).

event that is designed in view of this theological concept.[34] Besides, even if one under-
stands Exod 19:3–8 as a *secondary* interpretation of Exod 24 as a "priestly ordination," one
would still need to read this programmatic passage within its narrative context, i.e., within
the drama of salvation history characteristic of the non-Priestly Sinai pericope—and not as
general parenesis, the promises of which "are always and everywhere valid."[35]

Alternatively, one could consider the possibility that 2 Kgs 18:12 includes an
unspecific allusion to Exod 19. But the stereotypical use of language[36] does not
allow for such an assumption. What is important in making a judgment is that

---

34. The ritual can actually be understood solely as an inauguration rite *without* preexisting institutions: the acceptance of the covenant stipulations (24:3) is required before the
"young men"(!) can be commissioned for sacrifices; then the confirmation of the acceptance of the now literally documented "words of covenant" is needed in order to conduct
the covenant explicitly על כל הדברים האלה. The inauguration act, with application of blood
to the people, relies conceptually on a (priestly) consecration rite (but not literally on Lev
8), through its accommodation to the narrated situation (the application of the blood to
one individual at a time would be difficult to conceive of with regard to the entire people,
hence the mechanism of the sprinkling of the blood). Therefore, one can not argue on the
basis of the singularity of the formulation; cf., for instance, Aurelius, *Zukunft*, 161 n. 81.
Moreover, there are no compelling alternative explanations. W. Groß, *Zukunft*, 19, calls
to mind the conditioned (self-) curses connected with "cutting" treaties/covenants (cf.
Gen 15:9–21; Jer 34:18–19; *KAI* 222); but he remarks himself that in Exod 24 we do not
have any hint of such a meaning. Apparently the logic of sacrifice and blood application is
totally different in this case.
35. Aurelius, *Zukunft*, 168. According to him the actual addressee of Exod 19:5-6 represents "das nachstaatliche Israel," but—based on 2 Kgs 18:12—not all Israel, including the
North, rather a "rest of the people of Yнwн" in Judah (ibid., 108–9). Such an interpretation, however, provokes the question of how Exod 19:3b–4(!), 5–6 (and its context) could
lead postexilic readers to such a (directly applicable and restrictive) understanding.
36. In his argumentation Aurelius points to Jer 7:22–28 "als Vorbild für die Rahmung
der Geschichte durch Ex 19:3b–8 und 2 R 18:12" (*Zukunft*, 107). Jeremiah 7 contrasts
the promise, given after the exodus and conditioned by Israel's obedience (שמע בקול),
to Israel's enduring failure (3 x ולא שמעו). One must doubt, however, that Deuteronomistic
or post-Deuteronomistic tradents had any need for a *literary Vorlage* to arrive at such theological thinking. Aurelius is aware, of course, that Jer 7 does not "provide" all the important
theologumena of Exod 19:3–8—for instance, the term *berit*. He therefore proposes that Jer
11 and Judg 2:20 are further intermediary texts leading towards Exod 19:3–8 (ibid., 97–98,
104–06). Such an argumentation builds methodologically, however, on two far-reaching
presuppositions: (a) the identification of our OT texts with the tradition of ancient Israel as
a whole, combined with the view that Israel's tradition formed a hermetic universe of quo-
tations; (b) the postulate that all textual components in the OT bearing any phraseological
resemblance are literarily dependent on one another. Both presuppositions form, in my
view, unhistorical constructs; cf. already Erhard Blum, "Notwendigkeit und Grenzen historischer Exegese: Plädoyer für eine alttestamentliche Exegetik," in *Theologie und Exegese des
Alten Testaments / der Hebräischen Bibel: Zwischenbilanz und Zukunftsperspektiven* (ed.
B. Janowski; SBS 200; Stuttgart: Katholisches Bibelwerk, 2005), 11–40, esp. 26–28.

the verse and its related texts,[37] with their conceptual and compositional horizon, remain within the Deuteronomistic framework beginning in Deuteronomy.

In conclusion, the textual links discussed by Aurelius are at most conceivable on the level of eventual intertextual *receptions*, caused by similarities of theological stock language. In any case, the compositional construction of an Enneateuch would be too heavy a burden for a single verse like 2 Kgs 18:12.

A challenging proposal of R. G. Kratz addresses a completely different aspect of literary history.[38] He advocates the concept of an original Hexateuch, thereby decidedly drawing back to a position prior to the analytical turning point of M. Noth. According to Kratz, a Hexateuch extending into the book of Joshua marked the beginning of the literary history of bigger units in the realm of the Pentateuch. What at first could be seen as a return to Wellhausen proves on closer inspection to be something clearly different: the tradition of Genesis, for example, does not belong to this Hexateuch; rather, it comprises "Exod 2–Josh 12."[39] But this information could easily mislead as well, since according to the precise reconstruction of the layers,[40] there remain fewer than three pages of translated text for the primary form of this Hexateuch.

The ambitious undertaking to unearth such a small primary layer that is both complete and in its original wording within the massive textual entities of the Pentateuch and Joshua, on the basis of detailed analytical observations and successive literary-critical subtractions, will have difficulties gaining a wide consensus. Thus much, if not everything, depends on the plausibility of the results.

For that reason I will focus here on the passage in which the concept of the "Hexateuch" as a whole must be decided, and the evidence of which appears to be most important to Kratz: the transition from the time of Moses to the time of Joshua. The following textual elements[41] are postulated as belonging to the foundational source that extended from the wonder at the sea (Exod 14*; 15:20–22a) to the crossing of the Jordan and beyond:

---

37. In the summary of Aurelius (*Zukunft*, 208f.), 2 Kgs 18:5–7a; 21:7–9; 23:25–27 are also included.

38. Reinhard G. Kratz, *Die Komposition der erzählenden Bücher des Alten Testaments: Grundwissen der Bibelkritik* (Uni-Taschenbücher 2157; Göttingen: Vandenhoeck & Ruprecht, 2000), 129–30, 208–10, 215, 220–21 ; trans. as *The Composition of the Narrative Books of the Old Testament* (trans. J. Bowden; New York: T&T Clark, 2005); idem, "Der vor- und der nachpriesterschriftliche Hexateuch," in *Abschied vom Jahwisten: Die Komposition des Hexateuch in der jüngsten Diskussion* (ed. J. C. Gertz, K. Schmid, and M. Witte; BZAW 315; Berlin: de Gruyter, 2002), 295–323, esp. 316–319.

39. Cf. the chart in Kratz, *Kompositionen*, 331.

40. Ibid., 303 ("Sources" + "*Grundschrift* [E]" without later expansions).

41. Kratz, *Komposition*, 220, 302–3; and for Deut 34 see idem, "Hexateuch," 321.

Num 20:1* (…) and the people stayed in Kadesh. Miriam died there, and was buried there.

Num 22:1 The Israelites set out, and camped in the plains of Moab across the Jordan from Jericho.

Num 25:1a Israel stayed at Shittim. (…)

Deut 34:1a* Then Moses went up from the plains of Moab (…) to the top of Pisgah, which is opposite Jericho.

Deut 34:5–6* Then Moses (…) died there. (…) He buried him//he was buried in a valley (in the land of Moab) opposite Beth-Peor (…).

Josh 2:1–7, 15–16, 22–23; 3:1, 14a, 16

Then Joshua son of Nun sent two men secretly from Shittim as spies, saying, "Go, view the land, especially Jericho." So they went, and entered the house of a prostitute whose name was Rahab, and spent the night there (…).

The methodological questions connected with recovering such small textual fragments for the reconstruction of an original textual thread cannot be taken up in this context, nor can we deal here with the alleged narrative coherence of this thread.[42] Decisive for the whole hypothesis is the binding together of the episode of Rahab with Num 25 through the localization of the Israelites at Shittim. In the Documentary Hypothesis before M. Noth this relationship was dealt with by arranging Num 25* and Josh 2* together in one or more of the old sources.[43] In his redaction-historical model, Kratz claims exactly this connection within the itinerary as proof for a relatively old narrative connection between Moses and Joshua. The exact delimitation of this connection, however, proves to be difficult upon close inspection:

For one thing, the current version of the Rahab story in Josh 2, with Rahab's confession of Yhwh in 2:10–11, clearly belongs to a late- or post-Deuteronomistic context. Kratz solves this problem by means of a hefty literary-critical reduction of the narrative. The postulated base layer of Josh 2:1–7, 15–16, 22–23 is purely a profane text that is devoid of any theological theme, presenting itself as a sort of narrative facade, to the extent that one must ask oneself in the end, why the piece really should have been narrated. The preservation of the spies by Rahab remains without meaning, both

---

42. A variety of different literary-critical questions can be posed to Num 22:1; 25:1a and Deut 34:1*.

43. See especially Carl Steuernagel (*Das Buch Josua* [2d ed.; HKAT I/3/2; Göttingen: Vandenhoeck & Ruprecht, 1923], 212) who writes of Josh 2, "Die Haupterzählung stammt von E; das ergibt sich aus der Erwähnung von Schittim als Lagerort Israels (vgl. Num 25,1)."

for the characters as well as for the readers. For another thing, the supposed base text—like Josh 2 as a whole—stands in tension to the present main Deuteronomistic thread of the book of Joshua, as the source critics have long recognized: "Already Knobel had remarked in his commentary on Joshua from 1861 that Joshua's command to the guards to prepare the people to cross the Jordan in three days (1:11) finds its continuation, albeit not immediately, in 3:2. ... The narrative of the spies in chapter 2 is impossible between 1:11 and 3:2."[44] O. Eißfeldt accounted for this in one way by taking note of the established time period through 1:11 and 3:2, which the story of Rahab breaks up (2:22); and in another way by considering the narrative logic of 1:11.[45]

Now one could attempt to press the literary criticism still further and eliminate the Rahab narrative altogether. Then there would still remain the possibility of a connection between Num 25:1 and Josh 3:1 by means of the word "Shittim." But with this move, the problem becomes even more acute: As an assumed old element, Josh 3:1, along with its peculiar profile, functions as a foreign body within the fully consistent main narrative. In terms of redaction history, this does not make sense.

In contrast to Kratz's explanation, the whole issue is clarified simply if we consider the entire Rahab episode of Josh 2:1–3:1 as a post-Deuteronomistic addition to a previously established literary context concerned with Joshua.[46] Moreover, such a diachronic profile fits very well with the main point of the basic narrative, accounting for the non-Israelite Rahab's confession of YHWH, which points to a postexilic context.[47] From there it is also not difficult to explain the connection between Josh 2 and the location of the action in Num 25 as an intentional contrast between Rahab's exemplary fear of YHWH and the Moabite women, who seduced the Israelites into worship of Baal Peor at Shittim.

When one includes the larger context, it becomes immediately clear that the portions of the Rahab story included in the narrative of Jericho in Josh 6 represent an unmistakable insertion, and they are linked with elements that prepare the ground for the episode of

---

44. Eißfeldt, *Hexateuch-Synopse*, 66.

45. Ibid., 67: "In 1,11 ist der demnächstige, zeitlich schon bestimmte, Übergang fest beschlossene Sache. Dahinter hat die Erkundung Jerichos ... keinen Sinn." Eissfeldt employs classical source criticism, attributing 1:11 and 3:2–4 etc. to "E," and Josh 2 to his "L" and "J" source. Steuernagel (*Josua*, 192–193, 199–200), by contrast, allotted 1:10–18; 3:2–4* etc. to the main Dtr author ("D2"), while the "E" narrative of Josh 2 was inserted at a later time by "Rp."

46. See also John Van Seters, *In Search of History: Historiography in the Ancient World and the Origins of Biblical History* (New Haven: Yale University Press, 1983), 324–25; he attributes the chapter to his exilic Yahwist.

47. For detailed discussion see Erhard Blum, "Beschneidung und Passa in Kanaan: Beobachtungen und Mutmaßungen zu Jos 5," in *Freiheit und Recht* (ed. C. Hardmeier; Gütersloh: Kaiser, 2003), 292–322, esp. 296–97.

Achan's violation of the ban in Josh 7. Joshua 7, for its part, proves to be closely related to Josh 2 through a network of different elements and themes.[48] In this net of references, at the level of a post-Deuteronomistic redaction, one may evaluate the special profile of Josh 3:1 in terms of its function as leading up from the story of Rahab to the crossing of the Jordan: The peculiar statement, "they camped there before crossing over" (3:1b) is taken up in a clear manner in the speech of Joshua in 3:5 ("Sanctify yourselves; for tomorrow[!] Yнwн will do wonders in your midst"), which on the one hand stands in tension with the action of the שטרים who prepare the people (3:2) and on the other hand has its nearest correspondence in Josh 7:13.

Therefore, Josh 2:1–3:1 can hardly represent the thread of a pre-Deuteronomistic Hexateuch, but constitutes just the opposite, together with other building blocks (Josh 7:1; 5b–26; 5:1; and various passages in the narrative of the crossing of the Jordan); i.e., a late- or post-Deuteronomistic insertion and reworking that is altogether soaked in the problems of the postexilic period. Thus the question arises anew as to how the unmistakable references of this compositional layer to various pentateuchal traditions and texts are to be interpreted,[49] particularly with regard to the literary works they either constitute or presuppose. Are these references to be understood as components of a redaction within the boundaries of a Hexateuch or a Joshua/Former Prophets redaction that already had the almost complete Pentateuch as an independent source for reference? The references *per se* do not present a clear picture[50] unless they are combined with comprehensive literary hypotheses and models into a complex web of argumentation.

3

The basic problems concerning the evaluation of the literary connections that were noted in the first section have become more complicated in light of the examples in the second section, not least because of the lack of clarity with regard to assumed literary relationships and postulated dependencies. Despite these problems, exegetical analyses can certainly not help but rely on such text-immanent indicators. This will also become clear in the following discussion. Nevertheless, the focus here will be primarily on another sort of textual indicator.

---

48. Ibid., 295f.

49. To these references belongs naturally the localization of the Israelites at Shittim, but also in particular the recapitulation of the pentateuchal material by the Canaanite Rahab. See the examples, ibid., 298.

50. Likewise Kratz (*Komposition*, 224) rightly states on the basis of other large literary contexts that are presupposed in the text, "In vielen Fällen läßt sich kaum sagen, ob die Angleichungen der Verbindung dienen oder der Abtrennung der Bücher Rechnung tragen."

At the outset of this study I called attention to the enviably clear boundary markers in "primary" textual witnesses. In ancient texts those markers include such phenomena as titles or colophons. Their relatively high level of clarity results from the fact that they refer to the literary unity as a metatext whose subject is the unit itself. In our modern form of publication the title page or cover serves an analogous function. Such metatexts have generally been lost in the biblical literary tradition with its composite texts, except for a few places in the prophetic books and in the "writings."[51]

Within the realm of the Pentateuch there are no metatexts that exactly fit this category. But something similar does exist; namely, internal self-referential definitions of literary units. They are of immediate significance for our topic. For this reason it is surprising that they seldom play a role in the discussion.

The distribution of these references alone is significant: By far the majority are found in Deuteronomy, without a single one in the "Tetrateuch."[52]

We will consider as the first example a few verses in Deut 31:

> (9) Then Moses wrote down this Torah (התורה הזאת) and gave it to the Levitical priests who carried the ark of the covenant of YHWH, and to all the elders of Israel. (10) Moses commanded them: "Every seventh year ... (11) ... you shall read this Torah (התורה הזאת) before all Israel ... (13) ... so that they may hear and learn ... to observe diligently all the words of this Torah (כל דברי התורה הזאת) ...."

> (24) When Moses had finished writing down in a book (ספר) the words of this Torah (דברי התורה הזאת) to the very end (עד תמם), Moses commanded the Levites who carried the ark of the covenant of the LORD, saying, (26) "Take this book of the Torah (ספר התורה הזה) and put it beside the ark of the covenant of YHWH your God; let it remain there as a witness against you."

The text speaks of a Torah or a Torah book, which Moses wrote down immediately before his death and which therefore ends with the events of his lifetime. The near deixis expressed by the demonstrative pronouns (זה/זאת) can point only to the work itself (or its content), which included the cited verses in Deut 31.[53] Thus it could designate the entire Pentateuch or the book

---

51. Hayyim M. J. Gevaryahu ("A Set of Remarks about Scribes and Books in Biblical Time," *Beth Miqra* 43 [1990], 368–74 [Hebrew]) lists Jer 48:16; 51:64; Ps 72:20; Job 31:40b; and Prov 25:1 and in connection with Deut 31:24 points to the Akkadian colophon-notice *qati*; Michael Fishbane, "Varia Deuteronomica," *ZAW* 84 (1972), 349–52, esp. 350 n. 13, adds Dan 7:28a.

52. These references should be distinguished from designations for parts of texts, like Gen 5:1; Exod 17:14a, or also Lev 26:46; Num 36:13.

53. The assertions by Jean-Pierre Sonnet, *The Book Within the Book: Writing in Deuteronomy* (Biblical Interpretation Series 14; Leiden: Brill, 1997), 257, like "In Deuteronomy,

of Deuteronomy.[54] The research has tended to favor the latter option, with good reason. In both passages the role of the Levites is typical for Deuteronomy.[55] In addition, the implied order of the tablets of the Decalogue in the ark of the covenant, with the book of the Torah next to it (v. 24), corresponds exactly to the order of the Decalogue and the Deuteronomic law in Deut 5–6,[56] and picks up the connection between tablets, ark, and Levites in Deut 10:1–5, 8–9.[57] Moreover, the concept of learning linked with the Torah (Deut 31:9–13) is exclusively "Deuteronomic."[58] This concept holds also in relation to the king. In the Deuteronomistic law of the king (17:18–20), we find all of these features together again: a self-reference to Deuteronomy as "this Torah," which is to be copied by the king from the *Vorlage* that is in the care of the Levitical priests, and which must be studied by him.[59]

---

self-designation is systematically avoided at the level of the framing narrative, that is, at the level of Deuteronomy's Book" or "reference is systematically made to the represented act of communication, and not to the representational medium" are clearly disproved by Deut 31:9: It would be impossible for Moses to hand over an "act of communication" to the Levitical priests. Deut 31:24–26 also implies the identity of the written "words of this Torah" and the book of Torah given to the Levites (see also below notes 60 and 71). The statement by Dennis T. Olson, *Deuteronomy and the Death of Moses: A Theological Reading*, (OBT; Minneapolis: Fortress, 1994), 8: "Deuteronomy is in fact the only book of the Pentateuch that refers to itself as *torah*," quoted by Sonnet, ibid., must be confirmed unreservedly.

54. Eckart Otto, *Das Deuteronomium im Pentateuch und Hexateuch: Studien zur Literaturgeschichte von Pentateuch und Hexateuch im Lichte des Deuteronomiumrahmens* (FAT 20; Tübingen: Mohr Siebeck, 2000), 207 (and passim) claims a reference by his "Pentateuchredaktor" to Deuteronomy *and* the Holiness Code. This interpretation can, however, be excluded, not only for semantic reasons (the alleged selective deixis is impossible), but also on factual grounds: the so-called "Holiness Code" does not exist as a marked corpus, identifiable by the readers (against the "Covenant Code," Exod 24:7!), but only as a (disputed) literary-historical hypothesis.

55. Otto, ibid., 184–191, assigns Deut 31:9–13 to a "Pentateuchredaktor" (see preceding note) interpreting "Levitical priests" as a hint towards the alleged Zadokite origin of this redactor. The plausibility of this interpretation shall not be discussed here. Suffice it to remark that attributing this incognito to the Pentateuch redactor poses inter alia the mystery as to why there are no terminological or conceptual traces of the Levitical priests in the Pentateuch apart from Deuteronomy.

56. For the parallel in Exod 20 see above, nn. 26–27.

57. See also Sonnet, *Book*, 164–65.

58. See esp. the study of Georg Braulik, "Das Deuteronomium und die Gedächtniskultur Israels: Redaktionsgeschichtliche Beobachtungen zur Verwendung von למד," in *Biblische Theologie und gesellschaftlicher Wandel* (ed. G. Braulik, W. Gross, Sean McEvenue; Freiburg: Herder, 1993), 9–31. Again, the distribution of an expression like למד proves to be significant: "innerhalb des Pentateuch ist die Wurzel überhaupt nur in diesem Buch [Deut] belegt" (ibid., 10; see there n. 8 on additional terms of the semantic field).

59. Compare Deut 17:18–19: "When he has taken the throne of his kingdom, he shall write for himself a copy of this Torah (משנה התורה הזאת) from (the *Vorlage* which is) in

It is no less significant that this series of self-referential expressions starts in the introduction of the entire work, in Deut 1:5:

בעבר הירדן בארץ מואב הואיל משה באר את־התורה הזאת לאמר

Beyond the Jordan in the land of Moab, Moses undertook to expound this Torah clearly, saying:

There is much discussion over the verb באר (*pi'el*) which only appears within the Old Testament in this passage and in Deut 27:8 and Hab 2:2. In the other two instances the verb functions as a term of qualification next to כתב, which qualifies it as "writing clearly." One can surmise from this usage that the primary meaning is "to do something clearly." Here also, באר in Deut 1:5 qualifies the action that is designated with לאמר,[60] namely the Torah recital of Moses. Most of this has already been clarified by L. Perlitt.[61] In any case, the meaning of "to interpret,"[62] as a reflection on a preceding context,[63] cannot be based on the use of the term in biblical language.[64]

---

the presence of the Levitical priests (מלפני הכהנים הלוים). 19. It shall remain with him and he shall read in it all the day of his life, so that he may learn to fear YHWH his God, diligently observing all the words of this Torah. ..." How little the writer distinguishes between "the Torah" and the "book" is revealed in the use of the masculine pronominal suffix in v. 19, rather than the feminine (unless this reading is due to a scribal misinterpretation occurring with the orthographical change from בה to בו/בה).

60. That the main action "als inf. untergeordnet wird" is not unusual, compare Carl Brockelmann, *Hebräische Syntax* (Neukirchen-Vluyn: Neukirchener, 1956; 2d ed., 2004), 84–85; for the position of the object after the qualifying verb compare the position of מיהוה in Isa 29:15 (on this see Brockelmann, ibid., 30: "die näheren Umstände einer Handlung [werden] oft als selbständig aufgefasst und als die Hauptsache betrachtet"); in Isa 7:11 the main action is given in the preceding context. The seemingly elliptical application in Deut 1:5 may be due to the fact that two auxiliaries are combined here.

61. Lothar Perlitt, *Deuteronomium* (BKAT 5/1; Neukirchen-Vluyn: Neukirchener, 1990), 22–23. For translation he considers the options "deutlich lehren" or "(rechtswirksam) bezeugen;" the first one seems much more adequate.

62. Raik Heckl (*Moses Vermächtnis: Kohärenz, literarische Intention und Funktion von Dtn 1–3* [Arbeiten zur Bibel und ihrer Geschichte 9; Leipzig: Evangelische Verlagsanstalt, 2004], 65–66, 69) suggests yet another meaning: With "this Torah" in 1:5 is meant the following citation of YHWH's word in 1:6–8. But for what purpose should a clear command for departure be "explained" (so Heckl's meaning of באר *pi'el*), and where does this happen in Deut 1? Even more than that, where in the Old Testament would תורה be used for a situational demand? And why should התורה הזאת mean something different here than elsewhere in Deuteronomy?

63. Konrad Schmid, "Das Deuteronomium innerhalb der 'deuteronomistischen Geschichtswerke' in Gen–2 Kön," in *Das Deuteronomium zwischen Pentateuch und Deuteronomistischem Geschichtswerk* (ed. E. Otto and R. Achenbach; FRLANT 206; Göttingen: Vandenhoeck & Ruprecht, 2004), 193–211, esp. 199–200.

64. The postbiblical interpretation as "explain" (ancient translations and rabbinical tradition) suggested itself when Deut 1:5 was read within its canonical context (Pentateuch/Torah).

This opening in Deut 1:5 is therefore a kind of "integrated title" to the present book and serves at the same time to indicate to the reader what kind of book it is: a "Torah"—that is, an "instruction." This instruction includes, of course, the commands and the laws, but also the speech by Moses, beginning with Deut 1 with its parenesis and recounted narrative. We do not need to define here on which level of the literary history of Deuteronomy the metatextual elements of the framework of Deuteronomy should be located.[65] For our context three observations provide further guidance:

First, it is striking how clearly and exclusively the internal references to "this Torah" and to "this book" remain inner-Deuteronomic,[66] either through references to Moses' actual speech,[67] or through other specifically Deuteronomistic features.[68] This determination corresponds in a significant way with the complete absence of any similar self-referential formulas in Genesis through Numbers.[69]

Second, it is noteworthy that of the nine Deuteronomic references to the term "book (of the Torah)," six occur in the concluding section on blessings and curses,[70] as for example Deut 29:20: "... according to all the curses of this covenant (ברית), which are written in this book of the Torah." This

---

65. The explanation of the unmistakable relationship between Deut 4:10 and 31:12 (is this a one-sided dependency or from the same hand?) is quite important in this regard. For that it seems to me essential that Deut 4—which is certainly not a primary text in Deuteronomy—remains in its substance within an interior Deuteronomic horizon (with references back from the DtrG). This is not compromised by the literary dependence of Deut 4:16*–18 on Gen 1, as is frequently alleged following Michael Fishbane (initially noted in "Varia Deuteronomica," 349; where, however, he speaks of a shared "pattern"). Not only must Deut 4:16*–18 be seen as a secondary development, dependent on the ban on images in Deut 5:8 (and compare the inclusive resumption in 4:23; see also T. Veijola, *Das 5. Buch Mose: Deuteronomium: Kapitel 1,1-16,17* [ATD 8.1; Göttingen: Vandenhoeck & Ruprecht, 2004], 106), but the literary dependence of the addition from Gen 1 is in no way evident; the linguistic references are not close enough, and the Wisdom tradition presupposed here, as there, is not specifically Priestly enough.

66. The term "inner-Deuteronomic" denotes all Deuteronomistic redactions and insertions that are confined to Deuteronomy (and the subsequent historical works) and have no equivalents or connections in the so-called Tetrateuch.

67. So, for example, in Deut 1:5; 4:8; 28:61; 29:20.

68. Such as the "Levitical priests": 17:18; 31:9, 24–26.

69. Moreover, in the Tetrateuch there is only one example of *torah* used in the sense of "teaching, instruction" as is characteristic of Deuteronomy: this is the phrase תורת יהוה in Exod 13:9. Among the appearances of ספר in Gen 5:1; Exod 17:14; 24:7; 32:32–33; Num 5:23; 21:14, only Gen 5:1 is self-referential—not to the record as a whole, however, but to pieces or parts of the text. The same applies—in quite different ways—to the other texts (Exod 17:14 is not a counter-example, since the definite article is idiomatic here; compare Num 5:23).

70. Deut 28:58, 61; 29:19–20, 26; 30:10 (using the phrase "written in the book ...").

concentration is anything but coincidental, as is shown by the ancient Near Eastern vassal treaties; in which the warnings and sanctions, as well as the self-referential thematization of the treaty, in the closing sections represents an established structural element.[71] As is well known, this tradition of ancient Near Eastern treaty texts constitutes an essential context for the theological concept of the covenant in Deuteronomy, so that the elements of writing and self-reference probably belonged to that concept *from the beginning*.

Third, it is also apparent that in the Deuteronomistic tradition the respective texts are not qualified by the term "covenant," in the first place, but by the term "Torah." This is indicative not only of a new conceptual point of emphasis beyond the idea of treaties, but also of the constitution of a specific literary genre, namely, "the book of the Torah."

The fundamental forms of communication in the book of Deuteronomy—parenesis, and engaging and performative speech by Moses—cannot be separated from this concept of the Torah. This certainly corresponds to the pragmatics of ancient Near Eastern treaty documents, which are characterized by speeches such as parenetic exhortations or warnings directed towards the treaty partner, partly in the form of citations, but mostly with reference to the treaty document. While in these documents, however, the king involved can appear directly (though at times in the third person) as speaker and communicator of the treaty, which the gods "merely" guarantee, YHWH's promises and obligations are mediated through the teaching of Moses. This feature may have been one reason for preferring the term "Torah," in addition to its other potential uses as a means of parenesis, education, and so forth.

Whether the term "Torah" belonged to the Deuteronomic tradition from the beginning must remain an open question. It seems clear, however, that the term "Torah" in the comprehensive sense of "instruction, teaching" does not exist prior to Deuteronomy, and its later uses are dependent on Deuteronomy. "Torah" in this sense means, first of all, the covenant obligations binding upon Israel, but in addition, the narrative recounting of YHWH's actions on behalf of the people that provide the basis for the covenant relationship. This broad meaning is implied in the self-referential statements within the framework of the book (Deut 1:5; 31:9–13, 24–27).

No less important, the particular marking of the Deuteronomistic edition of Deuteronomy, as having been written down by Moses and given to the Levitical priests as a "book of the Torah," means that it is now defined as a

---

71. See also Sonnet (*Book*, 256–57) for examples. The Aramaic treaties from Sefire, which he cites, are interesting from another aspect as well: the terms for the content ("this contract"—עדיא אלן) and for the literary record ("this inscription"—ספרא זנה) are used in a similar way to "this Torah" and "this Torah book" in Deuteronomy, namely, with the identical references (see for example *KAI* 222B 7–8).

book that may be referenced and that, as such, may be integrated seamlessly into a larger work.[72] In its linkage of introductory speeches, legal corpora, and blessings and curses, it probably was thought of in this way from the beginning. In any case, the embedding of references to the citable Torah is underscored at the first compositional place of transition with the kind of clarity that one would desire; after the death of Moses, the warning is issued to his successor in Josh 1:8:

> "This book of the Torah (ספר התורה הזה) shall not depart out of your mouth! You shall meditate on it day and night, so that you may be careful to act in accordance with all that is written in it."

In its present canonical context this should undoubtedly be related to the Pentateuch as a whole. In its primary usage, however, it meant the Deuteronomistic Torah. This conclusion is based on the close compositional interweaving between the beginning of the book of Joshua and the texts in Deuteronomy that describe Moses' successor (Deut 1:37–38; 3:21–28; 31:2–6, 7–8),[73] a topic that twice functions as a peak in Moses' introductory speech in Deut 1–3.

In taking note of this evidence, we stand once again close to M. Noth's hypothesis of a Deuteronomistic History that began with the Deuteronomistic form of Deuteronomy. The various characteristic traits of Deuteronomy outlined here, which distinguish Deuteronomy from the Tetrateuch (and which also appear in relatively late stages of its composition), and its self-profiling as an independent "book of the Torah," are explained most easily within the model of Noth.[74]

---

72. Another prerequisite for this is the repeatedly noted blurring of the textual pragmatics of the work: the content of the Torah is mediated through the speech of Moses, cited by the anonymous narrator, whose remarks themselves belong to the book of Torah.

73. See the foundational study by Norbert Lohfink, "Die deuteronomistische Darstellung des Übergangs der Führung Israels von Moses auf Josue: Ein Beitrag zur alttestamentlichen Theologie des Amtes," *Schol* 37 (1962): 32–44. With regard to this "inner-Deuteronomistic" presentation it does not matter if, with Rudolf Smend ("Das Gesetz und die Völker: Ein Beitrag zur deuteronomistischen Redaktionsgeschichte," in *Probleme biblischer Theologie: Gerhard von Rad zum 70. Geburtstag* [ed. H. W. Wolff; Munich: Kaiser, 1971), 494–509, esp. 494–97), one sees in Josh 1:7–9 a reworking by a later Deuteronomistic hand. In addition to the evidence that the (primary or secondary) link of the theme of Torah with the appointment of Joshua as successor is found also in Deut 31, one should note the strictly Deuteronomistic features of the Joshua passages; compare, for example Josh 1:7–8 [originally without תורה, see LXX] with Deut 17:18–20. It is also significant that all the more or less content-specific references to "the Torah" in Joshua through Kings refer to Deuteronomy.

74. That is, in any case, true with regard to the beginnings of Deuteronomy and

Finally this conclusion is reinforced by the observation—noted already by Wellhausen[75]—that Deuteronomy, especially in its introductory speeches in Deut 1–3, presents itself as *the beginning of a work*. This conclusion is not weakened by the fact that these narrative portions are formed as recapitulations of the Moses-exodus-wilderness traditions and that knowledge thereof on the side of the addressees appears to be presupposed.

It is interesting that this aspect of the Nothian model has experienced strong opposition in recent analyses from different methodological and conceptual presuppositions. These analyses insist, using arguments that in part contradict one another, that Deut 1–3 is intended to be read as a literary continuation of the Tetrateuch.

Such a premise is a matter of course in an investigation of the final form of the text such as that undertaken by J.-P. Sonnet.[76] Over against this, the detailed investigation of R. Heckl on Deut 1–3 works from both synchronic and diachronic perspectives. Starting from rather "traditional" literary-historical presuppositions regarding Pentateuch and Hexateuch, Heckl arrives at far-reaching assumptions of intratextual connections between Deuteronomy and texts from the story of Abraham through Numbers.[77] Yet another example is provided by K. Schmid, who evaluates the apparent parallelism of the revelation of the Decalogue and the legal corpus in the Sinai pericope and in Deuteronomy and concludes: "Read in conjunction with Genesis–Numbers, Deuteronomy must be understood as the Mosaic interpretation of the divine law from Sinai, their agreement being secured through the two Decalogues."[78] He explains this coordination with the Sinai pericope diachronically by stating that, "as opposed to the classical theory of an independent work from Deuteronomy through 2 Kings, when the redactional integration of Deuteronomy into its literary surrounding took place, there was probably from the beginning a preceding context (first Exod through Num; and later Gen through Num), especially since Deuteronomy

---

Joshua. The stringency of the continuation of this feature through Judges and Samuel to Kings will not be discussed in this framework, nor will the questions of potential pre-stages, of inner layers, or of post-Deuteronomistic additions (the significance of which was underestimated by Noth).

75. Compare n. 90.

76. Cf. Sonnet, *Book*, 23–24, concerning the methodical premises of his work. Here one gets the impression that on the one hand, Sonnet presupposes the Pentateuch to be the canonical context of Deuteronomy; while on the other hand, he maintains the identity of Deuteronomy's "canonical and narrative claim." Just this identity, however, can not be proven as long as 1) the canonical context is presupposed in any particular interpretation, and 2) any examination of the diachronic profile of possible Pentateuch references is avoided.

77. Heckl, *Moses Vermächtnis*. Heckl's very detailed representation cannot be appreciated in this context. It seems to me, however, that some alleged references back, such as Deut 3:23ff. to Gen 13:14ff. (ibid., 398); or Deut 1:6–8 to Exod 20–33 (ibid., 373–74); or of Deut 1:18 to Exod 24:3 (ibid., 398), are highly artificial; in terms of methodology, one finds here again (see n. 36) the inference from similarities to genetic relations based implicitly on the view of Old Testament language and tradition as a hermetic space.

78. Schmid, *Deuteronomium*, 200.

does not offer a sufficient narrative beginning."[79] The structural correspondence between the Sinai legislation and the recapitulation in Deuteronomy is in fact obvious, but as can be demonstrated, it does not lead per se to this specific diachronic explanation.[80] This explanation depends essentially on the claim of the narrative insufficiency of the beginning of Deuteronomy.

The issues concerning this question are investigated by J. C. Gertz in a careful study.[81] For him the model of rereading (*relecture*) is fundamental to the understanding of the introduction(s) of Deuteronomy. Though this model "does not necessarily presuppose that it concerns a reception process within one and the same 'book,'"[82] he offers in favor of this possibility inter alia the following arguments: (1) the stylization of the whole book as a speech of Moses, which permits a coherent narrative integration into the entire context; (2) the view that "the textual references in Deut 1–3 exhibit the same intensity towards both sides of the literary context";[83] and in particular (3) the view that the design in question reflects "the redactional necessities of the integration of a previously independent Deuteronomy into the course of the narrative."[84] What serves Gertz to this end is the reevaluation of the detailed correlations between the Book of the Covenant and the Deuteronomic Law, along with the insight from R. Heckl[85] that the itinerary in Deut 1–3 marks the location of Moses' farewell address in terms of the integration of the proclamation of law and conquest as a (now successful) new Horeb edition.

In my opinion, however, none of these observations necessarily leads to the conclusion that Deut 1–3 is an insertion into the preceding literary context: (1) The stylization of Moses' speech represents, indeed, an important precondition for the possibility of the compositional integration of Deuteronomy into a comprehensive pentateuchal narrative. The *raison d'être* of this stylization, however, is twofold: (a) Deuteronomy as Moses' speech fits, as noted above, the pragmatics of a *Torah* book, the tradition-historical roots of which can be traced back to the ancient Near Eastern vassal treaties; and (b) only the stylization as Moses' speech enables the author to give a concise narrative recapitulation which can stand on its own, rather than confining himself to a short summary or presenting a full narrative (see below). (2) The volume of textual references is not decisive for the compositional integration; what is decisive is their function in the entire profile of the relevant text. Precisely in this regard the references in Deut 1–3 to the preceding and following contexts are not comparable, in so far as the recapitulative narrative in its entirety is aimed at the following context (see below). (3) The conceptual position of Deuteronomy over against the

---

79. Ibid., 209.

80. Cf. Blum, *Studien*, 197ff., esp. 199–200, where the hermeneutical "identification" of the Book of the Covenant and the Deuteronomic law in a protopentateuchal context is already stated, but combined with a different diachronic explanation.

81. Jan C. Gertz, "Kompositorische Funktion und literarhistorischer Ort von Deuteronomium 1–3," in *Die deuteronomistischen Geschichtswerke: Redaktions- und religionsgeschichtliche Perspektiven zur 'Deuteronomismus'-Diskussion in der Tora und den Vorderen Propheten* (ed. M. Witte et al.; BZAW 365; Berlin: de Gruyter, 2005).

82. Ibid., 116. For the unfolding of this thesis and the supporting arguments see ibid., 117–22.

83. Ibid., 117–18.

84. Ibid., 118.

85. Heckl, *Moses Vermächtnis*, 354.

Book of the Covenant,[86] and the theological topography of the Deuteronomic introductory speeches (see above), may be understood unreservedly as compositional necessities for the creation of an independent book of the Torah[87] *next to* an existing composition which encompassed the account of the Book of the Covenant.

Furthermore it seems decisive that the literary "sufficiency" of the narrative introductions of Deuteronomy actually stands out. Certainly Deut 1–10 presents itself as a recollection of events that are already known.[88] In this respect a basic knowledge of previous traditions by the reader is required, including the figure of Moses, the tradition of the exodus, the mountain of God as the place for the revelation of law, etc. Nevertheless the (pre-Priestly)[89] traditions are not simply recapitulated in a summary fashion. Rather they were narrated completely anew, and this was done in such a way that the readers are *not* dependent on the previous context of a book. Such a massive redundancy and pursuit of narrative sufficiency would make no sense in a speech by the central character, fashioned

---

86. Gertz's argument ("Funktion," 119) that an "Identifikation von Bundes-buch und Dtn bei Beibehaltung der tatsächlichen Unterschiede und gleichzeitiger Qualifikation beider Gesetze als göttliche Willenskundgebung ist … nur dort notwendig, wo beide Rechtskorpora nachträglich in ein und denselben literarischen Kontext zu stehen kommen," is not compelling, in my view. The hermeneutical identification of the two corpora also makes perfect sense if they originally belonged to separate texts, but nevertheless were both recognized as divine stipulations.

87. Among the scholars who prefer to see Deuteronomy as an insertion into something like a Hexateuch, only R. G. Kratz treats the matter of Deuteronomy's "Verselbständigung": "zur zitablen Größe innerhalb von Jos–Reg" (*Komposition,* 136, 221). According to Kratz, however, this "Verselbständigung" of Deuteronomy as Torah book marks the *end* of an extended growing process in the realm of Deut, after the elaborated formation of Gen–Num including P. Leaving aside some difficult implications of this view, I would like to point only to two of its suppositions that seem to me most doubtful: (1) the assumption of an quite early *Einschreibung* of a *Urdeuteronomium* into Kratz's pre-Dtr Hexateuch; (2) the claim to dependence of Deut 1–3 (etc.) on the Priestly-redacted Pentateuch. The alleged Hexateuch (1) has already been critically discussed (see above). The second supposition (2) must be questioned on account of a double set of objections: first, the very few references in Deut 1–3 to Priestly traditions in the Tetrateuch are ostensibly late adaptations, partly evident still in the textual history (see also below n. 91); second, only the non-Priestly Sinai pericope has been elaborated in accordance with Deuteronomy (see above nn. 25–26).

88. Norbert Lohfink, ("Darstellungskunst und Theologie in Dtn 1,6–3,29," *Bib* 41 [1960]: 105–34, esp. 108–9), concludes that the Dtr author not only had knowledge of material, but that he presupposed a specific "textual knowledge" of his sources on the part of his addressees, which would have allowed him to "play" with the texts. But it is not clear whether such modern exegesis, however excellent, can be assumed for ancient reception of the text.

89. Still clear and worthy of consideration is Wellhausen, *Composition,* 201: "Es muss feststehn, 1) dass das Deuteronomium *ausführlich* die ältere Geschichte von Exod. 19 an *reproducirt,* 2) dass es dabei ausschliesslich der jehovistischen Anschauung folgt und *bei allen Differenzen* die priesterliche vollkommen ignoriert, 3) dass diese völlige Einflusslo-sigkeit von Q auf das Ganze der Anschauung nur aus Unbekanntschaft mit dieser Schrift zu erklären ist …."

as the end of a narrative.[90] Instead, the narrative is self-sufficient to such a degree that, in individual cases, one must also reckon with the possibility of a Deuteronomic creation of traditions without a corresponding *Vorlage* in the older tradition.[91]

Last, but not least, Deut 1–3 is a "quoted" narrative, stylized in a remarkably concise way. Alongside the (rather implicit) introduction of the "repeated" communication of God's will, every detail addresses questions raised by the impending entrance into the land, where the regulations of the Torah should have value: What belongs to this land and what does not? Why should there be confidence, despite the Canaanites' superior power? And, above all, why should Joshua, and not Moses, lead the people west of the Jordan?[92] In short: Deuteronomy presents itself not only as an independent Torah or Covenant document in its main layers, including the postexilic layer of Deut 4*, but also as the self-sufficient beginning of a work, to which belongs at least the book of Joshua*; and to which further belongs, in my opinion, a basic text in Judges* to Kings*.

This overall position is confirmed when one asks what kind of elements may be recognized with sufficient clarity in positing a literary connection between Deuteronomy and a non-Priestly "Tetrateuch." With Wellhausen, one discovers primarily, and almost exclusively, specific parts of Deut 31.[93] In a double report of the Deuteronomistic account of the appointment of Joshua as

---

90. Also here Wellhausen's sharp insight is evident, when he states, concerning the integration of Deuteronomy into the Hexateuch, that this was "nur nach hinten durch äusserlich hervortretende Bindemittel (Kap. 31) erfolgt, nach vorn sind solche nicht sichtbar. Denn Kap. 1–4 hat offenbar nicht den Zweck, an die vorhergehende Erzählung anzuknüpfen, vielmehr sie ausführlich zu recapituliren, d.h. zu ersetzen" (ibid., 193). A different view is taken by Reinhard G. Kratz, ("Der literarische Ort des Deuteronomiums," in *Liebe und Gebot: Studien zum Deuteronomium* [ed. R.G. Kratz and H. Spieckermann; FRLANT 190; Göttingen: Vandenhoeck & Ruprecht, 2000], 101–20, esp. 109), who, however, gives no explanation for the profile of the recapitulation in Deut 1–3 so clearly highlighted by Wellhausen.

91. This seems to be the case with Deut 1:9–18, for known reasons. For the notice about Og there is the well-established idea that this text was taken over from Deut 3:1ff. into Num 21:33ff. An interesting, but more complicated, case is the Decalogue in Deut 5; compare Erhard Blum, "The Decalogue and the Composition History of the Pentateuch," in *The Pentateuch: International Perspectives on Current Research* (ed. K. Schmid, T. B. Dozeman, and B. Schwartz; FAT; Tübingen: Mohr Siebeck, forthcoming).

92. Compare Lothar Perlitt, ("Deuteronomium 1–3 im Streit der Methoden," in *Das Deuteronomium. Entstehung, Gestalt und Botschaft* [ed. N. Lohfink; BETL 68; Leuven: Leuven University Press, 1985], 149–63, esp. 162–63): "Mit der Resektion dieses 'Ergebnisses' der Landnahme [Deut 3:8ff.] fiele Dtn 2f. in sich zusammen, weil die Kapitel als Präludium und Kontrapunkt der westjordanischen Landnahme unter Josua verstanden werden sollen. … Auf die Kontrapunktik von Dtn 1–3 und Jos 1–11 bezieht sich das Fazit in Jos 12 in schöner Bestätigung. Mose präfiguriert Josua: Man kann Dtn 1–3 nur in seinem Großkontext auslegen."

93. For the following see Blum, *Studien*, 76–88; and (with modification) idem, "Die literarische Verbindung von Erzvätern und Exodus: Ein Gespräch mit neueren Endredaktionshypothesen," in *Abschied vom Jahwisten: Die Komposition des Hexateuch in*

the successor to Moses (Deut 31:7–8; compare 1:38; 3:28), one finds in Deut
31:14–15, 23 an element completely foreign to Deuteronomy, namely, the prophetic "tent of meeting." This oracular tent, which is not to be confused with
the Priestly tent of meeting/tabernacle, is introduced in Exod 33:7–11 and
from that point on remains connected with a web of earlier motifs (compare
Num 11 and 12).[94] It belongs to a postexilic elaboration of a pre-Deuteronomistic tradition concerning Moses and the exodus (from the seventh century
B.C.E.). This tradition, which was known to the Deuteronomistic tradents
of Deuteronomy (and their audience), served later on as the precursor of a
new composition, which I name "the D-Composition (KD)." With the insertion of the tent-of-meeting complex in Deut 31:14–15, 23 (24) (+ 34:10), this
D-Composition fastened itself compositionally to the end of the Deuteronomistic book of the Torah. As a result the farewell speech of Moses now
represents the final act of a larger narrative beginning with the exodus. At
the same time the D-Composition has oriented itself towards Deuteronomy,
especially in its elaboration of the mountain of God pericope. Thus the literary integration of Deuteronomy into the old/new tradition of the exodus and
Moses resulted in a doubling of the Torah structure (comprising salvation history and covenant obligations). Another consequence, which can hardly be
overestimated, was that the self-designation of Deuteronomy as the "book of
the Torah" now acquired a broader reference that included the entire composition from Exod 1 onward.

The entire narrative was held together through the prophetic depiction
of Moses found from Exod 3 on; he is presented as the father of all prophets
in Num 11 and at the same time, in Num 12 as a super-prophet, with whom
YHWH communicates face to face. When the new composition closed with
the clarification: "Never since has there arisen a prophet in Israel like Moses,
whom YHWH knew face to face" (Deut 34:10), the preceding Mosaic Torah
(now Exod* through Deut*) was authorized beyond comparison over against
all other traditions.

It is difficult to judge whether this expanded Torah book still stood in
some literary connection with Joshua, etc. This appears unlikely to me in spite
of some echoes of KD, especially in Josh 2, 3–5, and 7. This question, however, is of secondary importance: Whatever one decides on the basis of these
indications, which are not clear in that respect by themselves, the specifically
marked and independent context of this Torah, as a book, remains unaffected.

---

der jüngsten Diskussion (ed. J.C. Gertz, K. Schmid, and M. Witte; BZAW 315; Berlin: de
Gruyter, 2002), 119–56.
    94. In addition to the *Ohel Moed*, these include in particular: YHWH's approach in the
cloud; Moses' face-to-face communication with God; Moses and the prophecy/prophets;
and Joshua as helper of and successor to Moses.

On the basis of this, it is necessary to insist, against a more recent trend in research, that the Pentateuch did not come into being due to a late, more or less technical separation from the books of Joshua, etc. Rather the concept of the Mosaic Torah belonged to the genetic code of this tradition of origins at least from Deuteronomy onwards.

I come to a final set of reflections: What remains of the enduring discussion of the Pentateuch-Hexateuch problem in view of a model like the one described above? It would not be superficial to see here a question of perspective: In the outline of salvation history, the Pentateuch indeed remains a torso. For this reason G. von Rad always spoke of the theology of the Hexateuch, notwithstanding M. Noth. Within the concept of Torah, however, Joshua cannot be integrated following Deut 31; 34; i.e., after the constitution of a Mosaic document of the Torah. But even if the alternative can be traced back to the perspective of different "genres," the alternative does not simply go away because it is grounded in a tension that is inherent to the text. This is reflected lastly within the process of the creation of the tradition itself, in which a Hexateuch was in fact formed next to the Pentateuch. For this reason, allow me to return to an old *Ceterum censeo*.[95]

Already M. Noth had seen that Josh 24 is not integrated compositionally into the main narrative of the Deuteronomistic History. The chapter is about a covenant-making ceremony at Shechem, in which before his death Joshua reviews the entire history of salvation from the ancestors across the Euphrates River to the successful conquest of the land. The people are summoned to decide which God they will choose: Yʜwʜ or the strange gods of the Mesopotamians, Egyptians, and Amorites. Moreover it has long been recognized that Gen 35:1–7 (8), from the story of Jacob, including its formulations, is presented as a positive prelude to the assembly in Joshua: in addition to that, in the same context Jacob buys a piece land near Shechem where the bones of Joseph are buried at the end of Josh 24 (v. 32). The transfer of these bones is prepared for and carried out in individual notices (Gen 50:25–26; Exod 13:19). This is a verifiably late, but intentional redactional cross-linking that has as its goal Josh 24. One can in fact read this text, which von Rad identified as a "Hexateuch in miniature," as the resonant finale of a Hextateuch.

The recently expressed objection to such a view,[96] that Josh 24 refers also to the subsequent history of Israel (24:19–20), leads us back to the distinction that was stated in the

---

95. See already Erhard Blum, *Die Komposition der Vätergeschichte* (WMANT 57; Neukirchen-Vluyn: Neukirchener, 1984), 45–61.

96. Kratz, "Hexateuch," 295–323, esp. 303; and Schmid, "Deuteronomium," 193–94 n. 1. Why the decision for Yʜwʜ and against the foreign gods in Josh 24 should "dem Königtum Konkurrenz mache[n]" (ibid.), remains unclear to me: Shechem is neither the city in

first section between thematic/textual references/horizons on the one side and literary compositions on the other. In any case, it would definitely be puzzling if a programmatic text like Josh 24 did not have the later "history of Israel" in view.[97] We have analogous passages in the Mosaic Torah, and they are likewise of as little relevance there as here.

The confirmation in favor of the Hexateuch as an intentional literary work is in the end the fact that Josh 24 does indicate to which book it claims to belong no less explicitly than does Deuteronomy:

> Josh 24:25 So Joshua made a covenant with the people that day, and made statutes and ordinances (חק ומשפט) for them at Shechem.

> 26 Joshua wrote these things/words in the book of the Torah of God.

> ויכתב יהושע את־הדברים האלה בספר תורת אלהים

The phrase, הדברים האלה, cannot relate semantically to חק ומשפט.[98] Rather it is an internal self-reference to the text of Josh 24. Already the self-identification as "the book of the Torah of God," certainly excludes the possibility that only the book of Joshua is in view. In addition to that, the entire literary horizon of Josh 24 and the compositional relationships already noted refer to the broader context of a Hexateuch that includes the story of the ancestors.[99] A Hexateuch, however, could not be named the "Torah of Moses," because it would include the book of Joshua. It also could not be named the "Torah of Joshua," because in matters of Torah Moses is irreplaceable. Therefore, the

---

which kings are crowned (except for problematic ones like Abimelech and Jeroboam); nor would textual references to 1 Sam 10; 12 (here, however, one must differentiate; see provisionally Blum, *Komposition*, 51–53) balance the complete silence on the theme of kingship.

97. Concretely: If from its postexilic perspective(!) Josh 24:19–20 anticipates Israel's future breaking of the first command, this per se implies in no way an allusion to an "entsprechende erzählerische Fortsetzung" (Schmid, "Deuteronomium," 193–94 n. 1); nor would a clear reference to a narrative continuation indicate per se that Josh 24 was not intended to close a literary work. The proposed RC hypothesis of the Hexateuch actually implies that Josh 24 not only knew the established connection of Judges etc., but that this knowledge could also be presupposed for the addressees.

98. For discussion see Erhard Blum, "The Literary Connection between the Books of Genesis and Exodus and the End of the Book of Joshua," in *A Farewell to the Yahwist? The Composition of the Pentateuch in Recent European Interpretation* (ed. T. B. Dozeman and K. Schmid; SBLSymS 34; Atlanta: Scholars Press, 2006), 89–106, esp. n. 26.

99. Another feature confirms that Josh 24 was intended as the closing section of a literary work: According to the factual logic of the documentation of recording and presenting, the witnesses (compare Deut 31:26; Josh 24:27) cannot but stand at the end of the respective document.

entire work was named with the apparently singular but, in any case, fitting title, "the book of the Torah of God."

In this instance a Hexateuch *was* constituted. This fact is completely independent from the question of whether the author of Josh 24 had also inserted redactional material into other places, for instance, Judg 6:7–10 (which seems likely). In light of the above-noted observations about the "genetic code" of the whole tradition, it was inevitable that this formation of a Hexateuch would not be carried out under the mark of a *Geschichtswerk*, but through the attempt at a new definition of *the book of the Torah*.

At the same time this secondary hexateuchal Torah remains, as we know, a fleeting attempt. The exclusive connection between Moses and the book of the Torah was too solid to be broken up again. It had stood at the beginning and it remained in force at the end. That is the reason why the Former Prophets begin with Josh 1 and not with Judg 1.

"Empirical" Comparison and the Analysis of the Relationship of the Pentateuch and the Former Prophets

David M. Carr

This essay will address the question of the relationship between the Pentateuch and the Former Prophets by comparison of Samuel–Kings and Chronicles. Although the study of Samuel–Kings and Chronicles is a digression, the "empirical" comparison of overlapping historical narratives in the Hebrew Bible will provide a perspective on the relationship between the Pentateuch and Former prophets distinct from that of a mere internal textual analysis of the Enneateuch.

Although some precursor studies had done similar things, the term "empirical" began to be used in a new way in biblical studies in the wake of J. Tigay's edited volume, *Empirical Models for Biblical Studies*.[1] This volume contained a range of articles that explored how biblical studies might be informed through analysis of cases of textual growth where it appeared that multiple stages of such growth were documented by separate manuscript traditions. For example, the volume featured a reprint of the classic 1889 article by G. F. Moore which traced how the four gospels—attested in separate manuscript traditions—had been combined into the Diatessaron.[2] Tigay himself examined examples of the conflation of biblical laws in the so-called proto-Samaritan pentateuchal manuscripts at Qumran.[3] E. Tov provided

---

1. Jeffrey Tigay, ed., *Empirical Models for Biblical Criticism* (Philadelphia: University of Pennsylvania Press, 1985). Earlier studies along similar lines include Thomas R. W. Longstaff, *Evidence of Conflation in Mark? A Study in the Synoptic Problem* (SBLDS 28; Missoula, Mont.: Scholars Press, 1977) and Herbert Donner, "Der Redaktor: Überlegungen zum vorkritischen Umgang mit der Heiligen Schrift," *Henoch* 2 (1980): 1–30.

2. George F. Moore, "Tatian's *Diatessaron* and the Analysis of the Pentateuch," in Tigay, *Empirical Models*, 243–56.

3. Jeffrey Tigay, "Conflation as a Redactional Technique," in idem, *Empirical Models*, 61–83.

another case study, in which he described different manuscripts editions of Jeremiah witnessed to by the MT and Old Greek (along with some Qumran fragments).[4] The volume did not attempt a grand synthesis, but it began to illustrate the potential of drawing on documented examples of transmission history.

In general, I would identify two different ways in which these empirical analyses have informed the study of textual growth. First, scholars have found new ways to use documentation to understand particular cases of textual growth. For example, depending on how you understand the relationship of textual witnesses, the Old Greek forms of Exodus, Jeremiah, and Esdras/Ezra–Nehemiah, may attest generally earlier forms of their respective traditions, and thus they are useful for understanding the prehistory of the books now in the MT.[5] Second, as Tigay shows in his essay on conflation, the more one analyzes multiple cases of documented growth of texts in the Near East, the more certain trends appear. These trends can be used to develop models of textual growth and identify indicators that might be used to identify such growth, even in the absence of documented preliminary stages of a given text.

Both senses of "empirical" investigation will be relevant in the following discussion. First, documented dynamics of oral-written transmission can, I argue, illuminate the relationship between Chronicles and Samuel–Kings to confirm that the author(s) of Chronicles often followed a historical source (consisting in large part of material also found in Samuel–Kings) quite closely. Second, building on that analysis, I will suggest that Chronicles may, at points, provide insight into the earlier scope of the books of the Former Prophets. This second point will provide a springboard to evaluate anew the evolution of the relationship between the books of the Former Prophets and the Pentateuch.

EMPIRICAL COMPARISON AND THE ORAL-WRITTEN TRANSMISSION OF SAMUEL–KINGS AND CHRONICLES

I start with a premise concerning the character and use of ancient historical narratives like Samuel–Kings and Chronicles. In another context I have argued at length that such works were transmitted primarily in the context of writing-supported, family-centered education of elites, whether priestly,

---

4. Emanuel Tov, "The Literary History of the Book of Jeremiah in Light of Its Textual History," in Tigay, *Empirical Models*, 215–37.

5. For an overview of cases, brief discussion and an overview of scholarship, see Emanuel Tov, *Textual Criticism of the Hebrew Bible* (2d ed.; Minneapolis: Fortress, 2001), 313–50.

royal bureaucratic, or other.[6] Such texts might temporarily have other *Sitzen im Leben*, or they might imitate texts that have other contexts, but as soon as they entered the "Stream of Tradition" they were transmitted primarily and particularly in an educational context.

This model is relevant to the present study for two reasons. First, a prominent part of this model of transmission through education is that this educational system was focused on enabling *memorization* of the tradition through written and oral means. Early schooling focused on gaining the ability to reproduce the tradition accurately, a tradition often seen to be of divine origin, coming from a distant past, whose antiquity was marked by being written in a foreign language or an archaic dialect of the native language. Those who attained ultimate mastery of this tradition would not only reproduce older traditions, but also modify and extend them. When they did so, they often worked from their *memory* of the texts rather than from copies. This is evident in the types of variants that show up in parallel versions of texts: exchanges of words with similar meanings, meaningless shifts in word order, variation in syntactically equivalent expressions, etc. Studies in classics, medieval literature, psychology, and folklore have shown how these types of errors tend to occur in memory—based as they are in semantic equivalences. I term them "memory variants." This concept of memory variants will be important shortly.

The second reason the model of writing-supported memorization is relevant to the present study is that we have documentation outside Israel for the educational use of historical materials of the sort seen in Samuel–Kings (and Chronicles). By this I mean, not merely the case of the widespread use of royal inscriptions (or pseudo-royal inscriptions) in Old Babylonian education; or the use of various sorts of royal narratives and instructions in Egyptian and Mesopotamian education—e.g., the Sargon and Naram-Sin literature attested in school materials in the Old Babylonian period. Rather, following A. K. Grayson, we can recognize the didactic use of more extensive historical narratives in educational contexts during the first-millennium period of Mesopotamian education. Though such extensive historical narratives, e.g., the Babylonian Chronicle series, appear to have originated as scholarly reference resources for divination, Grayson, H. Tadmor, and others have argued that several such narratives were designed to serve a combination of propagandistic and educational goals.[7] These include: the Cuthean

---

6. David M. Carr, *Writing on the Tablet of the Heart: Origins of Scripture and Literature* (New York: Oxford University Press, 2005).

7. Albert Kirk Grayson, "History and Historians of the Ancient Near East: Assyria and Babylonia," *Or* 49 (1980): 189–90; Hayyim Tadmor, "Autobiographical Apology in the Royal Assyrian Literature," in *History, Historiography, and Interpretation: Studies*

legend of Naram-Sin, the Weidner Chronicle, the Chronicle of Nabonidus, the Epic of Tukulti Ninurta, and the Synchronistic Chronicle. Indeed, P. Gesche, in her study of first-millennium Babylonian education, has argued that royal historical texts such as these played a remarkably central role in the general education of all students.[8] Furthermore, my own study of parallel versions of these texts has found a remarkable level of memory variants in the transmission of these Akkadian texts that suggests the central role of memorization in the educational process.[9]

This comparative evidence strengthens a proposal already made in the early twentieth century by Norbert Peters that Israel's historiographic traditions originated in educational settings. Peters, followed by L. Dürr, M. Noth, A. Lemaire, and others, was struck by the unusually didactic form of the Deuteronomistic history, the way potentially earlier annalistic and other sources had been reshaped and framed by didactic speeches aiming to educate its users about God's purposes and their responsibilities.[10]

One thing these earlier scholars could not draw on was the above-discussed evidence of memory variants in the transmission of Israelite texts,

---

in Biblical and Cuneiform Languages (ed. H. Tadmor and M. Weinfeld; Jerusalem: The Hebrew University Magnes Press, 1984), 54–55.

8. Petra Gesche, Schulunterricht in Babylonien im ersten Jahrtausend v. Chr. (AOAT 275; Münster: Ugarit-Verlag, 2001), 147–52.

9. This study is not yet published. Provisionally, some studies outside the area of biblical literature that are relevant include Milman Parry's initial formulation in "Studies in the Epic Technique of Oral Verse-Making, I: Homer and Homeric Style," Harvard Studies in Classical Philology 41 (1930): 75–76; and subsequent studies in some other fields, such as Helmer Ringgren, "Oral and Written Transmission in the Old Testament: Some Observations," Studia Theologica 3 (1949): 34–59; Kenneth Sisam, "Notes on Old English Poetry: The Authority of Old English Poetical Manuscripts," Review of English Studies 257–268 (1953): 261; Albert C. Baugh, "Improvisation in the Middle English Romance," Proceedings of the American Philosophical Society 103 (1959): 418–54; idem, "The Middle English Romance: Some Questions of Creation, Presentation, and Preservation," Speculum 42 (1967): 1–31; Hendrik van der Werf, The Chansons of the Troubadours and Trouvères: A Study of the Melodies and their Relation to the Poems (Utrecht: Oosthoek, 1972), 26–31; Niek Veldhuis, Elementary Education at Nippur: The Lists of Trees and Wooden Objects (Groningen: Styx, 1997), 131–41; Raymond F. Person, "The Ancient Israelite Scribe as Performer," JBL 117 (1998): 601–609; Carr, Writing on the Tablet of the Heart, 42–45.

10. Norbert Peters, Unsere Bibel: Die Lebensquellen der Heiligen Schrift (Paderborn: Bonifacius, 1929), 208–10, see also Hubert Cancik, Grundzüge der hethitischen und alttestamentlichen Geschichtsschreibung (Abhandlungen des Deutschen Palästinavereins; Wiesbaden: Harrassowitz, 1976), 54–64 and André Lemaire, "Towards a Redactional History of the Book of Kings," in Reconsidering Israel and Judah: Recent Studies on the Deuteronomistic History (ed. G. N. Knoppers and J. G. McConville; Winona Lake: Eisenbrauns, 2000), 446–61 (including a survey of other studies with a similar viewpoint on pp. 459–60).

which has now become a resource in evaluating changes in textual traditions. This is the first type of "empirical" evidence to be considered in this essay. Take, for example, the Kings and Chronicles versions of the story of Solomon's dream at Gibeon. The two versions of the story open with similar statements about Solomon's thousands of offerings at Gibeon, but with different word order: 1 Kgs 3:4b has אלף עלות יעלה שלמה, while 2 Chr 1:6 has ויעל עליו עלות אלף. We see similar variation in word order in their introduction of Solomon's dream theophany: 1 Kgs 3:5a reads בגבעון נראה יהוה אל־שלמה בחלום הלילה, while 2 Chr 1:7a has בלילה ההוא נראה אלהים לשלמה. The introductions in 1 Kgs 3:5a//2 Chr 1:7a illustrate one of the common types of memory variants in the Hebrew Bible: alteration between אלהים and יהוה. Sometimes the variants are more substantial. For example, the description of the large number of the people in 1 Kgs 3:8 is עם רב אשר לא־ימנה ולא יספר מרב, while in 2 Chr 1:9 it is עם רב כעפר הארץ—similar ideas, but quite different ways of expressing them. The examples from this text (see chart 1) and others could be multiplied. My preliminary survey of close parallels across the Hebrew Bible, both in historical and other books, has indicated that the vast majority of variation in closely parallel texts is best interpreted as this sort of memory variation between relative equivalent phrases, rather than the sort of graphic variation characteristic of later stages in the process of the manuscript transmission.

Whether or not one situates the use of these texts in educational and related contexts, these memory variants are evidence that early versions of Chronicles and Samuel–Kings were transmitted in an environment where written texts were memorized and often accessed by means of memory. Scholars have long recognized how unwieldy ancient scrolls were, how difficult it was to find a given pericope in a scroll or to compare texts in multiple scrolls.[11] These memory variants suggest that ancient authors overcame this problem when composing a new work by using their memory to recall written texts that they wished to build on, revise, or cite. And their memory appears for the most part to be quite accurate, only occasionally exchanging words, switching lines, substituting similar expressions, and the like.

As a result, minor variations of this sort—typical of memory slips and switches—between Samuel–Kings and Chronicles may not point to subtle exegesis on the part of the author(s) of Chronicles but to the sorts of oral–written dynamics typical of the transmission of many ancient texts. Thus, rather than positing that switches in word order between Samuel–Kings and Chronicles represent a conscious attempt by the author of Chronicles to pro-

---

11. On this see especially the parody of traditional models in Susan Niditch, *Oral World and Written Word: Ancient Israelite Literature* (Library of Ancient Israel; Louisville: Westminster John Knox, 1996), 113.

duce a (highly occasional) "chiasm" between highly disparate texts,[12] one can allow that shifts such as those discussed above in 1 Kgs 3:5 occurred simply because of the variability of memory dynamics. The shift from the description of Solomon's great people as עם רב אשר לא־ימנה ולא יספר מרב (1 Kgs 3:8) to עם רב כעפר הארץ (2 Chr 1:9) comes not from the Chronicler's substitution of "more common phrasing" (Japhet) or some effort on the part of the Chronicler to avoid describing the people in a way similar to the sacrifices offered at the dedication of the temple (1 Kgs 8:5b; Kalimi), but just from the sort of free variation typical of texts transmitted through memory.[13] The authors of Chronicles themselves may have introduced such memory variants into their reproduction of earlier narratives or such variants may already have been developed in the version of such narratives that those authors used (different editions of Samuel–Kings).

To be sure, there are many larger variations between Chronicles and Samuel–Kings that are best explained as the result of conscious reshaping of prior tradition by the Chronicler. Nevertheless, the yield from this portion of the discussion is the insight that the author(s) of Chronicles may not have been as consistently creative as scholars sometimes think. Rather than explain *virtually every* variation between Chronicles and Samuel–Kings as the result of exegetical reshaping by the Chronicler, we may identify a subset of more minor changes (shifts in synonyms, word order, addition/subtraction of minor particles, etc.) which are as likely or more likely explained by memory dynamics in the transmission of Samuel–Kings and/or Chronicles. This means that in some respects the Chronicler has stayed closer to his sources than was previously supposed. This latter point will be relevant later in this essay, when we consider broader dynamics in the relationship between Chronicles and books of the Deuteronomistic History.

EMPIRICAL EVIDENCE FOR THE "TREND TOWARD EXPANSION"

Empirical comparison also documents a general trend of ancient authors to expand upon, rather than abbreviate, written sources that they were reproducing. This "trend toward expansion" is found in the later versions of the Gilgamesh tradition, which expand OB versions with a new prologue, flood

---

12. Cf. Isaac Kalimi, *The Reshaping of Ancient Israelite History in Chronicles* (Winona Lake: Eisenbrauns, 2005), 246–47, who also sees a diachronic shift in order of noun and modifier in Chronicles that (if it held) could point to conscious/unconscious linguistic updating on the part of the Chronicler.

13. Cf. Sara Japhet, *The Ideology of the Book of Chronicles and Its Place in Biblical Thought* (Frankfurt: Lang, 1989), 93–94; and Isaac Kalimi, *Reshaping*, 351–52.

tablet and conclusion (among other changes).[14] Similar trends toward expansion (in parallel sections) are documented in the late, standard Babylonian recension of the Anzu Epic, the Atrahasis Epic, the Tummal Inscription, and the Šumma Isbu birth omen series, and are also likely in several other Mesopotamian traditions (e.g., the Sumerian King List and the Code of Hammurabi).[15] Closer to ancient Israel, we see similar documentation of a trend toward expansion in successive redactions of the Pentateuch—the proto-MT, the so-called proto-Samaritan harmonizing version, and 4QRP. Even the *Temple Scroll* expands on its pentateuchal precursor sections, where it closely follows such precursors.[16] So also, the MT of the Jeremiah tradition is a good example of the multitude of ways in which expansion is attested in the manuscript traditions of the Hebrew Bible.[17] This trend is documented in other early Jewish works as well, as in the addition of the story of the three guards (Esd 3:1–5:6) to the Esdras/Ezra tradition.[18] In these cases and many others, the trend toward expansion is evident, in cases where later versions that closely follow their precursor text either reproduce or expand their precursor. Moreover, lest there be questions about circularity: in each case specific arguments independent of this "rule of supplementation" can be used

14. Jeffrey Tigay, *The Evolution of the Gilgamesh Epic* (Philadelphia: University of Pennsylvania Press, 1982), especially 103–5.

15. For discussion, see Tigay, *Gilgamesh Epic*, 104 (including nn. 76–78).

16. For a discussion of the scroll from this perspective, with citations of earlier literature, see David M. Carr, "Method in Determination of Direction of Dependence: An Empirical Test of Criteria Applied to Exodus 34,11–26 and its Parallels," in *Gottes Volk am Sinai: Untersuchungen zu Ex 32–34 und Dtn 9–10* (ed. M. Köckert and E. Blum; Veröffentlichungen der wissenschaftlichen Gesellschaft für Theologie 18; Gütersloh: Kaiser and Gütersloher Verlagshaus, 2001), 118–23.

17. Much of the literature and issues are surveyed in Tov, *Textual Criticism*, 319–27; although add, among others, Hermann-Josef Stipp, *Das masoretische und alexandrinische Sondergut des Jeremiabuches: Textgeschichtlicher Rang, Eigenarten, Triebkräfte* (OBO 136; Fribourg: Universitätsverlag; Göttingen: Vandenhoek & Ruprecht, 1994); and idem, *Jeremia, der Tempel, und die Aristokratie: Die patrizische (schafanidische) Redaktion des Jeremiabuches* (Waltrop: Spenner, 2000). For a survey of more potential cases of documented expansion, see Tov, *Textual Criticism*, 328–50.

18. The broader issue of the relationship of Esdras to Ezra is more complicated, but scholars are virtually unanimous on the late character of the "three guards" expansion. The textual development of the Qumran *Community Rule* might be taken as a prominent counterexample to this broader trend, since one of its most expansive editions, 1QS, is dated on paleographic grounds earlier than shorter recensions, such as 4QS[b] and 4QS[d]. Nevertheless, as argued by Sarianna Metso, *The Textual Development of the Qumran Community Rule* (STDJ 21; Leiden: Brill, 1997), a closer examination of the character of the differences between 1QS and the shorter recensions indicates that the later copies generally preserve earlier recensions of the material.

to establish the lateness of the expanded version, and it is extremely difficult to maintain that the direction of dependence is the reverse.

To be sure, there are clear cases of abbreviation, each of which has its special circumstances. For example, both folklore and psychological studies have shown an initial tendency toward abbreviation in *exclusively orally transmitted* traditions, such that later oral versions are often shorter than the original. So also, A. T. Olmstead, and more recently H. J. Tertel, have shown a tendency in Assyrian royal inscriptions to abbreviate the narration of earlier years in the later years of a king's reign.[19] And there are cases where a later tradition is quite loosely dependent on a precursor tradition; e.g., the free adaptation of some Sumerian Gilgamesh traditions in the Old Babylonian Gilgamesh epic, where it is not always clear that the later version is either longer or shorter than its precursors.[20] The correspondences between the Akkadian epic and its Sumerian precursors are not close. And in exceptional cases later works do abbreviate discrete aspects of earlier written traditions that they otherwise expand; for example, the later versions of the Gilgamesh epic eliminate a speech by the barmaid to Gilgamesh (OB X, 6–14) that does not conform to their new perspective on human mortality.[21] *Generally*, however, the trend toward expansion is far more prevalent *in cases where a later tradition reproduces large sections of an earlier tradition*, and cases of abbreviation or elimination in such cases of large-scale reproduction are the exception, rather than the rule.

The trend toward expansion affirms the status and value that was attributed to precursor traditions in ancient cultures, including Israel. They were seen as holy, from ancient times, etc.[22] Whether in Egypt, Greece, Mesopotamia, or Israel, there was a valuing of the canonical past that generally precluded wholesale deletion of portions of an ancient witness. One always had the option of writing a completely new account, and the opportunities for creative adaptation were greater when one was moving a precursor tradition from one language, e.g., Sumerian, to another, e.g., Akkadian. Nevertheless, if one was—in effect—producing a new version of the ancient tradition, the

---

19. Albert Ten Eyck Olmstead, *Assyrian Historiography: A Source Study* (Columbia, Mo.: University of Missouri Press, 1916) (especially p. 21), and Hans Jürgen Tertel, *Text and Transmission: An Empirical Model for the Literary Development of Old Testament Narratives* (Berlin: de Gruyter, 1994), 68–155.

20. Tigay, *Gilgamesh Epic*, 23–54.

21. There are other dynamics surrounding these shifts as well, which I plan to discuss in another context, such as an overall trend in the late version toward harmonizing the structure of the speeches at the end of Gilgamesh. Nevertheless, this is one of several clear examples where a later tradent appears to have failed to reproduce a significant swath of material in a written precursor text that he otherwise reproduces.

22. Carr, *Writing on the Tablet of the Heart*, 30, 71, 107.

tendency was to preserve that tradition in full, even as it might be expanded and revised through various additions.

THE CASE OF "EMPIRICAL COMPARISON" IN THE HEBREW BIBLE

The books of Chronicles provide one of the most prominent examples of empirical comparison in the Hebrew Bible. Already two hundred years ago Wilhelm Martin de Wette effectively argued that Chronicles was a late, often highly creative abbreviation, extension, and adaptation of material from Samuel–Kings.[23] His conclusion has remained dominant among the majority of biblical scholars for over a century, up to the present day.

Yet, after a long period of broad consensus, this picture is no longer so clear. Evidence emerging from Qumran, especially the 4QSam[a] scroll, has converged with evidence from the Septuagint and Josephus to suggest that the author of Chronicles was *not* dependent on the version of Samuel–Kings (or the Deuteronomistic History as a whole) that was eventually codified by the Masoretes. As Eugene Ulrich and others have shown, the Chronicler appears to have been dependent on a version of Samuel–Kings closer to that seen in the 4QSam[a] scroll and the one used by Josephus.[24] Meanwhile, in a pair of studies, H. Williamson has argued persuasively that some characteristics found toward the end of 2 Chronicles are best explained as the result of an extension of the Samuel–Kings tradition before it was used as a source by the Chronicler.[25] This has led to more global reevaluations of the relationship of Samuel–Kings and Chronicles, such as Steven McKenzie's attempt to use Chronicles to reconstruct the contours of a preexilic edition of the Deuteronomistic History.[26] Together, these studies suggest that the authors of Chronicles followed their sources for Samuel–Kings more closely than scholars once sup-

---

23. Wilhelm Martin L. de Wette, *Beiträge zur Einleitung in das Alte Testament* (2 vols.; Halle: Schimmelpfenning, 1806–1807).

24. See especially Eugene C. Ulrich, *The Qumran Text of Samuel and Josephus* (HSM 19; Missoula, Mont.: Scholars Press, 1978), and the publication and analysis of 4QSam[a] in Frank Moore Cross et.al., *Qumran Cave 4, 12: 1–2 Samuel* (DJD 17; Oxford: Clarendon, 2005). In addition, see Werner E. Lemke, "Synoptic Studies in the Chronicler's History" (Ph.D. diss., Harvard University, 1963); idem, "The Synoptic Problem in the Chronicler's History," *HTR* 58 (1965): 349–63.

25. Hugh Williamson, "The Death of Josiah and the Continuing Development of the Deuteronomic History," *VT* 26 (1982): 351–61; and idem, "Reliving the Death of Josiah: A Reply to C. T. Begg," *VT* 37 (1987): 9–15.

26. Steven McKenzie, *The Chronicler's Use of the Deuteronomistic History* (HSM 13; Atlanta: Scholars Press, 1984). Note also Lemke, "Synoptic Studies," and "Synoptic Problem."

posed, even as their edition of those traditions was quite distinct from that of the MT and other significant later witnesses for those books.

In the wake of these studies Graeme Auld proposed a yet more radical thesis: that the books of Chronicles were not based on a book like Samuel–Kings. Rather both Samuel–Kings and Chronicles were based on a common source, a postexilic "Book of the Two [Royal] Houses," which corresponded in the main with the material shared by Samuel–Kings and Chronicles. The "Book of the Two Houses" was, in a sense, much like the gospel source Q consisting of material shared by Matthew and Luke.[27] In this case, however, Auld's Hebrew Bible "Q" would have begun with an account of Saul's death, include extensive sections (shared by Chronicles and Samuel–Kings) concerning David and Solomon, and have continued with a narrative largely focused on Judah's kings up to the exile. In his 1994 book, *Kings Without Privilege*, and a series of essays published in various contexts, Auld has attempted to show how both Samuel–Kings and Chronicles can be seen as different outgrowths of this common source, building on the terminology and motifs of this "Book of the Two Houses" in distinctively different ways.[28]

Auld's proposal has received much attention and criticism, including significant reviews by Gary Knoppers, Hugh Williamson and Richard Coggins, as well as article-length treatments by Zippora Talshir, Christophe Nihan and Thomas Römer, and Steven McKenzie.[29] Many have found Auld's dating problematic and wondered why a postexilic author would add huge amounts of material about the North to a "Book of the Two Houses" as outlined by Auld. A further problem for many reviewers is the fact that the shared source begins with the conclusion of Saul's reign, an odd place, many think, for

---

27. Auld notes this analogy in one of his first presentations of the hypothesis: A. Graeme Auld, "Prophets through the Looking Glass: Between Writings and Moses," *JSOT* 27 (1983): 16.

28. A. Graeme Auld, *Kings Without Privilege: David and Moses in the Story of the Bible's Kings* (Edinburgh: T&T Clark, 1994); and idem, *Samuel at the Threshold: Selected Works of Graeme Auld* (SOTSMS; Burlington, Vt.: Ashgate, 2004).

29. Gary Knoppers, review of A. Graeme Auld, *Kings Without Privilege, ATJ* 27 (1995): 118–21; Richard J. Coggins, review of A. Graeme Auld, *Kings Without Privilege, Theology* 98 (1995): 383; Hugh Williamson, review of A. Graeme Auld, *Kings Without Privilege, VT* 46 (1996): 553–55; and Thomas C. Römer and Christophe Nihan, "Une source commune aux récits de rois et chroniques? À propos d'un ouvrage récent d'A. G. Auld," *ETR* 79 (1999): 415–22; McKenzie, "Chronicler as Redactor"; Zipora Talshir, "The Reign of Solomon in the Making: Pseudo-Connections Between 3 Kingdoms and Chronicles," *VT* 50 (2000): 233–49. Particularly relevant, as well, is the survey by Thomas Willi of potential places where Chronicles may presuppose material from Kings that is in the parallel material (*Die Chronik als Auslegung: Untersuchungen zur literarischen Gestaltung der historischen Überlieferung Israels* [FRLANT 106; Göttingen: Vandenhoeck & Ruprecht, 1972], 56–65).

the beginning of a "Book of the Two Houses." Finally, many reviewers have argued that material found in Chronicles—including some material shared by Chronicles and Samuel–Kings and thus part of Auld's hypothesized "Book of the Two Houses"—may presuppose earlier material that is found only in Samuel–Kings. Cases such as these would suggest that Chronicles actually did eliminate material found in its precursor text, a text that might look a lot like Samuel–Kings.

I too was quite skeptical about Auld's thesis when he initially presented it to me orally at a conference in the early 1990s, but I started to reconsider while doing an unrelated exercise for an introductory class on the Deuteronomistic and Chronistic Histories two years ago. In order to give students a flavor of the two histories (Chronicles and the Deuteronomistic History) and a sense of what it meant to talk of "Deuteronomistic redaction," I gave my students an English-language version of the story of Solomon's dream at Gibeon in two columns (similar to chart 1). The Kings version was on the left, with elements underlined that had been identified in my book, *From D to Q* as elements of a Deuteronomistic redaction. The Chronicles version was on the right. The analysis of the Deuteronomistic redaction in *From D to Q* had been done independently of Auld's analysis, and later portions of the book were based on the typical assumption that the Chronicler had the full Kings version in front of him.[30]

What becomes evident on more examination of chart 1 is the following: when one subtracts the underlined elements of putative Deuteronomistic redaction, the remainder—the posited pre-Deuteronomistic *Vorlage*—is almost identical to the material shared with Chronicles. Indeed, in 1993, just two years after my publication of *From D to Q* and apparently independently of knowledge of it, Auld published an article on the Gibeon story where he proposed—on the basis of his approach—that the Gibeon story material shared by Kings and Chronicles preceded both of them.[31] As G. Braulik noted in an article a few years later, Auld's identification of this pre-Deuteronomistic Gibeon story was virtually identical to mine.[32] The main difference was that Auld included an incomparability formula shared by Kings and Chronicles that I had excised—tentatively—on redaction-critical grounds, and my work has been criticized for doing so.[33] Aside from this

30. David M. Carr, *From D to Q: A Study of Early Jewish Interpretations of Solomon's Dream at Gibeon* (SBLMS 44; Atlanta: Scholars Press, 1991).

31. A. Graeme Auld, "Solomon at Gibeon," *ErIsr* 24 (1993): 1–7.

32. Georg Braulik, "Weisheit im Buch Deuteronomium," in *Weisheit ausserhalb der kanonischen Weisheitsschriften* (ed. B. Janowski; Gütersloh: Kaiser and Gütersloher Verlaghaus, 1996), 50 (n. 59).

33. This was one point on which my analysis in *From D to Q* was rightly criticized in

detail, my terminologically-oriented redaction-critical analysis and Auld's analysis of shared material produced similar results.

This led me to review Auld's work and that of his critics. As Auld acknowledges, he relates his research methodology to the work of Ulrich, Williamson, McKenzie, and others noted above, who argue that Chronicles is much closer to a version of Samuel–Kings than previously supposed. Where scholars once supposed that Chronicles had added material or changed it, it is now clear that such changes are already found in 4QSam[a] and/or the Old Greek. Chronicles was merely reproducing its precursor text at these junctures. The research on memory variants described above reinforces this insight. There are many loci where previous scholars have tried to find an exegetical reason why Chronicles would be modifying its *Vorlage* in Samuel–Kings, but where the difference can be plausibly explained as a form of memory variation. In sum, in places where Chronicles is parallel to Samuel–Kings, it appears that the author(s) of Chronicles stayed much closer to earlier sources than previously supposed. We cannot assume anymore that every difference between Chronicles and Samuel–Kings was produced by the Chronicler's exegetical and theological creativity.

This then raises a question about the extent to which Chronicles is an exception to the "trend toward expansion" that was described in the previous section. For example, with Auld we might ask why Chronicles—a text generally quite focused on the temple—would fail to reproduce significant sections in 1 Kings about the temple (e.g., 1 Kgs 6:4–18, 25–27, 28–32; 6:34–7:12, etc.), if such sections were in its source? As Auld points out, several parts of this portion of 1 Kings are placed differently in the Old Greek version, suggesting fluidity in the 1 Kings tradition about the temple up to a late point.[34] Similarly, why would the Chronicler eliminate traditions about Solomon's superior insight, such as the story of the prostitutes arguing over one baby (1 Kgs 3:16–28) or the later overview of Solomon's extraordinary wisdom (1 Kgs 5:9–14)? Of course, intelligent biblical scholars can work two hundred years and come up with explanations for all these minuses in Chronicles, but an alternative would be to say that the Chronicler may not have had these sections of the 1 Kings narrative when composing his work. Indeed, more generally, Chronicles may not have abbreviated its source where it has minuses in other parallel sections, but it *may* be a witness at points to a shorter version in its source.

Christa Schäfer-Lichtenberger, *Joshua und Salomo: Eine Studie zu Autorität und Legitimität des Nachfolgers im Alten Testament* (VTSup 58; Leiden: Brill, 1995), 266 (n. 234).

34. Auld, *Kings Without Privilege*, 23–26, see also Steven McKenzie, *The Chronicler's Use of the Deuteronomistic History* (HSM 33; Atlanta: Scholars Press, 1984), 108. Römer and Nihan, "Une source commune?" 422 (n. 29) note in an otherwise critical review of Auld's work that the temple narrative is one place where it offers the most potential.

This is not to say that the authors of Chronicles did not omit large swathes of the historical books used by it, and here Auld's more general position requires correction in my judgment.[35] We can most clearly see abbreviation in Chronicles in cases where Chronicles features *incomplete* abbreviation of portions of Samuel–Kings that has produced incongruities in the later text. For example, as many have observed—the existing text of 1 Chr 20:1–3, and thus the postulated shared text (cf. 2 Sam 11:1, 26, 30–31) starts with an otherwise dangling juxtaposition of David's presence in Jerusalem with Joab's campaign in Ammon (2 Sam 11:1//1 Chr 20:1). In Samuel, this ironic placement of David in Jerusalem away from the war "at the time when kings went to battle" already anticipates his misdeeds in the David and Bathsheba story that follows in 2 Samuel 11–12. Furthermore, as many have pointed out, the combination of materials in 1 Chr 20:1–3 jumps from Joab's conquering of Rabbah while David was still in Jerusalem (1 Chr 20:1//2 Sam 11:1, 26b) to David taking the crown of Milcom along with other booty out of Rabbah (1 Chr 20:2–3//2 Sam 12:30–31). David never travels to Ammon in this shared source. To be sure, there are a couple of Greek LXX manuscripts of Chronicles that preserve a form of Joab's invitation to David to come to Rabbah (as seen in 2 Sam 12:27–29), but most text-critics rightly propose that these are secondary harmonizations of these Chronicles manuscripts to Samuel in order to deal with the difficulty just observed. Furthermore, as Ralph Klein has observed, the Chronicles description of Joab's destruction of Ammon uses a verb, הרס that was featured in David's original order to Joab to conquer Ammon, found in special material in Samuel which is not included in Chronicles (2 Sam 11:25).[36] All this seems to indicate that the Chronicler knew of material in 2 Sam 11:25, 12:27–29 and the broader David-Bathsheba story, but omitted it in the process of producing this somewhat jumbled account of the conclusion of the Ammon campaign. The account in Chronicles is not just shorter, but jumbled in a way suggesting *incomplete* adaptation.[37] There are other loci where the text of Chronicles has incongruities that seem to result from incomplete abbreviation of its source text in Samuel–Kings. These include the mention in 1 Chr 14:3 of *more* wives that David took in Jerusalem (//2 Sam

---

35. Here my position has evolved from my cautious endorsement of the broader potential of Auld's proposal in David M. Carr, "Empirische Perspektiven auf das Deuteronomistische Geschichtswerk," in *Das deuteronomistische Geschichtswerk: Redaktions- und religionsgeschichtliche Perspektiven zur 'Deuteronomismus'-Diskussion in Tora und Vorderen Propheten* (ed. M. Witte et al.; BZAW 365; Berlin: de Gruyter, 2006), 13 (see more broadly the discussion on pp. 8–13).

36. Ralph W. Klein, *1 Chronicles: A Commentary* (Hermeneia; Minneapolis: Fortress, 2006), 407.

37. Willi, *Chronik als Auslegung*, 57–58; Talshir, "Reign of Solomon," 233–34.

5:13), despite the fact that Chronicles omits narratives in Samuel regarding earlier wives he had taken (e.g. 1 Samuel 25; 2 Sam 3:13-16),[38] the mention in 2 Chr 10:4 of Israel's complaint about Solomon's oppression without rebuttal by Rehoboam (//1 Kgs 12:4)—despite the lack of any previous description in Chronicles of Solomon's forced labor (cf. 1 Kgs 4:6b–7; 5:7–8 [ET 4:27–28], 27–28 [ET 5:13–14]);[39] and the assertion in 2 Chr 10:15 (//1 Kgs 12:15) that Rehoboam's failure to listen to Israel fulfilled Ahijah's prophecy, despite the fact that this prophecy (found in 1 Kgs 11:29–39) is not reproduced in Chronicles.[40] These cases, along with some issues regarding placement of material, such as the appendices to Samuel and the narrative about Micaiah,[41] suggest that the Chronicler knew of materials much like those now found in Samuel–Kings regarding David's reign in Hebron, the story of David and Bathsheba, Solomon's introduction of forced labor in Israel, the prophecy of Ahijah, and several parts of the Hezekiah narrative. As past reviewers of Auld's work have suggested, cases such as these give good reason to believe that the Chronicler did not attempt to reproduce these large sections of his *Vorlage*, for various reasons: they were there in the *Vorlage*, he knew them, but he did not preserve them. In at least these cases, the above-described "trend toward expansion" does not hold.

In sum, the relationship between the Deuteronomistic History and Chronicles is more complex than either the older traditional picture or Auld's initial proposal. The vast verbatim overlap between the two historical works shows a form of literary dependence, generally of Chronicles on parallels found in Samuel–Kings. Yet I have discussed text-critical and other evidence that suggests that Chronicles did not use a version of Samuel–Kings identical to the proto-MT or any version witnessed to in our current manuscripts. Indeed, there are points, such as the Chronicler's version of the Solomon narrative, where Chronicles may well have had a version of the narrative significantly shorter and/or different from that now seen in the Deuteronomistic History. The two narrative works are not simply different stages on the same literary trajectory, and cases of significant divergence—especially (given the trend toward expansion) cases where Chronicles lacks material found in the Deuteronomistic History—must be evaluated on a case by case basis.

---

38. Willi, *Chronik als Auslegung*, 57.

39. Willi, *Chronik als Auslegung*, 58–59.

40. Willi, *Chronik als Auslegung*, 58; McKenzie, "Chronicler as Redactor," 83.

41. For discussion of the appendices to Samuel, see Hugh Williamson, "A Response to A. Graeme Auld," *JSOT* 8 (1983): 36–37. For the Micaiah story, see Knoppers, review of Auld, 120; and Sara Japhet, *1 and 2 Chronicles* (OTL; Louisville: Westminster John Knox, 1993), 756–57.

CHRONICLES AND THE RELATIONSHIP BETWEEN THE
PENTATEUCH AND FORMER PROPHETS

So, where does this leave us with the question of the Pentateuch and the Former Prophets? First, given the previous discussion, it is not clear that everything now in Samuel–Kings was available to the Chronicler. Although I have reviewed several cases where it is clear that Chronicles eliminated material now found in Samuel–Kings, there are other places where the less expansive text in Chronicles—or less expansive shared material between Chronicles and Samuel–Kings—may provide access to an earlier, less expansive version of the material now seen in the Deuteronomistic History.[42] Given this, I propose the following "thought experiment," in which we compare links to the Pentateuch in material that is *shared* between Chronicles and the Deuteronomistic History with links to the Pentateuch *peculiar* to Chronicles and to DtrH, respectively.

First, if one focuses on material shared between Chronicles and the Deuteronomistic History, the links to the Pentateuch are relatively rare and general. Overall, the shared material in Chronicles and the Deuteronomistic History is dominated by literary structures linking the reigns of David and Solomon with those of their successors in Judah. Not only are there cross-references, but the narrative unfolds in ways that make clear that the descriptions and evaluations of the kings of Judah up to the exile were meant to be part of the same literary work that described David's founding of the dynasty and Solomon's building of the Jerusalem temple. In contrast, pentateuchal themes only rarely are mentioned in material shared by Chronicles and Samuel–Kings, and when they are mentioned, only in a tertiary way. For example,

---

42. Along these lines, it is unclear whether the Chronicler regarded Samuel–Kings as part of an extended literary work stretching back to include Genesis through Judges. Certainly Chronicles knows of these books, and the genealogical sections of 1 Chr 1–9, assuming they are part of an early layer of Chronicles, draw extensively on names and data in Genesis through Judges. Nevertheless, given the scope of the overlap between Chronicles and the Deuteronomistic History, it is easier to imagine Chronicles as created with Samuel–Kings in front it of, without Deuteronomy–Joshua–Judges, than to imagine Chronicles as recasting of the whole of the Primary History, but only reproducing verbatim the part of it limited to Samuel–Kings. Recently there has been an increasing chorus of voices raising questions about whether and when there ever was an overarching Deuteronomistic History (on this see the helpful summary and proposed "compromise" in Thomas Römer, *The So-Called Deuteronomistic History: A Sociological, Literary and Historical Introduction* [London: T&T Clark, 2005], 38–43). The selective reproduction of only one part of the Deuteronomistic History in Chronicles could be an additional datum suggesting that Samuel–Kings may have started out separate from Deuteronomy–Joshua as an account of Judah and Israel's monarchies.

the divine speech to Nathan briefly refers to Israel coming out of Egypt and God dwelling amidst Israel in a tent or tabernacle (2 Sam 7:2, 6//1 Chr 17:1, 5); Solomon refers in his temple dedication prayer to the exodus, to Horeb, and to the placement of tablets in the ark at Horeb (1 Kgs 8:9, 16, 21//2 Chr 5:10; 6:5, 11; note also 2 Kgs 9:9//2 Chr 7:22); and both 2 Kgs 14:6//2 Chr 25:4 and 2 Kgs 21:8//2 Chr 33:8 refer to the "Torah" of "Moses," with 2 Kgs 14:6//2 Chr 25:4 actually citing part of it (Deut 24:16). Yet, as pointed out by Erhard Blum, such references to other texts in themselves do not constitute proof that a given text is part of the same literary corpus as the narratives to which it refers.[43] Indeed, the references to the "book of the Torah of Moses" in 2 Kgs 14:6//2 Chr 25:4, and "all the Torah [and decrees and laws]" of "Moses" in 2 Kgs 21:8//2 Chr 33:8, seem to be links to a separately named and known work, as do the less specific references to the "[scroll of]Torah" (2 Kgs 22:8, 12//2 Chr 34:15, 20), "scroll of the covenant" (2 Kgs 23:2–3//2 Chr 34:30–31; cf. 2 Kgs 23:21), and "scroll" (2 Kgs 22:8, 10, 13, 16; 2 Chr 34:15, 18, 21, 24) in the shared material in the Josiah narrative. Moreover, certain parts of the shared material between Samuel–Kings and Chronicles, such as the description of the construction of Solomon's temple, show a striking *lack* of coordination with potentially related materials in the Tetrateuch.

All this changes significantly when we look at material that is peculiar to the Deuteronomistic History on the one hand and Chronicles on the other. For example, material specific to the books of Chronicles shows broad and deep connections to the Pentateuch far surpassing those found in the Chronicles material shared with the Deuteronomistic History. The genealogies of 1 Chr 1–9 echo in form and content many of the Priestly genealogies of Genesis and Exodus and show knowledge of details of books from Genesis through Samuel. The Priestly tabernacle appears at Gibeon in material specific to the Chronicles version of the story of Solomon's dream (2 Chr 1:3–5; note also 1 Chr 16:37–43, which prepares for it). The Aaronide priests, Levitical priests, and their practices in the Priestly version of the Moses story are prominently featured at numerous points of Chronicles that have no counterpart in Kings (e.g., 1 Chr 22:2–29:30; 2 Chr 13; 31; 35:1–19). Clearly Chronicles was not meant to be part of the same literary corpus as the Pentateuch, but material specific to Chronicles shows that its authors were highly interested

---

43. See Erhard Blum, "Pentateuch-Hexateuch-Enneateuch? Or: How Can One Recognize a Literary Work in the Hebrew Bible?" in this volume, 30–35. At this point I should note that I do not find persuasive Graeme Auld's arguments for the secondary character of many of these references to Moses in the shared material (Auld, *Kings Without Privilege*, 144–46).

in coordinating the story told there with central elements of the pentateuchal narrative.[44]

Turning to material specific to the Deuteronomistic History (and not paralleled by Chronicles), it is clear that this material is thoroughly linked with pentateuchal traditions. This starts with the book of Deuteronomy itself, with its extensive review of events from the tetrateuchal Moses story. As argued by Blum, such a review shows obvious knowledge of other literary works, but seems to constitute the beginning of a new literary work—hence the need for the review.[45] What is significant for our purpose is the prominent link with the preceding Moses traditions in Deuteronomy along with mention of the promise of land to the ancestors. Whatever preliminary links to these traditions might exist in the shared material, they are dwarfed by the range and extent of back-references in Deuteronomy to the Tetrateuch.

Furthermore, the material specific to the Deuteronomistic History (and not paralleled in Chronicles) develops a concept of the Mosaic Torah that is found not only in Deuteronomy, but also throughout much of the other material special to the Deuteronomistic History. This culminates in a Torah-focused rearrangement of the narration of Josiah's reform. According to the version of this story in 2 Kings (and in contrast to that in Chronicles), Josiah's purification of the cult and land all follows from and flows out of the discovery of the scroll of the Torah in the temple, and the making of a covenant on the basis of it.

These links to the Pentateuch, particularly Deuteronomy, are found in much of the rest of the material that is special to the Deuteronomistic History. The book of Joshua starts with the injunction for Joshua to recite the Torah continually (Josh 1:8), moves to an account of the Jordan crossing modeled on and recalling the Red Sea-crossing (Josh 3:1–5:12), and concludes with Joshua's own injunction to the people to follow the Torah (Josh 23), along with a review of many events in the Torah in the covenant at Shechem (Josh 24). Moreover, Josh 1–11 is, in large part, an execution of the divine conquest command in Deut 7, and many have observed the links between the tribal lists of Josh 13–22 and Priestly material now in the Pentateuch.

The Torah and other themes continue in Judges, particularly the framework of Judges that attributes the defeat of Israel to their disobedience of Yahweh's commands. For example, Judg 2:6–23 introduces the cycle with an overview of the transition from the exodus-wilderness generation to their children and the clarification that the subsequent defeat of the second generation results from their propensity to "follow other gods" (cf. the chil-

44. For more connections and discussion, see Auld, *Kings Without Privilege*, 130–31.
45. Blum, "Pentateuch-Hexateuch-Enneateuch?" 30–35.

dren's instruction in Deut 6:14–15). Here we see a more general trend: the most prominent links to the Pentateuch in the material special to the Deuteronomistic History are found in its framing material, while there are other traditions apparently used by the Deuteronomistic authors that do not have such widespread and intense coordination to the general theme of Mosaic law or to the particulars of the pentateuchal tradition.

This distinction is particularly evident in Samuel. We see explicit references back to the Torah in Samuel's speech in 1 Sam 12:8, as part of a narrative sequence extending into the period of the judges (1 Sam 12:9–11). Yet large sections of Samuel, including parts often assigned to the ark narrative or succession narrative, lack clear cross-references to previous material. Though scholars have often noted parallels between characters and plot in the succession narrative on the one hand and the material on Judah in Genesis on the other, the two tradition blocks are not explicitly coordinated with each other as part of a narrative sequence as they are in 1 Sam 12:8–11 and other framework settings particular to the Deuteronomistic History.

These links to the Pentateuch continue in the book of Kings, starting with David's reference to the "Torah of Moses" in 1 Kgs 2:3. The Deuteronomistic version of Solomon's dream at Gibeon, 1 Kings 3:2–15, links to the theme of the commandments in Deuteronomy, turning the story into one of Solomon gaining Deuteronomic Torah as wisdom (see underlined elements in chart 1); this wisdom is then demonstrated in the story of Solomon's judgment between the two prostitutes, a story unique to the Deuteronomistic History. The Deuteronomistic version of Solomon's temple dedication features additional references to Moses, including to God's fulfillment of all the good words spoken "through Moses" (1 Kgs 8:56). The Deuteronomistic account of Solomon also implicitly links to Torah in its special material about how Solomon became a bad king. According to the extra chapter in 1 Kgs 11 (especially 11:1–13), Solomon caused the eventual split of the kingdom by allowing foreign wives to turn him from obedience to the covenant, thus disobeying Deut 7:1–6. Looking more broadly at other parts of Kings, there is much special Deuteronomistic material, as in Samuel, that has few links with Deuteronomy or the Pentateuch more broadly, such as several large blocks of material about the North. Nevertheless, once again in the framing passages, such as the explanation of the North's downfall (2 Kgs 17) or the Deuteronomistic version of Josiah's reform (2 Kgs 22–23), the coordination with Torah and/or Pentateuch is much clearer for the books of the Former Prophets. Moreover, in a case like Solomon's dedicatory prayer for the temple (1 Kgs 8), where the material shared between Chronicles and Kings already links to the Pentateuch at several points (1 Kgs 8:9, 16, 21 //2 Chr 5:10; 6:5, 11), material specific to the Deuteronomistic History expands on these links (1 Kgs 8:51, 53, 56). Or, take the example of Hezekiah's reform, where 2 Kgs 18:4 features a reference to Hezekiah's destruction of the serpent that Moses made, which is lacking in its Chronicles counterpart. Finally, 2 Kings features praise of Hezekiah's (2 Kgs 18:5–6) and Josiah's (2 Kgs 23:25) Torah obedience that has no specific parallel in Chronicles.

Here we should recall again points made by Erhard Blum in earlier publications and—in particularly pointed form—in the essay published in this volume. If a text shows knowledge of facts from another text, this does not prove that both texts were always part of the same literary work. Instead, to *know* that they were connected, one needs evidence of compositional integration—so that elements at one point of a text provide the final unfolding of elements introduced at an earlier point. Moses giving of the Deuteronomic Torah at Moab, and the foregrounding of that Torah, especially in the version of Josiah's reform found in 2 Kings, is a potential case wherein an author has contributed compositional integration, so that Deuteronomy is now the centerpiece of the conclusion of Kings. In this respect Chronicles may witness to a stage of the narrative about Josiah that preceded the focus on Deuteronomic law in 2 Kings 22–23.

This leads back to a trend, documented in prior empirical studies, for later editions of works to manifest increasing levels of harmonization and coordination of disparate episodes. Let me give a range of examples from Mesopotamian traditions. Within the Gilgamesh epic we see such harmonization in the late version of Gilgamesh's dreams of Enkidu, the interchange between Enkidu and the harlot, the subsequent interchange between Shamash and Enkidu, the narrative introductions of Gilgamesh's dreams on the way to Cedar mountain, and the various expansions and abbreviations of Gilgamesh's final encounters with the barmaid and boatman after Enkidu's death.[46] In addition, later versions of the Atrahasis Epic contain several harmonizing expansions, such as in the description of the gods' response to human noise (SB 4.3, 7; cf. OB 1.356) and the interchange between Ea and Atrahasis (SB 5.27–30). The Etana Epic also features an addition that assimilates the warning by the eagle's offspring (LV 2.48–49) to an oath given earlier (LV 2.18–19).[47]

Turning to the other end of the chronological continuum, we may observe that the proto-Samaritan pentateuchal traditions are primarily characterized by the presence of plusses—previously known only in the Samaritan Pentateuch—that harmonize parts of Deuteronomy with parts of the Tetrateuch and vice-versa.[48] These harmonizations continue in 4QRP and related tradi-

---

46. On this, see in particular the early study, Jerrold Cooper, "Gilgamesh Dreams of Enkidu: The Evolution and Dilution of Narrative," in *Essays on the Ancient Near East in Memory of Jacob Joel Finkelstein* (ed. M. Ellis; Hamden, Conn.: Archon, 1977), 39–44.

47. Tertel, *Text and Transmission*, 33–36, 53–55.

48. Tigay, "Conflation."

tions. Finally, in the case of the *Temple Scroll*, many of the columns featuring verbatim parallels to biblical material harmonize sections from Deuteronomy with legislation and/or wording found in Deuteronomy, Leviticus, and elsewhere.[49] Notably, in my study of these examples of harmonization the level of verbatim agreement was higher for the base text, Deuteronomy, while there were a higher number of memory variants in the texts being integrated—suggesting that they were being quoted from memory.

These examples could be multiplied, but the dynamic should be clear. In many cases ancient tradents did not merely preserve the traditions before them, but coordinated different parts of these traditions with each other, thereby harmonizing them. I suggest that such harmonization involved what might be understood as a "hyper-memorization" of tradition where different parts of a textual tradition (or broader corpus) were understood to be so sacrosanct that they were not allowed to contradict each other.

Turning back to the case at hand, there may be places—especially where Chronicles and Samuel–Kings are closely parallel to each other—where one or the other tradition witnesses to a form of a given narrative not yet coordinated/harmonized with the Torah. For example, whether or not the material in Samuel–Kings was always connected to Deuteronomy through Judges, the Chronicles version of Josiah's reign may preserve a form of that narrative that was less harmonized with what preceded than the version now in 2 Kgs 22–23. Empirical documentation of harmonization gives us a different perspective on the Torah focus of the 2 Kgs 22–23 narrative than mere text-immanent analysis would.

In conclusion, the results from empirical comparison offer different forms of assistance in analyzing the links between the books of the Former Prophets and the Pentateuch. First, empirical comparison can uncover oral-written dynamics that explain minor divergences between Chronicles and Samuel–Kings, thus reinforcing scholarship based on other data (e.g., analysis of 4QSam[a] and other text-critical evidence) that show the Chronicler's remarkably close dependence on its sources in Samuel–Kings in parallel passages. Second, empirical comparison of texts can uncover broader dynamics in textual-transmission, such as the trend toward expansion and harmonization, that would suggest that some of the differences between Chronicles and Samuel–Kings were caused by expansion and/or harmonization of parts of Samuel–Kings with preceding material. Third, in so far as Chronicles (at least in overlapping sections) may provide access to an earlier form of Samuel–Kings, it offers one possible avenue for stratifying the links to the Pentateuch in the books of the Former Prophets. I have argued that those links to the

---

49. For discussion and citation of some earlier studies, see Carr, "Method."

Pentateuch are far less common in material shared between Chronicles and Samuel–Kings than they are in material specific to Chronicles on the one hand and Samuel–Kings on the other. Such empirical comparison may provide additional evidence of the authorial work that bound the Torah to Former Prophets, "harmonizing" the one with the other in ways consonant with modes used in many other examples of documented growth of ancient traditions.

Chart 1: Comparison of 1 Kings 3:2–15 with 2 Chronicles 1:1–13

Case Studies

1 Kings 3:2–15	**2 Chronicles 1:1–13**
	(1:1) ויתחזק שלמה בן־דויד על־מלכותו ויהוה אלהיו עמו ויגדלהו למעלה (1:2) ויאמר שלמה לכל־ישראל לשרי האלפים והמאות ולשפטים ולכל נשיא לכל־ישראל ראשי האבות
(3:2) <u>רק העם מזבחים בבמות כי</u> <u>לא־נבנה בית לשם יהוה עד הימים ההם</u>	
(3:3) <u>ויאהב שלמה את־יהוה ללכת</u> <u>בחקות דוד אביו רק בבמות</u> <u>הוא מזבח ומקטיר</u> (3:4) וילך המלך גבענה לזבח שם כי היא הבמה הגדולה	(1:3) וילכו שלמה וכל־הקהל עמו לבמה אשר בגבעון כי־שם היה אהל מועד האלהים אשר עשה משה עבד־יהוה במדבר (1:4) אבל ארון האלהים העלה דויד מקרית יערים בהכין לו דויד כי נטה־לו אהל בירושלם (1:5) ומזבח הנחשת אשר עשה בצלאל בן־אורי בן־חור שם לפני משכן יהוה וידרשהו שלמה והקהל (1:6) ויעל שלמה שם על־מזבח הנחשת לפני יהוה אשר לאהל מועד ויעל עליו עלות אלף
אלף עלות יעלה שלמה על המזבח ההוא (3:5) בגבעון נראה יהוה אל־שלמה בחלום הלילה ויאמר אלהים שאל מה אתן־לך (3:6) ויאמר שלמה אתה עשית עם־עבדך דוד אבי חסד גדול <u>כאשר הלך לפניך באמת ובצדקה</u> <u>ובישרת לבב עמך</u> <u>ותשמר־לו את־החסד הגדול הזה</u> <u>ותתן־לו בן ישב על־כסאו כיום הזה</u>	(1:7) בלילה ההוא נראה אלהים לשלמה ויאמר לו שאל מה אתן־לך (1:8) ויאמר שלמה לאלהים אתה עשית עם־דויד אבי חסד גדול
(3:7) ועתה יהוה אלהי אתה המלכת את־עבדך תחת דוד אבי ואנכי נער קטן	והמלכתני תחתיו (1:9) עתה יהוה אלהים יאמן דברך עם דויד אבי כי אתה המלכתני על־עם רב כעפר הארץ (1:10) עתה חכמה ומדע תן־לי ואצאה לפני העם־הזה ואבואה
לא אדע צאת ובא (3:8) <u>ועבדך בתוך עמך אשר בחרת</u> <u>עם־רב אשר לא־ימנה ולא יספר מרב</u> (3:9) ונתת לעבדך לב שמע לשפט את־עמך להבין בין־טוב לרע <u>כי מי יוכל לשפט את־עמך הכבד הזה</u>	[1:10a עתה חכמה ומדע תן־לי] כי־מי ישפט את־עמך הזה הגדול

1 Kings 3:2–15

(3:10) <u>וייטב הדבר בעיני אדני כי שאל</u>
<u>שלמה את־הדבר הזה</u>
(3:11) ויאמר אלהים אליו
יען אשר שאלת את־הדבר הזה
ולא־שאלת לך ימים רבים
ולא־שאלת לך עשר ולא שאלת נפש
איביך
ושאלת לך הבין לשמע משפט

(3:12) הנה עשיתי כדבריך
הנה נתתי לך לב חכם ונבון
<u>אשר כמוך לא־היה לפניך ואחריך</u>
<u>לא־יקום כמוך</u>
(3:13) וגם אשר לא־שאלת נתתי לך
גם־עשר גם־כבוד
אשר לא־היה כמוך איש במלכים
כל־ימיך
(3:14) <u>ואם תלך בדרכי לשמר חקי</u>
<u>ומצותי כאשר הלך דוד אביך</u>
והארכתי את־ימיך
(3:15) ויקץ שלמה והנה חלום
ויבוא ירושלם ויעמד
לפני ארון ברית־אדני ויעל עלות
ויעש אלמים ויעש משתה לכל־עבדיו

[3:16–28—King's "plus"—story about Solomon's wise judgment vis-á-vis dispute between prostitutes.]

(4:1) ויהי המלך שלמה מלך
על־כל־ישראל

2 Chronicles 1:1–13

(1:11) ויאמר־אלהים לשלמה
יען אשר היתה זאת עם־לבבך
ולא־שאלת עשר נכסים וכבוד ואת נפש
שנאיך וגם־ימים רבים לא שאלת

ותשאל־לך הכמה ומדע אשר תשפוט
את־עמי אשר המלכתיך עליו

(1:12) החכמה והמדע נתון לך

ועשר ונכסים וכבוד אתן־לך
אשר לא־היה כן למלכים אשר לפניך
ואחריך לא יהיה־כן

(1:13) ויבא שלמה לבמה אשר־בגבעון
ירושלם מלפני אהל מועד

[Chronicles "minus"—no story about wise judgment in dispute between prostitutes.]

וימלך על־ישראל

CASE STUDIES

The Envisioning of the Land in the Priestly Material:

Fulfilled Promise or Future Hope?

Suzanne Boorer

Several models have been proposed regarding the definition and place of the Priestly material within the formation of Genesis–Kings, since the broad acceptance of the concept of a Deuteronomistic History.[1] A key aspect of this debate is the nature of the Priestly material. Is it an originally independent source or a redaction? If it is the former, is it comprised of a basic P narrative (Pg),[2] to which supplements have been added, or not? Intimately related to this is the issue of its extent: does the Priestly narrative material that extends from Genesis–Numbers reach its conclusion in Joshua, or prior to this, before the narrative account of the entry into the land; that is, is the promise of the land fulfilled, or does it remain unfulfilled as a future hope? It is this last question that I will seek to address. However, this can only be done in the context of the broader debate on the nature of the Priestly material, for out of this discussion arise the parameters of my investigation which, though including literary considerations, will be primarily concerned with theological and hermeneutical arguments.

---

1. Hereafter referred to as DtrH.

2. Pg is the terminology used to refer to the independent P narrative material in Genesis–Numbers, as identified by Martin Noth (*A History of Pentateuchal Traditions* [trans. B. W. Anderson; Englewood Cliffs, N.J.: Prentice Hall, 1972], 8–19; trans. of *Uberlieferungsgeschichte des Pentateuch* [Stuttgart: Kohlhammer, 1948]). The designation has been taken up by a number of scholars; see those listed in Philip P. Jensen, *Graded Holiness: A Key to the Priestly Conception of the World* (JSOTSup 106; Sheffield: Sheffield Academic Press, 1992), 220–24.

I

Since the acceptance of the DtrH, the multitude of views put forward with regard to the nature, extent, and place of the Priestly material within the formation of Genesis–Kings falls roughly into four different models.[3]

Model 1

The first model maintains the existence of an originally independent P narrative (Pg) that basically spans Genesis–Numbers, ending with the Mosaic generation. Pg does not extend into Joshua; the promise of the land remains unfulfilled. Texts in P style in Joshua are late secondary additions to preexisting material, so any fulfillment of the land promise that is envisioned is the work of later supplementer(s). Texts in the latter half of the book of Numbers, which look towards the account of land fulfillment and distribution in Joshua, are also in large part later supplements, thought by most to have been added after the combining of Genesis–Numbers[4] with the DtrH.

Martin Noth originated this model.[5] According to Noth, Pg was originally an independent source that ended with the death of Moses.[6] This Pg, supplemented with secondary Priestly additions, was combined with the earlier JE to form a Tetrateuch. This was subsequently combined with the DtrH. There is no trace of Pg in Joshua: the P-style texts in Joshua[7] are isolated additions to already existing material, whether to DtrH or other material subsequently inserted into the DtrH.[8] Furthermore, texts reminiscent of P in the second half of Numbers, in particular the bulk of Num 32–35, which have much in common with Josh 13–21, represent in large part expansions after the amalgamation of the (JEP) Tetrateuch with the DtrH.[9]

---

3. I will be focusing here primarily on the Priestly material, with some attention to how it relates to the DtrH.

4. Which by this stage had already been combined with the non-P (J) material.

5. See Martin Noth, *The Chronicler's History* (trans. H. G. Williamson; JSOTSup 50; Sheffield: JSOT Press, 1987), 107–48; trans. of *Überlieferungsgeschichtliche Studien, Teil 2* (Halle: Niemeyer, 1943); idem, *A History of Pentateuchal Traditions*, 8–19; idem, *Das Buch Josua* (2d ed.; HAT 1/7; Tübingen: Mohr [Siebeck], 1953).

6. Num 20:22b, 23a*, 25–29; 21:4a*; 22:1b; 27:12–23; Deut 34:1a*, 7–9; see Noth, *A History of Pentateuchal Traditions*, 19.

7. The texts that Noth examines in particular are: Josh 4:15–17, 19; 5:10–12; 9:14, 15b, 17–20; 14:1b; 18:1; 19:51a; 20; 21:1–42; 22:9–34. See Noth, *The Chronicler's History*, 111–19.

8. The preexisting material to which P-like additions have been added is itself quite complex in Noth's view; see Noth, *The Chronicler's History*, 115–19.

9. See the complex discussion of these Numbers texts in Noth, *The Chronicler's History*, 121–48, and in particular the chart on p. 148.

Noth's basic position, especially the idea that Pg concludes with the death of Moses, has been followed by a number of scholars.[10] A recent variation is the view of E. Cortese.[11] According to Cortese, Pg was an originally independent document that ended with the death of Moses. A Priestly redactor (Ps) revised a document behind Josh 13–21, appended it to Pg (or perhaps J + Pg) at the end of Numbers, and inserted material into Leviticus and Numbers. This Ps was quite separate from the DtrH; indeed, prior to the composition of the DtrH. Subsequently, then, a second Priestly redactor (Pss) combined the text made up of J + Pg + Ps with the DtrH, by inserting some material into the Genesis–Numbers and into Josh 13–21 and transferring the latter into the DtrH.[12]

---

10. See for example, Karl Elliger, "Sinn und Ursprung der Priesterlichen Geschichtserzahlung," *ZTK* 49 (1952): 121–43; Peter Weimar, "Struktur und Composition der priesterschriftlichen Geschichtsdarstellung," *BN* 23 (1984): 81–134; 24 (1985): 138–62; and the chart in Jensen, *Graded Holiness*, 220–24. See also A. Graeme Auld (*Joshua, Moses and the Land: Tetrateuch–Pentateuch–Hexateuch in a Generation since 1938* [Edinburgh: T&T Clark, 1980], 52–116), who is in line with Noth but presents an even more complex picture. He identifies five narrative strata within Josh 13–19 (with P-like texts such as Josh 14:1b–3; 19:51; 20; 21:1–42 belonging to the latest stratum). The last ten chapters of Numbers represent a series of redaction levels that are dependent on the second half of Joshua. He therefore sees all P-like texts in the second half of Numbers and Joshua as very late.

11. Enzo Cortese, *Josua 13–21: Ein priesterschriftlicher Abschnitt in deuteronomistischen Geschichtswerke* (OBO 94; Fribourg: Universitätsverlag; Gottingen: Vandenhoeck & Ruprecht, 1990).

12. Thus Cortese differs from Noth, seeing the work of Ps in Josh 13–21 as much more substantial than Noth's isolated P-like additions, and attributing more of the material towards the end of Numbers (e.g., Num 35) to Ps, *prior* to combination with DtrH, rather than to stages of redaction after the combination of Genesis–Numbers with the DtrH. In both cases, however, the chapters in the latter half of Numbers, like Josh 13–21, to which they are closely related, are not seen as part of Pg but as representing later supplements. Subsumed under this model are also, for example, the views of Thomas C. Römer, who maintains that Pg was an originally independent source that ended with the tabernacle (Lev 9); and that P-style texts in Joshua are the work of a Dtr-Priestly group who, by combining Pg with the DtrH, sought to promote a Hexateuch. See Thomas C. Römer, *The So-Called Deuteronomistic History: A Sociological, Historical, and Literary Introduction* (London: T&T Clark, 2005), 82, 178–80; idem and Mark Z. Brettler, "Deuteronomy 34 and the Case for a Persian Hexateuch," *JBL* 119 (2000): 401–19. See also Albert de Pury ("The Jacob Story and the Beginning of the Formation of the Pentateuch," in *A Farewell to the Yahwist? The Composition of the Pentateuch in Recent European Interpretation* [ed. T. Dozeman and K. Schmid; SBLSymS 34; Atlanta: Society of Biblical Literature, 2006], 51–72), who sees Pg (following T. Pola) as an originally independent source, but as ending in Exod 40*. The position of Erhard Blum (*Studien zur Komposition des Pentateuch* [Berlin: de Gruyter, 1990], passim, and especially pp. 224–28) with regard to the Priestly material represents something of an anomaly, in that he sees his KP as a "Komposition" that is neither a source nor a redaction, and which indeed incorporates his KD. However, although his view has affinities with the redactional model (that is, Model 4), to be discussed shortly, his position

Model 2

The second model maintains that the Priestly material is an originally independent source (P) that spans Genesis to Joshua. This source therefore reaches its conclusion with the fulfillment of the promise of the land. Little account is taken of distinctions between an original P narrative and possible secondary supplements, with the Priestly material tending to be treated as a whole. This Priestly material includes the chapters in the latter half of Numbers, as well as the account of the distribution of the land in the second half of Joshua (Josh 13–22). This Priestly material in Joshua was subsequently worked into the Deuteronomistic History.

Sigmund Mowinckel, following in the footsteps of Gerhard von Rad,[13] is the main proponent of this model.[14] According to Mowinckel, P as an originally independent narrative included passages in the latter half of Numbers, in particular Num 32; 33:50–34:29; 35:9–15; passages in Joshua, in particular Josh 4:19; 5:10–12; 9:15b–21; and the whole of Josh 12–19 and 21, for which he sees P as the author. Hence the texts in Numbers that look towards the distribution of the land in Joshua, as well as the Joshua account of coming into the land and the distribution of the land are all the work of P. P was combined with the earlier JJv[15] to form a Hexateuch (JJvP). When this Hexateuch was combined with the DtrH the parts of JJvP that dealt with Joshua and land settlement were worked into the corresponding part of the DtrH.

More recent, and closely related, is the view of J. E. Petersen.[16] For Petersen, P consisted of the Priestly *Grundschrift* in the Pentateuch and six core units,[17] joined with eleven units edited by P (comprising early lists of boundaries and cities) to form the bulk of Josh 13–22. This hypothesis maintains that P was

---

has much in common with Model 1: he distinguishes KP, which he sees as extending only as far as Num 27 and as representing a coherent and intentional theology, from later post-P supplements in P style, both in the Pentateuch, including Num 31–35, and in Joshua (e.g., Josh 5:10–12; 14:1–2; 18:1; 19:51).

13. See for example, Gerhard von Rad's 1943 essay, "The Promised Land and Yahweh's Land in the Hexateuch," in *The Problem of the Hexateuch and Other Essays* (trans. E. W. Trueman Dicken; Edinburgh: Oliver & Boyd; 1966; repr. London: SCM Press, 1984; trans. of *Gesammelte Studien zum Alten Testament* [TB 8; Munich: Kaiser, 1958]), 79–93.

14. Sigmund Mowinckel, *Tetrateuch–Pentateuch–Hexateuch: Die Berichte über die Landnahme in den drei altisraelitischen Geschichtswerken* (BZAW 90; Berlin: Töpelmann, 1964); and see Auld, *Joshua, Moses and the Land*, 27–31.

15. Jv stands for "Jahwista variatus," which is in essence the material traditionally attributed to E.

16. J. E. Petersen, "Priestly Materials in Josh 13–22: A Return to the Hexateuch?" *HAR* 4 (1980): 131–46.

17. These comprise: Josh 13:15–32; 18:1; 14:1–5; 19:51; 17:3–6; 20:1–9; 21:1–42; 22:9–34.

earlier than the DtrH, and that in consequence, the editor of the DtrH detached this P account of the land allocation from the rest of P, edited it, and interpolated it into his account of the conquest and settlement of the land.[18]

Model 3

The third model is represented by the view of Norbert Lohfink, in particular, although the position of Joseph Blenkinsopp with regard to P can also be classified here.[19] Like the first model, this view maintains the existence of an originally independent P narrative (Pg) that is distinguished from subsequent secondary supplementation in P style. However, unlike the first model, this model maintains that this Pg extends into Joshua and may be discerned there in at least a few texts (e.g., Josh 4:19; 5:10–12; 14:1–2*; 18:1; 19:51).[20] Thus Pg reaches its conclusion with the fulfillment of the promise of the land. Both Pg and DtrH were edited before they were combined, hence the presence of secondary P and secondary Dtr texts; and after they were combined more post-P/DtrH editing also occurred.[21]

Model 4

The fourth model is represented by the position of John Van Seters.[22] This view distinguishes itself from the first three models in maintaining a view of the Priestly material as a redaction of non-Priestly material, rather than as an

---

18. Thus Petersen and Mowinckel have very similar views regarding the nature and extent of P, but differ on the dating of P and the relationship of P to DtrH. A variation of Petersen's view is that of John E. Harvey, *Retelling the Torah: The Deuteronomistic Historian's Use of Tetrateuchal Narratives* (London: T&T Clark, 2004), especially 100 n. 5. Harvey argues that a Tetrateuch comprised of JP and P in Joshua preceded DtrH; Dtr edited this JP + P corpus and appended his own history (much of which was modeled on JP + P), also interpolating P material in Josh 13–22, to produce Genesis–Kings.

19. Norbert Lohfink, "The Priestly Narrative and History," in *The Theology of the Pentateuch: Themes of the Priestly Narrative and Deuteronomy* (trans. L. M. Maloney; Edinburgh: T&T Clark, 1994), 136–72; idem, "The Strata of the Pentateuch and the Question of War," in *The Theology of the Pentateuch*, 173–226, especially 199–201, 211, 216–18; Joseph Blenkinsopp, "The Structure of P," *CBQ* 38 (1976): 275–92; idem, *Sage, Priest, Prophet: Religious and Intellectual Leadership in Ancient Israel* (Louisville: Westminster John Knox, 1995), 68–69, 104–5, 109.

20. Lohfink, "The Priestly Narrative and History," 145 n. 29; "The Strata of the Pentateuch and the Question of War," 200–201. Note that Lohfink also includes Num 34:1–18 as part of his Pg.

21. Lohfink, "The Strata of the Pentateuch and the Question of War," 211, 216–18.

22. John Van Seters, *In Search of History: Historiography in the Ancient World and the Origins of Biblical History* (New Haven: Yale University Press, 1983), 322–42.

originally independent source. As redaction, this Priestly material tends to be treated as a single composition. It is seen to extend from Genesis through Joshua, and even Judg 1–2. It therefore describes extensively the account of the fulfillment of the promise of the land both in the many texts attributed to the hand of the P redactor in Joshua[23] and in the earlier non-P material in Joshua that the P redactor incorporated. Since, according to this view, DtrH was supplemented and extended by J (which extends from Genesis–Joshua), and this P redaction is later than J, the Priestly redactor supplemented both the J and Dtr material to form the account from Genesis–Joshua (and Judg 1–2) in its present form.[24]

Clearly in terms of my topic—whether the Priestly material envisions the possession of the land as fulfilled promise or future hope—models two, three and four come down firmly on the side of fulfilled promise: Priestly material in Joshua, to a greater or lesser extent, is in continuity with that in Genesis–Numbers (in one form or another) and represents the conclusion and completion of the movement of the narrative as a whole. Model one stands alone in maintaining that the basic Priestly narrative in Genesis–Numbers does not find its completion in Joshua: In this schema, Pg is confined to the Mosaic generation and the promise of the land remains ultimately unfulfilled, as a future hope.

II

In light of these models it is necessary to define the parameters and the specific approach within which I will explore the issue of whether the land envisioned in the Priestly material represents fulfilled promise or future hope.

First, I do not intend to address here the fourth model, which sees the whole of the Priestly material as redaction. I am assuming with many scholars that an originally independent Priestly source can be discerned at

---

23. The texts listed by Van Seters (*In Search of History*, 324–42) as P supplements in Joshua are: Josh 3:1, 4b–5, 6–7, 9–10a, 11b, 15–19; 5:2–9, 10–12; 6:1–3, 4ab, 5, 6a, 7, 10–11, 14–16aa, b, 17a, 20b, 21, 24a, 26–27; 7:1–26; 9:14, 15b, 17–21, 23; Josh 12; 13–19; 20:6, 9bb; 21; 22:7–34; 24:32–33; and Judg 1:1–2:5.

24. Thomas Dozeman (*God at War: Power in the Exodus Tradition* [New York: Oxford University Press, 1996], 104, 106–7, 109, 89 n. 146, 135 n. 13, 19) also sees P as a redaction that extends into Joshua, including especially the chronology in Josh 4:19, and 18:1; 19:51 (and possibly the structure of Joshua 18–19). However, he attributes much less text to P within Joshua than Van Seters, and underplays the significance of this material considerably, maintaining that for P the death of Moses is more significant than conquest and indeed that P is more oriented to creation than conquest.

least within Genesis–Numbers.[25] The reasons for this are the many strong
parallels between Priestly and non-Priestly narrative texts throughout Genesis–Numbers, and the coherence of this Priestly narrative material in
Genesis–Numbers, especially in terms of structure.[26]

Secondly, what primarily separates model two from models one and three
is the lack of a distinction within the Priestly material between Pg and later
supplements. In relation to this, what particularly impinges on our issue is
whether or not the texts in P style in the latter half of Numbers, especially
Num 32–35, are included as part of the basic Priestly narrative spanning
Genesis–Numbers. This issue is important because these chapters have many
similarities with P-style texts in Joshua, and indeed anticipate, and are fulfilled
by, the Joshua texts, especially within Josh 13–21. The proponents of model
two *do* include Num 32–35, which strengthens the claim that the Priestly
material in Genesis–Numbers reaches its conclusion and fulfillment in the
account of the occupation and distribution of the land as described in Joshua.
The proponents of models one and three see the chapters in the latter half of
Numbers as supplements that are later than Pg.[27] This not only excludes them
from Pg, but also excludes the closely related material in Joshua that has to do

---

25. For example, Noth, *A History of Pentateuchal Traditions*, 8–19; Sean McEvenue,
The Narrative Style of the Priestly Writer (Rome: Biblical Institute Press, 1971); Lohfink,
"The Priestly Narrative and History," 144–47; John A. Emerton, "The Priestly Writer in
Genesis," *JTS* 39 (1988): 381–400; Ernest W. Nicholson, "P as an Originally Independent
Source in the Pentateuch," *IBS* 10 (1988): 192–206; Antony F. Campbell, "The Priestly Text:
Redaction or Source?" in *Biblische Theologie und gesellschaftlicher Wandel: Für Norbert
Lohfink SJ* (ed. G. Braulik, W. Gross, S. McEvenue; Freiburg: Herder, 1993), 32–47; Ludwig
Schmidt, *Studien zur Priesterschrift* (BZAW 214; Berlin: de Gruyter, 1993); Joseph Blen-
kinsopp, *The Pentateuch: An Introduction to the First Five Books of the Bible* (London:
SCM Press, 1992), 78; idem, *Sage, Priest, Prophet*, 108; David M. Carr, *Reading the Frac-
tures of Genesis: Historical and Literary Approaches* (Louisville: Westminster John Knox,
1996), 46–47; Graham I. Davies, "The Composition of the Book of Exodus: Reflections on
the Theses of Erhard Blum," in *Texts, Temples, and Traditions* (ed. M. V. Fox et al.; Winona
Lake: Eisenbrauns, 1996), 71–85; and see Jensen, *Graded Holiness*, 20–24.

26. See especially the movement from creation to uncreation to the (re)appearance
of land in both the cosmic section in Gen 1–9* (P) and the story of the nation in Exod
1–Num 14* (P); the strong parallels between Gen 1:1–2:4a and Exod 25–31; the deliberate
structuring of Gen 1–Exod 1:7* (P) in terms of genealogies and that of Exod 6–Num 14*
(P) at least in terms of itineraries; and the division of the material into eras where God is
referred to as Elohim in relation to the cosmos (Gen 1–10*[P]), as El Shaddai in relation
to the ancestors (Gen 11–50*), and as Yhwh in relation to the nation from Moses onwards
(Exod 6 and onward). See Suzanne Boorer, "The Earth/Land (*'rts*) in the Priestly Material:
The Preservation of the "Good" Earth and the Promised Land of Canaan Throughout the
Generations," *ABR* 49 (2001): 19–33, especially 20–21.

27. Lohfink ("The Priestly Narrative and History," 145 n. 3) does seek to include Num
34:1–18 as part of Pg, but his argument as a whole does not depend on this.

with the occupation of the land. Thus, under models one and three, these texts cannot be used to provide evidence for any account of the fulfillment of the land promise in Pg. There are, however, other P-style texts in Joshua that have much in common, linguistically and thematically, with texts in Genesis–Numbers that lie outside the contentious chapters in the latter half of Numbers and are recognized as belonging to Pg by the proponents of model one. These texts are identified by the proponents of model three, and Lohfink in particular, as: Josh 4:19; 5:10–12; 18:1; 19:51.[28] These texts are also among those that are specifically debated, though ultimately excluded, by Noth, who originated model one, as the texts most likely, if there were to be any in Joshua, to belong to Pg.[29] Since the chapters in the latter part of Numbers are so contentious, and it is not possible here to engage with the extensive and complex literary debate surrounding them,[30] it will be more constructive for our purposes to focus on those texts in Joshua identified by Lohfink as belonging to Pg, rather than the wider net of texts advocated by the proponents of model two: i.e., the passages in Num 28–36 and those corresponding to them in Josh 13–21 that appear to be in P-style.[31] The texts identified by Lohfink represent a minimalist position that will, however, still enable us to test whether Pg, as the basic Priestly narrative identified in Genesis–Numbers (excluding Num 28–36), does indeed continue into Joshua and contain an account of the fulfillment of the land promise. That is, in order to address our issue, I will not engage with model two directly, but rather effectively dialogue with models one and three.

Thirdly, the debate as to whether Pg envisions the land as fulfilled promise or future hope cannot be decided on literary grounds alone. It is surely reasonable to expect that if Pg was an originally independent source, some sort of theological coherence or horizon that accounts for its major components would be discernable. Hence, it might be expected that theological consider-

---

28. Lohfink, "The Priestly Narrative and History," 145 n. 29; "The Strata of the Pentateuch and the Question of War," 200–201. Blenkinsopp ("The Structure of P," 288–89) identifies these texts, and also Josh 4:9, 19; 9:15–21; 11:15, 20; 14:1–5; 21:1–8; 22:10–34; 24:33 (although he maintains that 19:51 formed the original ending of P). Elements that these texts have in common with Pg in Genesis–Numbers include: the dating in Josh 4:19; 5:10–11 in association with the Passover (see Exod 12:3, 6); the reference to the "tent of meeting" in Josh 18:1; 19:51 (see Exod 25–31); and the use of the verb כבשׁ in Josh 18:1 (see Gen 1:28).

29. Noth, *The Chronicler's History*, 111–17, and see n. 7. Joshua 14:1–2; 18:1; 19:51 are also singled out by Richard D. Nelson (*Joshua: A Commentary* [Louisville: Westminster John Knox], 9) as texts in P style, along also with Josh 21:1–2; 22:9–34; 3:4; 9:15b, 18–21.

30. See Noth, *The Chronicler's History*, 121–34, 148; Auld, *Joshua, Moses and the Land*, 72–84.

31. See Auld, *Joshua, Moses and the Land*, 30; Petersen, "Priestly Materials in Josh 13–22," 138.

ations would also be important alongside literary analysis. How is the motif of the promise of the land, which has some prominence in Pg within Genesis–Numbers (Gen 17:8; Exod 6:4, 8; and see the itineraries within Exodus and Numbers), to be accounted for theologically within the shape of Pg as a whole? This is another aspect that separates model one, especially as represented by Noth, and model three, as represented by Lohfink in particular, but also Blenkinsopp: for Noth neither the land promise nor its lack of fulfillment is of significance within the theological horizon of Pg, whereas for Lohfink and Blenkinsopp the land promise and its fulfillment are essential within Pg's structure, theology, and for Lohfink, its hermeneutics.

For Noth, the founder of model one, the extent of Pg was determined primarily, indeed solely, on the grounds of literary and redactional analysis.[32] This contrasts sharply with model two, for whose proponents, in particular Mowinckel, and before him von Rad, but also Petersen, arguments in terms of form and theology are vitally important. These scholars assumed that, given the emphasis on the promise of the land throughout the Priestly material, this theme must reach its conclusion and fulfillment in the conquest and allotment of the land.[33] Noth's attempt to account for the lack of a conquest and land distribution narrative as the fulfillment of the land promise is hardly adequate. He argued that Pg's primary concern was the setting up of the institutions at Sinai for the national and cultic community, and that in the narrative unfolding of the promise of the land, Pg was merely following the inherited (JE) tradition; once the cult was set up, anything after that was not important.[34] Similarly, those scholars who follow Noth's literary analysis (and they are in the majority) have had, it seems to me, only limited success in attempting to account theologically for the shape of a Pg as a whole that ends with the Mosaic generation: the key to the theological interpretation of Pg tends to focus on only a part of Pg, not all the components of Pg in its entirety; that is, either the Sinai material and its institutions,[35] or the narrative frame within which the Sinai material is set.[36] In the case of the latter analytical framework,

32. Noth (*The Chronicler's History*, 136) states this explicitly, " ... we must not tailor our literary findings by a particular preconception of P, but rather our conception of P by the literary findings ...."

33. See Auld, *Joshua, Moses and the Land*, 30; Petersen, "Priestly Materials in Josh 13–22," 137.

34. Noth, *The Chronicler's History*, 138; *A History of Pentateuchal Traditions*, 240–42.

35. For example, Ralph W. Klein, "The Message of P," in *Die Botschaft und die Boten: Festschrift für Hans Walter Wolff zum 70. Geburtstag* (ed. J. Jeremias and L. Perlitt; Neukirchen-Vluyn: Neukirchener, 1981), 57–66; Schmidt, *Studien zur Priesterschrift*, 259; Blum, *Studien zur Komposition des Pentateuch*, 287–332.

36. For example, Elliger, "Sinn und Ursprung der Priesterlichen Geschichtserzahlung," 121–43; Walter Brueggemann, "The Kerygma of the Priestly Writers," in *The Vitality of Old*

where the land promise is seen as significant, the lack of its fulfillment is not adequately accounted for, except insofar as it is considered appropriate in addressing the exilic generation who are as yet outside the land.[37]

In contrast to Noth, the proponents of model three, Lohfink and Blenkinsopp, place at least equal importance on structural and theological arguments alongside literary arguments in support of their claim that Pg continues into Joshua. Blenkinsopp argues for an account of the fulfillment of the land promise in Joshua on the grounds of literary coherence and theological structure, which are inseparably linked. He identifies structural indicators that have certain literary formulations in common, and that occur at key points; these are indicative of the structure and theology of Pg as a coherent whole. Blenkinsopp identifies formulaic expressions for the successful completion of a work at three key points:[38] creation of the world, Gen 2:1, 2;[39] construction of the sanctuary, Exod 39:32; 40:33;[40] and the distribution of the land along with the setting up of the sanctuary at Shiloh, Josh 19:51.[41] This conclusion formula (along with the more common execution formula)[42] gives special, structural prominence to these points in the narrative. Moreover, further linguistic links between these structural points in the narrative are found in that: God/Moses "sees" and "blesses" in relation to both the finishing of the creation (Gen 1:31; 2:3) and the construction of the sanctuary (Exod 39:43);[43] the verb כבש (subdue) is used in relation to the earth/land in the creation narrative in Gen 1:28 and in relation to the distribution of the land in Josh 18:1, which is closely linked with Josh 19:51.[44] P therefore has a triadic structure that shows "interdependence within P of creation, construction of the sanctuary, and occupation of the land."[45] This triadic structure is underscored by

---

Testament Traditions (ed. W. Brueggemann and H. W. Wolff; Atlanta: John Knox, 1982), 101–13, 159–67.

37. See, for example, Brueggemann, "The Kerygma of the Priestly Writers," 101–13; Elliger, "Sinn und Ursprung der Priesterlichen Geschichtserzahlung," 141–42.

38. Blenkinsopp, "The Structure of P," 275–76.

39. "Thus the heavens and the earth were finished and all the host of them .... God finished his work which he had done."

40. "Thus all the work of the tabernacle of the tent of meeting was finished ... so Moses finished the work."

41. "So they finished dividing the land."

42. "X did according to all that YHWH (God) commanded him;" Blenkinsopp, "The Structure of P," 276.

43. Blenkinsopp ("The Structure of P," 284–86) also argues for a link between the creation/flood and the construction of the sanctuary in terms of the parallel pattern in ancient Near Eastern myths which link the creation (by victory over watery chaos) with the building of a temple for the god.

44. Blenkinsopp, "The Structure of P," 290.

45. Ibid., 282. Further evidence cited by Blenkinsopp in support of his conclusion is

the fact that some undisputed P passages in the Pentateuch, such as the land promise, the purchase of the cave of Machpelah, the mission of the spies, and the census and ordering of the camp, are unintelligible if P had no interest in the occupation of the land.[46] These literary and theological features constitute Blenkinsopp's primary argument for the extension of Pg into Joshua. He concludes that, "The structural correspondence in P between creation–deluge, construction of the wilderness sanctuary, and the setting up of the same sanctuary in the occupied land of Canaan," confirms that the P narrative originally ended with the conquest and occupation of the land.[47]

Lohfink puts forward literary, theological, and hermeneutical arguments in favor of seeing Pg as extending into, and concluding in, Joshua, on the evidence of Josh 4:19; 5:10–12; 14:1–2*; 18:1; 19:51.[48] He makes the general observation that an account of the occupation of the land is to be expected "since so much in Pg has pointed towards this moment."[49] In view of this, he seeks to assess whether the texts he has identified in the style of P within Joshua belong to Pg.[50] The literary criterion is the extent to which these Joshua texts may be anticipated, in light of the narrative system of Pg.[51] Lohfink argues that in Josh 18:1, two major themes of Pg are brought to a conclusion: first, in that the tabernacle is set up; and, second, that the land has been subdued (כבשׁ), in fulfillment of Gen 1:28 (where כבשׁ is also used). In addition, Josh 5:10–12 is in continuity with Pg in Genesis–Numbers in its reference to the Passover and in the notice of the cessation of the manna, which forms a link to Exod 16:35.[52] Furthermore he argues that all the elements within Gen 1:28 are fulfilled within Pg: the multiplying motif is fulfilled in Gen 47:27;

---

the reference to the divine spirit in relation to the creation of the world (Gen 1:2), the construction of the sanctuary (Exod 31:3; 35), and the commissioning of Joshua (Num 27:18; Deut 34:9) which has in view the occupation of the land; see ibid.

46. Ibid., 287.

47. Ibid., 289.

48. Lohfink justifies basing his view that Pg contains an account of the entry into, and occupation of, the land on only these few texts by making the preliminary observation that only a few texts in Joshua are sufficient to establish Pg's presence: Pg may have reported the entry into Canaan succinctly (as in the account of the exodus in Exod 12:40–42), especially given Pg's lack of emphasis on military aspects; and in any case, since Pg did not form the redactional basis for other material in Joshua in the same way as in Genesis–Numbers it could be imagined that not all of the original Pg account of the occupation of the land has been preserved; see Lohfink, "The Priestly Narrative and History," 146 n. 30; idem, "The Strata of the Pentateuch and the Question of War," 199–200.

49. Lohfink, "The Strata of the Pentateuch and the Question of War," 199.

50. I.e., Josh 4:19; 5:10–12; 14:1–2*; 18:1; 19:51.

51. Lohfink, "The Priestly Narrative and History," 146 n. 30.

52. Lohfink, "The Strata of the Pentateuch and the Question of War," 200–201; "The Priestly Narrative and History," 146 n. 30. The texts closely related to Josh 18:1, i.e. Josh

Exod 1:7, and dominion over the animals in Gen 9:1–7. Likewise the Abra-hamic promise of descendants is fulfilled in Exod 1:7, and the promise to be their God is fulfilled in the Sinai pericope. Therefore it makes sense, and it is to be expected, that the promise in relation to the land, referred to in Gen 1:28 (since כבשׁ, he believes, is to be interpreted in terms of land possession by the nations) and in the Abrahamic covenant promises, is also fulfilled within Pg.[53] This is evidenced in Josh 18:1 which echoes Gen 1:28 in its use of כבשׁ, and so forms "a literary parenthesis around the whole work."[54] Hence, Lohfink con-cludes, within Pg "there is no hint of a promise that has not been fulfilled".[55]

Clearly literary and theological arguments are inseparably related here: the theological expectation of a symmetrical fulfillment of all three promises (of multiplying/descendants, relationship with God, and land possession), and the literary analysis, interact with and support each other. Lohfink, however, goes beyond this, using not only theological but hermeneutical arguments to further explore further the implications of the shape of Pg, wherein all the promises, including that of the land, are fulfilled.

Hermeneutically, he speaks of the Pg material in terms of the "trans-parency" of presentation: although narrated in the guise of the past, what is communicated are theological concepts and guidance that address the situ-ations, experiences and problems of the readers (the exiles), and perhaps all possible future readers.[56] Events or situations narrated are "paradigmatic" in the sense that they repeatedly recur—in the past, present, and future. Lohfink says,

> Every event is transparently narrated. What once was can also return. The structural congruence illuminates the readers' present—and perhaps every possible present … there is, in a certain sense, a storehouse of paradigmatic world situations, all of which existed at one time and can recur again.[57]

Another way in which Lohfink describes this "transparency," or recurring repetition of "paradigmatic situations" in Pg, is through the terminology of "myth" (*Mythus*). He uses "myth" in the sense of that which "tells of things that happened in the timelessness of primeval time, that are true always and everywhere and therefore can also explain the Now,"[58] and as such, "we get

---

19:51 and 14:1, Lohfink sees as fulfilling Numbers 34, which he sees as part of Pg in con-trast to Noth.

53. Lohfink, "The Priestly Narrative and History," 166–69.

54. Ibid., 167.

55. Ibid., 169.

56. Ibid., 159–60.

57. Ibid., 161.

58. Ibid., 162.

the impression that, in spite of the temporal sequence, we are ... looking at a great picture collection assembled on artistic principles."[59] In view of this conception, Lohfink sees parallels between the nature and shape of Pg and that of the Atrahasis myth, in that both show a movement from a restless phase to a stable world. In Pg, however, this occurs twice over, not only from pre-Flood to post-Flood, but also, as exemplified by Israel, from wilderness sojourn to possession of the land.[60] With the possession of the land "the status proposed by God is achieved. Here the narrative stops .... The world is now the way it should be and needs no further changes."[61] The possession of the land, therefore, represents the "stability of the world, which God has brought to its perfected form."[62]

For Pg, then, there is no eschatology in the sense of an expectation of new events or new actions of Yahweh in the future that surpass the past and are as yet unknown, as found in the prophets.[63] Rather, what is offered in Pg is a vision of a static world that is already known and can be repeatedly returned to. Hope, therefore, is not based on an eschatological future, but "is founded on what our world has already received from God since the crossing of the Jordan and, as far as God is concerned, can never lose."[64] This vision of a stable or static world of settlement in the land, already known in the past, however, does not simply legitimate things as they are. The (exilic) readers did not live in the "land," within the stable, peaceful order planned for them by God: that is, "the world can fall repeatedly from its perfect form into the imperfection of becoming."[65] In that case the pattern must be repeated and the paths of the dynamic phase trodden again in order to embody the stable final state of the world already brought about by God.[66] In short, "The ideal shape of the world is known, it has already existed before. From the point of view of God it is always present, and all that is necessary is to return to it."[67]

It is clear from the foregoing that the fulfillment of the promises in Pg, and in particular that of the land, through the portrayal of its possession in Joshua, is foundational to the way in which Lohfink conceives of Pg, both theologically as representing the stable world in perfected form that God has brought into being; and hermeneutically in the way the narrative can be seen

---

59. Ibid.
60. Ibid., 170–71.
61. Ibid., 171.
62. Ibid.
63. Ibid., 164, 172.
64. Ibid., 172.
65. Ibid.
66. Ibid.
67. Ibid.

to function, both for its original audience, and also for all other audiences thereafter, as the ideal already brought about by God that needs to be embodied.

So far, if theological as well as literary considerations must be taken into account in deciding whether Pg extends into Joshua, then the advocates of model three—those who argue for the fulfillment of the land promise in Pg on interrelated literary and theological/hermeneutical grounds—would seem to have presented the more persuasive case, in contrast to model one. Noth's focus on literary analysis alone, and both his and his followers' inability to account for the lack of the fulfillment of the land promise within the theological horizon of Pg, shows a failure to mount a decisive case for the envisioning of the possession of the land in Pg as an unfulfilled hope. In what follows, however, I will seek to argue for the position of model one, i.e., that Pg does not extend into Joshua and thus that the possession of the land remains an unfulfilled hope; and I will attempt to do this on both literary and theological/hermeneutical grounds. The theological and hermeneutical grounds will, however, be my primary focus, for I do not believe that this issue can be decided on literary grounds alone; and more importantly, it is in the area of theology and hermeneutics that the major weakness of the arguments for this position thus far lie. Therefore, while taking into account literary analysis, I will seek primarily to provide theological and hermeneutical arguments in support of an unrealized eschatology in relation to the land in Pg.

In terms of literary analysis, I will focus on those texts in Joshua attributed to Pg by Lohfink, viz., 4:19; 5:10–12; 14:1–2*; 18:1; 19:51, since, as noted above, these are also the significant texts identified by Noth as closest to Pg in Genesis–Numbers. Thus, they represent a minimalist position that still enables us to test whether Pg does indeed continue into Joshua and therefore contain an account of the fulfillment of the land promise. The criterion that will be used to discern whether these texts belong to Pg will be that advocated by Lohfink, noted above, i.e., the extent to which these texts and their contents ought to be expected in light of the narrative system of Pg;[68] that is, whether or not these texts in Joshua cohere with Pg in Genesis–Numbers in terminology and in terms of narrative motifs and specific theological content.[69] This analysis will involve a critique of both Lohfink's arguments in relation to these texts and Blenkinsopp's arguments in relation to Josh 19:51. It

---

68. Ibid., 146 n. 30.

69. The other criterion cited by Lohfink ("The Priestly Narrative and History," 146 n. 30), whether the P-like texts in Joshua seem to have been secondarily inserted into their context and so do not presuppose their present contexts, is not of primary significance, since the way P-like texts in Joshua relate to their contexts depends on one's model of how DtrH relates to the Priestly material within the formation of Genesis–Kings.

will be argued that, rather than cohering decisively with Pg in Genesis–Numbers, the narrative motifs in the Joshua texts display a certain disjunction with their corresponding texts, as they are portrayed in narrative sequence in Genesis–Numbers; this disjunction, then, raises doubts as to whether they should therefore be seen as belonging to Pg.

More importantly and decisively, in terms of theological and hermeneutical arguments, my starting point will be Lohfink's position. A critique and an extension of his hermeneutical arguments, in particular, will lead to the conclusion, in direct contrast to Lohfink's view, that intrinsic to the very nature of Pg hermeneutically and theologically is the positive conviction that the land promise is yet *unfulfilled*, and is rather a future vision or unrealized eschatological hope.

III

Beginning our literary analysis with Josh 4:19; 5:10–12, clearly a number of similarities with Pg in Genesis–Numbers are apparent. These comprise: the dating of the Passover on the fourteenth day of the month in Josh 5:10 (see Exod 12:6), and coordinated with this the reference to the tenth day of the first month in Josh 4:19 (see Exod 12:3); the association of eating unleavened bread with the Passover, and as linked to the day after the Passover in Josh 5:11 (see Exod 12:1–20);[70] the reference to the cessation of the manna upon entry into the land, which is described as "the land of Canaan" in Josh 5:12 (see Exod 16:35 which seems to anticipate this).

However, there are also some anomalies in Josh 4:19; 5:10–12 in relation to Pg in Genesis–Numbers. With regard to the Passover celebration, it is said in 5:10 to occur "in the evening (בערב)" on the fourteenth day, which is more in line with Deut 16:4, 6 than with Pg, which consistently uses "between the evenings (בן הערבים)" (Exod 12:6; and see Lev 23:5; Num 9:3, 5, 11); and it is a national celebration here (see Deut 16; 2 Kgs 23:21–23) rather than a family one as in Pg (Exod 12:3–4)[71]. There is no mention of the eating of unleavened bread for seven days as in Pg (Exod 12:14–20), but instead the reference to unleavened bread is linked with parched grain (קלוי) as the produce of the land, with the word "produce" (מעבור) (Josh 5:11, 12) occurring only here in the Hebrew Bible.

Given these features and repetitions within Josh 5:10–12, such as the references to the lack of manna (twice, vv. 12aαβ) and to their eating of the

---

70. On the timing of Passover in relation to eating unleavened bread in Exod 12:1–20, see Brevard S. Childs, *Exodus* (OTL; London: SCM Press, 1974), 197.

71. See Nelson, *Joshua*, 79.

produce/crops of the land (3 times, vv. 11b, 12aα, b), many have concluded that there are different layers of composition in the text.[72] Though there is debate about the details,[73] almost all who see different compositional layers distinguish between earlier non-Priestly material and later Priestly additions or editing.[74] At the very least the chronological references to the fourteenth day in v. 10 and the day after the Passover in v. 11 are attributed to P editing,[75] but it has also been argued that the reference to the Passover itself in v. 10, as well as the repetition of the detail concerning the lack of manna linked with eating the crops of the land in v. 12aβb, are due to P editing.[76]

This proposal that the passage involves earlier non-P level(s) of composition overlaid with Priestly redaction is quite feasible, given both the mixture of Priestly and non-Priestly traits in the text, and the repetitions. For example, v. 12b clarifies the unusual reference to "produce" (מעבור) in vv. 11b, 12aα using the more common term "crops" (מתבואת); the reference to the "land" in vv. 11b, 12aα is clarified through the use of common P terminology, the "land of Canaan." If this is the case, then the Priestly traits in Josh 5:10–12 are themselves redactional and do not represent evidence for the continuation of Pg, as an originally independent narrative, into Joshua.[77]

The content of Josh 4:19 and Josh 5:10–12 also provides evidence that these verses are not a continuation of Pg, since it is not coherent with Pg's

---

72. See for example, Noth (*The Chronicler's History*, 112); and recently, Jan A. Wagenaar, "The Cessation of the Manna: Editorial Frames for the Wilderness Wandering in Ex 16,35 and Josh 5,10–12," *ZAW* 112 (2000): 192–209. Wagenaar cites E. Otto, M. Rose, as well as Noth as distinguishing an earlier non-P level (whether Noth's *Sammler*, or Otto's J, or Rose's Dtr) from P additions; and Wagenaar himself distinguishes two earlier levels of text before P editing which he sees in Josh 5:10aβb (excluding "in the plains of Jericho") and Josh 5:12aβb.

73. Leading Nelson (*Joshua*, 78) to remark that vv. 10–12 "reflect a complicated pre-history, the details of which are elusive."

74. An exception is Chris Brekelmans ("Joshua V 10–12: Another Approach," in *New Avenues in the Study of the Old Testament* [ed. A. S. Van der Woude; Leiden: Brill, 1989], 89–95), who sees Josh 5:10–11 (minus "on the day after the Passover, on that very day") as P, on the same level as Exod 16:35, and 5:10 as a later addition.

75. Noth, *The Chronicler's History*, 112.

76. See Wagenaar, "The Cessation of the Manna," 192–209.

77. Lohfink ("The Strata of the Pentateuch and the Question of War," 201 n. 66), engages with arguments against seeing Josh 5:10–12 as a whole as belonging to Pg; he comments only on the expression "in the evening" (v. 10), which, as already noted, is used in Deut 16:4, 6, but differs from the usual expression of "between the evenings" found in Pg. Lohfink argues that "in the evening" is also used by Pg in Exod 12:18; 16:(8), 13; Lev 6:13; 23:32. However, this argument does not hold, since in none of these references does "in the evening" refer to the time of the Passover as in Josh 5:10; it is never used in relation to the Passover in Pg.

narrative system.[78] The details that these verses have in common with Pg are presented in a different pattern and combined with elements not found in Pg. Hence, the dating given in Exod 12:3 and 6—the tenth day of the first month for the selection of the lamb and the fourteenth day for the slaughter of the lamb for the Passover—is transferred in Josh 4:19 and Josh 5:10 to the times of the coming up out of the Jordan and camping at Gilgal, and the keeping of the Passover, respectively; indeed this timing links Josh 4:19 and 5:10–12 together,[79] but distinguishes these verses from Pg in Genesis–Numbers. The narrative sequence of Pg in Exod 12:1–20 and Exod 16*—the account of the Passover and Unleavened bread rite followed by that of the appearance of the manna, with the notice of its continuance until they came into the land—has been conflated into a different pattern in Josh 5:10–12. The parallel sequences in Exodus 12 and 16 of eating meat (Passover/quail) followed by bread (unleavened bread/manna) has been conflated into one episode in Josh 5:10–12, where the eating of the Passover is followed by the eating of unleavened bread (with no mention of duration) along with parched grain, coincident with the cessation of the manna.[80] And so, the elements of Passover, unleavened bread, the continuance of the meat/manna until arrival at the border of the land of Canaan, all of which occur in Pg's account within a sequence of episodes in Exod 12 and 16, have been telescoped in Josh 4:19; 5:10–12, in a manner that diverges from Pg. Joshua 4:19; 5:10–12, though it has elements in common with Pg, does not fulfill or cohere with the specific combination of motifs in the narrative sequence and the theology of Pg in Exod 12 and 16, but presents its own unique perspective. Therefore, Josh 4:19; 5:10–12 is not the expected extension of Pg in Genesis–Numbers, but reads more like a closely related but later redaction that portrays the extension or fulfillment of the narrative movement of Pg in a different direction, through telescoping and conflation.

Leaving aside the complex debate surrounding redactional levels of composition in Josh 13–19, and therefore the issue of whether Josh 14:1–2; 18:1; 19:51 are redactional,[81] we will focus on Josh 14:1–2; 18:1; 19:51 in terms of

---

78. For this criterion see above; and Lohfink, "The Priestly Narrative and History," 146 n. 30.

79. Nelson, Joshua, 70.

80. It is interesting to note also that the reference to the "border (קצה) of the land of Canaan" in Exod 16:35, is echoed both in Josh 4:19 in relation to Gilgal as being on the east "border" (קצה) of Jericho, and in Josh 5:12 in the reference to "the land of Canaan;" see Wagenaar, "The Cessation of the Manna," 207.

81. See for example, Noth (The Chronicler's History, 113–17) who sees Josh 14:1a as part of the earliest textual layer; Josh 19:51b as an addition to 19:49b–50 which belongs to the second layer; and Josh 14:1b; 18:1; 19:51a as additions belonging to the third layer; Auld (Joshua, Moses and the Land, 63, 67) who sees Josh 14:1b–3; 19:51 as belonging to

our primary criterion as to whether they cohere with, and are expected by, the narrative system of Pg in Genesis–Numbers.

Clearly, Josh 14:1–2; 18:1; and 19:51 are interrelated. Joshua 14:1b–2a and 19:51a refer to the inheritance distributed according to lot by the priest Eleazar, Joshua, and the heads of the families of the tribes of the Israelites. Both Josh 18:1 and 19:51 refer to the location of Shiloh and to the tent of meeting. Indeed Josh 19:51 would seem to bring together elements from Josh 14:1–2a and Josh 18:1 into a summary conclusion.[82] Priestly terminology and motifs in these verses that are also found in Pg in Genesis–Numbers comprise: the "land of Canaan" in Josh 14:1; "Eleazar" as priest (see Num 20:25–29), including his primacy over Joshua, linked with the motif of decision by lot (see Num 27:15–23)[83] in Josh 14:1–2a and Josh 19:51a;[84] the reference to the "congregation" (עדה) in Josh 18:1; more significantly, the reference in Josh 18:1 to the "land" (ארץ) having been "subdued" using the terminology of כבש (see Gen 1:28, which also uses כבש in relation to ארץ); the reference to the "tent of meeting" (אהל מועד) (see Exod 25–31); and the notice that the leaders had "finished" dividing the land (see Gen 2:2; Exod 40:33).[85] The last three motifs are the most significant, and as we have seen, it is these that figure prominently in the arguments of Lohfink and Blenkinsopp for the extension of Pg into Joshua. So it will be helpful to critique their arguments as a step

---

the latest, fifth level of redaction and Josh 18:1 as belonging to one of the latest strata in the book of Joshua; and Volkmar Fritz (*Das Buch Josua* [Tübingen: Mohr (Siebeck), 1994], 177, 179, 200) who sees these verses as later P or post-P redaction. That these verses are redactional is likely, given the material that they seem to bracket, which in all likelihood comprises earlier layers of material; and note in particular the repetition of Josh 19:49a by 19:51b concerning the "finishing" of the distribution.

82. See Nelson, *Joshua*, 176, 226; Fritz, *Das Buch Josua*, 200–201; Robert G. Boling, *Joshua* (AB 6; New York: Doubleday, 1982), 469.

83. Although Num 27:15–23 may be a secondary addition to Num 27:12–14, given that it breaks the common pattern in Pg of divine command and execution: Moses is portrayed as taking the initiative and praying for a successor, and in response to this initiative, Yhwh appoints Joshua in a subordinate role to Eleazar. See also the comments on this passage by Noth, *Numbers* (Philadelphia: Westminster, 1968), 213; Römer and Brettler ("Deuteronomy 34 and the Case for a Persian Hexateuch," 401–19, especially 407–8), who argue that Deut 34:9, which refers to Joshua and is closely related to Num 27:15–23, is part of a Priestly-Deuteronomistic Hexateuchal redaction that is later than Pg; and Auld (*Joshua, Moses and the Land*, 84) who argues that Joshua's subordination to Eleazar is in line with very late levels within Joshua.

84. The land distribution by lot in Josh 14:2a; 19:51 is anticipated by Num 26:55; 33:54; 34:13; however, these contentious chapters in Numbers lie outside the parameters within which we are addressing the issue.

85. Blenkinsopp, "The Structure of P," 275–76.

towards assessing whether these verses are anticipated by, and cohere with, Pg in Genesis–Numbers.

Lohfink argues that in Josh 18:1, two themes that have a major role in Pg—the tabernacle and the כבש of the land, set up programmatically in Gen 1:28—are brought together and reach their conclusion.[86] The argument has some merit: the motif of the tabernacle is central within Pg, and so its mention in Josh 18:1 and Josh 19:51 would seem to be significant. The use of the verb כבש in relation to taking land is uncommon,[87] and, if Josh 18:1 is part of Pg, this verb is strategically placed at the beginning and end, thus bracketing the whole.[88] However, closer scrutiny casts a considerable amount of doubt on Lohfink's line of reasoning.

Lohfink's argument regarding כבש in Gen 1:28 and Josh 18:1 is not as strong as it may at first seem. The use of the same term does not necessarily mean that the texts represent the same layer of composition: one may be copying the other.[89] Indeed, Auld argues that the text in Joshua may have been drafted later with Gen 1:28 in mind and could be late, since the closest formulation to that in Josh 18:1 is in 1 Chr 22:18; or even that Gen 1:28 might have been supplemented with Joshua in mind, since כבש does not fit easily within Gen 1:28,[90] and unlike the first three verbs in Gen 1:28 is not referred to repeatedly within Pg (see e.g., Gen 9:1, 7; Exod 1:7).[91]

Moreover, Lohfink's argument relies to a large extent on his view that כבש is to be understood in the sense of taking possession of the land, so that the occurrence of the term in Gen 1:28 refers to the nations possessing their own lands. In that case, the land promise to Abraham in Gen 17:8, even though it uses different terminology, is an extension of Gen 1:28, which is therefore seen to be fulfilled in Josh 18:1.[92] In this way, as noted above, Lohfink sees all the elements of Gen 1:28, and therefore all the promises, as being fulfilled in Pg. Lohfink's interpretation of כבש as denoting land possession, in continuity with the land promise to Abraham, is, however, a weak argument; כבש more commonly refers to military conquest, enslavement, and even rape.[93]

---

86. Lohfink, "The Priestly Narrative and History," 167;

87. The closest parallels are found in Num 32:22, 29; 1 Chr 22:18; see Auld, *Joshua, Moses and the Land*, 63.

88. See Lohfink, "The Strata of the Pentateuch and the Question of War," 200; "The Priestly Narrative and History," 167.

89. See Suzanne Boorer, *The Promise of the Land as Oath: A Key to the Formation of the Pentateuch* (Berlin: de Gruyter, 1992), 444–46.

90. The *qal* of כבש occurs nowhere else the Hebrew Bible in relation to *'rṣ*.

91. A. Graeme Auld, *Joshua Retold: Synoptic Perspectives* (OTS; Edinburgh: T&T Clark, 1998), 65–66; *Joshua, Moses and the Land*, 120 n. 30.

92. Lohfink, "The Priestly Narrative and History," 167.

93. See Auld, *Joshua Retold*, 68; Norman Habel, "Geophany: The Earth Story in

This meaning does not cohere well with the rest of Pg, and in particular with Pg's account of the surveying of the land in Num 13–14*—where, since the surveyors fail and are punished for slandering the land (Num 13:32; 14:36–37), the land is clearly to be valued. Furthermore, in the new creation order after the flood in Pg (Gen 9:1–7), although the terminology of being fruitful, multiplying, and filling the earth (9:1, 7), and the theme of having dominion over the creatures (9:2–6), are picked up from Gen 1:28, there is no reference to כבש in relation to the earth at all; this lack suggests that this element is no longer part of the new created order within which the Abrahamic covenant promises will unfold.

All these arguments combine to raise significant doubts concerning Lohfink's argument regarding כבש, which, along with the reference to the tent of meeting, is his primary indicator for seeing Pg in Joshua.

With regard to the reference to "the tent of meeting" in Josh 18:1 (and Josh 19:51), there are also some anomalies by comparison with Pg in Genesis–Numbers: the fleeting references to the tent in Joshua contrast with the central role it plays in Pg in Exod 25–Num 9;[94] the verb used in relation to its erection in Josh 18:1, שכן (hipʿil), differs from that used in Exod 40:2, 17 (קום) (hipʿil/hopʿal);[95] and the localization of the portable tent of meeting at Shiloh would seem to point forward to Shiloh traditions in 1 Sam 1–3, rather than back to any anticipation of this particular location, of which there is no mention in Genesis–Numbers.[96] Cumulatively these anomalies create some doubt that the reference to "the tent of meeting" in Josh 18:1 and Josh 19:51 forms an extension of and conclusion to Pg in Genesis–Numbers.

Lohfink's only other argument for the anticipation of these Joshua texts by Pg in Genesis–Numbers rests on the foreshadowing in Num 34 (which I have excluded from consideration within the parameters of this discussion) of the leaders listed in Josh 14:1; 19:51.[97] It may be concluded that Lohfink's claims concerning the anticipation of Josh 14:1–2; 18:1; and 19:51 by Pg in Genesis–Numbers are questionable, and at the very least, open to doubt.

Blenkinsopp draws a parallel between Gen 2:1–2; Exod 39:32; 40:33; and Josh 19:51, on the basis of their use of the language of "finishing," in support of his view that the distribution of the land in Josh 19:51 forms a structural correspondence with the creation of the world and the construction of the

---

Genesis 1," in The Earth Story in Genesis (ed. N. Habel and S. Wurst; Sheffield: Sheffield Academic Press, 2000), 34–48, especially 46–47.

94. See Blum, Studien zur Komposition des Pentateuch, 227–28.

95. Ibid.; Auld, Joshua, Moses and the Land, 63.

96. Blum, Studien zur Komposition des Pentateuch, 227–28.

97. Lohfink, "The Priestly Narrative and History," 145 n. 3.

sanctuary, and therefore represents the extension of Pg into Joshua.[98] On closer examination this parallel does not carry much weight. Whereas the creation of the world (Gen 1:31; 2:1, 2, 3) and the construction of the sanctuary (Exod 39:32, 43; 40:33) do display multiple strong links—viz., the heavens and the earth/all the work of the tabernacle "was finished," God/Moses "finished" the work, God/Moses "saw," God/Moses "blessed"—the only point of comparison in Josh 19:51 is that they "finished" dividing the land. This looks like pale copying, by means of a catchword only, to create a connection with the deliberately crafted parallel between the creation of the world and the construction of the sanctuary in Pg's narrative pattern, and therefore gives the impression of being a secondary addition rather than an integral part of Pg.

In a similar way to Josh 4:19; 5:10–12, the verses in Josh 14:1–2; 18:1; 19:51 seem to conflate various elements found in different places in Pg throughout Genesis–Numbers, such as the "subduing" of the earth (Gen 1:28), the "tent of meeting" (Exod 25–31), and the notice of "finishing" (Gen 1:2; Exod 40:33), and to have combined these with, for example, the localization at Shiloh. The impression gained, as in Josh 4:19; 5:10–12, is that of a closely related but later redaction that portrays the extension or fulfillment of the narrative movement of Pg in a slightly different way through telescoping and conflation.

However, arguments on literary grounds alone for the view that Pg does not extend into Joshua, are not conclusive. More decisive are theological and hermeneutical arguments that can be brought to bear in support of the view that inherent within the nature and shape of Pg in Genesis–Numbers is the positive conviction that the land promise is yet unfulfilled. These theological and hermeneutical arguments redress the inadequacy of attempts by those adhering to model one to account for the lack of a fulfillment of the land promise within the horizon of Pg. My arguments are based on a critique and extension of the hermeneutical arguments of Lohfink outlined above, but ironically reach opposite conclusions.[99]

Inherent within Lohfink's hermeneutics is a conception of Pg as comprised of timeless scenarios or scenarios that transcend time and can speak to every situation, whether this quality is expressed in terms of "transparency" or "paradigmatic situations" or "myth." As an extension of this conception, I

---

98. Blenkinsopp also argues on the grounds of the common terminology between Josh 18:1 (which is closely associated with Josh 19:51) and Gen 1:28, in terms of the earth and the word כבש—see Blenkinsopp, "The Structure of P," 290, and the discussion above.

99. For a fuller discussion of the nature and hermeneutics of Pg as I understand them, see Suzanne Boorer, "The 'Paradigmatic' and 'Historiographical' Nature of the Priestly Material as Key to its Interpretation," in *Seeing Signals, Reading Signs: The Art of Exegesis* (ed. M. O'Brien and H. Wallace; London: T&T Clark, 2004), 45–60.

would argue that scenarios within Pg may indeed be seen as timeless or tran-
scending time in the sense that they combine past tradition and future vision:
that is, older traditions are taken up and reshaped in combination with visions
for the future, in "paradigmatic scenarios" that can speak to ongoing present experience.[100] An illustration will clarify this concept. The description or
picture drawn in Pg of the tabernacle and its cult consists of the combination of distinct past traditions conflated with future ideals. Examples of past
traditions include: old tent traditions, Jerusalem temple traditions and their
corresponding modes of presence, the figure of Aaron, and (albeit in relation
to the priesthood) royal anointing and clothing traditions.[101] The future ideals
comprise the leadership of the community by the Aaronide priesthood. This
presents something unique: a picture that would have been partially recog-
nizable by P's (probably exilic) audience through the various past traditions,
but that is here conflated with and taken up into a new vision for the future.
The result is that P's picture of the tabernacle and its cult transcends time,
spanning past and future such that past traditions are redeemed and trans-
formed and integrated with programmatic ideals to present an integral whole,
or seemingly "timeless" vision.[102]

---

100. I am assuming, with the majority of scholars, that Pg is exilic/early postexilic,
and therefore that the present experience of Pg's original audience would be that of exile.
See, for example, Elliger, "Sinn und Ursprung der Priesterlichen Geschichtserzahlung," 141;
Klein, "The Message of P," 58; Ronald E. Clements, God and Temple: The Idea of the Divine
in Ancient Israel (London: SCM Press, 1965), 111, 122; McEvenue, The Narrative Style
of the Priestly Writer, 186; Lohfink, "The Priestly Narrative and History," 148; Terence E.
Fretheim, "The Priestly Document: Anti-Temple?" VT 18 (1968): 313–29, 313; Volkmar
Fritz, "Das Geschichtsverstandnis der Priesterschrift," ZTK 84 (1987): 426–39, 427; Blen-
kinsopp, The Pentateuch, 238; idem, Sage, Priest, Prophet, 68; David M. Carr, Reading the
Fractures of Genesis, 136–37.

101. See, for example, Roland de Vaux, Ancient Israel: Its Life and Institutions
(London: Dartman, Longman & Todd, 1961), 295–97, 301–2, 347, 450; Menaham Haran,
"Shiloh and Jerusalem: The Origin of the Priestly Tradition in the Pentateuch," JBL 81
(1962): 14–24; Clements, God and Temple, 114; Gerhard von Rad, "The Tent and the Ark,"
in idem, The Problem of the Hexateuch and Other Essays, 103–4; Fretheim, "The Priestly
Document: Anti-Temple?" 315; Frank M. Cross, "The Priestly Tabernacle," in Old Testa-
ment Issues (ed. S. Sandmel; London: SCM Press, 1968); 40–67; Trygge N. D. Mettinger,
The Dethronement of Sabbaoth: Studies in the Shem and Kabod Theologies (ConBOT 18;
Lund: Gleerup, 1982), 81–96; Richard E. Friedman, "Tabernacle," in ABD 6: 292–300; Blenkinsopp, Sage, Priest, Prophet, 66–97.

102. See Boorer, "The 'Paradigmatic' and 'Historiographical' Nature of the Priestly
Material," 47. Another example is the description of the Passover/Unleavened Bread Festival of Exod 12:1–20. The account appears to telescope a complex history concerning the
probably originally distinct traditions of Passover and unleavened bread, and rituals surrounding the firstborn into one coherent festival, as the primary means of the ongoing
celebration of the exodus. Moreover, this account, which collapses into one the various

However, as already noted, Lohfink sees these scenarios of which Pg is comprised in terms of "a great picture collection assembled on artistic principles."[103] For Lohfink, the narrative sequence is in effect incidental and unimportant. E. Blum's criticism of Lohfink in this regard is well-founded, for, as he argues, a central characteristic of the Priestly material is its portrayal of a specific, cause-and-effect contingent, sequence of "events."[104] Given this factor, as Blum rightly maintains, individual scenarios cannot be taken out of their sequential context and simply applied "paradigmatically" or "transparently" to the contemporary situation in isolation, as Lohfink has a tendency to do, but must rather be interpreted within their narrated sequence. The trajectory along which the scenarios are placed is also essential to the shape, theology, and I would argue, hermeneutics of Pg. This trajectory comprises, in relation to the story of Israel: the unfolding of the Abrahamic covenant promises of descendants (Gen 17:1–8; an extension, specific to the nation Israel, of the command to multiply in Gen 1:28; 9:1, 7); the promise of divine presence; and the promise of everlasting possession of the land of Canaan. The scenarios relating to the nation of Israel, therefore, represent the unfolding of these promises. But if the scenarios can be seen as "paradigmatic" and time-transcendent, in that they collapse together past tradition and future vision to speak to the ongoing present, could not this also be said with regard to the trajectory along which they are arranged? That is, can the trajectory itself also be seen as "paradigmatic" in a way similar to that of the individual scenarios, and indeed in interaction with them, since these scenarios are components of the unfolding of the promises—partially known or fulfilled in the past, and yet inseparably linked for their contemporary audience with visions for their future?

---

stages of past tradition, is recounted in a form that also collapses together the description of the rite as instituted in the past with its ongoing celebration in the present and into the future: as such it is timeless. The narrative does this by making no distinction in time between the narrative event set at the exodus and the ongoing celebration of the ritual: these become one. In contrast to the earlier non-P material in Exod 12–13 (e.g., 12:29–39; 13:3–16), where narration of the event in the past and its ongoing celebration in the future through rite or law are clearly distinguished in time, P's description makes no such distinction: "The instructions and description of events for the exodus night is the (present and future) cultic celebration … the narrative is the cultic rite/law and the present celebration of Passover and Unleavened Bread is that of the time of the exodus from Egypt." See Boorer, *The Promise of the Land as Oath*, 143–202, especially 159–60, 164–65; "The 'Paradigmatic' and 'Historiographical' Nature of the Priestly Material," 46–47.

103. Lohfink, "The Priestly Narrative and History," 162.

104. Blum (*Studien zur Komposition des Pentateuch*, 331) does not of course use the term "history" (*Geschichte*) as Lohfink initially set it up—i.e., as the narration of what has actually happened—and therefore questions the dichotomy Lohfink articulated between "history" and "paradigm"; Blum maintains that all biblical *Geschichte* tends towards paradigm.

I believe that this is precisely the case. Indeed, all three promises, including the promise of the land, are portrayed in their unfolding scenarios and their particular trajectory as inseparably comprising past and future, partial embodiment and future vision. In terms of this paper it is particularly important to make this case in relation to the land promise, but it will be helpful also to discuss the other two promises in this regard, in order to show that the theology and hermeneutics for all three promises in Pg are consistent.[105] And so, in opposition to Lohfink's view of Pg's hermeneutical theology, in which the land promise and all the promises are fulfilled, I will argue that inherent within Pg's hermeneutic the land promise, indeed all three promises, though partially fulfilled, contain a future dimension yet to be realized.

The promise of descendants (Gen 17:1–6; foreshadowed in Gen 1:28; 9:1, 7) is unfolded along its trajectory, partially fulfilled in Exod 1:7,[106] and further unfolded in Num 1–2 with the census and arrangement of the tribes around the sanctuary. In the scenario of Num 1–2, past tradition—seen, for example, in the prominence given to Judah, which reflects the late preexilic situation—is an inseparable component within a paradigm that surely portrays for Pg's (exilic) audience a future vision of all twelve tribes unified in an ordered pattern around the sanctuary (itself comprised of past tradition and future vision), as the vehicle for God's presence. Hence the promise of descendants, particularly in this paradigmatic scenario of Num 1–2, comprises past tradition inseparably combined with future vision in a way that suggests partial fulfillment but yet looks forward to a goal that is yet to be realized.[107]

The promise to be the God of Abraham's descendents (Gen 17:7–8) is unfolded in Pg in the exodus and manna scenarios (Exod 6–16*); in the recognition by both the Egyptians and the Israelites that "I am Yhwh" (Exod 6:2, 6, 8; 14:7, 18; 16:12); and in Exod 25–31, 35–40 concerning the construction of the tabernacle as the means of the presence of God. Since, as we have seen,

---

105. See Lohfink, "The Priestly Narrative and History," 166–69. As we have seen, it was important to Lohfink to see a consistency and symmetry between all three promises of the Abrahamic covenant (two of which, descendants and land, he related back to Gen 1:28) in terms of their fulfillment within Pg.

106. Cf. Lohfink ("The Priestly Narrative and History," 167), who sees the motif of multiplying in Gen 1:28 as fulfilled in Exod 1:7. It is interesting to note that David Carr ("What is Required to Identify Pre-Priestly Narrative Connections between Genesis and Exodus? Some General Reflections and Specific Cases," in Dozeman and Schmid, *A Farewell to the Yahwist?* 159–80, 173) suggests Exod 1:7 (along with Josh 18:1) may be a post-P redaction because of the mixture of P and non-P language that it contains.

107. Cf. Josh 13–19, which not only does not cohere closely with what is envisioned in Num 1–2, but would seem to consist, to a large extent, of traditional material that has been taken up (city lists and boundary lists), rather than an integrated paradigm as envisioned by Pg in Num 2 in particular.

the latter scenario in particular[108] comprises past traditions reshaped in combination with programmatic elements to present a vision for the future, this promise of God's presence, as it unfolds along its trajectory, is also partially fulfilled and yet looking forward to an envisioned future.[109]

So it is also with regard to the promise of the land (Gen 17:8). The trajectory of the land promise as it is unfolded comprises past tradition inseparably combined with future vision in such a way that it is partially fulfilled but yet forward-looking, to a future goal that is yet to be realized. The past tradition that shows the partial fulfillment of the land promise is expressed in terms of the foothold gained in the land by the ancestors: Pg shapes this tradition to portray Abraham and the other ancestors as resident aliens in the land in their lifetime, but as buried in the land in a plot that they own (Gen 23; 25:7–11; 49:29–32). The unfolding of the land promise in the itineraries of Exodus and Numbers also shows its partial fulfillment, but in such a way that the ultimate vision and realization still lie in the future. Pg's paradigmatic scenario, within Pg's trajectory that is structured by itineraries, that focusses on the land, is the episode of the surveying of the land in Num 13–14*. Pg's scenario takes up elements of the older tradition found in the non-P material in Num 13–14 and reshapes them to show that the unfolding of the land promise is halted here because of the slandering of the land by the spies (Num 13:32), in which the people are complicit (Num 14:1a, 2–3, 10a): at this point in the trajectory, the fulfillment of the promise envisioned as "everlasting possession of the land of Canaan" (Gen 17:8) is unrealized for them, but open to be fulfilled in the future—it is the future fulfillment of the land promise itself which constitutes the future vision of this paradigmatic scenario. But this episode also features a rejection by the people of the future envisioned within the paradigmatic scenarios relating more specifically to the unfolding of the promise of descendants and the divine presence: in Num 14:35 the congregation is described as "gathered together against me," symbolizing the reversal and rejection of the formation of the twelve tribes gathered in order around the sanctuary (Exod 25–Num 4*).[110] And so with this paradigmatic scenario, the future envisioned in relation to all three promises—the presence of God in relation to the sanctuary and its cult, with its inherent programmatic vision; the formation of the descendants as twelve unified tribes around this envisioned sanctuary; and their entrance into the promised land as

---

108. The same could be said of Exod 6–16* (Pg), but it is beyond the scope of this paper to expand upon these scenarios.

109. Cf. Lohfink ("The Priestly Narrative and History," 169), who sees the promise to be the people's God as fulfilled at Sinai.

110. See Boorer, "The Earth/Land (*'rts*) in the Priestly Material," 31.

the beginning of their everlasting possession of it—remains in the realm of unrealized hope, as a three-fold goal that yet lies in the future.

Thus, it seems to me that, inherent in the very nature or theological hermeneutics of Pg as a whole, past and future dimensions are inseparably linked to address ongoing present experience. And this applies to all aspects of Pg, in both its individual paradigmatic scenarios and the trajectory along which they are arranged, as they interact with one another in the unfolding of all three promises, There is therefore a future dimension or vision inherent within every aspect of Pg, in its scenarios and its narrative trajectory, and therefore with regard to all three promises—of descendants, of divine presence, and of the everlasting possession of the land. Thus the land promise envisaged in Pg, as with the other promises, has a future dimension as yet unrealized: though partially fulfilled and glimpsed through the tradition, the complete fulfillment of Pg's promise of everlasting possession of the land is a future vision.

Given the hermeneutics of Pg in Genesis–Numbers, the fulfillment of the land promise in Joshua, and in particular the texts we have examined in Josh 4:19; 5:10–12; 14:1–2*; 18:1; 19:51, hardly comprises a fitting conclusion to this dynamic. Given Pg's built-in dimension of future fulfillment at every point, a conclusion and complete fulfillment is not really to be expected, since this would be at odds with the visionary nature of the narrative. Even if we were to seek a conclusion, these texts in Joshua do not conform to Pg's theological hermeneutics, but, as we have seen in our literary analysis, rather telescope and conflate certain disparate elements of Pg in Genesis–Numbers in a way that is anomalous to its narrative system. In short, the texts in Joshua, with their motif of fulfillment of the land promise, do not present a conclusion that is coherent with Pg in Genesis–Numbers— literarily, theologically, or hermeneutically.

IV

In conclusion, it has been argued that, in line with model 1, Pg does not extend into Joshua: the promise of the land, according to Pg, remains unfulfilled. The arguments for this position have involved theological and hermeneutical considerations in tandem with literary analysis, in order to redress the weaknesses of the arguments put forward by the proponents of model one. It has been shown that the P-style texts examined from Joshua (Josh 4:19; 5:10–12; 14:1–2*; 18:1; 19:51), although similar to aspects of Pg in Genesis–Numbers, show a lack of coherence or are anomalous, with respect to both the narrative system and theological hermeneutics of Pg's interactive paradigmatic trajectory and scenarios, which by their very nature put forth a future vision at every point. The promise of the land, as an important component, along with the other two promises of descendants and divine presence, is envisaged within Pg's theological hermeneutic as partially glimpsed but as yet unfulfilled: the fulfillment of the promise of everlasting possession of the land of Canaan in Pg is a future vision of hope, as yet unrealized in all its completeness.

It might be imagined that later redactors are responsible for the P-like texts in Joshua, perhaps in an attempt to align the return to the land in postexilic times with Pg's vision; and perhaps in this way, at some stage, such redaction represents an attempt to formulate a Hexateuch.[111] But exploration of this question, which would involve an examination of these P-like texts in Joshua in relation to their surrounding material, and an exploration of the place of the Deuteronomistic History in relation to these broader issues, lies outside the scope of this investigation. Therefore, no conclusions can be drawn from our discussion with regard to the wider issue of the place of the Priestly material within the formation of Genesis–Kings, and in particular with regard to its relationship to the Deuteronomistic history, the question with which I began in outlining the models. However, it *can* be said, it seems to me, that at some stage, probably in exilic times, there existed an originally independent Priestly source (Pg) that concluded with the Mosaic generation and envisioned the promise of the land, along with the other promises, as not yet fully realized, as a future hope. Furthermore, it would seem that this Pg formed a precedent for the shape of the later Pentateuch as a whole: the hermeneutical theology of both works conceptualizes the fulfillment of the land promise as an unrealized future vision, perhaps in line with other voices in the early and later postexilic period that seem to have conceived of an unending exile, even after the return to the land.[112]

---

111. See for example, Römer, *The So-Called Deuteronomistic History*, 179–80; Römer and Brettler, "Deuteronomy 34 and the Case for a Persian Hexateuch," 409–15.

112. See for example, John Hill, "'Your Exile Will Be Long': The Book of Jeremiah and the Unended Exile," in *Reading the Book of Jeremiah: A Search for Coherence* (ed. M. Kessler; Winona Lake: Eisenbrauns, 2004), 149–61.

ON THE COHESION AND SEPARATION OF BOOKS WITHIN THE ENNEATEUCH

*Christoph Levin**

SINGLE BOOKS OR LARGE REDACTIONAL UNITS?

As the retelling of the history of Israel, the great biblical work contained in the books of Genesis to Kings constitutes a continuous unit. The sequence of events which begins with the creation of the world and ends with the Babylonian exile can at no point be rationally broken off and begun afresh. Spinoza already drew attention to this fact in the eighth chapter of his *Tractatus theologico-politicus* of 1670: "These books are so intertwined with one another that from this alone we can perceive that they contain the account of only a single historian."[1]

At the same time, however, it is obvious that the Enneateuch is a collection, which brings together diverse material with a multiform previous history. The selection, arrangement, and assembly have been made intentionally, and it makes sense to ascribe this work to one or several redactions. That is what Spinoza did when he traced back the whole Enneateuch to Ezra, as its presumed author.

Recently, the great redaction-historical hypotheses are being called in question. Attention is focused on blocks of tradition, such as the Primeval History, the history of the patriarchs, the Joseph story, the exodus tradition, the conquest of the promised land, the stories about the Judges, and the account of the monarchical era. These are supposed to have been put together only at a late stage, and then in several steps. Thus the Deuteronomistic His-

---

* English translation by Margaret Kohl.
1. "Hi enim libri ita invicem connectuntur, ut ex hoc solo dignoscere possimus eos non nisi unam unius historici narrationem continere." Benedictus de Spinoza, *Opera I: Tractatus theologico-politicus* (ed. G. Gawlik and F. Niewöhner; Darmstadt: Wissenschaftliche Buchgesellschaft, 1979), 298.

tory is said to have originally comprised only the books of Samuel and Kings: "The beginning lies in Samuel–Kings."[2] For the narrative about the conquest of the land in the books of Deuteronomy and Joshua a separate redaction is postulated, which created an independent work.[3] The book of Judges was supposedly interposed later between Joshua and Samuel, in order to establish the connection between Deuteronomy and Joshua, on the one hand, and Samuel and Kings, on the other.[4] With regard to the Tetrateuch, there is a growing widespread view that the book of Genesis was not separated from the rest but was made to precede it at some later point.[5] What all these hypotheses come down to is that the narrative sequence as a whole was not a starting point; it was a terminus. According to Reinhard Kratz, the complex as a totality is no earlier than the Torah, which developed out of the First Commandment: "If we remove this presupposition and take away the connecting links based on it, the whole historical construction collapses into loose, disconnected individual parts."[6]

It is doubtful whether this revival of the Fragment Hypothesis constitutes an advance in our knowledge. That the narrated material is made up of different and formerly independent units was never in dispute. But if the whole structure is accounted for merely as the outcome of later literary combinations, then a problem solved by the earlier redaction-historical hypotheses,

---

2. Reinhard G. Kratz, *The Composition of the Narrative Books of the Old Testament* (trans. J. Bowden; London: T&T Clark; New York: Continuum, 2005), 158. In current research this opinion is increasingly shared. See also Ernst Würthwein, "Erwägungen zum sog. deuteronomistischen Geschichtswerk," in idem, *Studien zum Deuteronomistischen Geschichtswerk* (BZAW 227; Berlin: de Gruyter, 1994), 1–11.

3. See esp. Norbert Lohfink, "Kerygmata des Deuteronomistischen Geschichtswerks," in *Die Botschaft und die Boten: Festschrift für Hans Walter Wolff zum 70. Geburtstag* (ed. J. Jeremias and L. Perlitt; Neukirchen-Vluyn: Neukirchener, 1981), 87–100, esp. 92–96; repr. in idem, *Studien zum Deuteronomium und zur deuteronomistischen Literatur II* (SBAB 12; Stuttgart: Katholisches Bibelwerk, 1991), 125–42, esp. 132–37.

4. See esp. Kratz, *The Composition of the Narrative Books*, 191.

5. See esp. Konrad Schmid, *Erzväter und Exodus: Untersuchungen zur doppelten Begründung der Ursprünge Israels innerhalb der Geschichtsbücher des Alten Testaments* (WMANT 81; Neukirchen-Vluyn: Neukirchener, 1999); Kratz, *Composition*, 281; Jan Christian Gertz, "The Transition between the Books of Genesis and Exodus," in *A Farewell to the Yahwist? The Composition of the Pentateuch in Recent European Interpretation* (ed. T. B. Dozeman and K. Schmid; SBLSymS 34; Atlanta: Society of Biblical Literature, 2006), 73–87. Schmid, *Literaturgeschichte des Alten Testaments: Eine Einführung* (Darmstadt: Wissenschaftliche Buchgesellschaft, 2008), 158–59, presents a short summary of this position wherein the shortcuts are clearly seen. Contrary to all of them see Christoph Levin, "The Yahwist and the Redactional Link between Genesis and Exodus," in Dozeman and Schmid, *A Farewell to the Yahwist?* 131–41.

6. Kratz, *The Composition of the Narrative Books*, 155.

returns. The course of the historical events as they are presented is not in itself self-evident, but is rather to a large degree fictitious: "A gigantic structure such as this, the whole conforming to one single plan, does not grow up naturally of its own accord."[7] Gerhard von Rad established this principle, and we do not refute his insight by ignoring it. It is highly unlikely that the overall historiographical concept came into being only through the subsequent linking together of books, which were for the most part already independent.

In pentateuchal research of the mid-twentieth century, scholars explored the possibility that the sequence followed a traditional pattern, which supposedly had its *Sitz im Leben* in the *memoria* used in the cult.[8] This solution has simply proved untenable. The credal formulas, which, it had been assumed, provided the original structure for this pattern, have proved to be late summaries. They do not precede the redactional compilations; they presuppose them, and without them are inconceivable.[9] The cohesion of the whole can be explained only in the light of redaction history. Spinoza's conclusion is still valid.

However, Martin Noth had already disputed the existence of redactions that encompassed the entire Enneateuch from the outset by cutting the ground from under the feet of earlier attempts to trace the sources of the Pentateuch as far as the books of Kings.[10] His hypothesis of a Deuteronomistic History comprising the books of Deuteronomy to Kings excludes the possibility that

---

7. Gerhard von Rad, "The Form-Critical Problem of the Hexateuch," in idem, *The Problem of the Hexateuch and Other Essays* (trans. E. W. Trueman Dicken; Edinburgh: Oliver & Boyd, 1966; repr. London: SCM Press, 1984), 1–78, p. 52.

8. See von Rad, "The Form-Critical Problem of the Hexateuch," 3–8 and 50–53.

9. See esp. Wolfgang Richter, "Beobachtungen zur theologischen Systembildung in der alttestamentlichen Literatur anhand des 'Kleinen geschichtlichen Credo,'" in *Wahrheit und Verkündigung* (ed. L. Scheffczyk et al.; Paderborn: Schöningh, 1967), 1:175–212; Brevard S. Childs, "Deuteronomic Formulae of the Exodus Traditions," in *Hebräische Wortforschung* (ed. B. Hartmann et al.; VTSup 16; Leiden: Brill, 1967), 30–39, esp. 39.

10. For the book of Joshua this detection of pentateuchal materials follows from the earlier hypotheses concerning the Hexateuch. See Abraham Kuenen, *An Historico-Critical Inquiry into the Origin and Composition of the Hexateuch: Vol. 1* (trans. P. H. Wicksteed; London: Macmillan, 1886; Dutch original 1861; 2d ed. 1885); and Julius Wellhausen, *Die Composition des Hexateuchs* (4th ed.; Berlin: de Gruyter, 1963; originally published 1876–1878)—both of them rather hesitantly. For sources in Judges, see esp. Karl Budde, *Die Bücher Richter und Samuel, ihre Quellen und ihr Aufbau* (Gießen: Ricker, 1890); followed by George F. Moore, *A Critical and Exegetical Commentary on Judges* (ICC; Edinburgh: T&T Clark, 1895); Charles Fox Burney, *The Book of Judges with Introduction and Notes* (London: Rivingtons, 1918); Otto Eißfeldt, *Die Quellen des Richterbuches* (Leipzig: Hinrichs, 1925). For Samuel and Kings see esp. Immanuel Benzinger, *Jahvist und Elohist in den Königsbüchern* (Stuttgart: Kohlhammer, 1921); Gustav Hölscher, "Das Buch der Könige, seine Quellen und seine Redaktion," in *Eucharistērion: Studien zur Religion und*

the Enneateuch came into being as a single historical work. In at least one point there must be a secondary join, rather than a secondary division. Noth detected this caesura between the books of Numbers and Deuteronomy. There is a sound argument in favor of this theory, even apart from Noth's hypothesis: at the beginning of the book of Deuteronomy we find in chapters 1–3 the most extensive recapitulation link in the books of the Enneateuch. This great bridge would not exist unless it had been required by some deep gulf.

THE SIZE OF THE SCROLLS

One possible objection to continuous redactions rests on the compass of the present text. It would seem reasonable to expect that a work which emanated from a redaction would, as a literary unit, have comprised a single scroll. The extent of today's text of the Enneateuch, or even of only the Tetrateuch and the Deuteronomistic History, exceeds by far the compass of any scrolls known to us. The Isaiah scroll from Qumran is the longest ancient biblical manuscript extant, and it could accommodate not more than a quarter of today's Torah. The finished Enneateuch is more than six times longer than the longest book in the Bible, the Psalms.[11] It may well be that "judging by the manufacture of the ancient scrolls ... a scroll that would accommodate a whole text of the size of Genesis to 2 Kings was not an impossibility."[12] But the fact that the sequence of historical events was distributed over nine books shows that any such major scroll was unknown to the Second Temple scribes. "In the circumstances of the period in which these works first appeared ... there was no possibility whatsoever of containing them on only one scroll."[13] "The fact that the biblical books, and even the smallest of them, were kept from the outset on separate scrolls is also a conclusive proof of the basic rule,

---

Literatur des Alten und Neuen Testaments: Hermann Gunkel zum 60. Geburtstage (ed. H. Schmidt; 2 vols.; FRLANT 36; Göttingen: Vandenhoeck & Ruprecht, 1923), 1:158–213.

11. See the arguments about the size of the scrolls in Konrad Schmid, "Buchtechnische und sachliche Prolegomena zur Enneateuchfrage," in *Auf dem Weg zur Endgestalt von Genesis bis II Regum* (ed. M. Beck and U. Schorn; BZAW 370; Berlin: de Gruyter, 2006), 1–14, esp. 5–9; idem, "Une grande historiographie allant de Genèse à 2 Rois a-t-elle un jour existé?" in *Les dernières rédactions du Pentateuque, de l'Hexateuque et de L'Ennéateuque* (ed. T. Römer and K. Schmid; BETL 203; Leuven: Peeters, 2007), 35–45.

12. Schmid, *Erzväter und Exodus*, 29. In Qumran a few number of scrolls were found that contain more than one book of the Torah, such as 4QGen-Exod[a], 4QpalaeoGen-Exod[l], 4QExod-Lev[f], 4QLev-Num[a]. These are exceptions. See Emanuel Tov, *Textual Criticism of the Hebrew Bible* (2d ed.; Minneapolis: Fortress, 2001), 203–4.

13. Menahem Haran, "Book-Size and the Device of Catch-Lines in the Biblical Canon," *JJS* 36 (1985): 1–11, esp. 2.

that each complete work was to be written on its own scroll."[14] Taking these two preconditions together, we must conclude that the first redactional form of the historical works—which form the basis of the Enneateuch—must have been considerably shorter than the present text in its full extent.

From this it follows that Reinhard Kratz's theory turns the literary history upside down: "Insight into the gradual growth of the Deuteronomistic redaction in (Deuteronomy) Joshua–Kings removes the basis from Noth's hypothesis."[15] The very opposite is true: The "gradual growth" of the Deuteronomistic History—as well as of the Yahwist's History and the Priestly Code—is the presupposition without which these redactional units are quantitatively inconceivable.

The individual books (or complexes of books) did not precede the literary growth; they are its outcome. The joins show "that the division of Genesis to 2 Kings into books must be earlier than the conclusion of the productive shaping of the text."[16] Indeed it must have been very much earlier. In relation to the literary process as a whole, the division was already made early on, then in its turn becoming the presupposition for further growth.[17] As soon as the material from one scroll was distributed between two, there was again room for new literary expansions, until the text had grown so much that it was once more distributed between separate scrolls.

In this process the division between the books was not made programmatically but followed practical criteria. It was intended to make the continually expanded scroll or scrolls manageable once more. During the copying process, the text was broken off at a particular place, and a new scroll was begun, deviating from the *Vorlage*. This very likely did not take place in a single act. Each of these caesuras follows its own rules. The division of Samuel and Kings into two books each, took place for the first time only in the Septuagint. This does not exclude the possibility that the sequence of separate single books created a meaningful division of epochs as we find it today.

_____

14. Menahem Haran, "Book-Size and the Thematic Cycles in the Pentateuch," in *Die Hebräische Bibel und ihre zweifache Nachgeschichte* (ed. Erhard Blum et al.; Neukirchen-Vluyn: Neukirchener, 1990), 165–76, esp. 166.

15. Kratz, *The Composition of the Narrative Books*, 216. Cited affirmatively by Jan C. Gertz, "Kompositorische Funktion und literarischer Ort von Deuteronomium 1–3," in *Die deuteronomistischen Geschichtswerke: Redaktions- und religionsgeschichtliche Perspektiven zur "Deuteronomismus"-Diskussion in Tora und Vorderen Propheten* (ed. M. Witte et al.; BZAW 365; Berlin: de Gruyter, 2006), 103–23, esp. 107.

16. Schmid, *Erzväter und Exodus*, 31.

17. The conclusion of Haran, however, proves to be wrong: "There should be no doubt that this fivefold division was imprinted in this work from its very beginning" ("Book-Size and the Thematic Cycles in the Pentateuch," 172).

The condition for the distribution of the material between several scrolls was that the pragmatic connection was preserved in the process. Consequently the gaps between the books which had newly come into being had to be bridged by way of links in the content. In several cases what had gone before was recapitulated in the succeeding scroll.

However, here we must differentiate. The recapitulations could serve both to bridge secondary divisions and to create original connections which did not previously exist. These two possibilities are not even mutually exclusive. For today's narrative complex, it is not absolutely necessary that the beginning was, so to speak, an Enneateuch torso. That this was so is in fact highly improbable. To this extent, the recent theories are not from the outset unjustified; they merely exaggerate the state of affairs. Even Noth's hypothesis did not presuppose one single major composition but two: the Tetrateuch, Genesis to Numbers, on the one hand, and the Deuteronomistic History, Deuteronomy to Kings, on the other. Here it was assumed that in the book of Deuteronomy the two works were dovetailed, since the death of Moses in Deut 34 was still assigned to the narrative in the Tetrateuch. In this way the term "Pentateuch" also retained its justification.

Thus, we have to scrutinize each individual link in order to decide whether the link was intended to bridge some connection that had broken down, or whether its purpose was to establish for the first time a connection that had not hitherto existed. We shall first work backwards from the book of Kings to the book of Deuteronomy, and then forward from the book of Genesis to the book of Numbers, finishing with the transition between Numbers and Deuteronomy.

Samuel and Kings

The caesura between the books of Samuel and Kings is clearly secondary. It splits up a single preredactional work: the collection of narratives about the kings, which describe the presuppositions and circumstances under which the rule of David was passed on to Solomon. Solomon's accession to the throne, with which the new book begins in 1 Kgs 1, is the final point of a development that commences in 2 Sam 10–12 with Solomon's birth.[18] It was preceded by the story of Sheba's rebellion in 2 Sam 20, which was originally the final text in this series of events.

---

18. See Leonhard Rost, *The Succession to the Throne of David* (trans. M. D. Rutter and D. M. Gunn; Sheffield: Almond Press, 1982).

2 Sam 20 [Succession narrative: The rebellion of Sheba]
   2 Sam 21:1–14 [Burial of Saul and Jonathan]
      2 Sam 21:15–22 [David's heroes fighting against the Philistines]
         2 Sam 22 [David's song of deliverance (quoting from Ps 18)]
         2 Sam 23:1–7 [David's last words]
      2 Sam 23:8–39 [David's mighty men]
   2 Sam 24 [David's census and punishment. He finds the place to build
the temple.]

   1 Kgs 1–2 [Succession narrative: Solomon ascends to the throne.]

Today no fewer than four chapters have been appended to 2 Sam 20, forming
an "appendix"[19] to the David account in the books of Samuel. This appendix
was added only after the books had been separated. It presupposes that extra
sheets have been tacked on to the now separate Samuel scroll. The additional
columns contain a whole sheaf of material. "2 Sam. 21–24 is full of additions,
which gradually accumulated after Dtr.'s history had been divided into separate books."[20] "These chapters … are composed of different elements; 21:1–14
belongs together with 24:1–25; 21:15–22 is related to 23:8–39; left over in the
middle are the two songs 22:1–51 and 23:1–7."[21]

   This convoluted process of growth must have extended over a considerable period: "2 Sam. 21:1–14 and 24:1–25 were the first passages to be added,
as we can tell from the thematic connection between 24:1a and 21:1–14."[22]
The story about David's census in 2 Sam 24 refers at the beginning to the story
about the fate of the house of Saul in 2 Sam 21:1–14. "This connection was
later broken by the interposition of the anecdotes and lists of David's 'mighty
men' (2 Sam. 21:15–22 and 23:8–39). This latter complex of traditional material, held together by its subject matter, was then split in two when the poetic
passages (ch. 22 and 23:1–7) were inserted";[23] that is, David's song of deliverance (which repeats Ps 18), and David's last will.

   Taken together, these six large sections amount to no less than 139 Masoretic verses. From this it can be deduced that the books of Samuel and Kings
had been separated long before the end of the literary process.

---

   19. Julius Wellhausen, *Die Composition des Hexateuchs*, 263.
   20. Martin Noth, *The Deuteronomistic History* (trans. J. Doull et al.; JSOTSup 15;
Sheffield: Sheffield Academic Press, 1981); trans. of *Überlieferungsgeschichtliche Studien: Die sammelnden und bearbeitenden Geschichtswerke im Alten Testament* (Halle:
Niemeyer, 1943; 2d repr. ed., 1957; 3d repr. ed.: Darmstadt: Wissenschaftliche Buchgesellschaft, 1967), 124 n. 3.
   21. Wellhausen, *Die Composition des Hexateuchs*, 260.
   22. Noth, *The Deuteronomistic History*, 124–25 n. 3.
   23. Noth, *The Deuteronomistic History*, 125 n. 3.

JUDGES AND SAMUEL

(a) At present the opinion is gaining ground that the Deuteronomistic History originally consisted only of the books of Samuel and Kings. "The beginning of the Deuteronomistic redaction does not lie in Deuteronomy but in Samuel–Kings and from here extends forwards into (Genesis–)Deuteronomy, Joshua and Judges."[24] The most important reason for this view is that in the book of Judges the religious practice of the Israelites seems to be subjected to a different standard from that enjoined in the books of Kings for the religious practice of the kings. "Whereas in Samuel–Kings the First Commandment has become the criterion for assessing the kings only at a secondary stage and has replaced ... the criterion of the unity of the kingdom and the cult, in Deuteronomy itself as in Joshua and Judges, more or less from the beginning it is the criterion of the 'Deuteronomistic' ... revisions."[25] The cyclical outline of history also differentiates the book of Judges from the books of Samuel and Kings, with their linear presentation. Consequently von Rad had already maintained: "It is difficult to think that the editing of the Book of Judges and that of the Book of Kings could have taken place as a single piece of work."[26]

However, the redactor did not have a free hand everywhere; he was dependent on the tradition he used. For the account of the era of the Judges, which is his own redactional invention, he arranged the material freely; for the period of the monarchy, on the other hand, the course of events was fixed by the progress of history as it is documented in the annals of the kings, specifically in the excerpts of these annals which provide the framework of the account. Nevertheless, even in the case of the kings of Judah, the redaction created a cyclical order of eras alternating between godliness and apostasy. Sin was dominant in the case of Rehoboam (1 Kgs 14:22) and Abijam (15:3), Jehoram (2 Kgs 8:18) and Ahaziah (8:27), and among the last kings from Jehoahaz (23:32) to Zedekiah (24:19). Godliness ruled from Asa (1 Kgs 15:11) to Jehoshaphat (22:43) and from Jehoash (2 Kgs 12:2) to Jotham (15:34).[27]

---

24. Kratz, *The Composition of the Narrative Books*, 158. Earlier, see esp. Würthwein, "Erwägungen zum sog. deuteronomistischen Geschichtswerk."

25. Kratz, *The Composition of the Narrative Books*, 157–58.

26. Gerhard von Rad, *The Theology of Israel's Historical Traditions* (trans. D. M. G. Stalker; vol. 1 of *Old Testament Theology*; New York: Harper, 1962), 347.

27. See Christoph Levin, "Die Frömmigkeit der Könige von Israel und Juda," in *Houses Full of All Good Things* (ed. J. Pakkala and M. Nissinen; Publications of the Finnish Exegetical Society 95; Helsinki: Finnish Exegetical Society; and Göttingen: Vandenhoeck & Ruprecht, 2008), 129–68, esp. 160.

With regard to the nature of the offences, the difference between Judges and Kings is not as great as has been maintained. In the books of Kings, too, the earliest Deuteronomistic redaction already reports the introduction of foreign cults; i.e., the worship of Baal (1 Kgs 16:31–32; 22:53; 2 Kgs 8:18, 27; 10:28), and of "the host of heaven" (2 Kgs 21:3bβγ).[28] On the other hand, in the book of Judges the sin is only occasionally described more precisely as an infringement of Yhwh's claim to sole allegiance (Judg 2:11; 10:6).[29] In most cases sin remains undefined (Judg 3:12; 4:1; 6:1; 13:1) and is only judged according to its consequence, the historical disaster.

(b) If the Deuteronomistic History had begun with 1 Sam 1, the caesura between the books of Judges and Samuel would mark not a secondary division but a secondary amalgamation. In that case it would be surprising that the fusion should have been made by way of a simple parataxis, for—in just the same way as in 1 Kgs 1, but in marked contrast to Deut 1–3, and also in distinction from Exod 1 and Judg 1—a recapitulation of what must have gone before is missing. "In the whole sequence of the historical books, 1 Sam 1:1 offers for the first time after Gen 1:1 a completely independent beginning to the narrative."[30] This abrupt beginning is one reason for the theory that the work of the Deuteronomist originally began in 1 Sam 1. But that is to judge by appearances, since of course the stories about Samuel and Saul belong within the whole sequence of the Israelite history. From this standpoint the book of Samuel lacks an exposition. The fact that the context is not recapitulated therefore actually speaks against 1 Sam 1 being a new beginning, and in favor of a secondary literary cut.

On the other hand the book of Judges presses emphatically forward to the introduction of the monarchy: "In those days there was no king in Israel; every man did what was right in his own eyes" (*'îš hayyāšār bĕ'ênāyw ya'áśeh*) (Judg 17:6; RSV)—that is to say, not in the eyes of Yhwh. The thrust of this judgment, which touches closely on the usual Deuteronomistic judgment about godliness, is that the king is needed to put in order the Israelites' relationship to God. Interpreted in this light, the narrative relating the establishment of the sanctuary in Dan in Judg 17–18 provides a reason for the demand for a

---

28. These notes were later given a comprehensive expansion. The kings were accused in lavish detail of violating the First Commandment, see Levin, "Die Frömmigkeit der Könige von Israel und Juda," 138–51. Kratz, on the other hand, believes that all the mentions of apostasy are later additions (*The Composition of the Narrative Books*, 162), including 1 Kgs 16:31; 2 Kgs 10:28; 21:3. He provides no literary-critical reasons for his view (see pp. 165, 166, 169).

29. Texts such as Judg 2:1–5; 2:12–3:7; 6:7–10, 25–32; 8:24–27, 33–35; 10:6*, 10b–16 were added only later.

30. Schmid, *Erzväter und Exodus*, 31.

king.[31] The prelude to the introduction of the monarchy, which the redaction has constructed in 1 Sam 8, links up explicitly with the era of the Judges.[32] "If we disregard the secondary division of the books, we have to extend the Deuteronomistic era of the Judges to the emergence of the monarchy (1 Sam 8–12)."[33]

(c) That the books originally formed a literary unit is even more evident on the level of the preredactional sources than on the level of the redaction:

Judg 13–16 [The *wayĕhî 'îš* collection (1): The Samson narratives]
Judg 17–18 [The *wayĕhî 'îš* collection (2): The founding of the sanctuary at Dan]
Judg 19 [The story about the Levite's concubine]
Judg 20 [Benjamin and Israel at war]
Judg 21 [Wives for the Benjaminites]

1 Sam 1–3 [The *wayĕhî 'îš* collection (3): The Samuel narratives] ...
1 Sam 9:1–10:16 [The *wayĕhî 'îš* collection (4): The Saul narratives]

The stories about Samson (Judg 13–16), about the setting up of the sanctuary in Dan (Judg 17–18), about the childhood of Samuel (1 Sam 1–3), and about Saul (1 Sam 9–14) all start off in a very similar way: *wayĕhî 'îš ('eḥad) min ... ûšĕmô ...* "There was a (certain) man of ... whose name was ..." (Judg 13:2; 17:1; 1 Sam 1:1; 9:1). In the Old Testament this narrative beginning is confined—apart from the two secondary examples Judg 19:1b und Job 1:1—to these four narrative complexes.[34] Since in addition these follow immediately upon one another, it is virtually certain that they belonged to a common preredactional compilation. That would also explain why some of the material does not fit in with the intention of the whole as we have it today; for example, the stylization of Samson the hero as deliverer. "It is easier to understand how a story like that of Samson should have been included in the Deuteronomic Book of Judges, if the author found it in the earlier work on which he based his own, than to imagine that he introduced it for himself from some other source."[35]

31. See Timo Veijola, *Das Königtum in der Beurteilung der deuteronomistischen Historiographie* (AASF 198; Helsinki: Suomalainen Tiedeakatemia, 1977).
32. See Veijola, *Das Königtum*, 68.
33. Veijola, *Das Königtum*, 28.
34. The beginning of the Job narrative joins together the same building blocks but in a different style: *'îš hāyâ bĕ ... ... šĕmô* "There was once a man in ... whose name was ...." The beginning of the narrative in Judg 19:1b imitates 17:1: *wayĕhî 'îš ... bĕ* "There was a man ... in ...." Here, too, the differences predominate.
35. Moore, *A Critical and Exegetical Commentary on Judges*, xx. Noth, *The Deuteronomistic History*, 52, on the other hand considers "the possibility that the Samson

Traces of the compiler are still evident: Samson's birth (Judg 13) has been put in front of the earlier Samson traditions,[36] just as the promise of Samuel's birth (1 Sam 1) has been made to precede the birth of Samuel, and the story about Saul and the asses (1 Sam 9:1–10:16) has been placed before the stories about Saul's kingdom (which begin with 1 Sam 11). Everything suggests that this compilation was incorporated by the redaction into a single undivided work. If today it is distributed between the books of Judges and Samuel, this shows that the books were separated at a secondary stage.

(d) In this case, too, the division of the books has made it possible to add an appendix to the separate book of Judges. Again this appendix has grown to a considerable size. The story about the establishment of the sanctuary in Dan (Judg 17–18) was probably not yet part of the expansion. It is not just that the beginning of the story shows that it is part of the earlier compilation itself; in addition, the story is fitted into the conception of the Deuteronomistic redaction by way of the note 17:6 (= 18:1a) stating that at that time Israel lacked a king and that consequently everyone did whatever pleased himself (and not YHWH).

The chapters of Judg 19–21 are different. The narratives about the shameful act at Gibeah, about the fight of the Israelites against Benjamin, and about the rape of the women for the benefit of the Benjaminites are strongly dependent on other biblical traditions, which they modify in midrashic style.[37] The concept of the people of God, which is premised here, belongs to the latest phase of Old Testament literary history. The foundation itself is already close to Chronicles, as Wellhausen rightly pointed out. As Walter Groß remarks, "It is a late postexilic testimony of scribal work."[38] The three chapters, containing 103 Masoretic verses in all, were added only after the books had been separated; and in addition, these chapters themselves evidently developed in several stages.

---

stories were not added to Dtr.'s account until later." Noth was followed by Hartmut Gese, "Die ältere Simsonüberlieferung (Richter c. 14–15)," *ZTK* 82 (1985): 261–80, esp. 261–62; Markus Witte, "Wie Simson in den Kanon kam—Redaktionsgeschichtliche Beobachtungen zu Jdc 13–16," *ZAW* 112 (2000): 526–49; and others. However, the additions of the Deuteronomistic editor in Judg 13:1, 5b; 15:20; 16:31 irrefutably show that the Samson cycle was part of the Deuteronomistic History right from the beginning.

36. See also Judg 6:11–24 as a prologue to the Gideon narratives. The original narratives began in 6:33.

37. See Wellhausen, *Die Composition des Hexateuchs*, 229–33. Burney, *The Book of Judges*, 444–45, demonstrates in detail the dependence on Gen 19 and 1 Sam 11.

38. Walter Groß, *Richter* (HTKAT; Freiburg: Herder, 2009), 879. See also Uwe Becker, *Richterzeit und Königtum* (BZAW 192; Berlin: de Gruyter, 1990), 257–99.

Joshua and Judges

The fact that the books of Joshua and Judges were once joined is shown by the double account of Joshua's death. A book of Judges subsequently interposed between the books of Joshua and Samuel would certainly not have repeated this report. A. Graeme Auld rightly stresses: "It is more than likely that in the original Deuteronomist's conception his short transitional passage linking his account of Joshua to that of the Judges appeared but once."[39] When today's book begins with the words: *wayĕhî ʾaḥărê môt yĕhôšuaʿ* "After the death of Joshua," and only then goes on to recount that Joshua died, it is a crass contradiction which can only be explained by the secondary separation of the books.

The original report of Joshua's death must therefore be the one given in Judg 2:7–10; this can also be shown by details in the text.[40] The account was anticipated in Josh 24:29–31 in order to provide a conclusion for the now separate book, in the same way that the book of Deuteronomy ends with the death of Moses. The beginning of today's book of Judges follows the pattern of the book of Joshua. "The first four words of Jud. i 1, *wyhy ʾhry mwt yhwšʿ*, appear to have been modelled on the corresponding words of the book of Joshua. It is likely therefore that they at least belong to this later editorial stage of 'book' division."[41] The transition is an imitation of the transfer of leadership from Moses to Joshua.

> Josh 11:23b And the land had rest from war.
>> Josh 12 [The kings defeated by Joshua]
>>> 13:1–21:42 [The distribution of the land]
>> 21:43–45 [Another summary of the conquest, repeating 11:23b with regard to Josh 12]
>>> Josh 22 [The tribes east of the Jordan]
>>> Josh 23 [Joshua's charge to Israel]
>> 24:1–2, 15–18, 22 [At Shechem, the Israelites elect Yhwh as their God.]
> 24:28 Then Joshua sent the people away, every man to his inheritance.
>>> 29 After these things Joshua the son of Nun, the servant of Yhwh, died, being a hundred and ten years old. 30 And they buried him in his own inheritance at Timnath-serah, which is in the hill country of Ephraim, north of the mountain of Gaash. 31 And Israel served Yhwh all the days of Joshua, and all the days of the elders who outlived Joshua and had known all the work which Yhwh did for Israel. [= Close to the book of Joshua]

---

39. A. Graeme Auld, "Judges I and History: A Reconsideration," *VT* 25 (1975): 261–85, esp. 263.

40. See Auld, "Judges I and History," 264.

41. Auld, "Judges I and History," 265.

32 [The bones of Joseph=link to the end of the book of Genesis.]

Judg 1:1 After the death of Joshua the Israelites inquired of YHWH, Who shall go up first for us against the Canaanites, to fight against them? [= New book-heading]
1:2–36 [Because the narrative sequence of the chapter depends wholly on v. 1, its oldest parts are already later than the separation of the books.]

2:1 Now the angel of YHWH went up from Gilgal. ... And he said, I brought you up from Egypt, and brought you into the land that I had sworn to give to your fathers. ... 2 And you shall make no covenant with the inhabitants of this land; tear down their altars. ... 6 Then Joshua sent the people away. And the people of Israel went every man to his inheritance to take possession of the land. [V. 6 is recapitulating Josh 24:28 in order to knot the narrative thread.]

2:7 And the people served YHWH all the days of Joshua. ... 8 And Joshua the son of Nun ... died at the age of one hundred and ten years. 9 And they buried him within the bounds of his inheritance in Timnath-heres, in the hill country of Ephraim, north of the mountain of Gaash.

Once again, the join shows that the separation took place relatively early on; for the entirety of Judg 1—that is, the account of the occupation of the land by the tribe of Judah (1:1–20), the capture of Bethel (1:22–26), and the list of notes which place on record the failures to settle Canaan (1:21, 27–36)—is dependent on the book's present heading, and is inconceivable without it. The attempt to restrict the redactional join between the books to the four words *wayĕhî 'aḥărê môt yĕhôšuaʻ*, "After the death of Joshua,"[42] cannot be supported by literary-critical criteria. Why is Joshua suddenly missing, so that the Israelites are compelled to question YHWH directly? The conclusion would be that the very basis of Judg 1 is already bound up with the redactional process in which the Hexateuch and the book of Judges were separated. "It is not unlikely that this new preface is contemporaneous with the division of the long Deuteronomistic History into the now familiar separate books."[43]

In the framework of the newer Documentary Hypothesis, Judg 1 has sometimes been thought to be the account of the conquest in source J.[44] Although mistaken, this conclusion could nevertheless be based on solid

---

42. Thus most recently argued by Mareike Rake, *"Juda wird aufsteigen!" Untersuchungen zum ersten Kapitel des Richterbuches* (BZAW 367; Berlin: de Gruyter, 2006), 131–33, along with many others before (see ibid. 132 n. 420).

43. Auld, "Judges I and History," 285.

44. See esp. Eduard Meyer, "Kritik der Berichte über die Eroberung Palästinas," *ZAW* 1 (1881): 117–46; Budde, *Die Bücher Richter und Samuel, ihre Quellen und ihr Aufbau*, 1–89.

observation, since Judg 1 is related to the non-Priestly sections of the book of Genesis. There, too, the land is presented as populated by the Canaanites,[45] there too the precedence of Judah is stressed,[46] and it is in Gen 50:8 that the term "the house of Joseph" (Judg 1:22, 23, 35) originates.

Prior to the division of the books, the "compositional nexus" was Judg 2:1–5, which was subsequently inserted between the account of the conquest and the death of Joshua, as can be detected from the resumptive repetition of Josh 24:28 in Judg 2:6. "The Mal'ak episode has demonstrably not been constituted as the end and theological interpretation of Judg 1."[47] The literary horizon of the scene in Bochim belongs to another level. It is intended to link the Tetrateuch's historical account with the Deuteronomistic History. In Judg 2:1, the angel, who is none other than the angel of Exod 3:2, points to the promise in Exod 3:17, which he quotes word-for-word,[48] in order to establish that it has been fulfilled through the conquest described in Josh 2–11. This reminder is followed in v. 2a by the admonition not to enter into any alliance with the people of the country, indeed to destroy their cultic places. The Israelites are to cut themselves off completely from the other inhabitants of the country.[49] This is in sharp contrast to the original form of the Deuteronomistic History, for which all the inhabitants of the country are understood to be Israelites. And as in the Deuteronomistic History (and in sharp contrast to the Yahwist's History, see Gen 12:7–8; 13:18; 28:10–19), the Israelites are to destroy the many altars in the country, in order to obey the command for the centralization of the cult according to Deut 12. Thus Judg 2:1–6 constitutes a compromise full of tension, the aim of which is to balance the theological programs of the two histories.

In addition, in the case of the books of Joshua and Judges, the division has made it possible to expand the last part of the previous scroll considerably—that is to say, the part which later became the book of Joshua. Only a very minimal part of this account is the work of the Deuteronomistic editor. He notes the end of the occupation in Josh 11:23b: "And the land had rest from war." "Dtr. has already (Jos. 11:23a^b) mentioned the distribution of the conquered area among the tribes—briefly, to be sure, but in terms suggesting

---

45. Gen 12:6; 13:7; 24:3, 37; 34:30; 50:11.

46. Gen 37:26–27; 38:27–30; 43:3–5, 8–10; 44:14–34; 46:28.

47. Erhard Blum, "Der kompositionelle Knoten am Übergang von Josua zu Richter: Ein Entflechtungsvorschlag," in *Deuteronomy and Deuteronomic Literature* (ed. M. Vervenne and J. Lust; BETL 133; Leuven: Peeters, 1997), 181–212, esp. 182.

48. This explains the imperfect 'a'āleh, which in fact must be read as a preterite (LXX: ἀνεβίβασα).

49. This is possibly the first occurrence of the commandment not to join into a covenant with the inhabitants of the country. The other instances, Deut 7:1–6; Exod 34:12–15, and Exod 23:23–33, may depend on this.

that he has finished with the topic."[50] After that Joshua dismisses the people to their homes: "And Joshua sent the people away, every man to his inheritance" (24:28). Then he dies (Judg 2:7–10).

Some of the expansions still presuppose that the books formed a single unit. The list of the defeated kings in Josh 12 is an expansion of 11:23. It is linked with the summary in 21:43–45, which substantially repeats and emphasizes 11:23. This was probably followed by the assembly in Josh 24, at which Joshua binds the people to YHWH as its God.[51] Later on, Joshua's testament in Josh 23 was interpolated, and in this Joshua makes the fulfillment established in 21:43–45 the occasion for a warning to the people before he dies. The model was the aged Abraham, cf. Gen 24:1. Once again, the literary horizon also includes the book of Genesis.

It was only after the books had been separated that the report of the distribution of the land in Josh 13:1–21:42 and ch. 22 was interpolated. In order to fit it into the course of events, the augmenter anticipated and repeated in 13:1 the scene of 23:1.[52] The ten chapters contain a number of passages that are parallel to the report of the conquest in Judg 1. Mareike Rake has shown (contrary to Graeme Auld and others) that for the most part Judg 1 was the source text for the Joshua parallels, not vice versa.[53] Since, as we saw above, Judg 1 came into being in connection with the separation of the books, or as a consequence of the separation, we must deduce that Josh 13–22* was added only after the books had been divided. The expansion as a whole comprises 303 Masoretic verses, exactly the same length as the first twelve chapters of the book. That means that, apart from the last two chapters, half of today's book came into being after the separation. Once again we see that it was the separation into independent books that provided the precondition for the later growth of the text.

DEUTERONOMY AND JOSHUA

Since Joshua's assumption of office is closely related to the death of Moses (Josh 1:1–2, 5b), and is also prepared for in Num 27:12–23 and Deut 31:1–8, in this case, too, the separation of the books is unquestionably secondary. "At

---

50. Noth, *The Deuteronomistic History*, 40.

51. For the earliest form of this chapter, see Reinhard Müller, *Königtum und Gottesherrschaft* (FAT 2/3; Tübingen: Mohr Siebeck, 2004), 215–31, esp. 224. See also Uwe Becker, "Endredaktionelle Kontextvernetzungen des Josua-Buches," in Witte et al., *Die deuteronomistischen Geschichtswerke*, 139–61.

52. See Noth, *The Deuteronomistic History*, 40–41.

53. See the detailed discussion by Rake, *"Juda wird aufsteigen!"* 34–60.

any rate, Josh 1 is certainly not the beginning."[54] It is even doubtful whether the separation ever took the form of a specific act. To continue with a new scroll after the death of Moses could at some point have taken place simply as a matter of course, since for the later picture of the history, the beginning of Joshua's official leadership clearly meant the start of a new epoch.

> Deut 34:5* And Moses died there, 6* and was buried. [= End of the Yahwist's History]
>> 9 And Joshua the son of Nun was full of the spirit of wisdom, for Moses had laid his hands upon him; so the Israelites obeyed him, and did as YHWH had commanded Moses. [= Link to the separate book of Joshua]
>>> 10 And there has not arisen a prophet since in Israel like Moses, whom YHWH knew face to face, 11 none like him for all the signs and the wonders which YHWH sent him to do in the land of Egypt, to Pharaoh and to all his servants and to all his land, 12 and for all the mighty power and all the great and terrible deeds which Moses wrought in the sight of all Israel. [= Close to the Torah, added later]

> Josh 1:1 After the death of Moses YHWH said to Joshua the son of Nun, Moses' minister, 2 Moses my servant is dead; now therefore arise, go over the Jordan, you and all the people, into the land which I am giving to them.
>> 3 Every place that the sole of your foot will tread upon I have given to you, as I promised to Moses. [= Refers to the promises of the land in Deuteronomy in order to link the separated books]
> 5b As I was with Moses, so I will be with you; I will not fail you or forsake you. ... 2:1 And Joshua the son of Nun sent two men secretly from Shittim as spies, saying, Go, view the land. [Here the narrative thread of Num 20:1aβb; 25:1a; Deut 34:5*–6* is picked up. This may be the narrative link of the Yahwist's and the Deuteronomist's Histories.]

As casually as this caesura may have come about, its consequence is far-reaching—even if this consequence made itself felt only at a much later time. It was thus that "the Book of the Torah of Moses" (*sēper tôrat mōšeh*, Josh 8:31; 23:6; 2 Kgs 14:6; Neh 8:1) came into being as an independent, outstanding part of the canon.[55] The consequences appear most clearly in the history of the textual transmission. In the books of Genesis to Deuteronomy the text has, largely speaking, been transmitted without great deviations; from Josh 1 onwards, on the other hand, the Hebrew text at once begins to show a consid-

---

54. Noth, *The Deuteronomistic History*, 12.

55. See esp. Erhard Blum, "Pentateuch–Hexateuch–Enneateuch? Oder: Woran erkennt man ein literarisches Werk in der Hebräischen Bibel?" in Römer and Schmid, *Les dernières rédactions du Pentateuque, de l'Hexateuque et de L'Ennéateuque*, 67–97, esp. 71–72.

erable amount of additional material compared with the Greek. The writer's attitude has changed: outside the Torah, concern for a topical thrust has been given rather more scope, over against the desire to conserve,[56] because the religious dignity of the text was less.

The join between the books was bridged at a later point by the addition of Deut 34:9, a reference to Joshua as Moses' successor, following the latter's death. The praise of Moses as *the* wholly incomparable prophet, which ends the Torah in vv. 10–12, is the addition of a later hand and already presupposes the existence of the Pentateuch. On the other side of the join, by quoting Deut 11:24, Josh 1:3–4 establishes a link with Deuteronomy's promises of the land.

In the case of Deuteronomy, too, the possibility emerged of expanding the now separated scroll. But of course, the report of Moses' death still had to end the book, so that later additions have to be looked for in the previous chapters. What come into question as expansions of this kind are passages that reflect a "pentateuchal" perspective. One such passage is in all probability Moses' blessing in Deut 33, "which is not related to anything that comes before or after it."[57] The Song of Moses in 32:1–43 may likewise have been added, including its frame in 31:27b–30; 32:44–45, and the later introduction in 31:16–22.[58]

Genesis and Exodus

To turn now to the beginning of the Enneateuch: The books of Genesis and Exodus were also separated at a later point. It is true that with the Joseph story in Gen 37; 39–45, and the stories about Moses in Exod 2–4, two independent complexes have undoubtedly met each other. But these preredactional compositions had already been redactionally linked at the time when the books were separated. The link even existed at several levels: on the one hand at the level of the Priestly Code (which today is widely accepted as being a continuous source and which spans at least the books of Genesis and Exodus); and before that at the level of the Yahwist's History, which in the framework of its historical conception brought the story of Joseph and the Moses story into a narrative sequence for the first time. This means that the separation of the books was also preceded by the redactional linking of these

---

56. For this antagonism, which guides the textual transmission, see the famous statement of Martin Noth, *Die Welt des Alten Testaments* (4th ed.; Berlin: Töpelmann, 1962), 267.

57. Noth, *The Deuteronomistic History*, 35.

58. See also Reinhard G. Kratz, "Der literarische Ort des Deuteronomiums," in *Liebe und Gebot: Studien zum Deuteronomium* (ed. R. G. Kratz and H. Spieckermann; FRLANT 190; Göttingen: Vandenhoeck & Ruprecht, 2000), 101–20, esp. 102–3.

two historical works in the so-called "final redaction" (R) or, more precisely, the "redaction R^{JP}."

> Gen 50:1 J: Then Joseph threw himself on his father's face, and wept over him and kissed him. ... 7 And Joseph went up to bury his father, ... 10 and he observed a time of mourning for his father for seven days. ...[59] 14 And Joseph returned to Egypt ... after he had buried his father. ... 22b P: And Joseph lived for one hundred and ten years. ...
>
> > 25 So Joseph made the Israelites swear, saying, When God comes to you, you shall carry up my bones from here. [= link to Josh 24:32]
>
> 26 J: Then Joseph died, R^{JP}: being one hundred and ten years old.
> > He was embalmed and placed in a coffin in Egypt. [= link to Josh 24:32]
>
> Exod 1:1 These are the names of the sons of Israel who came to Egypt with Jacob, each with his household: 2 Reuben, Simeon, Levi, and Judah, 3 Issachar, Zebulun, and Benjamin, 4 Dan and Naphtali, Gad and Asher. 5 The total number of people born to Jacob was seventy. Joseph was already in Egypt. 6 Then Joseph died, and all his brothers, and that whole generation. 7 But the Israelites were fruitful and prolific; they multiplied and grew exceedingly strong; so that the land was filled with them. [= New book heading and link to the previous history, quoting from Gen 35:22-26; 46:26-27; 47:27; 50:22a, 26a]
> 8 J: Now a new king arose over Egypt, who did not know Joseph. 9 He said to his people, Look, the Israelite people are more numerous and more powerful than we. 10 Come, let us deal shrewdly with them, or they will increase. ... 11 Therefore they set taskmasters over them to oppress them with forced labor. ... 12 But the more they were oppressed, the more they multiplied and spread, so that [the Egyptians] came to dread the Israelites. 13 P: The Egyptians became ruthless in imposing tasks on Israelites, 14 and made their lives bitter with hard service in mortar and brick and in every kind of field labor. They were ruthless in all the tasks that they imposed on them.

In the Yahwist's history, the Joseph story, which originally ended with the message to Jacob that "Joseph is still alive" (Gen 45:26aα), is continued by way of Joseph's reencounter with his father (46:29–30) and Jacob's move to Egypt (47:1a, 5a, 6a, 11*); the aim of the continuation is to link the patriarchal narratives with the exodus story. One presupposition, without which the

---

59. The report about the burial in Gen 50:12–13 is generally assigned to P. But it has meanwhile emerged that this report already presupposes the combination of J and P. See Christoph Levin, "Abraham erwirbt seine Grablege (Genesis 23)," in *"Gerechtigkeit und Recht zu üben" (Gen 18, 19)* (ed. R. Achenbach and M. Arneth; BZABR 13; Wiesbaden: Harrassowitz, 2009), 96–113, esp. 107.

combination of the material would not have been possible, is that after his death Jacob was brought back to the land of the promise in order to be buried there (47:29a, bβ, 30b–31a). Once Joseph has sworn to ensure this, Jacob dies (47:31b): "Then Joseph fell on his father's face, and wept over him, and kissed him. And Joseph went up to bury his father, and he made a mourning for his father seven days. And Joseph returned to Egypt after he had buried his father. Then Joseph died. Now there arose a new king over Egypt, who did not know Joseph" (Gen 50:1, 7a, 10b, 14aα*, b, 26aα; Exod 1:8). This sequence is certainly redactional but constitutes a self-contained order of events.

On the level of the Priestly Code, a continuous thread begins only with Exod 1:13–14. It continues unaltered in Exod 2:23aβb–25; 6:2–7:13. In Gen 50, on the other hand, the combining redaction R[JP] has taken over only Jacob's age (110 years) from the Priestly Code (Gen 50:22b P), attaching it to the Yahwist's account with the help of 50:26aβ R[JP]. We can see this procedure at work in other passages, too.[60] Thus, no more than remnants of the Priestly Code's stories about the patriarchs have remained[61]—although this does not mean that we should have to conclude that the source P never existed.

The severance between the books was made after the account of the death of Joseph. This caesura corresponds to that of the books of Deuteronomy and Joshua, which conclude with the death of Moses or Joshua, respectively; at this point, too, the division leads to a structuring of the epochs, which makes good sense. Later, the motif of Joseph's bones, Gen 50:25, 26b, also establishes a link with the end of the conquest in Josh 24:32, which draws a frame around the Hexateuch.

In order to heal the split between Genesis and Exodus, a new beginning was put in front of the book of Exodus. This recapitulates the events in the book of Genesis in so far as these are essential for an understanding of the now independent book. Under the heading, "These are the names of the Israelites who came to Egypt with Jacob," the list of Jacob's sons in Gen 35:22b–26 is repeated.[62] The style is reminiscent of the Priestly Code. But that is deceptive: the list is a later quotation.[63] It is immediately followed by a recollection

---

60. See Gen 16:3aβγ, 16; 21:2b, 4–5; 25:19–20, 26b; 41:46a; 47:28.

61. See esp. Rolf Rendtorff, *The Problem of the Process of Transmission in the Pentateuch* (trans. J. J. Scullion; JSOTSup 89; Sheffield: Sheffield Academic Press, 1990).

62. The frequent assertion that Exod 1:1–5 is a recapitulation of Gen 46:8–27 (e.g., Gertz, *Tradition und Redaktion in der Exoduserzählung*, 349) is clearly wrong; see Christoph Levin, "Das System der zwölf Stämme Israels," in idem, *Fortschreibungen: Gesammelte Studien zum Alten Testament* (BZAW 316; Berlin: de Gruyter, 2003), 111–23, esp. 118.

63. See Christoph Levin, *Der Jahwist* (FRLANT 157; Göttingen: Vandenhoeck & Ruprecht, 1993), 315; and see previously, Georg Fohrer, *Überlieferung und Geschichte des Exodus* (BZAW 91; Berlin: de Gruyter, 1964), 9; and others. The number given of "seventy

in v. 6 of the end of the now-detached book of Genesis: the death of Joseph (Gen 50:26aα).[64] The statement about the increase of the people in v. 7 substantially repeats Gen 47:27 and at the same time anticipates Exod 1:9b.[65] This verse is a striking mixture of the language of P and J, showing that at this time the Yahwist's history and the Priestly Code had already been combined.

Once again the separation has made it possible to expand the latter part of the previous book, this time the book of Genesis. One such expansion is clearly the list of the Israelites who have migrated to Egypt, Gen 46:8–27, which is an extended anticipation of Exod 1:1–4.[66] Jacob's blessing in Gen 49:1–28a, b*, which presupposes the system of the twelve tribes—in fact, a very late development—may also be seen as an expansion of this kind; its purpose would be to round off the book of Genesis, which as a result may be read as an independent account of the beginnings of God's people.

Exodus and Leviticus

The caesura between the books of Exodus and Leviticus comes between the account of the building of the tabernacle, on the one hand, and that of its consecration through the first sacrifices, on the other. The fact that this separation is secondary emerges unequivocally from the wilderness itinerary. The narrative, which is broken off at the end of Exod 34, is continued in Num 10:11.

> Exod 35:1–39:31 [The completion of the tabernacle, inserted after the separation of the books.]
> Exod 39:32 P Thus all the work of the tabernacle of the tent of meeting was finished; and the Israelites had done according to all that YHWH had commanded Moses; so had they done. ... 42 According to all that YHWH had commanded Moses, so the Israelites had done all the work. 43 And Moses saw all the work, and behold, they had done it; as YHWH had commanded, so had they done it. And Moses blessed them.

---

persons" (v. 5a) was added later, together with v. 1bβ. It is taken from Gen 46:26–27. The method of numbering there is slightly modified: Jacob himself is no longer included.

64. See Levin, *Jahwist*, 315, followed by Gertz, *Tradition und Redaktion in der Exoduserzählung*, 363.

65. Erhard Blum, "Die literarische Verbindung von Erzvätern und Exodus," in *Abschied vom Jahwisten: Die Komposition des Hexateuch in der jüngsten Diskussion* (ed. J. C. Gertz et al.; BZAW 315; Berlin: de Gruyter, 2002), 118–56, esp. 145–48, has clearly shown, contrary to Gertz, *Tradition und Redaktion in der Exoduserzählung*, 352-57, and Schmid, *Erzväter und Exodus*, 70–71, that Exod 1:7 does not belong to the Priestly Code.

66. See Levin, *Der Jahwist*, 305.

> 40:1-16 [anticipates Lev 8-10 in order to connect the separated books (Exod 35:1-39:31 still not present, at this stage).]
>
> 40:17 P And in the first month in the second year, on the first day of the month, the tabernacle was erected.
>
> 40:18-33 [Details of the tabernacle, as completed according to Exod 25-31]
> 40:34-38 [anticipates the wanderings in the desert, Num 9-10]
>
> Lev 1-7 [Laws of the offerings, probably inserted after the separation of the books.]
> Lev 8-10 P [The consecration of the priests. The first offering]

The text that preceded the severance between Exodus and Leviticus was the note concerning the completion, in Exod 40:17: "And in the fifth month in the second year, on the first day of the month, the tabernacle was erected." Compared with this note, the detailed listing in vv. 18-33 is already an addition. By repeated reminders, this passage looks back to the instructions given to Moses in Exod 25-31, "as YHWH has commanded Moses" (vv. 19b, 21b, 23b, 25b, 27b, 29b, 32b). It can be detected here that at this time the detailed account of the building of the tabernacle in Exod 35-39 was not yet in existence.[67]

The instruction for the consecration in 40:1-16 was also still missing. This passage is later than vv. 18-33, and is not concerned solely with the tabernacle, which is to be adorned with the furnishings that have been prepared; vv. 12-16 also anticipate the anointing of Aaron, which is reported in Leviticus 8. Martin Noth rightly suggests, "Perhaps even the division of the Pentateuch into 'books' had already taken place, so that the need arose to bring the theme of the furnishing of the sanctuary to an end of some kind at the end of the Book of Exodus."[68] Right at the end of the present book, in 40:34-38, a glance forward to the journeyings in the wilderness was added, thus establishing a narrative link with Num 9.

At the time when the books were separated, the account of the construction of the tabernacle in Exod 35-39 was undoubtedly still missing. These 176 Masoretic verses were added very late. The fluid form of the text in these chapters is striking, compared with the Samaritan Pentateuch and the Septuagint. Since Exod 40:12-16 points forward to Lev 8, in order to bracket together the books of Exodus and Leviticus, this suggests the further possibil-

---

67. It was Julio Popper, *Der biblische Bericht über die Stiftshütte* (Leipzig: Hunger, 1862), who first recognized that Exod 35-40 is secondary to Exod 25-31. The main arguments are set forth by Brevard S. Childs, *The Book of Exodus* (OTL; London: SCM Press, 1974), 533-37.

68. Martin Noth, *Exodus: A Commentary* (trans. J. S. Bowden; OTL; London: SCM Press, 1962), 283.

ity that the sacrificial laws Lev 1–7 were put at the beginning of Leviticus after this book had already become independent.

LEVITICUS AND NUMBERS

The caesura between the books of Leviticus and Numbers is evidently dependent on the Holiness Code in Lev 17–26, the end of which in Lev 26, with blessings and curses, forms a natural break.

> Lev 11–15 [Prescriptions concerning purity, some of them possibly inserted after the separation of the books]
> Lev 16 P [The Day of Atonement]
> Lev 17–26 [Holiness Code, possibly inserted after the separation of the books]
>> Lev 27 [Law concerning vows (= annexes to the separate book)]
>
>> Num 1–8 [The order of the camp. Law of the Levites, and other legal material. At least some of this material was inserted after the separation of the books.]
> Num 9–10 P+J [Resumption of the wanderings in the desert]

"The chapters Lev. xvii.–xxvi. … form a work of a peculiar character by themselves, … which harmonises but little with the Priestly Code."[69] In tradition history this law book occupies a central position between Deuteronomy, the book of Ezekiel, and the Priestly Code. Whether it was once independent or originated from the outset as a supplement to its context is debated.

It is usually assumed that it was the Priestly Code into whose literary context the Holiness Code was inserted. That can neither be proved nor disproved, the less so since it is only with difficulty that the original substance of the Priestly Code can be distinguished from either the additions introduced into it while it was still independent, or from the expansions that were added after it was redactionally linked with the other Pentateuch source.[70] But that a new scroll would have been begun after the conclusion of Lev 26 with its blessing and curse seems so obvious that we can even consider whether the separation of the books may have gone hand in hand with the interpolation of Lev 17–26. Today the final sentence Lev 26:46: "These are the statutes and ordinances and laws that YHWH established between himself and the Israelites

---

69. Julius Wellhausen, *Prolegomena to the History of Israel* (trans. J. S. Black and A. Menzies; Edinburgh: Black, 1885), 376.

70. See Martin Noth, *Leviticus: A Commentary* (trans. J. E. Anderson; OTL; Philadelphia: Westminster, 1965), 13.

on Mount Sinai through Moses," constitutes something like a summing up of the Sinaitic legislation in general.

After the separation of Leviticus from the book of Numbers, the final chapter was added as an appendix: "For the appended chapter on dedicatory gifts (ch. 27), one can only surmise that the Pentateuch's division into 'Books' was already projected and that it was simply placed as an isolated fragment at the end of a 'Book.'"[71]

NUMBERS AND DEUTERONOMY

Among all the examples that have to be examined here, the transition between the books of Numbers and Deuteronomy presents a special case. Here, unity such as that which obtains between the material of Samuel and Kings, or between the books of Judges and Samuel, is lacking. There is no earlier redactional thread, such as links Josh 24:28 with Judg 2:6, and Gen 50:26aα with Exod 1:8. There is no direct connection, as obtains between Deut 34:5–6* and Josh 1:1. And there is no bridge comparable with that between Exod 40:12–16 and Lev 8, and between Exod 40:34–38 and Num 9–10.

Instead, Deut 1–3 presents an unusually expansive recapitulation of the events that have gone before, in Num 11–32. Surprisingly, this recapitulation is not stated from the narrator's perspective but is given the form of a speech made by Moses. It assumes the style of the law book that follows in Deuteronomy.

> Num 20:1aβb J^Q And the people stayed in Kadesh; and Miriam died there, and was buried there. ...
> Num 22–24 J^{Q+R} [The Editor of the Yahwist's History inserted the story of Balaam into the itinerary of the wilderness.]
> Num 25:1b J^Q And Israel dwelt in Shittim. ...
>> Num 25–32 [Narrative and legal material inserted later]
>> Num 33–36 [Annexes after the separation of the books.]
>
> Deut 1:1a These are the words that Moses spoke to all Israel beyond the Jordan. [= Heading to insert Deuteronomy into the sequence of history]
>> Deut 1–3 [The narrative of Num 11–32 is resumed as part of Moses' speech to the people.]
>> [The Corpus of Deuteronomy]
>> Deut 31–33 [Preparations for Moses' death]
> Deut 34:5* J^Q And Moses died there, 6* and was buried. [= End of the Yahwist's History]

---

71. Noth, *Leviticus*, 14.

The heading, "These are the words that Moses spoke to all Israel beyond the Jordan," shows that the purpose is to incorporate Moses' speech, which then follows, into the sequence of historical events.[72] The style of the heading already suggests that in this case the narrative continuity has been created, not disrupted. Even in its shortest form this was never "the heading only for the legislative and parenetic core of Deuteronomy, but always already provided the link between that and the literary outline of the early history, from the journeyings through the wilderness to the conquest."[73] That linkage is the very reason why the preceding events described in Num 11–32 are recapitulated in Moses' speech. As a rule, here Deuteronomy is the receptive part.[74] That does not exclude the possibility that in terms of their details the parallels might also have been harmonized in the reverse direction.

Earlier research assumed that the pentateuchal sources continue, following Moses' address. This view was seemingly contradicted by Martin Noth's hypothesis that the Deuteronomistic History begins in Deut 1. But the earlier view remains correct, even though it has emerged that the Priestly Code has no share in Deut 34.[75] The note concerning the death of Moses in Deut 34:5*–6* may be linked with the note about Israel's sojourn in Shittim in Num 25:1a, just as Miriam's death is linked with the sojourn of the Israelites in Kadesh in Num 20:1aβb.[76] It is at just this point that the narrative about the conquest begins; in Josh 2, Joshua sends out the spies *from Shittim* to Jericho. The notes about the death of Miriam in Kadesh and the death of Moses in Shittim probably marked the end of the Yahwist's History.[77] It is possible that traces of the link between the Yahwistic and the Deuteronomistic redactions might be found in Deut 34 and Josh 2. Of course the precise way in which these two threads are interwoven requires further investigation, and it may

---

72. Lothar Perlitt, *Deuteronomium* (BKAT 5.1; Neukirchen-Vluyn: Neukirchener, 1990), 4.

73. Perlitt, *Deuteronomium*, 6.

74. See Perlitt, *Deuteronomium*, 38; Timo Veijola, *Das fünfte Buch Mose: Deuteronomium Kapitel 1,1–16,17* (ATD 8.1; Göttingen: Vandenhoeck & Ruprecht, 2004), 16; Gertz, "Kompositorische Funktion und literarhistorischer Ort von Dtn 1–3," 112.

75. Cf. Lothar Perlitt, "Priesterschrift im Deuteronomium?" *ZAW* 100 (1988) Supplement: 65–88, esp. 76–86.

76. Kratz, "Der literarische Ort des Deuteronomiums," 119 n. 73.

77. Wellhausen, *Die Composition des Hexateuchs*, 116: "It is worth mentioning that J suddenly breaks off after Balaam's blessing. It is only in Num 25:1–5 and Deut 34 that we might perhaps claim to find some traces of this marvellous narrative book." Similarly Levin, *Der Jahwist*, 50; idem, "The Yahwist: The Earliest Editor in the Pentateuch," *JBL* 126 (2007): 209–30, esp. 217.

never be possible to clarify this process completely.[78] About the fact of the link there can be no doubt.

If it is correct that the thread of the history runs in some way or other from Num 25 to the book of Joshua by way of Deut 34, then the Deuteronomic law can only have been inserted into the course of the historical events at a later point. The Deuteronomistic History did not begin with the book of Deuteronomy. That may also be assumed for an external reason: for if the Deuteronomistic History had included the Deuteronomic law from the very beginning, it would have been too extensive for a single scroll. Noth's hypothesis—in this respect—requires correction, and the earlier Hexateuch hypotheses are—in this respect—right. That does not mean, however, that we should carry the pentateuchal sources forward into the historical books, as was usual before Noth, any more than it means that we should dispute the existence of the Deuteronomistic History.

The historicization of the Deuteronomic law, which is the outcome of its incorporation into the sequence of historical events, is undoubtedly secondary; and with it the Moses fiction, too.[79] If the centralization of the cult was the occasion for the creation of the Deuteronomic law, which all the evidence suggests, then it is in the wrong place in the present form of the account: in the land of Moab before the conquest and long before the building of the Temple. In the light of its original intention, the Deuteronomic law for its part is unsuited as a program for life in the promised land.[80]

On the other hand the historicization must already have taken place early on, for it is presupposed by commandments such as Deut 17:14–20; 18:9–22; 19:8–10, 14; and 26:1–15. For later tradition, the fact that the Deuteronomic law was not proclaimed on Sinai like all other laws presented a great difficulty (see Deut 5:3; 28:69); but the account could no longer be moved. As an expedient, the Decalogue of Exod 20:2–17 was therefore repeated later in Deut 5:6–21, in order to demonstrate the identity between the Deuteronomic law and the law given on Sinai.[81] In this way, the Deuteronomic law like the Sinaitic one is presented as an interpretation of the Decalogue.

In view of these considerations, the case of Deut 1–3 presents the paradoxical possibility that the books of Numbers and Deuteronomy were

---

78. Blum, "Pentateuch–Hexateuch–Enneateuch?" 80–82, points out, over against Kratz, that the connection between Num 25:1a and Josh 2:1 is neither smooth nor without an alternative.

79. The suggestion that Deuteronomy was created for its context (Kratz, *The Composition of the Narrative Books*, 123–24) can be ruled out.

80. See Christoph Levin, *Die Verheißung des neuen Bundes* (FRLANT 137; Göttingen: Vandenhoeck & Ruprecht, 1985), 85–87.

81. See Levin, *Die Verheißung des neuen Bundes*, 97.

separated *in order* to be linked together. The purpose of the book's new beginning was to fit the Deuteronomic law into the sequence of historical events. The beginning of the book of Deuteronomy is in fact both independent and nonindependent. When, in the debate about Deut 1–3, these two possibilities are supposed to be mutually incompatible, an alternative is maintained which is no alternative at all. Since the Deuteronomic law was fitted into the historical framework early on, however, we have to reckon with the possibility that the historical narrative that follows the original heading of Deut 1:1 was later expanded considerably.

Again, the preceding book has received extensive additions. The latest additions to the Torah found a home in the book of Numbers rather than in Deuteronomy, as the final sentence in Num 36:13 shows: "These are the commandments and the ordinances which Yнwн commanded by Moses to the Israelites in the plains of Moab by the Jordan at Jericho." This notice locates the proclamation of the subsequently added commandments at the same place as the proclamation of Deuteronomy. How much was added between Num 25:1b and 36:13 before the books were separated, we neither can nor must decide. All that is unequivocally clear is that Num 33–36 no longer found an echo in Deut 1–3.

Conclusions

1. The fact that the Enneateuch was distributed between nine individual books was due to the technical requirements of the scrolls; the process of division was at the same time the precondition for further gradual literary growth.

2. The individual books cannot have preceded this growth, nor can the distribution of the material have taken place in one or several acts after the growth was complete. The idea that the text of the Enneateuch was at the end divided proportionately between different scrolls is as wrong as the suggestion that the material was distributed between different scrolls from the outset.[82] "The usual division of this historical complex into 'books' … was undoubtedly a secondary process in the history of the tradition."[83]

3. The narrative coherence of the material is based on the coherence of the first redactions. Therefore, the original form of the text, which the first redactions produced, must have been very much shorter than what we have today. There must have been room for these initial versions on a single scroll.

4. The obviously secondary character of the separation of the books is incompatible with all kinds of hypotheses maintained among exegetes, concerning preliminary stages of the Enneateuch. At no time was there an

---

82. Contrary to Haran, "Book-Size and the Device of Catch-Lines in the Biblical Canon."

83. Noth, *The Deuteronomistic History*, 4.

original Hexateuch from Genesis to Joshua; or a work comprising the books of Exodus to Joshua; or a narrative about the conquest consisting of Deuteronomy and Joshua; or a Deuteronomistic History composed only of the books of Samuel and Kings.

5. At the same time, the possibility that the Enneateuch goes back to a foundational single work is excluded, since the first two redactions, the Yahwist in Genesis to Numbers (+ Deuteronomy) and the Deuteronomist in (Deuteronomy +) Joshua to Kings, diametrically contradict each other in their attitudes to the place of the cult. For the Deuteronomistic redaction, the central sanctuary in Jerusalem is the principal norm. Its aim is the reinstatement of the Davidic dynasty in order that it should restore the temple. The Yahwist redaction, on the other hand, upholds the concerns of Diaspora Judaism, and proclaims the omnipresence of the God YHWH, so that his worship might be made possible worldwide. The occasionally expressed opinion that the Yahwist "approximates to the Deuteronomic-Deuteronomistic form of tradition and to its literary work,"[84] or even that it builds on the Deuteronomist,[85] is out of the question. There must therefore be a "compositional nexus" in today's total work, a point at which the two first redactions are bound together.[86] If it is correct that the death of Moses still belongs to the Yahwist's History, this nexus must for preference be looked for in proximity to that event. This does not rule out the possibility that the end of the Yahwist's History (which had probably even then been united with the Priestly Code) and the beginning of the Deuteronomistic History had been intertwined.

6. The Tetrateuch, for its part, rests on the linking of two redactional works, the Yahwist's History and the Priestly Code. In the context of the growth of the text as a whole, these must have been linked very early on, and space must originally have been found for both of them on one and the same scroll.[87] Recent literary-critical investigations have shown that the bulk of the text was added *after* the two Pentateuch sources had been amalgamated.[88]

7. The eight caesuras between the nine books differ very considerably from one another. The transitions between the books of Exodus and Leviticus,

---

84. Hans Heinrich Schmid, *Der sogenannte Jahwist: Beobachtungen und Fragen zur Pentateuchforschung* (Zurich: Theologischer Verlag, 1976), 167.

85. Martin Rose, *Jahwist und Deuteronomist: Untersuchungen zu den Berührungspunkten beider Literaturwerke* (ATANT 67; Zurich: Theologischer Verlag, 1981).

86. This is the grain of truth in Blum's interpretation of Judg 2:1–5; see his "Der kompositionelle Knoten am Übergang von Josua zu Richter."

87. The thesis, recently renewed by Raik Heckl, *Moses Vermächtnis: Kohärenz, literarische Intention und Funktion von Dtn 1–3* (Arbeiten zur Bibel und ihrer Geschichte 9; Leipzig: Evangelische Verlagsanstalt, 2004), that Deut 1–3 did not yet presuppose the Priestly Code, greatly overestimates the age of the *Vorlage* in Num 11–32.

88. See *pars pro toto* Christoph Levin, "Die Redaktion R^{IP} in der Urgeschichte," in Beck und Schorn, *Auf dem Weg zur Endgestalt von Genesis bis II Regum*, 15–34, esp. 18–23.

and between Leviticus and Numbers, are made almost casually. These books have no individually constituted beginnings. The same is true of the books of Samuel and Kings. The caesuras between the books of Genesis and Exodus and between Joshua and Judges are different. The books of Exodus and Judges were in each case given a new beginning, and the book of Joshua a new ending.[89] The transition between Deuteronomy and the book of Joshua following the death of Moses marks a clear caesura, but not necessarily a deliberately constructed commencement for a new book. The expansive beginning of the book of Deuteronomy should probably be viewed as an exception.

8. In the case of each of the caesuras, the preceding scroll has been expanded by addenda after the separation. These expansions are most extensive in the book of Joshua (chs. 13–22). But they are extremely pronounced in the books of Exodus (chs. 35–39; 40*), Numbers (chs. 33–36), Judges (chs. 19–21), and Samuel (chs. 21–24), as well. These expansions show that in the growth process seen as a whole, the books were separated relatively early on.

9. Since the separation of the books is at once the *result* of the literary growth and the *condition* which made the literary growth possible, the books have been separated successively. The question about the sequence in which the caesuras were made is a necessary question but one difficult to answer. It would seem that Genesis and Exodus were divided quite early, since the book of Genesis presents itself as a clearly defined entity, and was from early on relatively extensive. Joshua and Judges also seem to have been separated quite early; for the cross-connections between Joshua 24 and Genesis 50 show that a Hexateuch as point of reference had already existed for some time. The separation of Leviticus and Numbers could be earlier than the separation of Exodus and Leviticus.

10. Since the separation of the books was primarily undertaken for technical reasons, we have to consider the paradoxical possibility that books were separated in order that the material could be combined. For, if large amounts of material were to be joined, this was only possible if that material was distributed over several scrolls, which had then for their part to be linked in terms of content. This may have been the case with the Holiness Code in Lev 17–26: its interpolation may have led to the separation of the books of Leviticus and Numbers. The other such instance is the interpolation of the Deuteronomic law, which must also in some way or other have gone hand in hand with the linking of the Tetrateuch to the Deuteronomistic History. The question of whether Deut 1–3 marks an independent beginning or a secondary bridge is perhaps a false alternative: the beginning of this book may have functioned as both at the same time.

---

89. Erhard Blum, *Studien zur Komposition des Pentateuch* (BZAW 189; Berlin: de Gruyter, 1990), 363, notes the comparability of the two book transitions.

FROM EDEN TO BABYLON:
READING GENESIS 2–4 AS A PARADIGMATIC NARRATIVE*

Cynthia Edenburg

While working on this paper, I have felt like the eponymous hero of Jorge Luis Borges' tale, "Pierre Menard, Author of the *Quixote*," who sought to recreate Cervantes' work, word-for-word. But while Menard deliberately thought to reproduce someone else's work, I had the vanity to think that my initial independent observation was new; namely, that the basic scheme, sin and exile, is already introduced in the Eden and Cain stories, and thereby presents a coherent thematic framework for the entire narrative from Genesis to the end of Kings. *Zeitgeist*, or the spirit of the times, had prepared me to conceive what was for me, at least, previously inconceivable—that the so-called "Yahwistic" stories in Gen 2–4 enter into dialogue with the conclusion to the DtrH. Although it quickly became clear that others had already explored this intellectual territory, the new currents in research of the non-Priestly materials in the Pentateuch present good cause for reexamining the purpose and literary history of Gen 2–4, in order to investigate the implications of the sin and exile theme for the compositional history of Genesis–2 Kings as a whole. In the following, I shall examine the relationship between the Eden and Cain stories; their place within the Primeval History; their referent; and their function within differing literary contexts. Since the Eden story in Gen 2:4b–3:24 has received exhaustive treatment by others, I shall focus most of my comments on the story of Cain.

Classical source criticism attributes the formation of the Primeval History in Gen 1–11 to a single author, the Yahwist (J), who compiled his composition from traditional materials. J's Primeval History was but the opening to his more extensive narrative, which continued through the patriarchs, the

---

* This essay was prepared during a research leave supported by the Research Fund of The Open University of Israel.

exodus, and the desert wanderings, thus providing the narrative backbone for what subsequently became Genesis, Exodus and Numbers.[1] As long as J was thought to represent a preexilic source from sometime between the tenth and mid-eighth centuries B.C.E.,[2] it remained inconceivable that the Primeval History might somehow anticipate the end of the monarchy, the destruction of the temple, and the exile from the land. With the rise of form criticism, the interest in the complete stories was diverted to the supposedly independent units comprising the narratives, particularly when literary criticism could help demonstrate the complex origin of the final composition. Thus, Gunkel and others focused on the etiological aim of the separate strands they isolated in the Eden narrative—a creation story and an account of how the hardships inherent in human existence had originated—while the Cain story was broken down into a simple ethnic etiology for the nomadic Kenites, which was later theologized by the addition of the dialogues between YHWH and Cain.[3]

However, the tendency of source and redaction criticism to explain the few discrepancies in the stories as deriving from combining sources or from editorial manipulation of an early narrative, makes us forget that both the Eden narrative and the story of Cain can be read with no significant difficulty as coherent narratives (and have been so read for centuries);[4] in contrast, for

---

1. See Gerhard von Rad, "The Form-Critical Problem of the Hexateuch," in idem, *From Genesis to Chronicles: Explorations in Old Testament Theology* (ed. K. C. Hanson; Minneapolis: Augsburg Fortress, 2005), 40–48.

2. See, e.g., von Rad, "Problem," 53–54; Otto Eissfeldt, The Old Testament: An Introduction (trans. P. R. Ackroyd; New York: Harper & Row, 1965), 200; Walter Brueggemann, "David and His Theologian," CBQ 30 (1968): 156–81.

3. See, e.g., Hermann Gunkel, *Genesis* (trans. M. E. Biddle; Macon: Mercer University Press, 1997), 2–4, 27–31, 44–49; Nicolas Wyatt, "Interpreting the Creation and Fall Story in Genesis 2–3," *ZAW* 93 (1981): 11–12; David M. Carr, "The Politics of Textual Subversion: A Diachronic Perspective on the Garden of Eden Story," *JBL* 112 (1993): 577–88; Markus Witte, *Die biblische Urgeschichte: Redaktions- und theologiegeschichtliche Beobachtungen zu Genesis 1:1–11:26* (BZAW 265; Berlin: de Gruyter, 1998), 155; cf. Claus Westermann, *Genesis 1–11: A Commentary* (trans. J. J. Scullion; Minneapolis: Augsburg, 1984), 190–97, 284–87; John Van Seters, *Prologue to History: The Yahwist as Historian in Genesis* (Louisville: Westminster John Knox, 1992), 109–19, 135–41; Reinhard G. Kratz, *The Composition of the Narrative Books of the Old Testament* (trans. J. Bowden; London: T&T Clark, 2005), 252–54.

4. See, e.g., Van Seters, *Yahwist*, 109–16, 143; Eckart Otto, "Die Paradieserzählung Genesis 2–3: Eine nachpriesterschriftliche Lehrerzählung in ihrem religionshistorischen Kontext," in *"Jedes Ding hat seine Zeit . . .": Studien zur israelitischen und altorientalischen Weisheit: Diethelm Michel zum 65. Geburtstag* (ed. A. A. Diesel et al.; BZAW 241; Berlin: de Gruyter, 1996), 173–74; Konrad Schmid, "Die Unteilbarkeit der Weisheit: Überlegungen zur sogenannten Paradieserzählung Gen 2f. und ihrer theologischen Tendenz," *ZAW* 114 (2002): 24–27; Jan Christian Gertz, "Von Adam zu Enosch: Überlegungen zur Entstehungsgeschichte von Gen 2–4," in *Gott und Mensch im Dialog: Festschrift für Otto Kaiser zum*

example, to the flood story, where contradictions necessitate compositional or source analysis. Moreover, some scribe—be he the author of the stories, or their collector, or redactor—imparted a similar structure to the Eden and Cain stories and even invoked similar language.[5] The conflict in both stories derives from a divine command or warning (Gen 2:17, cf. 3:1–5; 4:6–7) which is abrogated (3:6–7; 4:8); God in response initiates a judicial confrontation and interrogation (3:9–13; 4:9–10), but the guilty parties initially deny guilt (3:12, 13b; 4:9); God pronounces judgment (3:14–19; 4:10–12), and punishes both the man and Cain by cursing the ground (3:17–19; 4:11–12) so that the land will not yield produce (3:18; 4:12); however, despite the punishment, God demonstrates concern and care for the transgressors (3:21; 4:13–15); both stories conclude with expulsion (3:23, 24; 4:16), following which, the characters dwell east of Eden (3:24; 4:16).[6] Shared language includes:

3:16b; 4:7b: [y]-ב ימשל/ת [x]-ו דך/תשוקתו [x] אל

3:9b; 4:9a: איכה/אי

3:14; 4:11: -מ אתה ארור

3:17; 4:11: בעבורך האדמה ארור/האדמה מן אתה ארור

3:23: האדמה את לעבד [x]-מ וישלחהו ;3:24: האדם את ויגרש //

4:14: האדמה פני מעל גרש

The extent of these similarities goes beyond the vague thematic echoes found elsewhere within the Primeval History. This might indicate that these two stories were designed to be read together, notwithstanding a certain amount of tension between them.[7]

---

80. *Geburtstag* (ed. M. Witte; BZAW 345; Berlin: de Gruyter, 2004), 1:223–24, 232; Trygge N. D. Mettinger, *The Eden Narrative: A Literary and Religio-historical Study of Gen 2–3* (Winona Lake: Eisenbrauns, 2007), 13–14, 41.

5. On the concept of author, see Van Seters, *Yahwist*, 4, 110–11, 143, 329; on that of collector, see Gunkel, *Genesis*, lxx–lxxiii, 49; on that of redactor, see, e.g., Witte, *Urgeschichte*, 59–60, 79–85, 151–55, who distinguishes a proto-J layer from J and post-P final redactions.

6. Cf. Westermann, *Genesis*, 285–86, 303; Alan J. Hauser, "Linguistic and Thematic Links between Genesis 4:1–16 and Genesis 2–3," *JETS* 23 (1980): 297–305; Frank Crüsemann, "Die Eigenständigkeit der Urgeschichte: Ein Beitrag zur Diskussion um den Jahwisten," in *Die Botschaft und die Boten: Festschrift für Hans Walter Wolff zum 70. Geburtstag* (ed. J. Jeremias and L. Perlitt; Neukirchen-Vluyn: Neukirchener, 1981), 15; Van Seters, *Jahwist*, 139–40; Witte, *Urgeschichte*, 153; Gertz, "Gen 2–4," 235.

7. This tension is evident mainly in Gen 4:14–15, which presumes a fully populated world, in contrast to the genealogical notice at the beginning of 4:1, which presents Cain as the firstborn son of the first couple of mankind. In the Cain narrative, the man and his wife Eve figure only in the opening birth notice (4:1), after which Adam and his wife reappear at the head of the Sethite genealogy (4:25), which already presumes the story of the fratricide.

To be sure, scholars have sought a unifying theme for the Eden and Cain stories, and likewise for the Primeval History as a whole; but for a long time, their efforts were governed by the view that J was composed prior to the demise of the northern kingdom. Thus, it was thought that the conflicts at the heart of the two stories should be read within the context of the entire Primeval History, and must relate to a universal crime and punishment theme, intended to explain the condition of humanity as a whole.[8] Within this context, the Eden and Cain narratives also served to explain the origin and nature of human society (origin of labor, professions, division of humankind into nations, etc.) before the Yahwist continued on to relate the history of a specific branch of humankind and its exclusive relationship with YHWH. However, this view of a universal theme and purpose for the Eden and Cain stories neglects the distinction between subject, theme, tendency and purpose:[9]

Subject deals with *what* the work is talking about within the fictive world it constructs. For example, the subject of the Cain story is fratricide, and this subject is developed through combining the motifs of rivalry between brothers and blind parental preference, with YHWH cast in the part of parent.

Theme is the abstract idea conveyed by the sum of a work's content and form. Theme is constructed by a *reader* who activates interpretive skills in order to unravel the meaning implied by the content and means of expression within the text. One might object that construction of theme is a subjective enterprise, and that different readers may construe the theme according to their particular understanding. Nonetheless, there is a way out of the endless proliferation of personal readings by remembering that an author is also the first reader of a text. For our purposes, the author is not limited to the poet who created a work like the Cain story, but can also signify a scribe who revised a previous text or composed a new synthesis out of different materials. We may presume that an author, as a first reader, has subsequent readers in mind when devising his work, and troubles himself to weave signs into the text which help direct readers to reconstruct the theme as he conceived it.

This is best explained by assuming that the Cain story was originally independent from its present context and that the Seth birth notice was expanded in 4:25b in order to tighten the link between Cain and Adam; and see, e.g., Gunkel, *Genesis*, 47, and Van Seters, *Yahwist*, 136, against a literary-critical solution like that of Witte, *Urgeschichte*, 152–55, or a harmonistic approach like that of Westermann, *Genesis*, 311.

8. See, e.g., von Rad, "Problem," 48–49; Frank Crüsemann, "Autonomie und Sünde: Gen 4:7 und die 'jahwistische' Urgeschichte," in *Traditionen der Befreiung: Sozialgeschichtliche Bibelauslegungen* (ed. W. Schottroff and W. Stegemann; Munich: Kaiser, 1980), 67–72; George W. Coats, *Genesis: With an Introduction to Narrative Literature* (FOTL 1; Grand Rapids: Eerdmans, 1983), 35–39; Westermann, *Genesis*, 53, 66–67.

9. For other discussions of subject, theme and purpose, see David J. A. Clines, "Theme in Genesis 1–11," *CBQ* 38 (1976): 286–89; and Mettinger, *Eden*, 42–47.

Tendency indicates the attitude of an author towards his subject. The Cain story does not condone Cain's behavior, but at the same time, Cain is not threatened with penalty of death. Some have thought that the story polemicizes against blood vengeance,[10] but this view misreads Gen 4:14–15. Cain does not state in v. 14 that he fears vengeance, but that as an outcast banished from the divine presence, he will fall victim to random violence. Furthermore, Yhwh's reply in v. 15 does not refute blood vengeance, but in fact invokes it as a means to deter other people from taking Cain's life. Others have held that Yhwh mitigates Cain's punishment.[11] However, Yhwh neither rescinds nor revises the curse on Cain; Cain still must wander in search of sustenance, since his occupation of tilling the ground will no longer yield produce, and neither is he to be readmitted into the divine presence. The view that the mark of Cain somehow represents a mitigation of the punishment is not evident from the text itself, but rather is based upon the preconception that all the stories in the Primeval History entail mitigation.[12]

I think that these snags in understanding the tendency behind Cain's punishment derive from a series of ambiguities built into the story, which reflects the author's attitude towards Cain. At different junctures within the text the reader must fill in gaps and choose between alternative interpretations that allow for different characterizations of Cain. For example, not only is the rejection of Cain's offering left unexplained, but neither is any background supplied for bringing the offerings. The narrator does not relate that Yhwh demanded offerings, and the mention of Cain's offering first may imply that Cain in a burst of spontaneous piety and thankfulness decided by himself to offer some of the fruit of his labor to Yhwh. When Abel saw this, then he *too* brought some of the firstborn from his flock (4:3–4). This short word, *too* (גם), is significant, for not only does it characterize Abel as a "copycat," but it also allows us to infer that Cain's offering was comprised of the firstfruits, just as Abel's was of the firstborn. According to this reading, there is not anything intrinsically better about Abel's offering, and Yhwh's rejection of Cain's firstfruits is arbitrary.[13] This type of ambiguity invites the reader to identify with

---

10. See, e.g., Umberto Cassuto, *From Adam to Noah: A Commentary on the Book of Genesis I–VI (Part One)* (trans. I. Abrahams; Jerusalem: The Hebrew University Magnes Press, 1961), 184–85, 221–27; cf. Westermann, *Genesis*, 311–12.

11. See, e.g., Westermann, *Genesis*, 287, 308–12; Hauser, "Links," 303–4.

12. See, e.g., von Rad, "Problem," 49; Brueggemann, "David," 175; Westermann, *Genesis*, 605; Clines, "Theme," 290–91; Crüsemann, "Eigenständigkeit," 22–25; Jože Krašovec, "Punishment and Mercy in the Primeval History (Gen 1–11)," *ETL* 70 (1994): 5–33.

13. Cf. Frank A. Spina, "The 'Ground' for Cain's Rejection (Gen 4): '*adāmāh* in the context of Gen 1–11," *ZAW* 104 (1992): 320–21. However Spina subsequently undermines this insight by linking the rejection of Cain's offering to the curse upon the ground in Gen 3:17–19.

Cain, for who would *not* be downcast under similar circumstances? In v. 7
Yʜᴡʜ warns Cain about "doing good," but at this point in the story both Cain
and the reader are confused about what, if anything, he has done wrong. This
ambiguity in the depiction of Cain continues in v. 13. Does Cain complain
here that his *punishment* (עון) is too great to bear (מנשוא), or does he admit
that his *sin* is too great to be *forgiven* (לשאת עון)?[14] Lastly, since text-critical
principles do not provide an explanation for the famous lacuna in v. 8, the
possibility should not be dismissed out of hand that the author of Gen 4:1–16
might have deliberately omitted Cain's words to Abel so that readers would
weigh alternative characterizations of the crime—was it premeditated murder
or overly violent reaction to a provocation?[15] This series of ambiguities with
regard to the author's attitude towards Cain raises the question—who really is
Cain? Does the narrative indeed intend for us to view him as an eponymous
tribal father?[16]

Finally, *purpose* deals with the aim towards which the text is directed, or
why it was written. There is an historical aspect inherent in the concept of
purpose, since it is based upon assumptions about the situation in the world
of the text's target audience. To be sure, the explanation of the origin of the
evils which plague the human condition is a theme inherent in the Eden and
Cain stories. But why was it necessary for a learned guild of scribes to com-
pose, copy, and edit these stories as part of a national "history"? This is the
question that must be considered if we are to give an adequate account of the
purpose of the Eden and Cain stories.

The answer to this question hinges on the way the sum of the elements
in both stories works together within their context. Since most scholars
have assumed from the outset that the pre- (or non-)Priestly Primeval History was created by one author or collector-editor, they have concentrated on
uncovering a common thematic structure that unites the whole.[17] However,
given the diversity of the materials in the Primeval History, such a common
theme or structure can only be stated in very general terms, such as "crime
and punishment" or "sin–punishment–mitigation."[18] By contrast, a very tight
common structure is shared by the Eden and Cain narratives, as was shown

---

14. See, e.g., Westermann, *Genesis*, 309, for the argument that the meaning of "sin" is
presumed by the translation of עון as punishment, and cf. Cassuto, *From Adam to Noah*,
who rightly points out the idiomatic usage of לשאת עון with the meaning, "to forgive sin";
and see, e.g., Exod 28:43; 34:7; Lev 5:1; Mic 7:18; Ps 32:5.

15. Cf. *Gen. Rab.* 22:8–9.

16. See, e.g., Westermann, *Genesis*, 317–18.

17. See, e.g., von Rad, "Problem," 48–49; Westermann, *Genesis*, 47–53, 66; Van Seters,
Yahwist, 189–91; Clines, "Theme," 289–306.

18. Cf. Westermann, *Genesis*, 66–67, 193; Clines, "Theme," 289–304.

above. Moreover, in addition to the striking parallels in formulation, the two stories also share motifs and themes absent from the rest of the Primeval History. Only in these two stories does YHWH directly confront the wrongdoers, implying a personal relationship that is not characteristic of the divine-human relationship elsewhere in the Primeval History. More significantly, the two stories share the theme of divine testing. Various scholars have argued that the prohibition in the Eden story is arbitrary, but to the best of my knowledge, only Mettinger has tied the nature of this command to the idea of the divine test to which God subjects the human being in order to ascertain obedience.[19] The concept of the test assumes that the subject is ignorant of being tested and has free choice, and that the outcome of the test is not known in advance.[20] In order to test blind obedience and fear of God, it is essential that the conditions of the test be arbitrary, so that the subject not be swayed by the justification given for a command, prohibition, or other trial. In my opinion, the idea of the divine test is also fundamental to the story of Cain, for only within the setting of a test is it possible to make sense of the arbitrary dealings of God with Cain.

Together, the two stories deal with two different types of tests to which the first family was subjected. In the Eden story, an explicit injunction is issued which tests obedience, and the nature of the offence is violation of YHWH's command; acquisition of knowledge and sexual awareness are but results of the violation.[21] Cain's story, by contrast, lacks an explicit command, and instead only admonishes Cain that if he "does good," he will have no cause to be downcast. Cain is not instructed "to do what is good in the eyes of YHWH" (cf., e.g., Deut 12:28), but simply to "do good," without further elaboration. This "doing good" implies basic normative behavior (cf. Pss 34:15; 37:3, 27). Both Cain and the reader are immediately aware that he has failed to "do good" when he kills Abel, even though the narrator refrains from comment and leaves the value judgments to YHWH. Thus it is evident that Cain's deed is an abrogation of essential social norms.[22] Hence, the two stories illustrate the consequences to be expected from archetypal offenses: violation of YHWH's

---

19. Mettinger, *Eden*, 23, 52–58. On the arbitrary nature of the prohibition in the Eden story, see Westermann, *Genesis*, 223–24; Carr, "Politics," 588–89; Bernard M. Levinson, *"The Right Chorale": Studies in Biblical Law and Interpretation* (FAT 54; Tübingen: Mohr Siebeck, 2008), 44.

20. Cf. Jacob Licht, *Testing in the Hebrew Scriptures and in Post-Biblical Judaism* (Jerusalem: The Hebrew University Magnes Press, 1973), 17 [Hebrew].

21. Westermann, *Genesis*, 223–24; Crüsemann, "Autonomie," 66; Van Seters, *Yahwist*, 126.

22. Cf. Crüsemann, "Autonomie," 66; Bernard Gosse, "L'inclusion de l'ensemble Genèse–II Rois, entre la perte du jardin d'Eden et celle de Jérusalem," *ZAW* 114 (2002): 204–9.

explicit commands on the one hand, and breaching the basic norms necessary for maintaining society on the other hand.

The point of the two stories further indicates their purpose. In most biblical texts, as well as other traditional literature, the point of a text is generally brought to the fore at its conclusion.[23] If this is so, then both stories together make the point that exile and alienation from YHWH is the inevitable consequence of violating YHWH's commandments and of failure to maintain essential social norms.[24] Stated in these terms, it becomes evident why these stories should be included in a national "history." In my opinion, even though these stories stand at the front of the pre- or non-Priestly Primeval History, their protagonists are not intended to represent humanity as a whole. Instead, the intimate relationship between YHWH and the man, woman, and Cain imply that they are conceived as prototypes for the relationship between YHWH and Israel, as *Israelite Urmenschen*.[25]

A final factor related to the purpose of the stories is their place within the context of the Bible. The story of Cain, as either an etiology or a morality story about a fratricide, does not require a setting at the beginning of the saga of humankind. In fact, Cain's fear that anyone happening by during his wanderings might kill him, presumes a world populated by other human beings, not a world occupied by only one nuclear family. The origin and first context for the Cain story is a matter for speculation; more interesting to me is the fact that it was designed to be read together with the Eden narrative at the head of the Primeval History. I propose that the purpose of the two stories is to establish an exemplar for the pattern carried out in the rest of the biblical narrative, somewhat similar to the programmatic introduction to the "period of the Judges" in Judg 2:11–19, which sketches the cyclic outline of the stories to come.

As others recently have noted, the recurring crime–punishment–exile theme in these narratives foreshadows the structure of the Deuteronomistic History.[26] The man was created outside the garden and was placed within it

---

23. See, e.g., Gunkel, *Genesis*, 33.

24. Cf. David N. Freedman, *The Unity of the Hebrew Bible* (Ann Arbor: University of Michigan Press, 1993), 8, 13; Van Seters, *Yahwist*, 190–91; Joseph Blenkinsopp, "A Post-exilic Lay Source in Genesis 1–11," in *Abschied vom Jahwisten: Die Komposition des Hexateuch in der jüngsten Diskussion* (ed. J. C. Gertz, et al.; BZAW 315; Berlin: de Gruyter, 2002), 51, 60; Gosse, "L'inclusion," 204–9; Christoph Levin, "The Yahwist: the Earliest Editor in the Pentateuch," *JBL* 126 (2007): 218; Mettinger, *Eden*, 58–59.

25. Cf., by contrast, the universalistic interpretation exemplified by Westermann, *Genesis*, 66–67.

26. See, e.g., Freedman, *Unity*, 8, 13; Konrad Schmid, "Buchtechnische und sachliche Prolegomena zur Enneateuchfrage," in *Auf dem Weg zur Endgestalt von Genesis bis II Regum* (ed. M. Beck and U. Schorn; BZAW 370; Berlin: de Gruyter, 2006), 4; Gosse,

by Yhwh, but he was banished from the garden and from Yhwh's immediate presence after breaking the single condition incumbent upon him. The paradise story thus plotted roughly parallels the DtrH in which Yhwh takes the people from Egypt and brings them into the land, which they conditionally possess and then lose after repeatedly breaking their treaty with Yhwh.[27] Similarly, Cain's banishment from the land which he had worked, as a result of shedding his brother's blood, foreshadows the justification given for the conquest and destruction of Judah in 2 Kgs 24:3–4 (cf. 21:16): "Thus Yhwh determined to cast Judah from his presence due to the all the sins committed by Manasseh, as well as the innocent blood which he shed. For he filled Jerusalem with innocent blood and Yhwh would not forgive." Moreover, given that the conclusions of both the Eden and Cain stories (Gen 3:24; 4:14, 16) foreshadow the conclusion of the DtrH in 2 Kgs 25:21 ("Thus, Judah was exiled from its land"), the Eden and East of Eden stories have been thought to play a central role in constructing a thematic frame for reading Genesis–2 Kings as an Enneateuch or Primary History.[28]

As I have shown, there is justification for viewing Gen 2-4 as opening a thematic *inclusio* that ends with the description of the Babylonian conquest and exile in 2 Kgs 24:1–25:21. However, it is possible to suggest other endpoints for an *inclusio* that opens with Eden and Cain—endpoints that bracket, not the historical work, but rather the body of pentateuchal law. For example, Deut 30:15–20 speaks of choosing between good and evil, between life and death, in order to dwell and live long in the land. Thus, Gen 2-4 might be viewed as an archetypical example illustrating the point of the paranetic oratory in Deut 30:15–20.[29] The placement of the closing bracket of the *inclusio* at Deut 30:15–20, of course, implies a pentateuchal frame of reference. Another possibility that suggests itself is Lev 26, which echoes several phrases and motifs in the Eden and Cain stories.[30] Here, the frame of reference for the *inclusio* is neither pentateuchal nor tetrateuchal. In both cases, Gen 2-4 illus-

---

"L'inclusion"; Thomas Römer and Konrad Schmid, "Introduction: Pentateuque, Hexateuque, Ennéateuque: Exposé du problème," in *Les dernières rédactions du Pentateuque, de l'Hexateuque et de l'Ennéateuque* (ed. T. Römer and K. Schmid; BETL 203; Leuven: Leuven University Press and Peeters, 2007), 4; cf. Otto, "Paradieserzählung," 179–83; Martin Emmrich, "The Temptation Narrative of Genesis 3:1–6: A Prelude to the Pentateuch and the History of Israel," *EvQ* 73 (January 2001): 3–20.

27. The analogy is already drawn in *Lam. Rab.* proem 4:1, dating to the seventh century c.e.; cf. Van Seters, *Yahwist*, 127–28.

28. See, e.g., Freedman *Unity*, 8, 13; Römer and Schmid, "Introduction," 4; Gosse, "L'inclusion," 204–9.

29. Cf. Mettinger, *Eden*, 52; Levinson, "The Right Chorale," 46.

30. For example, compare Lev 26:4 with Gen 2:5, 9; 3:17–18; Lev 26:5 with Gen 3:19; Lev 26:12 with Gen 3:8; Lev 26:20 with Gen 3:17–19, 4:12; Lev 26:31 with Gen 4:5.

trates in concrete terms the theoretical repercussions of violating divine law. If these alternative frames are equally as valid as the reading which brackets the so-called "Primary History," then how can we determine that the *inclusio* running from Eden to Babylon signifies that Genesis–2 Kings was conceived as a compositional unit or Enneateuch?

Ultimately, frames are a device for constructing meaning, and bracketing a text presents it as a meaningful unit. When the brackets are formulated in parallel language and the unit is relatively short, there is little doubt that the frame is being employed to mark a compositional unit. However, when the perception of a frame is based upon thematic rather than verbal parallels, then subjective criteria come into play, particularly when the frame is thought to bracket a large and diverse expanse of text, such as the entire Pentateuch and Former Prophets.[31] In other words, frames are deliberately employed by authors during the compositional process, but readers also have a tendency to bracket off long texts in order to uncover unifying themes and messages. A legally oriented reader might be more sensitive to the echoes of Eden and Cain in the epilogues to the Deuteronomic and Priestly law corpora, while a reader bored by law is more likely to concentrate on finding a meaningful frame for the historical narrative. Diachronic considerations also come into play in determining the extent of the text that a reader will bracket. Did the reader's text comprise a preexilic J and D? Or J and the DtrH? Or J, the DtrH and P? Does Gen 2–4 presume P, as some suggest?[32] If the non-P material in the Primeval History was composed and compiled to supplement P, then one could argue with justification that Gen 2–4 deliberately evokes Lev 26. Otherwise, the reverse is more than likely; namely that the author of Lev 26 echoed motifs and expression in Gen 2–4 in order to demarcate the extent of his Torah. Here we reach an impasse, for the frames perceived are employed as evidence for the history of the sources while at the same time diachronic preconceptions lead us to look for frames which will support our theses.

I suggest that consideration of the technical aspects of scroll production may provide a way out of this impasse. First, although Schmid cites a few instances of extremely long scrolls from Greece and Egypt, these undoubtedly represent exceptional cases.[33] As Haran and Tov point out, the maximum length a scroll was likely to run can be inferred from the length of the longest

---

31. Cf. Chris Wyckoff, "Have We Come Full Circle Yet? Closure, Psycholinguistics, and Problems of Recognition with the *Inclusio*," *JSOT* 30 (2006): 475–505.
32. See Otto, "Paradieserzählung"; Blenkinsopp, "Post-exilic"; Andreas Schüle, "Made in the 'Image of God': The Concepts of Divine Images in Gen 1–3," *ZAW* 117 (2005): 7, 19; and Mettinger, *Eden*, 50, countered by Levin, "Yahwist," 210–11.
33. Schmid, "Buchtechnische," 5–6.

scrolls from Qumran or from the length of the longest biblical books.[34] But in any event, I think that the concept of an Enneateuch is *not* related to the question of whether Genesis–2 Kings might have been inscribed upon one monstrous scroll. The concept of "book" or composition is not equivalent to "scroll," just as a "book" or a composition is not the same as a "volume." Moreover, in cuneiform literature a single composition could take up several tablets, such as the *Enuma Elish* and the Gilgamesh epic. In actuality, there is no empirical evidence that lengthy compositions like the DtrH were originally written on a single scroll. This means that neither length alone, nor the number of scrolls that would have been required for the so-called "Primary History," can function as indicators as to whether Genesis–2 Kings was considered a compositional unit.

Secondly, technical limitations impede the revision of scrolls. Large additions of several lines or columns could be inserted into scrolls either when recopying the entire scroll,[35] or by cutting the scroll and sewing in an entire new sheet, which would have been inscribed in advance. In that case, it would be necessary to plot the layout of the text and recopy sections of the columns into which the new text would be inserted.[36] However, the easiest way to add material would be to take advantage of the cover sheets at the beginning and end of a scroll, and if necessary to add new cover sheets.[37] Thus, I think that the phenomenon of appendices and secondary introductions arose by necessity, as scribes resorted to producing new editions by appending new prologues or endings to scrolls in order to redirect readers' efforts at decoding the message of the work as a whole.

These considerations lead me to conclude that Gen 2–4 was added to a Genesis scroll at the latest pre-P stage, or at least before the addition of the

34. Menahem Haran, "Book-Size and the Device of Catch-Lines in the Biblical Canon," *JJS* 36 (1985): 1–5; Emanuel Tov, "Copying of a Biblical Scroll," *JRH* 26 (2002): 192–94, 207.

35. Emanuel Tov, "The Writing of Early Scrolls: Implications for the Literary Analysis of Hebrew Scripture," *DSD* 13 (2006): 340–44, 47; Karel van der Toorn, *Scribal Culture and the Making of the Hebrew Bible* (Cambridge, Mass.: Harvard University Press, 2007), 126–27, 146–49.

36. Cf. Tov, "Copying," 190, 197.

37. See Tov, "Copying," 190, 203, 205; idem, *Scribal Practices and Approaches Reflected in the Texts Found in the Judean Desert* (STDJ 54; Boston: Brill, 2004), 111–18, on cover or handle sheets attached at the beginning and ends of the Qumran scrolls. Tov observes that in the Qumran scrolls these sheets were left empty and not utilized for revision, even though they sometimes had been ruled in advance. However, it should be noted that the Qumran scrolls derive from a postredactional stage in the evolution of the biblical texts, and therefore do not falsify the proposition that biblical scribes might have employed the cover sheets in order to revise existing copies of scrolls without recourse to extensive recopying.

Priestly creation account in Gen 1:1–2:4a. According to the new "block" paradigm for understanding the formation of the Pentateuch, the earliest compositional layer began with the Exodus and focused on deliverance, law-giving, and sustenance.[38] The pattern of crime, punishment, and exile is not inherent in the pentateuchal narrative, although the theme of punishment for transgressing divine commands does occasionally occur. The narrative was later extended back in time with the addition of the stories of the patriarchs, in which migration and the promise of the land play a prominent part. However, only with the Primeval History does the theme of exile, dispersion, and alienation from Yhwh come to the fore. If the block paradigm holds, then only after the addition of the Primeval History was it likely that readers would interpret Genesis–2 Kings as a continuous narrative. Therefore, it is likely that Gen 2–4 was composed for the present context and was appended to the opening of Genesis at a late stage in the development of the pre-Priestly literature in Genesis–2 Kings. Accordingly, the concept of a "Primary History" would be a pre-Priestly interpretive strategy devised by a post-Deuteronomistic scribe who thought to intimate that the causality which shaped the history of Israel and Judah had already been worked out at the beginning of humanity.

In conclusion, since there are no references to the Primeval History elsewhere in the Pentateuch, and given the major break between the Primeval History and the stories of the patriarchs, I concur with the view that the Primeval History was added at a late phase in the development of Genesis.[39] My comments regarding the technical aspects involved in revising scrolls also support this view. I cannot say at this point whether the Primeval History ever existed as an independent composition, or whether it was purposely drafted for its present context. Internal inconsistencies as well as the diverse nature of the materials comprising the Primeval History might speak against the view that a single author composed the whole.[40] Although I am still troubled by

---

38. See, e.g., Erhard Blum, "The Literary Connection between the Books of Genesis and Exodus and the End of the Book of Joshua," in *A Farewell to the Yahwist? The Composition of the Pentateuch in Recent European Interpretation* (ed. T. B. Dozeman and K. Schmid; SBLSymS 34; Atlanta: Society of Biblical Literature, 2006), 89–106; Levin, "Yahwist," 209–17, with additional literature there.

39. See, e.g., Witte, *Urgeschichte*, 192–99; Blenkinsopp, "Post-exilic," 52; Levin, "Yahwist," 209; cf. Otto, "Paradieserzählung," 174. Previously Crüsemann, "Eigenständigkeit," had argued persuasively for the independence of the Primeval History; however, he still thought that the Primeval History was composed in the tenth century B.C.E. (see pp. 26, 28).

40. See above for the tension between the Cain story and its context in the Primeval History. In addition, the Table of Nations (Gen 10:1–32) and the Babel story (11:1–9) can hardly derive from the same hand. The Table of Nations anticipates the division of

the question of the Cain story's original context, I am convinced that the Eden and Cain narratives were placed at the head of the Primeval History at the latest pre-P stage, and I tend to think that the Eden narrative was penned to serve as a partner to the Cain story in this context. Although I do think that these two stories were added to the beginning of the Genesis scroll in order to provide an interpretive key to the narrative of the history of Israel leading up to the exile, I am doubtful that the scribe ever thought of the large narrative block from Genesis to 2 Kings as a compositional unit or Enneateuch. In my opinion, the concept of an Enneateuch is best understood as a reading strategy for uncovering a significant message within a set of authoritative scrolls.

---

humankind, the separation of languages, and the dispersion of the nations (10:5, 18–21, 25, 31–32), while the Babel story opens with a united humankind speaking a common language (11:1). The two texts also display wholly different attitudes towards the subject of the division of humankind. A neutral attitude is evident in the Table of Nations, which explains the division as the result of propagation and natural increase. By contrast, the Babel story conveys a negative attitude to this process, representing the division and dispersion as a measure forced upon humankind by YHWH.

Exodus 32–34 and the Quest for an Enneateuch

Michael Konkel

1

Recent research is characterized by its renewed interest in the theory of an Enneateuch, namely, a narrative covering the books from Genesis–2 Kings. If you take a look at some recently published Old Testament textbooks in Germany you will find that they consistently assume the existence of such an Enneateuch (cf. the textbooks by J. C. Gertz, R. G. Kratz, K. Schmid, H.-C. Schmitt or E. Zenger).[1] Some of these scholars connect their theory to a somewhat modified model of a Deuteronomistic History starting with the book of Deuteronomy (e.g., H.-C. Schmitt, T. Römer),[2] whereas others simply dismiss the theory of a Deuteronomistic History (e.g., E. Zenger, R. G. Kratz, K. Schmid).[3]

Even though all these models do differ significantly as regards the details of their reconstruction of an Enneateuch, it seems nonetheless that a new consensus is within reach. Having said that, however, it needs to be further stated

---

1. Jan C. Gertz, ed., *Grundinformation Altes Testament: Eine Einführung in Literatur, Religion und Geschichte des Alten Testaments* (Uni-Taschenbücher 2745; Göttingen: Vandenhoeck & Ruprecht, 2006); Reinhard G. Kratz, *Die Komposition der erzählenden Bücher des Alten Testaments* (Uni-Taschenbücher 2157; Göttingen: Vandenhoeck & Ruprecht, 2000); Konrad Schmid, *Literaturgeschichte des Alten Testaments: Eine Einführung* (Darmstadt: Wissenschaftliche Buchgesellschaft, 2008); Hans-Christoph Schmitt, *Arbeitsbuch zum Alten Testament: Grundzüge der Geschichte Israels und der alttestamentlichen Schriften* (Uni-Taschenbücher 2146; Göttingen: Vandenhoeck & Ruprecht, 2005); Erich Zenger et al., *Einleitung in das Alte Testament* (7th ed.; Kohlhammer Studienbücher Theologie 1/1; Stuttgart: Kohlhammer, 2008).

2. Schmitt, *Arbeitsbuch*; Thomas Römer, *The So-Called Deuteronomistic History. A Sociological, Historical and Literary Introduction* (London: T&T Clark, 2007).

3. Kratz, *Komposition*; Konrad Schmid, *Erzväter und Exodus: Untersuchungen zur doppelten Begründung der Ursprünge Israels innerhalb der Geschichtsbücher des Alten Testaments* (WMANT 81; Neukirchen-Vluyn: Neukirchener, 1999).

that in the present discussion the enneateuchal perspective on pentateuchal texts is often more suggested than properly demonstrated. Furthermore, convincing evidence of a distinct enneateuchal redaction within the Pentateuch has not yet been discovered.[4]

In the following, I will focus on a small but nevertheless significant text, in order to analyze its most important intertextual references within the framework of an Enneateuch. I have chosen Exod 32–34, which is at the heart of the Pentateuch. At the same time this passage shows a characteristic mix of Deuteronomistic and Priestly language, so that we can assume late redactional work within these chapters. Nevertheless even the classification of these undisputed late redactional passages is a matter of debate: Are the Dtr passages pre- or post-Priestly? Are they part of a Pentateuch, a Hexateuch or an Enneateuch? H.-C. Schmitt and T. B. Dozeman assign Exod 32, for example, to a late Deuteronomistic redaction of an Enneateuch.[5] Schmitt assumes an earlier composition that he attributes to an exilic Jahwist (Exod 32:1–6, 15a*, 19–24, 30–34*); that composition was then reworked in a late Dtr redaction that linked the pre-Priestly Tetrateuch with P as well as with the Deuteronomistic History. Dozeman, for his part, assigns the composition of Exod 32 to a single, late, but nonetheless pre-Priestly author. On the other hand, E. Otto finds in Exod 32 the hand of a post-Priestly Pentateuch redactor, whereas R. Achenbach ascribes the chapter to a post-Priestly Hexateuch redactor.[6] They both strictly deny the existence of an Enneateuch-redaction.

2

Let us first look at the general outline of Exod 32–34: After the making of the covenant in Exod 24, Moses ascends the mountain in order to receive

---

4. Cf. Erik Aurelius, *Zukunft jenseits des Gerichts: Eine redaktionsgeschichtliche Studie zum Enneateuch* (BZAW 319; Berlin: de Gruyter, 2003), for the most far-reaching attempt to date.

5. Hans-Christoph Schmitt, "Die Erzählung vom Goldenen Kalb Ex. 32 und das Deuteronomistische Geschichtswerk," in *Theologie in Prophetie und Pentateuch: Gesammelte Schriften* (ed. U. Schorn and M. Büttner; BZAW 310; Berlin: de Gruyter, 2001), 311–25; Thomas B. Dozeman, "The Composition of Ex 32 within the Context of the Enneateuch," in *Auf dem Weg zur Endgestalt von Genesis bis II Regum* (ed. M. Beck and U. Schorn; BZAW 370; Berlin: de Gruyter, 2006), 175–89.

6. Eckart Otto, "Die nachpriesterschriftliche Pentateuchredaktion im Buch Exodus," in *Studies in the Book of Exodus: Redaction–Reception–Interpretation* (ed. M. Vervenne; BETL 126; Leuven: Peeters, 1996), 196–222; Reinhard Achenbach, "Grundlinien redaktioneller Arbeit in der Sinai-Perikope," in *Das Deuteronomium zwischen Pentateuch und Deuteronomistischem Geschichtswerk* (ed. idem and E. Otto; FRLANT 206; Göttingen: Vandenhoeck & Ruprecht, 2004), 56–80.

the stone tablets (Exod 24:12–13). Moses then stays on the mountain for forty days and forty nights (24:18). Meanwhile, just before the return of Moses, the people call on Aaron to build a golden calf. The calf is acclaimed as god and a feast with sacrifices is celebrated. When Moses returns he destroys the tablets and the calf (Exod 32:19–20). After long and tough negotiations (Exod 32:30–33:23), Moses manages to wrest a new version of the tablets together with a renewal of the covenant (Exod 34).

Within this framework there is embedded a system of three successive Mosaic intercessions:

32:11–13: The first intercession takes place while Moses is still on the mountain, where he is informed by the Lord about the events happening at the foot of the mountain. This intercession is successful: Moses manages to avert an immediate destruction of Israel by reminding God of the oath that he swore to the patriarchs.

32:31–32: The second intercession takes place after the destruction of both the tablets and the calf. This time, Moses prays for remission—and this time his intercession fails: He can only achieve a reprieve, but remission properly speaking is denied to him by the Lord.

34:8–9: The third intercession takes place after long and, from a rhetorical point of view, masterly structured negotiation between the Lord and Moses. Exodus 33 is a real masterpiece of ancient Israelite court rhetoric, in which Moses manages to achieve the remission that was formerly denied, in the form of a renewal of the covenant.

It is important to see how each intercession actually builds upon the preceding: the second intercession is not merely a doublet of the first one.[7] The first intercession succeeds insofar as it averts the immediate destruction of Israel—but no more. The second intercession for remission, on the contrary, fails; it is only after tough negotiations that Moses gets the chance for another intercession. That third and final intercession achieves the renewal of the covenant, a renewal which, in turn, amounts to remission, as Num 14:17–20 explicitly states.

---

7. This assessment by no means implies the redactional integrity of the system of three intercessions. The redactional composition of the three intercessions is deliberate and artful. Nonetheless there is still convincing evidence that the second intercession is chronologically prior, whereas the first and third intercession are late and composed to envelope the older one. For a detailed analysis see Michael Konkel, *Sünde und Vergebung: Eine Rekonstruktion der Redaktionsgeschichte der hinteren Sinaiperikope (Exodus 32–34) vor dem Hintergrund aktueller Pentateuchmodelle* (FAT 58; Tübingen: Mohr Siebeck, 2008).

3

Let us examine, using a synchronic methodology, the most important inter-textual references within Exod 32–34 from Genesis to the end of 2 Kings:[8]

Exodus 32:4, 8 → 1 Kings 12:28

> This he took from them and cast in a mold, and made it into a molten calf. And they exclaimed, "These are your gods, O Israel, who brought you out of the land of Egypt!" (Exod 32:4)

The first such reference that we find is in Exod 32:4 (which is later taken up by the Lord in 32:8). The story of the golden calf is linked with the cultic measures enforced by Jeroboam. The formula, "These are your gods, O Israel, which brought you up out of the land Egypt," cites 1 Kgs 12:28. The reference to several gods makes good sense within the context of 1 Kings, because it refers to the two calves of Jeroboam; in Exod 32, however, there is only one calf. Thus, the formula used in Exod 32 only makes sense if it entails a subtle reference to the story in 1 Kings, a story which is now reinterpreted in Exod 32 to convey that, at Sinai, all of Israel was involved in the service of the calf—and not only the northern kingdom. In other words, Exod 32 extends the guilt of the northern kingdom to all of Israel.[9]

Genesis 12:2 ← Exodus 32:10

> So now, leave me alone, so that my anger can burn against them and I can destroy them, and I will make from you a great nation. (Exod 32:10)

This next reference points back to Genesis: The sentence, "I will make from you a great nation," conforms almost literally to the promise to Abram in Gen 12:2—but now with Moses as subject. Generally this is taken as a real offer to Moses—as the possibility of starting the story of God and his people anew. Nevertheless I take this citation of Gen 12:2 to be a subtle hint for Moses that he should intercede for Israel by referring to the patriarchal oath. Indeed, this is exactly what Moses does immediately following.

---

8. For a synchronic survey of all significant intertextual references in Exod 32–34, see Konkel, *Sünde und Vergebung*, 51–104.

9. Cf. Jan C. Gertz, "Beobachtungen zu Komposition und Redaktion in Ex 32–34," in *Gottes Volk am Sinai: Untersuchungen zu Ex 32–34 und Dtn 9–10* (ed. M. Köckert and E. Blum; Veröffentlichungen der Wissenschaftlichen Gesellschaft für Theologie 18; Gütersloh: Gütersloher, 2001), 88–106.

Exodus 32:12 → 2 Kings 23:26

> Let not the Egyptians say, "It was with evil intent that he delivered them, only to kill them off in the mountains and annihilate them from the face of the earth." Turn from your blazing anger, and renounce the plan to punish your people. (Exod 32:12)

The demand to "turn from your blazing anger" occurs here for the first time in the Pentateuch. The expression refers exclusively to the anger of God. Therefore, within the framework of an Enneateuch, it is legitimate to look for the last occurrence of this phrase in the book of Kings. We find it in 2 Kgs 23:26, where the fate of Judah is sealed. Thus, we have here an intertextual link that connects the Sinai pericope with the end of the book of Kings. The *inclusio* thus created indicates the difference between the two situations: at Sinai Israel had the intercessor Moses, who saved Israel from the anger of the Lord, but after the sin of Manasseh there was no longer an intercessor who was able to save Israel and preserve them from God's wrath.

Genesis 13:14–17; 17; 22:17 ← Exodus 32:13

> Remember your servants, Abraham, Isaac, and Jacob, how you swore to them by your self and said to them: "I will make your offspring as numerous as the stars of heaven, and I will give to your offspring this whole land of which I spoke, to possess forever." (Exod 32:13)

The reference to the oath that the Lord swore to the patriarchs marks the climax of Moses' intercession in Exod 32. Moses first refers to Gen 22:15–18 and cites Gen 22:17 ("I will multiply your descendants as the stars of heaven"). It must be noted, however, that the promise of the land does not agree with Gen 22. Rather, Moses' speech in Exod 32:13 states that Israel shall inherit the land "forever." This statement can refer either to the covenant with Abraham in Gen 17 or, alternatively, to Gen 13:14–17, the other reference where the promise of the land is explicitly marked as "eternal."

Genesis 6:6–7 ← Exodus 32:12, 14

> And the Lord renounced the punishment he had planned to bring upon his people. (Exod 32:12)

This is a very important reference: Gen 6:6–7 is the first and only occurrence of the verb נחם with God as subject, prior to Exod 32. In that respect, we do have a clear connection between the two passages. While in the story of the flood "it repented the Lord that he had made man on earth," in Exod 32, the

Lord "repented over the evil which he had planned to do unto his people." The characterization of God in Exod 32 differs from that in the Flood-story: here God does not destroy Israel, but rather repents of the "evil" that he had considered bringing upon his people.

Genesis 34:25–26 ← Genesis 49:5–7 ← Exodus 32:26–29 → Deuteronomy 33:8–11

> 26 Moses stood up in the gate of the camp and said, "Whoever is for the Lord, come here!" And all the Levites rallied to him. 27 He said to them, "Thus says the Lord, the God of Israel: 'Each of you put sword on thigh, go back and forth from gate to gate throughout the camp, and slay brother, neighbor, and kin.'" 28 The Levites did as Moses had bidden; and some three thousand of the people fell that day. 29 And Moses said, "Dedicate yourselves to the Lord this day—for each of you has been against son and brother—that he may bestow a blessing upon you today." (Exod 32:26–29)

Exodus 32:26–29 is a *crux interpretum*. How does the judgment of the Levites relate to the judgment the Lord announces later in 32:34? How can the Levites be exempted from the judgment, even though they were obviously involved in serving the golden calf? What does the figure of 3,000 people denote? Whatever the answers, I think that this passage serves a distinct function within the composition of the Pentateuch. The book of Genesis includes the cursing of Levi by Jacob in Gen 49:5–7:

> 5 Simeon and Levi are a pair; Their weapons are tools of lawlessness. 6 Let not my person be included in their council, Let not my being be counted in their assembly. For when angry they slay men, And when pleased they maim oxen. 7 Cursed be their anger so fierce, and their wrath so relentless. I will divide them in Jacob, scatter them in Israel. (Gen 49:5–7)

The background for this curse is the episode of the revenge of Simeon and Levi against the people of Shechem as recounted in Gen 34. However, the question is how this curse relates to the motif of Levi's election, such as we can find it in the other books of the Pentateuch—especially with respect to the Priestly cult, as well as in the blessing of Moses in Deut 33:8–11:

> 8 And of Levi he said, Let your Thummim and Urim be with your faithful one, whom you tested at Massah, challenged at the waters of Meribah; 9 who said of his father and mother, "I consider them not." His brothers he disregarded, ignored his own children. Your precepts alone they observed, and kept your covenant. 10 They shall teach your laws to Jacob and your instructions to Israel. They shall offer you incense to savor, and whole-offerings on your altar. 11 Bless, O Lord, his substance, and favor his undertakings. Smite the loins of his foes; let his enemies rise no more. (Deut 33:8–11)

My own view is that Exod 32:26–29 actually comprises the necessary link that reconciles the theme of Levi's curse at the end of Genesis with the theme of the distinctive status assigned to Levi in the other books of the Pentateuch. We have then an intertextual line starting with Gen 34 and ending with Deut 33.

Genesis 12:7 ← Exodus 33:1–3 → Deuteronomy 34:4

> 33:1 Then the Lord said to Moses, "Set out from here, you and the people that you have brought up from the land of Egypt, to the land of which I swore to Abraham, Isaac, and Jacob, saying 'I will assign it to your offspring.' 2 I will send a messenger before you, and I will drive out the Canaanites, the Amorites, the Hittites, the Perizzites, the Hivites, and the Jebusites—3 a land flowing with milk and honey. But I will not go in your midst, since you are a stiff-necked people, lest I destroy you on the way." (Exod 33:1–3)

Now it is the Lord himself who refers, in his speech to Moses, to the oath previously made to the patriarchs (cf. Exod 32:13). The divine speech takes up Gen 12:7, a text which comprises the first promise of the land in the book of Genesis. But there is yet another intertextual reference: indeed, the end of Exod 33:1 conforms exactly to Deut 34:4:

> And the Lord said to him, "This is the land of which I swore to Abraham, Isaac, and Jacob, saying 'I will assign it to your offspring.' I have let you see it with your own eyes, but you shall not cross there." (Deut 34:4)

Just before his death, Moses sees the fulfillment of the things promised to him in Exod 33.Here, we have yet another line starting in Gen 12 and coming to an end in Deut 34. At the same time a hexateuchal perspective is opened up, through the reference to the combined motifs of the messenger (מלאך) and the driving out of the nations before Israel in Exod 33:1–3 (cf. Exod 23:20–33).

Exodus 33:4–6 → Judges 2:1–5

> 33:4 When the people heard this harsh word, they went into mourning, and none put on his finery. 5 The Lord said to Moses, "Say to the Israelite people, 'You are a stiff-necked people. If I were to go in your midst for one moment, I would destroy you. Now, then, leave off your finery, and I will consider what to do to you.'" 6 So the Israelites remained stripped of the finery from Mount Horeb on. (Exod 33:4–5)

The nearest structural parallel to this difficult passage is in Judg 2:1–5:

> 2:1 A messenger of the Lord came up from Gilgal to Bochim and said, "I brought you up from Egypt and I took you into the land which I had promised on oath to your fathers. And I said, 'I will never break my covenant with you. 2 And you, for your part, must make no covenant with the inhabitants of this land; you must tear down their altars.' But you have not obeyed me—look what you have done! 3 Therefore, I have resolved not to drive them out before you; they shall become your oppressors, and their gods shall be a snare to you." 4 As the messenger of the Lord spoke these words to all the Israelites, the people broke into weeping. 5 So they named that place Bochim, and they offered sacrifices there to the Lord. (Judg 2:1-5)

After the conquest, the messenger who was announced in Exod 33 (cf. Exod 23:20, 23) speaks to Israel. The people react in the same way as they did in Exod 33, namely, by mourning and weeping. Even though the Hebrew root that is used differs in Exod 33 and Judg 2, the intertextual link between Exod 33 and the beginning of the book of Judges is nonetheless unmistakable.

Combining the above observations on the connections between Exod 33, Deut 34 and Judg 2, we can therefore state the following: Within Exod 33:1–6, we have a perspective that encompasses the end of the Pentateuch (Deut 34), the conquest of the land, and even the book of Judges.

Exodus 34:8–9 → 2 Kings 24:3–4

> 34:8 Moses hastened to bow low to the ground in homage, 9 and said, "If I have gained your favor, O Lord, pray, let the Lord go in our midst, even though this is a stiff-necked people. Pardon our iniquity and our sin, and take us for your own!" (Exod 34:8–9)

Let us finally turn to the third intercession of Moses in Exod 34. For the first time within Exod 32–34, the theologically significant root סלח is used. If we look for the last occurrence of this root within the Enneateuch we come to 2 Kgs 24:3–4, where the fate of Judah is sealed:

> 24:3 All this befell Judah at the command of the Lord, who banished [them] from his presence because of all the sins that Manasseh had committed, 4 and also because of the blood of the innocent that he shed. For he filled Jerusalem with the blood of the innocent, and the Lord would not forgive. (2 Kgs 24:3–4)

Here we have an intertextual link between Exod 34 and the end of 2 Kings. It is a kind of negative correspondence to the intertextual link between Exod 32:12, 14 and Gen 6:6–7. However it is difficult to interpret: Moses' intercession at Sinai leads to forgiveness, but in 2 Kgs 24 it is stated that "the Lord would not forgive." Does this imply that, as in the connection between Exod

32:13 und 2 Kgs 23:26, without the intercessor Moses Israel could not be saved? I think the situation here is different, because Moses' plea for remission in Exod 34 does not target only the sin of the golden calf. It also aims for a deeper forgiveness of Israel, because it is a "stiff-necked" people. So we thus have to ask: If Moses achieved a general forgiveness for the "stiff-necked" nature of Israel in Exod 34, then why did the Lord not forgive the sin of Manasseh in 2 Kgs 24? We will skip this question for the moment and return to it later.

There is one final network of references, which signifies an enneateuchal-perspective: the motif of the stone tablets. This first occurs in Exod 24:12, where Moses is commanded to ascend the mountain to receive the stone tablets. Exodus 31:18 notes the delivery of the tablets to Moses. Exodus 31:15–16 describes the tablets in a unique manner as the "work of God" written with the "writing of God." Exodus 32:19 notes the destruction of these divine tablets. Exodus 34:1–4 states that Moses is commanded to create new tablets. So the second tablets are not the "work of God" like the first ones, but God himself writes on them "the words of the covenant, the ten words" (Exod 34:28).[10] These tablets are deposited in the ark. Thus, Exod 32–34 marks the beginning of a line of narrative tension that does not come to an end until the depositing of the ark, with the tablets, in the temple, in 1 Kgs 8:9.

4

In the wake of this synchronic survey, we may now reexamine these passages from the perspective of redaction criticism. The references under discussion occur within passages that are usually attributed to late, particularly Deuteronomistic redactions within Exod 32–34, namely, Exod 32:7–14; 32:26–29; Exod 33:1–11; and Exod 34:8–10.[11]

Of course there is as always the exception to the rule, namely, the quotation of 1 Kgs 12:28 in Exod 32:4. However it can be shown that this quotation is a later addition:[12]

---

10. It is not clear who is the subject in Exod 34:28. However, in 34:1 God announces that he himself will write on the tablets hewn by Moses. Therefore, in the text in its final shape, God must be the subject of Exod 34:28.

11. See Konkel, *Sünde und Vergebung*, for the current state of research and a detailed analysis.

12. Konkel, *Sünde und Vergebung*, 107–8; cf. Heinrich Holzinger, *Exodus*, (KHC 11; Tübingen: Mohr 1900), 109; Peter Weimar, "Das Goldene Kalb: Redaktionsgeschichtliche Erwägungen zu Ex 32," *BN* 38/39 (1987): 121–22; and others.

32:4a And he took (it) from their hand,
32:4b And cast in a mold (?)[13]
32:4c And made it a molten calf.
32:4d And they said:
32:4e These are your gods, O Israel, which brought you up out of the land
    of Egypt.
32:5a And *Aaron* saw (it),
32:5b And he built an altar before *it*.
32:5c And *Aaron* announced and said:
32:5d Tomorrow will be a feast to the Lord.

We have some problems within v. 5: The suffix of the third person singular in v. 5b (לפניו) can only refer to עגל מסכה in v. 4c. This is grammatically possible; however, the citation of 1 Kgs 12:28 disrupts the connection between v. 4c and v. 5b. This corresponds to another problem: Aaron is explicitly named twice even though this would not be necessary. The twofold naming of Aaron can be accounted for if vv. 4d–5a are secondary: Once the quotation of 1 Kgs 12:28 was introduced in v. 4d–e, it was necessary to mention Aaron once more, in v. 5a. Thus, we can reconstruct an older text that only included v. 4a–c and v. 5b–d:

32:4a And he took (it) from their hand,
32:4b And cast in a mold (?)
32:4c And made it a molten calf,
32:5b And he built an altar before it.
32:5c And Aaron announced and said:
32:5d Tomorrow will be a feast to the Lord.

Therefore, Exod 32:4 provides no argument for regarding Exod 32 in its entirety as Deuteronomistic. It still seems reasonable to assume a pre-Dtr version of the story;[14] later, that pre-Deuteronomistic account in Exod 32 was

---

13. The translation is not certain. Cf. for the range of possibilities Joachim Hahn, *Das "Goldene Kalb": Die Jahwe-Verehrung bei Stierbildern in der Geschichte Israels* (Europäische Hochschulschriften 23/154; Frankfurt: Lang, 1981), 144–71.

14. The pre-Dtr account includes Exod 32:1–4c, 5b–6c, 15b, 19a–c (without ומחלת), 19d, 20, 30, 31abc, 32–34b, d, (35a?); i.e., the making of the calf, its destruction by Moses, and his intercession to achieve a reprieve. As Gertz, *Beobachtungen*, has shown, this story not only refers to the northern kingdom, but to Israel in its entirety. He therefore proposes an exilic date for this composition. Nevertheless this account shows no direct influence of Dtr theology, as can be easily seen by a comparison with the Dtr parallel in Deut 9–10. I think a preexilic date for Exod 32* is still tenable if one sees here not only a reflection of the fall of the northern kingdom (722 B.C.E.), but also of the campaign of Sennacherib against Judah in 701 B.C.E. Contrary to the Dtr account in 2 Kgs 18–19, this campaign was a deliberate attack to destroy the infrastructure of Judah, from which it never completely

reworked by adding Exod 32:7–14, together with Exod 32:4.

Regarding Exod 32:7–14, it can be shown that this passage presumes the incorporation of the Priestly source or, if one prefers, of the Priestly texts.[15] The introduction of the speech in Exod 32:7 is typically Priestly.[16] Exodus 32:8 implies the insertion of the Decalogue in Exod 20.[17]

The reference to the patriarchal oath in Exod 32:13 culminates in referring to the promise of the land as "eternal." As was shown above, there are only two possible references in Genesis for this statement: either Gen 17:8, which belongs to P, or Gen 13:14–17. The latter verses are commonly regarded as pre-Priestly.[18] However the statement of v. 14 that Lot was separated from Abram presumes the separation of Abram and Lot in v. 11b. This verse is commonly seen as a part of P.[19] This observation means that Gen 13:14–17 has to be a post-Priestly addition within Gen 13. Therefore, whether the reference is to Gen 13:14–17 or to Gen 17, Exod 32:13 has to be post-Priestly as well.

Certainly some scholars acknowledge the post-Priestly provenance of Exod 32:13, but they make this an argument to see the verse as secondary.[20] But such an addition would disrupt the rhetorical outline of Exod 32:7–14:

---

recovered. Beyond that, the first deportations from Judah took place in the context of Sennacherib's campaign. So for people living in Judah in the seventh century, it may have been plausible to interpret their experiences as a fulfillment of a judgement that was prophesied by the Lord himself at Sinai. The Babylonian exile was not the first crisis in the history of Judah that could be interpreted as a divine judgment.

15. For a detailed analysis, see Konkel, *Sünde und Vergebung*, 147–62.

16. Cf., e.g., Exod 6:10, 13, 29; 14:1; 16:11; 25:1, etc.

17. Matthias Franz, *Der barmherzige und gnädige Gott: Die Gnadenrede vom Sinai (Exodus 34,6–7) und ihre Parallelen im Alten Testament und seiner Umwelt* (Stuttgart: Kohlhammer, 2003), 179; Konkel, *Sünde und Vergebung*, 148.

18. Cf., e.g., Erhard Blum, *Die Komposition der Vätergeschichte* (WMANT 57; Neukirchen-Vluyn: Neukirchener, 1984), 289–97; Matthias Köckert, *Vätergott und Väterverheißungen: Eine Auseinandersetzung mit Albrecht Alt und seinen Erben* (FRLANT 142; Göttingen: Vandenhoeck & Ruprecht, 1988), 250–55, 320–21; Schmid, *Erzväter*, 111–29.

19. E.g., Gerhard von Rad, *Das erste Buch Mose: Genesis* (10th ed.; ATD 2/4; Göttingen: Vandenhoeck & Ruprecht, 1976 [original: 1949]), 130; Thomas Pola, *Die ursprüngliche Priesterschrift: Beobachtungen zur Literarkritik und Traditionsgeschichte von PG* (WMANT 70; Neukirchen-Vluyn: Neukirchener, 1995), 343 n. 144.

20. Cf. Jacques Vermeylen, "L'affaire de veau d'or (Ex 32–34): Une clé pour la 'question deuteronomiste'?" *ZAW* 97 (1985): 16 n. 40; Weimar, *Das Goldene Kalb*, 124–25; Thomas Römer, *Israels Väter: Untersuchungen zur Väterthematik im Deuteronomium und in der deuteronomistischen Tradition* (OBO 99; Fribourg: Universitätsverlag; Göttingen: Vandenhoeck & Ruprecht, 1990), 258–65; Gertz, "Beobachtungen," 96; Norbert Lohfink, "Deuteronomium 9,1–10,11 und Exodus 32–34: Zu Endtextstruktur, Intertextualität, Schichtung und Abhängigkeiten," in Köckert and Blum, *Gottes Volk am Sinai*, 68; Aurelius, *Zukunft*, 165, 199–202.

Moses' argumentation is very prudent. First he pays respect to the Lord's mighty acts of salvation (v. 11), he then appeals to God's honor (v. 12). But it is only the third argument that "makes the face of the Lord soft" and manages to avert the sudden annihilation of Israel: the reference to the patriarchal oath is the essential reason why the intercession succeeds. If one takes this passage as secondary, one cuts off the climax of Moses' intercession. We can conclude, therefore, that Exod 32:7–14 in its entirety is post-Priestly.[21]

Exodus 32:7–14 is the nucleus of the so-called 'Dtr' redactions in Exod 32–34. Exodus 33:1–6 depends on Exod 32:7–14 and seems to be constructed to reconcile the non-Priestly tradition of the tent outside of the camp (Exod 33:7–11) with the Priestly tent inside the camp.[22] Due to the God's withdrawal from Israel's midst, the tent outside the camp becomes a transitional institution until the erection of the Priestly tent in Exod 40. Exodus 34:8–10 itself builds on Exod 33:1–6. The passage is clearly composed as a counterpart to Exod 32:7–14, so that the two intercessions in 32:11–13 and 34:8–9 frame the pre-Dtr intercession in 32:30–34*. Summing up, we can conclude that even though the three passages—Exod 32:7–14; 33:1–6; and 34:8–10—make heavy use of Dtr language, at the same time they presuppose the incorporation of P.

We have seen that some of the references discussed here suggest a pentateuchal perspective, while others suggest a hexateuchal or even an enneateuchal perspective. At first sight, it seems reasonable to assign these different perspectives to different redactions. However, I do not think that things work this way. The composition of two Mosaic intercessions to frame the pre-Dtr intercession (Exod 32:30–34*) is deliberate. The two passages clearly belong together and cannot be separated. Exodus 33:1–6 paves the way for the long negotiations that lead to the third intercession. At the same time this passage is essential for combining the Priestly and the non-Priestly tent-traditions. Only Exod 32:26–29 is not an essential part of the composition of Exod 32–34. But, if our reading of this passage is correct, then Exod 32:26–29 is necessary within the composition of the Pentateuch, to reconcile the Levi tradition in Genesis with the Levi tradition from Exodus to Deuteronomy.

The same holds true for the motif of the tablets. If you take a closer look at this motif you will find a mixture of Priestly (לחת העדות: 31:18; 32:15b–16; 34:29) and Deuteronomistic (לחת אבנים: 34:1–4, 28) language. Within the passages dealing with the tablets, it is not possible to separate a Deuteronomistic,-pre-Priestly strand from a post-Priestly one without destroying the narrative line of the motif.[23] Rather, it appears that the

---

21. Exodus 32:9, which is missing in LXX, may be a still later harmonizing addition from Deut 9:13.

22. Konkel, *Sünde und Vergebung*, 251–52.

23. Konkel, *Sünde und Vergebung*, 237–43.

redaction that incorporates the tablets into the narrative is able to use Deuteronomistic as well as Priestly language, depending on the context. Thus, in Exod 31:18, that redaction uses Priestly language at the end of Exod 25–31 because the latter is part of P; while in Exod 34, Deuteronomistic language is used through the citation of the parallel text of Deut 10, which has itself no counterpart in the Priestly texts.

At the moment, then, I cannot see a compelling reason to distinguish between separate redactions within the passage under discussion. Exodus 32–34 in its entirety is a very deliberately composed text that integrates older material. So, even though we can observe different intertextual horizons, the passages we have discussed, and the insertion of the motif of the stone-tablets, belong to one single redaction that mixes Dtr und Priestly language.

5

In a recent study, E. Aurelius has presented the most elaborate attempt to date, to demonstrate the existence of an Enneateuch redaction.[24] He proposes a redactional envelope created by Exod 19:3b–8 and 2 Kgs 18:12: "Die auffälligen Entsprechungen zwischen diesen zwei Texten beruhen nicht auf Zufall, sondern auf dem Willen eines Redaktors, der im Anschluß an Jer 7,22–28 die Geschichte Israels durch Ex 19,3b–8 und 2 R 18,12 gerahmt hat."[25] Based on that, Aurelius reconstructs a deeply stratified redaction history of the Enneateuch.

E. Blum and R. Achenbach have rightly criticized this thesis.[26] Exodus 19:3b–8 may be composed with 2 Kgs 18:12 in mind, but it is not possible to ascribe both texts to the same redaction. Exodus 19:3b–8 presupposes 2 Kgs 18:12. The supposed envelope does not exist: The promised status of Israel as a ממלכת כהנים (Exod 19:6) is fulfilled in Exod 24 and gambled away in Exod 32. 2 Kings 18:12 is the counterpart, not of Exod 19:3b–8, but of Exod 32.

Prima facie it seems that the passages discussed here can offer the evidence for an Enneateuch redaction that the model of Aurelius is lacking: We have evidence for a late post-Priestly redaction within Exod 32–34 that has unquestionable intertextual links to the books of Kings. But we have to be cautious.

---

24. Aurelius, *Zukunft*.

25. Aurelius, *Zukunft*, 208.

26. Erhard Blum, "Pentateuch–Hexateuch–Enneateuch? Oder: Woran erkennt man ein literarisches Werk in der hebräischen Bibel?" in *Textgestalt und Komposition: Exegetische Beiträge zu Tora und Vordere Propheten* (ed. W. Oswald; FAT 69; Tübingen: Mohr Siebeck, 2010); Reinhard Achenbach, "Pentateuch–Hexateuch–Enneateuch," *ZABR* 11 (2005): 122–54.

The following passages show intertextual links that pass the limits of the Hexateuch: Exod 32:4, 7–14 (1 Kgs 12:28); Exod 32:12 (2 Kgs 23:26); Exod 33:4–6 (Judg 2:1–5); Exod 34:8–9 (2 Kgs 23:3–4). It is clear that none of these references in the books of Kings can be attributed to the same post-Priestly redaction that we have in Exod 32–34. In other words, the references in 1 and 2 Kings are older. They are pre-Priestly and belong to the core of the Dtr history. So we have the same result as in the relationship seen between Exod 19:3b–8 and 2 Kgs 18:12: A late redaction of the Sinai pericope has established intertextual links to existing texts within the books of Kings. The status of Judg 2:1–5, however, is difficult to ascertain.[27] The text is definitely late, but it is hard to decide whether Exod 33:1–6 presupposes Judg 2:1–5 or vice versa. But one thing is for sure: Both texts cannot be ascribed to the same redaction.

The same applies, finally, to the motif of the stone tablets. Even though this motif provides the strongest conceptual link between the Sinai pericope and the books of Kings, the mention of the tablets in 1 Kgs 8:9 cannot be attributed to the same redaction that inserted the motif into the Sinai pericope. Rather, 1 Kgs 8:9 establishes a redactional link to Deut 5; 9–10, where the motif of the tablets is anchored. The insertion of the motif into the Sinai pericope extends this existing line from Deuteronomy to 1 Kings, backwards to Exodus.

The conclusion is hence complex. First, these observations contradict the assumption of the existence of a pre-Priestly Enneateuch (cf. the theories of R. G. Kratz and E. Zenger). All intertextual links between Exod 32–34 and the books of Kings are post-Priestly. The post-Priestly redaction that gave Exod 32–34 its final shape has in view the whole history of Israel from Genesis to the end of 2 Kings and therefore has an enneateuchal perspective. At the same time there is no evidence that the same post-Priestly redaction in Exod 32–34 can be detected in Deuteronomy–2 Kings. So it seems reasonable to conclude that intertextual links have been established from Exod 32–34 to an independent Deuteronomistic History. But does this, then, constitute an Enneateuch?

To answer this question we have to look more closely at the theology of the composition of Exod 32–34 in its final shape.[28] Essential is the third intercession of Moses in Exod 34. After the theophany and the revealing of the so-called "*Gnadenformel*" (Exod 34:6–7), the text continues:

> 8 Moses hastened to bow low to the ground in homage 9 and said, "If I have gained your favor, O Lord, pray, let the Lord go in our midst, even though this is a stiffnecked people. Pardon our iniquity and our sin, and take us for

---

27. Regarding Judg 2:1–5, see now the detailed analysis by Walter Groß, *Richter* (HTKAT; Freiburg: Herder, 2009), 155–78.

28. For the following see Konkel, *Sünde und Vergebung*, 289–304.

your own!" 10 He said: "I hereby make a covenant. Before all your people I will work such wonders as have not been wrought on all the earth or in any nation; and all the people who are with you shall see how awesome are the Lord's deeds, which I will perform for you." (Exod 34:8–10)

Moses here takes the chance to ask for remission once again after his first attempt has failed (Exod 32:30–34). He calls Israel a "stiff-necked people." This characterization is first used by the Lord in Exod 32:9 to justify the intended sudden annihilation of Israel. The characterization occurs again in Exod 33:1–3 after the failure of the first plea for forgiveness, to justify the Lord's decision not to accompany Israel to the land. Now Moses takes up this characterization of Israel and makes it the basis of his own intercession. It is tempting to say: Not *even though* Israel is "stiff-necked," should the Lord forgive, but rather *because* Israel is "stiff-necked." Moses, who was not involved in the service of the golden calf, identifies himself with the people: "Pardon *our* iniquity und *our* sin." The topic of the intercession in Exod 34 is not only forgiveness for the sin of the golden calf. It is about more, namely a further extension of the forgiveness that Israel requires because of its "stiff-necked" nature.

This time the Lord accepts the request of Moses, and he does this through the renewal of the covenant. The initiative is completely on the side of God, even though an obligation towards the law follows (Exod 34:11–28). But repentance as a condition for forgiveness is not mentioned. Also, Israel is not changed in its nature. It is still a "stiff-necked" people.

This concept can no longer be labeled "Deuteronomistic." Even in a late Dtr framework, repentance is the *conditio sine qua non* for forgiveness (cf. e.g., Deut 4:29–31; 30:1–10; 1 Kgs 8:33–34). What we have here is a synthesis of the Priestly theology of grace with the Dtr obligation to the law.

Thus we come back to the intertextual link between Exod 34:8–9 and 2 Kgs 24:3–4: If Moses achieved a far-reaching forgiveness that transcends the horizon of single event (cf. Num 14:17–20), why did God not forgive the "sin of Manasseh"? I think the answer to this question is found in 2 Kgs 24:4: "the blood of the innocent" was the sin that the Lord could not forgive. This kind of guilt was not included in the forgiveness at Sinai. Nevertheless for a reader from the postexilic period onward this was a message of hope: Exodus 34 does not establish an assurance of salvation. Nevertheless, based on the prior forgiveness at Sinai, a prospect of hope for Israel in exile is opened that is distinct from the Deuteronomistic theology of judgment.

So we must concede a paradox: There are intertextual references reaching from the Sinai pericope into the books of Kings. But just these references ensure that the time of Joshua onward is distinguished from the time of Moses. At Sinai a future for Israel is opened that breaks up the framework of the Deuteronomistic theology of repentance. This is articulated by reading Exod 32–34 in relation to the Deuteronomistic history. In such a framework, the time of Moses, represented by the Pentateuch, is distinguished from the following history as fundamental and paradigmatic.

An enneateuchal redaction in Exod 32–34 cannot be demonstrated. Paradoxically it is precisely the enneateuchal perspective of the late redaction in Exod 32–34 that establishes the basis for the constitution, not of an Enneateuch, but rather of a Pentateuch. So, we have continuity and discontinuity at the same time: The Torah is the foundation of the following Former Prophets.

THE BOOK OF JOSHUA AS AN INTERTEXT IN THE MT AND THE LXX CANONS

Thomas B. Dozeman

1. CONTEXT AND COMPOSITION IN THE STUDY OF JOSHUA

The identification of literary works within the Pentateuch and the Former Prophets has been a central focus of research from the outset of the modern period of interpretation.[1] And, as one might expect, the book of Joshua has played a significant role in this research, because of its pivotal location between the Pentateuch and the Former Prophets. As a consequence, literary context has dominated the interpretation of Joshua, raising questions of whether its history of composition should be read more closely with the Pentateuch or with the Former Prophets. The result has been the identification of a variety of literary works that relate the Pentateuch to the Former Prophets in distinct ways. Already in the seventeenth century C.E., B. de Spinoza identified a literary Enneateuch on the basis of the death notices at the outset of Joshua and Judges, which assign the separate books to the eras of Moses, Joshua, the judges, and so forth.[2] J. Wellhausen located the conclusion of the pentateuchal sources in Joshua, with the fulfillment of the promise of land, thus creating an original Hexateuch.[3] M. Noth, on the other hand, detached

---

1. See the article by Suzanne Boorer in this volume.

2. Baruch de Spinoza, *A Theologico-Political Treatise* (ed. J. Israel; Cambridge Texts in the History of Philosophy; Cambridge: Cambridge University Press, 2007 [original 1670]).

3. Julius Wellhausen, *Die Composition des Hexateuchs und der Historischen Bücher des Alten Testaments* (2d ed.; Berlin: Reimer, 1889), 118–36. Wellhausen interprets Joshua in the section, "The Narrative of the Remaining Books of the Hexateuch," which includes Exodus through Joshua. In this way he excludes Joshua from the Former Prophets. The interpretation of Joshua concludes this section, under the title, "The Conquest and Division of Canaan under Joshua." The section on the "Historical Books" includes Judges through Kings. For a summary of the history of interpretation of Joshua within the Hexa-

the composition of Joshua from the pentateuchal sources, creating the literary categories of the Tetrateuch and the Deuteronomistic History.[4]

The increasingly later dating of pentateuchal literature has cast doubt on the identification of an early Hexateuch in source criticism and on the Tetrateuch in M. Noth's Deuteronomistic History hypothesis, which, in turn, raises new questions about the interpretation of Joshua in its literary context. R. Kratz has recently returned to the hypothesis of a Hexateuch as the original literary framework for interpreting the story of the exodus and conquest, to which the narrative of Rahab in Joshua 2 provides the conclusion.[5] J. Blenkinsopp advocates a literary Enneateuch extending from Genesis 1 through 2 Kings 25, as a national epic that recounts "a continuous history from creation to exile."[6] K. Schmid interprets Joshua as a hinge for the Enneateuch, such that Joshua 24 functions as a pivotal text to create the era of salvation (initially extending from the exodus to the conquest, but eventually stretching from the story of origins to the conquest) and the era of decline (from the period of the judges to the end of the monarchy).[7] Over against this, E. Blum interprets Joshua 24, with its reference to the "book of the Torah of God" in v. 26, not as hinge within the Enneateuch but as a conclusion that reflects a

---

teuch see Ernst Jenni, "Zwei Jahrzehnte Forschung an den Büchern Josua bis Köinge," *TRu* 27 (1961): 1–32, 87–146; and the more recent study by Edward Noort, *Das Buch Josua: Forschungsgeschichte und Problemfelder* (EdF 292; Darmstadt: Wissenschaftliche Buchgesellschaft, 1998), 25–92.

4. M. Noth, *Das Buch Josua* (2d ed.; HAT 1/7; Tübingen: Mohr [Siebeck], 1971), 7–17. Noth interprets the composition of Joshua entirely within the context of the Deuteronomistic History, including pre-Dtr; Dtr1; Dtr2; post-Dtr; and late glosses. On the central role of Joshua in Noth's construction of the Deuteronomistic History hypothesis see Brian Peckham, "The Significance of the Book of Joshua in Noth's Theory of the Deuteronomistic History," in *The History of Israel's Traditions: The Heritage of Martin Noth* (ed. S. McKenzie and M. Graham; JSOTSup 182; Sheffield: Sheffield Academic Press, 1994), 213–34.

5. Reinhard G. Kratz, *The Composition of the Narrative Books of the Old Testament* (trans. J. Bowden; New York: T&T Clark, 2005), 133–49, et passim. The original Hexateuch identified by Kratz includes an early version of the account of the exodus and conquest. The connection between Joshua and the pentateuchal literature is evident in the setting of Shittim, which relates Num 25:1a; Deut 34:5; and Josh 2:1; 3:1.

6. Joseph Blenkinsopp, *The Pentateuch: An Introduction to the First Five Books of the Bible* (New York: Doubleday, 1992), 34 et passim.

7. Konrad Schmid, *Erzväter und Exodus: Untersuchungen zur doppelten Begründung der Ursprünge Israels innerhalb der Geschichtsbücher des Alten Testaments* (WMANT 81; Neukirchen-Vluyn: Neukirchener, 1999); idem, "The So-Called Yahwist and the Literary Gap Between Genesis and Exodus," in *A Farewell to the Yahwist? The Composition of the Pentateuch in Recent European Interpretation* (ed. T. B. Dozeman and K. Schmid; SBLSymS 34; Atlanta: Society of Biblical Literature, 2006), 29–50.

weak attempt to create a Hexateuch in the wake of the formation of the Torah of Moses.[8]

This research highlights the continuing ambiguity over the appropriate literary context for interpreting the composition of Joshua. The studies clarify that past models, such as the Hexateuch of source criticism or the hypothesis of the Deuteronomistic History, which once served as fixed points for interpreting the composition and literary context of Joshua, no longer hold the center or provide orientation for current research. The absence of an overarching model, moreover, is generating methodological confusion as significantly new hypotheses are proposed concerning the role of Joshua in the formation of the Pentateuch and the Former Prophets.[9]

The research also clarifies that interpreters are moving increasingly toward redaction criticism to identify the literary context of Joshua, rather than towards the source criticism of J. Wellhausen or the tradition history of M. Noth. Redaction criticism has focused attention on the late composition of Joshua to identify the literary contours of the Pentateuch, Hexateuch, Deuteronomistic History, or Enneateuch. The starting point of the redaction critic is with the "given" text of Joshua, rather than with reconstructed traditions or recovered original sources. This contrasts to source criticism and tradition history, which often begin with the identification of the earliest text or tradition before tracing the formation of the book to its present structure. The presupposition of redaction criticism is that the identification of the *Tendenz*, the horizon, or the contextual profile of late literary strands will indicate the relationship of Joshua to the Pentateuch and/or the Former Prophets and thus provide some control for the interpretation of its overall history of composition and its function within the larger literary context.[10]

---

8. E. Blum, "The Literary Connection between the Books of Genesis and Exodus and the End of the Book of Joshua," in Dozeman and Schmid, *A Farewell to the Yahwist?* \89–106. See also his identification of a "Josua 24 Bearbeitung" in *Die Komposition der Vätergeschichte* (WMANT 57; Neukirchen-Vluyn: Neukirchener, 1984), 39–61; idem, *Studien zur Komposition des Pentateuch* (BZAW 189; Berlin: de Gruyter, 1990), 363–65. Also see Erich Zenger (*Einleitung in das Alte Testament* [4th ed.; Studienbücher Theologie 1; Stuttgart: Kohlhammer, 2004], 100–106), who sees Josh 24 as the end of a Hexateuch; but he considers it the "historical work of a Jerusalem" author.

9. In a recent review of the changing landscape in biblical methodology, E. Blum ("Pentateuch-Hexateuch-Enneateuch? Oder Woran erkennt man ein literarisches Werk in der Hebraischen Bibel?" in *Les dernieres redactions du Pentateuque, de l' Hexateuque et de l'Enneateuque* [ed. T. Römer and K. Schmid; BETL 203; Leuven: Leuven University Press and Peeters, 2007], 69) mused that anything seems possible, and that all options appear to be open as far as deciding which of the literary works—Pentateuch, Hexateuch, Enneateuch, or Deuteronomistic History—has literary-historical priority.

10. For discussion of redaction criticism see, among others, Mark E. Biddle, "Redaction Criticism, Old Testament," in *Dictionary of Biblical Interpretation* (ed. J. H. Hayes;

But the ambiguity of the literary context of Joshua continues to exercise redaction critics. E. Otto and R. Achenbach account for the shifting literary boundaries between the Pentateuch and Joshua as the result of an initial Hexateuchal redaction focused on the promised land followed by a Torah-oriented pentateuchal redaction, both of which occured during the Persian period.[11] E. A. Knauf locates the book of Joshua in a larger Moses-exodus narrative in a similar manner to R. Kratz, and identifies five distinct endings in Joshua that reflect its history of composition from the sixth century B.C.E. into the Hasmonean period.[12] R. Albertz provides yet another reading of the late composition of Joshua by attributing a series of Priestly motifs to a mid-fourth/third century B.C.E. redaction that presupposes the Pentateuch,[13] while U. Becker interprets the late redactional stages of Josh 24 in a similar manner to K. Schmid, where it functions as a hinge that positions Joshua within the larger literary context of the Enneateuch.[14]

The growing prominence of redaction criticism for interpreting the composition of Joshua raises two related problems among researchers that will be the focus of my study. The first is whether redaction criticism is an appropriate methodology for interpreting the late composition of Joshua, where editors are identified as creative authors. This theory of composition continues to be

---

Nashville: Abingdon, 1999), 1:373–76; Rolf Knierim, "Criticism of Literary Features: Form, Tradition, and Redaction," in *The Hebrew Bible and Its Modern Interpreters* (ed. D. A. Knight and G. M. Tucker; Philadelphia: Fortress, 1985), 123–66; Thomas Krüger, "Anmerkungen zur Frage nach den Redaktionen der Grossen Erzählwerke im Alten Testament," in Römer and Schmid, *Les dernieres redactions*, 47–66, esp. 51–57; and Mark A. Christian, "Openness to the Other Inside and Outside of Numbers," in *The Books of Leviticus and Numbers* (ed. T. Römer; BETL 215; Leuven: Leuven University Press and Peeters, 2008); 579–608, esp. 585–602.

11. Eckart Otto, *Das Deuteronomium im Pentateuch und Hexateuch: Studien zur Literaturgeschichte von Pentateuch und Hexateuch im Lichte des Deuteronomiumrahmens* (FAT 30; Tübingen: Mohr Siebeck, 2000); and Reinhard Achenbach, *Die Vollendung der Tora: Studien zur Redaktionsgeschichte des Numeribuches im Kontext von Hexateuch und Pentateuch* (BZABR 3; Wiesbaden: Harrassowitz, 2003); idem, "Pentateuch, Hexateuch und Enneateuch: Eine Verhältnisbestimmung," *ZABR* 11 (2005): 122–54.

12. Ernst A. Knauf, "Buchschlüsse in Josua," in Römer and Schmid, *Les dernieres redactions*, 217–24; idem, *Josua* (ZBK 6; Zurich: Theologischer Verlag, 2008), 1–40. Knauf's literary-critical reconstruction eliminates the hypothesis of the Deuteronomistic History altogether as a framework for interpretation.

13. Rainer Albertz, "Die Kanonische Anpassung des Josuabuches: Eine Neuwertung seiner sogenannten "Priesterschriftlichen Texte," in Römer and Schmid, *Les dernieres redactions*, 199–216.

14. Uwe Becker, "Endredaktionelle Kontextvernetzungen des Josua-Buches," in *Die deuteronomistischen Geschichtswerke: Redaktions- und religionsgeschichtliche Perspektiven zur "Deuteronomismus"-Diskussion in Torah und Vorderen Propheten* (ed. M. Witte et al.; BZAW 365; Berlin: de Gruyter, 2006), 139–61.

debated by source critics,[15] and it has also been challenged recently by J. Van Seters, who rejects any assessment of redactors as creative composers, writing: "Only in a very limited sense do editors revise—for clarity, to correct mistakes, or to overcome difficulties in the text." [16] The second problem is the focus on the present form of the text as the starting point for redaction criticism of Joshua. The difficulty, according to T. Krüger, is in determining the end form or the given text of any biblical book or collection of books.[17] U. Becker builds on the conclusion of Krüger, adding that the notion of a final redaction of the book of Joshua merges the methodologies of textual and literary criticism, because of its complex textual history in the MT, the LXX, and the Dead Sea Scrolls.[18]

My aim in the following study is to evaluate whether redaction criticism is an appropriate methodology for discerning the composition and literary context of Joshua; and if so, with what final form of Joshua does one initiate the process of interpretation? I will begin with the problem of determining the final form of Joshua as a starting point for redaction criticism, before turning to the implications of the final or "end" form for discerning the narrative context of Joshua and the identification of the literary works, Pentateuch, Hexateuch, Enneateuch, or Deuteronomistic History.

2. The Final Form of Joshua in the MT and the LXX

What is the final form of the book of Joshua? As we have seen, the answer to this question is important in redaction criticism both for identifying an editor or author within a particular text and for recognizing the larger scope of that editor's work by tracing the *Tendenz*—the horizon or contextual profile of the redaction. The tendency among recent redaction critics is all too often to privilege or even limit research to the MT in determining the final

---

15. See, for example, Wellhausen, *Composition*, 118–36; or more recently, W. H. Propp, *Exodus 1–18* (AB 2A; New Haven: Yale University Press, 1999), 47–53.

16. J. Van Seters, *The Edited Bible: The Curious History of the "Editor" in Biblical Criticism* (Winona Lake: Eisenbrauns, 2006), 26. In a recent defense of source criticism, J. S. Baden (*J, E, and the Redaction of the Pentateuch* [FAT 68; Tübingen: Mohr Siebeck, 2009], 94) quotes Van Seters's rejection of the creative role of redactors in the composition of biblical literature approvingly and concludes: "This states my vision of the biblical redactor almost perfectly."

17. Krüger, "Anmerkungen," 57–58.

18. Becker, "Endradaktionelle Kontextvernexzungern des Josua-Buches," 140–41. See the discussion of E. Blum ("Gibt es die Endgestalt des Pentateuch?" in *Congress Volume: Leuven 1989* [ed., J. A. Emerton; VTSup 43; Leiden: Brill, 1991], 46–57, esp. 46–47), who questions whether there is such a thing as an "end form," at least with regard to the Pentateuch.

form of Joshua or any book for that matter. But, as T. Krüger and U. Becker have recently noted, the problem of determining the "end form" of a biblical book goes beyond the study of the MT, since one must decide if the given text is the MT or the LXX, which often differ from each other.[19] When the question of the "end form" is broadened in this way, the once distinct methodologies of textual and literary criticism become related within redaction criticism, since both methodologies may provide insight into the composition of the text. This is especially true in the case of Joshua, where the MT and the LXX often diverge from each other in what appears to be creative ways that lead to distinct interpretations of the book.

E. Ulrich reinforces the conclusions of Krüger and Becker by working in the reverse direction, from textual to literary criticism. He, too, underscores the problem of determining the "end form" of a biblical book, especially in light of the "pluriformity" in biblical manuscripts from Qumran, the MT, and the versions. Ulrich notes instances where textual variants exceed individual occurrences to form a coherent pattern.[20] In such cases, he concludes, textual criticism is actually part of the literary process that results in the variant editions of certain books at Qumran, or in the MT and the LXX. Ulrich defines variant (or multiple) literary editions as texts or even whole books that appear "in two or more parallel forms ... , which one author, major redactor [or] major editor completed and which a subsequent redactor or editor intentionally changed to a sufficient extent that the resultant form should be called a revised edition of that text."[21] The definition underscores the close relationship between certain forms of scribal practice and redaction criticism.[22] S.

---

19. Krüger, "Anmerkungen," 57–58.

20. Eugene Ulrich, "Double Literary Editions of Biblical Narratives and Reflections on Determining the Form to be Translated," in *Perspectives on the Hebrew Bible: Essays in Honor of Walter J. Harrelson* (ed. J. L. Crenshaw; Macon: Mercer University Press, 1988) 101–16; idem, "The Canonical Process, Textual Criticism, and Latter Stages in the Composition of the Bible," in *Sha'arei Talmon: Studies in the Bible, Qumran, and the Ancient Near East Presented to Shemaryahu Talmon* (ed. M. Fishbane, E. Tov, and W. W. Fields; Winona Lake, Ind.: Eisenbrauns, 1992), 267–91; idem, "Multiple Literary Editions: Reflections Toward a Theory of the History of the Biblical Text," in *Current Research and Technological Developments on the Dead Sea Scrolls: Conference on the Texts from the Judean Desert, Jerusalem, 30 April 1995* (ed. D. W. Parry and S. D. Ricks; STDJ 20; Leiden: Brill, 1996), 78–105. See the reprint of many of these articles in idem, *The Dead Sea Scrolls and the Origins of the Bible* (2 vols.; Studies in the Dead Sea Scrolls and Related Literature; Grand Rapids: Eerdmans, 1999).

21. Ulrich, "Canonical Process," 278; idem., "Multiple Literary Editions," 78–105, esp. 89–90.

22. Interpreters seek to classify the different types of literary editing into various categories, including redaction, revision, *Fortschreibung* (a continuous process of addition and reinterpretation), *Bearbeitung* (editing and adapting), recension, rewriting, and even

Talmon concludes from this intermingling of "lower" and "higher" forms of criticism that "authors and copyists were not clearly separable classes of literary practitioners."[23]

The interweaving of textual and literary criticisms is especially apparent in the book of Joshua, where the MT and the LXX present significantly different "given texts," as noted by any number of textual critics[24] and underscored most recently by U. Becker.[25] The "sizable extent of the differences between the MT and the LXX," according to E. Ulrich, even "makes it plausible that multiple editions of the full book did exist," which, he notes further, is reinforced by 4QJosh[a], where the different narrative sequence of Joshua's first altar in the promised land may connote yet another variant literary edition of the

translation. For an overview see Christian, "Openness to the Other," 583–605; and E. Earle Ellis, *The Old Testament in Early Christianity: Canon and Interpretation in the Light of Modern Research* (WUNT 54; Tübingen: Mohr Siebeck, 1991), 3–50.

23. Shemaryahu Talmon, "Textual Study of the Bible—A New Outlook," in *Qumran and the History of the Biblical Text* (ed. F. M. Cross and S. Talmon; Cambridge, Mass.: Harvard University Press, 1975), 336.

24. The significant differences between the MT and the LXX already presented a problem for interpreters in the late nineteenth and early twentieth centuries. August Dillmann (*Die Bücher Numeri, Deuteronomium und Josue* [Leipzig: Hirzel, 1886]) and Max A. Margolis (*The Book of Joshua in Greek* [Paris: Geuthner, 1931–36]) favored the priority of the MT, and he accounted for the differences in the LXX as corruptions of the MT. Samuel Holmes (*Joshua: The Hebrew and Greek Texts* [Cambridge: Cambridge University Press, 1914]) argued instead for the literary priority of the LXX. This debate has continued into the present. J. Alberto Soggin (*Joshua: A Commentary* [OTL; Philadelphia: Westminster Press, 1972]) and Marten H. Woudstra (*The Book of Joshua* [NICOT; Grand Rapids: Eerdmans, 1981]), for example, continue to favor the priority of the MT. Harry M. Orlinsky ("The Hebrew *Vorlage* of the Septuagint of the Book of Joshua," in *Congress Volume: Rome 1968* [ed. G. W. Anderson; VTSup 17; Leiden: Brill, 1969], 187–95); A. Graeme Auld, (*Joshua Retold: Synoptic Perspectives* [OTS; Edinburgh: T&T Clark, 1998]); Alexander Rofé, "The Piety of the Torah-Disciples at the Winding-Up of the Hebrew Bible: Josh 1:8; Ps 1:2; Isa 59:21," in *Bibel in jüdischer und christlicher Tradition: Festschrift für Johann Maier zum 60. Geburtstag* [ed. H. Merklein, K. Müller; and G. Stemberger; BBB 88; Bonn: Hahn, 1993], 78–85); and Lea Mazor ("The Septuagint Translation of the Book of Joshua: Abstract of Thesis Submitted for the Degree Doctor of Philosophy to the Senate of the Hebrew University, Jerusalem," *BIOSCS* 27 [1994]: 29–38) argue that the *Vorlage* of the LXX is the more ancient version of Joshua and that the MT represents the latest textual development. Eugene Ulrich, ("Pluriformity in the Biblical Text, Text Groups, and Questions of Canon," in *The Madrid Qumran Congress: Proceedings of the International Congress on the Dead Sea Scrolls, Madrid 18–21 March, 1991* [ed. J. Trebolle Barrera and L. V. Montaner; STDJ 11; Leiden: Brill, 1992], 23–41) has introduced the possibility of variant literary editions of Joshua on the basis of the differences between 4QJosh[a] and the MT or the LXX, in terms of the order of the narrative.

25. Becker, "Endredaktionelle Kontextvernetzungen des Josua-Buches," 140.

book.[26] This research suggests that a redaction-critical study of Joshua, as a means for identifying its function within a larger literary work, whether the Pentateuch, Hexateuch, Deuteronomistic History, or Enneateuch, must begin with a comparison of the MT and the LXX in order to determine the "given text." An exhaustive comparison of Joshua in the versions far exceeds the boundaries of the present study. Yet a more limited comparison of the beginning and ending of Joshua may provide enough information to illustrate the problem of determining an "end text" of Joshua and show how the textual variants in the MT and the LXX create distinct literary contexts for the book, which in turn may lead to the identification of different literary works such as the Pentateuch or Enneateuch.

2.1. The Beginning of Joshua

Joshua 1 presents a range of text-critical problems that influence the interpretation of the text, with the MT presenting a text expanded by nearly ten percent over the LXX. M. van der Meer states the problem of interpretation for Joshua 1 as follows: "Since no convincing explanation of scribal error can be adduced for these quantitative variants, it is clear that they must be the result of deliberate literary initiatives."[27] The difference between the longer MT and the more compact LXX has fueled debate over the textual history of Joshua 1. A. G. Auld notes five significant pluses in the MT of Josh 1:1–4 ("servant of YHWH," v. 1; "this" Jordan, v. 2; "to the people of Israel," v. 2; "this" Lebanon, v. 4; and "all the land of the Hittites," v. 4), by comparison with the absence of any pluses in the LXX. On the basis of these and the many other pluses in the MT of Joshua, Auld argues for the priority of the Hebrew *Vorlage* to the LXX.[28] H. M. Orlinsky reaches the same conclusion, arguing that many of the MT pluses cannot be explained as scribal error, even though they often disrupt the syntax of the MT.[29] A. Rofé adds that the MT pluses, such as "all the Torah" in v. 7, indicate a nomistic or legal ideol-

26. Eugene Ulrich, "4QJoshua[a] and Joshua's First Altar in the Promised Land," in *New Qumran Texts and Studies: Proceedings of the First Meeting of the International Organization for Qumran Studies, Paris 1992* (ed. G. J. Brooke and F. García Martínez; Leiden: Brill, 1994), 89–104; idem, "4QJosh[a]," in *Qumran Cave 4.IX: Deuteronomy, Joshua, Judges, Kings* (ed. E. Ulrich et al.; DJD IX; Oxford: Clarendon, 1995), 143–52.

27. Michaël N. van der Meer, *Formation and Reformulations: The Redaction of the Book of Joshua in the Light of the Oldest Textual Witnesses* (VTSup 102; Leiden: Brill, 2004), 161; idem, "Textual Criticism and Literary Criticism in Joshua 1:7 (MT and LXX)," in *X Congress of the International Organization for Septuagint and Cognate Studies, Oslo, 1998* (ed. B. A. Taylor; SBLSCS 51; Atlanta: Scholars Press, 2001), 355–71.

28. Auld, *Joshua Retold*, 8–9.

29. Orlinsky, "The Hebrew *Vorlage*," 187–95, esp. 188.

ogy underlying the present form of the longer text.[30] L. Mazor builds on the insight of Rofé, detecting further ideological motivation in the expansionistic geographical reference in the MT of v. 4.[31]

The debate over textual priority need not be resolved in order to recognize that the differences between the MT and the LXX raise a problem for determining the "end form" of Joshua 1. Indeed, however one conceptualizes the textual history, whether in terms of the priority of the MT, the priority of the *Vorlage* of the LXX, or the "pluriformity" of textual versions, the research suggests the interweaving of textual and literary factors in the formation of Joshua 1, which is especially apparent in the presentation of Moses and the role of Torah.

Moses is idealized in both the MT and the LXX as the mentor of Joshua (v. 1),[32] who enjoyed the special presence of God (v. 5);[33] received the divine

---

30. A. Rofé, "The Nomistic Correction in Biblical Manuscripts and its Occurrence in 4QSamᵃ," *RevQ* 14 (1989): 247–54, esp. 248. For further discussion see also idem, "The Piety of the Torah-Disciples," 78–85; and idem, "The Editing of the Book of Joshua in the Light of 4QJoshᵃ," in *New Qumran Texts and Studies: Proceedings of the First Meeting of the International Organization for Qumran Studies, Paris 1992* (ed. G. J. Brooke; STDJ 15; Leiden: Brill, 1994), 73–80.

31. Mazor, "The Septuagint Translation of the Book of Joshua," 29–38. See also Mazor's additional research on the ideological influence of textual transmission in "The Origin and Evolution of the Curse upon the Rebuilder of Jericho—A Contribution of Textual Criticism to Biblical Historiography," *Textus* 14 (1988): 1–26; and idem, "A Nomistic Reworking of the Jericho Conquest Narrative Reflected in LXX to Joshua 6:1-20," *Textus* 18 (1995): 47–62.

32. The Hebrew describes Joshua as an "assistant" or perhaps "novice" of Moses, using the word, מְשָׁרֵת, from the root, שׁרת. The term can designate cultic service, of the Aaronide priests (Exod 28:35, 43; 29:30; 35:19; 39:41) and especially the Levites (Num 1:50; 3:6, 31; 8:26; 18:2; see also Deut 10:8; 18:5; 21:5). The Greek ὑπουργός reinforces the leadership or mentor role of Moses.

33. The Deity states to Joshua in Josh 1:5: "As I was with Moses, I will be with you." The special status of Moses is also indicated in the MT of v. 1 by the phrase, "Moses, servant of Yʜwʜ," which is absent in the LXX. The plus in the MT is difficult to evaluate, especially since the epithet occurs in both the MT and the LXX an additional fourteen times (Josh 1:7, 13; 8:31, 33 [=LXX 9:2b, d]; 11:12; 12:6; 13:8; 14:7; 18:7; 22:2, 5). Interpreters vary in their evaluation of the textual problem and its meaning. Robert G. Boling (*Joshua: A New Translation with Notes and Commentary* [AB 6; New York: Doubleday, 1982], 114) suggests haplography in the LXX. Emanuel Tov (*The Greek and Hebrew Bible: Collected Essays on the Septuagint* [VTSup 72; Leiden: Brill, 1999], 394) attributes the epithet to a secondary expansion in the MT, under the influence of Deuteronomy. In this case, the presence of the epithet may be part of the redaction that occurred when Joshua was placed in its present narrative context. Klaus Bieberstein (*Josua—Jordan—Jericho: Archeologie, Geschichte und Theologie der Landnahme-erzählungen Josua 1–6* [OBO 143; Fribourg: Universitätsverlag; Göttingen: Vandenhoek & Ruprecht, 1995], 85) suggests that the MT plus reflects the growing status of Moses in postexilic literature. Van der Meer

promise of land (v. 3); and taught Joshua laws that would lead to his successful leadership in the land (vv. 7–8). Yet there are also differences between the MT and the LXX in the idealization of Moses, especially in the description of his instruction in vv. 7–8. Redaction critics have long suspected that these verses represent a late literary addition to Joshua. R. Smend described vv. 7–9 as a nomistic redaction that reinterprets the divine command in v. 6, where Joshua is called to be courageous in war because of God's unconditional promise to the ancestors. The reinterpretation in vv. 7–9, according to Smend, qualifies the unconditional promise of v. 6 with the word "only," which leads to the reevaluation of success in war as conditional on obedience to the law. The law is further defined in v. 8 as the "book of the law."[34] Such a nomistic reinterpretation of a previously unconditional promise indicates an intentional change to Joshua 1, which in turn suggests the work of a separate author or editor in the composition of Joshua 1. But this in itself does not represent the "final form" of Joshua 1.

Although the nomistic reinterpretation in vv. 7–8 is in both the MT and the LXX, there are also differences in v. 7, which have prompted past interpreters to suspect that the versions represent still further creative changes to the text that have influenced interpretation. The divine speech to Joshua in the MT of v. 7 states:

רק חזק ואמץ מאד לשמר לעשות ככל־התורה אשר צוך
משה עבדי אל־תסור ממנו

> Only be courageous and very strong by observing and doing all the Torah which Moses, my servant, commanded you. Do not turn from it.

The MT describes the commandments of Moses as "all the Torah." This Torah was given to Joshua alone (צוך), and it is referred to at the close of the divine statement in the singular, "do not turn from it" (ממנו). Thus the MT has a clearly defined understanding of Moses' commandments as "all the Torah," in the possession of Joshua. This phrasing suggests a book that Joshua must study for success in leadership, rather than a need to recall past teaching from his lived experience with Moses. But the MT presents a problem, noted already by the Masoretes:[35] the masculine singular suffix on the preposition ממנו ("from it") does not correspond to its antecedent, the femi-

---

(*Formation and Reformulations*, 183) reverses the argument, advocating instead "stylistic shortening" in the LXX to avoid the redundancy of the epithet in the MT.

34. Rudolf Smend ("Das Gesetz und die Völker," in *Probleme biblischer Theologie: Gerhard von Rad zum 70. Geburtstag* [ed. H. W. Wolff; Munich: Kaiser, 1971], 494–504) included Josh 1:7–9; 13:1bβ–6; and 23, as part of the nomistic redaction of Joshua.

35. See the marginal note, סביר ממנה.

nine noun התורה ("Torah"). The textual problem of the MT is compounded by the absence of the phrase, "all the Torah" in the LXX:

ἴσχυε οὖν καὶ ἀνδρίζου φυλάσσεσθαι καὶ ποιεῖν καθότι ἐνετείλατό σοι Μωυσῆς ὁ παῖς μου καὶ οὐκ ἐκκλινεῖς ἀπ᾽ αὐτῶν ...

Be strong and manly to observe and to do as Moses, my servant, commanded you and do not turn from them...

The absence of "all the Torah," in the LXX is accompanied by one other difference from the MT: when the LXX refers to the Mosaic instruction at the close of the statement it uses the plural, "do not turn from them" (ἀπ᾽ αὐτῶν).

The textual variations in Josh 1:7 have given rise to debate over the relationship between the MT and the LXX. Many modern interpreters judge the phrase, "all the Torah," in the MT to be a later addition: either as a gloss, as according to M. A. Margolis,[36] in which case it would provide little or no insight into the larger interpretation of Joshua or its literary context;[37] or as part of a more comprehensive reinterpretation that is later than the LXX. In the latter case, the reference to "all the Torah" would represent a more significant reinterpretation of Joshua. E. Tov, for example, judges the reference, "all the Torah," to be a secondary post-LXX addition to Joshua under the influence of the book of Deuteronomy.[38] A. Rofé agrees, noting that the addition of Torah observance (a nomistic interpretation of revelation) is foreign to and disruptive of the book of Joshua, where the central character receives direct divine commands.[39] M. van der Meer also argues that Josh 1:7–8 is a "nomistic re-edition of the Deuteronomistic (DtrH) composition," but he adds that the absence of "all the Torah" in v. 7, and the replacement of the restrictive particles, רק ("only") and מאד ("very"), with the inferential conjunction, οὖν ("thus, therefore"), is an innovation by the Greek translator that is meant to harmonize vv. 7–8 with Josh 1:2–6.[40]

The debate over the priority of the *Vorlage* of the LXX or the MT is difficult to resolve on the basis of such a limited comparison of textual variants.

---

36. Margolis, *The Book of Joshua in Greek*, 6.

37. This would also presumably be the position of Van Seters, *The Edited Bible*, 331 et passim. Although Van Seters does not address Josh 1:7–9 in particular, he utilizes the research of William McKane on Jeremiah (*A Critical and Exegetical Commentary on Jeremiah* [ICC; Edinburgh: T&T Clark, 1986], 1:lxxxi–lxxxii et passim), who states that editorial differences—such as those evident in this case between the MT and the LXX—are triggered by single verses and present no overarching reinterpretation of material.

38. Tov, *The Greek and Hebrew Bible*, 390.

39. Rofé, "The Nomistic Correction," 248.

40. Van der Meer, *Formation and Reformulations*, 214–22.

Yet even without a resolution to this problem, the differences do suggest continuing literary activity in the transmission of the textual versions that change the "final form" of Joshua 1 beyond the nomistic redaction of vv. 7–8. The different reinterpretations in the MT and the LXX do not revolve around *whether* there is a "book of Torah," since both versions refer to such a book in v. 8. A closer examination of v. 7 in the following section will illustrate that the differences have more to do with the literary context of Joshua in the emerging MT and the LXX canons, especially the issue of how the book of Joshua is meant to relate to the literature of the Pentateuch. We will return to the interpretation of the context of Joshua in the MT and the LXX in the following section after a comparison of the ending of Joshua in the MT and the LXX.

2.2. The Ending of Joshua

The MT and the LXX also provide different endings to the book of Joshua, which continue to raise the problem of the "end form" of Joshua. These differences include both the narrative sequence and the content of the ending of Josh 24. The MT concludes the book with the notice of three burials: those of Joshua (Josh 24:29–30); the bones of Joseph (Josh 24:32); and Eleazar (Josh 24:33). The MT's closing portrait of the Israelite people is positive: "Israel served YHWH all the days of Joshua" (Josh 24:31). The LXX concludes the book of Joshua with the notice of four burials—those of Joshua (Josh 24:30–31); the bones of Joseph (Josh 24:32); Eleazar (Josh 24:33); and Phinehas (Josh 24:33a)—while its closing portrait of the Israelites is one of faithlessness, which leads to their oppression by Eglon, the king of Moab (Josh 24:33b). These contrasting conclusions are further complicated by the additional account of the death and burial of Joshua in Judg 2:6–10, which may provide a window into an even earlier stage in the composition of Joshua than the different endings of the MT and the LXX.[41] The earlier redaction-critical stage of composition in the double account of Joshua's death (Josh 24:28–33; Judg 2:6–10) will be excluded from our study in order to remain focused on the literary context of the MT and the LXX and the problem of determining

---

41. For a range of solutions see Albrecht Alt, "Josua," in *Werden und Wesen des Alten Testament: Vorträge gehalten auf der internationalen Tagung alttestamentlicher Forscher zu Göttingen vom 4.–10, September 1935* (ed. P. Volz, F. Stummer, and J. Hempel; BZAW 66; Berlin: Topelman, 1936), 13–29; A. Graeme Auld, "Judges 1 and History: A Reconsideration" *VT* 25 (1975): 261–85; Erhard Blum, "Der kompositionelle Knoten am Übergang von Josua zu Richter: Ein Entflectungsvorschlag," in *Deuteronomy and Deuteronomic Literature: Festschrift C. H. W. Brekelmans* (ed. M. Vervenne and J. Lust; BETL 133; Leuven: Leuven University Press and Peeters, 1997), 181–212; and Mareike Rake, *"Juda wird aufsteigen?": Untersuchungen zum ersten Kapitel des Richterbuches* (BZAW 367; Berlin: de Gruyter, 2006).

the "end form" of the book. The different endings of Joshua can be illustrated in the following manner:

MT Josh 24:29-33	LXX Josh 24:30-33
Departure of the Israelites	*Departure of the Israelites*
28 Joshua sent the people away to their inheritances.	**28** Iesous sent the people away and they went each to his place.
	Faithfulness of the Israelites
	29 And Israel served the Lord all the days of Iesous and all the days of the elders during the time of Iesous and who knew all the work of the Lord, which he did for Israel.
(1) Burial of Joshua	(1) Burial of Iesous
29 And after these words, Joshua the son of Nun the servant of YHWH died. He was one hundred and ten years old. **30** And they buried him in the territory of his inheritance in Timnath-serah, which is in the highland of Ephraim, north of Mount Gaash.	**30** And it happened after these things, Iesous the son of Naue the servant of the Lord died, one hundred and ten years old. **31** And they buried him at the border of his allotment in Thamnatharaschara in the highland of Ephraim from the north of Mount Gaas.
	31a There they placed with him in the tomb in which they buried him, the flint knives with which he circumcised the sons of Israel at Galgala, when he led them out of Egypt as the Lord commanded them. And there they are until this day.
Faithfulness of the Israelites	
31 Israel served YHWH all the days of Joshua and all the days of the elders whose days extended beyond Joshua, and who knew the work that YHWH did for Israel.	
(2) Burial of Joseph's Bones	(2) Burial of Joseph's Bones
32 The bones of Joseph that the Israelites brought up from Egypt were buried in Shechem in the section of the field that Jacob bought from the sons of Hamor, the father of Shechem for one hundred Qesitah. They belonged to the sons of Joseph as an inheritance.	**32** And the bones of Joseph the sons of Israel brought up from Egypt and buried in Sikima in the part of the field which Jacob brought from the Amorites who dwelt in Sikima for one hundred ewe-lambs. And he gave it to Joseph as a portion.

MT Josh 24:29-33	LXX Josh 24:30-33
(3) Burial of Eleazar	(3) Burial of Eleazar
33 And Eleazar the son of Aaron died. And they buried him in Gibeah of Phinehas his son, which was given to him in the highland of Ephraim.	**33** And it happened after this, Eleazar the son of Aaron, the high priest died and was buried in Gabaath of Phinees of his son, which he gave him in the highland of Ephraim.
	(4) Burial of Phinees
	33a On that day the sons of Israel took the ark of God and carried it around in their midst.
	(And Phinees was priest after his father Eleazar until he died and was buried at Gabaath, which belonged to him.
	Departure of the Israelites
	33b The sons of Israel departed each to his own place and to his own city.
	Unfaithfulness of the Israelites
	And the sons of Israel worshipped Ashtaroth and the gods of the nations round about them. And the Lord gave them over to the hand of Eglon the king of Moab. And he ruled over them for eighteen years.

The MT of Josh 24:28–33 begins with Joshua sending the Israelites to their respective tribal lands (v. 28), after which he dies at the age of one hundred and ten years (v. 29) and is buried at Timnath-serah (v. 30). Verse 31 provides the closing portrait of the Israelites as being faithful not only during the lifetime of Joshua, but also during "all the days of the elders whose days extended beyond Joshua." The MT version follows this ideal portrait of the Israelites with the account of the burial of Joseph's bones (v. 32), and lastly, that of Eleazar (v. 33), who represents the priesthood during the lifetime of Joshua and his generation. Thus, the burial of Joshua and Eleazar punctuates the time period in salvation history, within which the MT version of Joshua is to be read. The focus is on the second generation of the Israelites who had left Egypt; they represent the ideal of faithfulness. This generation is to be compared to the first generation of Israelites, who die in the wilderness, and to the later generation(s), whose apostasy is narrated in Judges.

The "end form" of the LXX provides a very different closing to Joshua. The LXX includes two accounts of the return of the Israelites to their respective tribal lands (LXX Josh 24:29 and 33b), as opposed to the single mention in the MT (MT Josh 24:32). Joshua sends the Israelites away for the first time (LXX Josh 24:28–29) before his death (LXX Josh 24:30) and burial at "Thamnatharaschara" (LXX Josh 24:31). The death and burial of Joshua in the LXX also includes the additional notice that the flint knives with which he circumcised the Israelite males in Josh 5:4–5 are also buried with him (LXX Josh 24:31a). The LXX then records the burial of Joseph's bones and of Eleazar (LXX Josh 24:32-33), as in the MT (Josh 24:32–33). But the LXX also extends the timeline to another generation by including a procession with the ark and the burial of Phinehas (LXX Josh 24:33a), before concluding the book with the notice of Israel's second return to their tribal lands, at which time they act unfaithfully toward Yhwh and are oppressed by Eglon, king of Moab (LXX Josh 24:33b).

The final forms of the ending of Joshua in the MT and the LXX are decidedly different. The inclusion of the flint knives in the LXX version of Joshua's burial (LXX Josh 24:31a) indicates literary activity in the transmission of the textual versions. The presence of this detail at the conclusion of the book links the burial of Joshua with the LXX version of the story of circumcision in Josh 5:4–6 and the LXX addition to the account of the Levitical cities (LXX Josh 19:42a–b). A. Rofé concluded that the motif of the flint knives in the LXX of Josh 24:31a is the more original ending of Joshua, and that their removal in the MT is an instance of late nomistic editing to remove a reference to religious relics that had become offensive to the editors of the MT.[42] M. Rösel, on the other hand, favors the priority of the MT, noting that the flint knives are an important motif throughout the LXX version of the book of Joshua.[43] C. G. den Hertog agrees with M. Rösel, noting that the flint knives represent the concerns of the translator about the status of uncircumcised Jews in Alexandria.[44] However one decides the priority of the MT and the LXX, it is clear that editors have influenced the final form of the text of Joshua and that they are part of the history of composition. We will build on this insight in the following section by interpreting the divergent sequence of the burials in the MT and the LXX of Joshua as editorial creations aimed at fashioning distinct literary contexts for the book of Joshua.

42. A. Rofé, "The End of the Book of Joshua according to the Septuagint," *Henoch* 4 (1982): 17–36, esp. 24–25.

43. Martin Rösel, "The Septuagint-Version of the Book of Joshua," *SJOT* 16 (2002): 15–16.

44. Cornelis G. den Hertog, "Jos 5,4–6 in der griechischen Übersetzung," *ZAW* 104 (1992): 601–6.

3. The Literary Context of Joshua in the MT and the LXX

The textual differences in the MT and the LXX result in two different "end forms" in the beginning and ending of Joshua. The differences are motivated in part by content. There is an emphasis on Torah and on the leadership of Joshua in the MT of Joshua 1 that exceeds that of the LXX, where the reference to Torah is missing in Josh 1:7 and where the people assume a more prominent role alongside Joshua. The emphasis on the flint knives of circumcision in the LXX ending of Joshua may reflect special concerns of the Greek scribal translators—or the absence of this motif in the MT may be the result of fears by the MT scribes about worshiping relics. A comparison of content alone, however, does not probe the full extent of the differences between the MT and the LXX. My aim in this section is to employ the additional criterion of literary context to account for the different "end forms" of the beginning and ending of Joshua in the emerging MT and LXX canons.

3.1. The Beginning of Joshua

The comparison of Josh 1:7–8 in the MT and the LXX underscores two differences in the textual versions of v. 7: (1) the reference to "all the Torah" as the teaching of Moses in the MT and its absence in the LXX; and (2) the contrasting references to the teaching of Moses in the singular (ממנו) in the MT and in the plural (αὐτῶν) in the LXX. There may indeed be an emphasis on Torah in the MT version as noted above. But that emphasis is only minor, when we note that the "book of the Torah" is specifically mentioned in both the MT and the LXX in v. 8. Thus, both versions emphasize the authority of Torah in the story of Joshua. When the comparison is expanded from simply content to include literary context, it becomes clear that the authority of Torah functions differently in the MT and the LXX versions of Joshua.

The reference to the instruction of Moses in the MT of Josh 1:7 as "all the Torah" suggests a single corpus of law as the object to which Yhwh is drawing Joshua's attention. This reading is reinforced when the Deity refers to the Torah in the singular, in the command that Joshua "not turn from it." These unique features define the authority of Torah in the MT, which in turn influences the relationship of Joshua to Moses and the book of Joshua to the Pentateuch. The reference to "all the Torah," conceived as a singular entity, suggests that revelation consists in the study of the book, Torah, by the leader, Joshua. The study of Torah distances Joshua in time from Moses, the author of the Torah. The literary effect of the MT is to separate the book of Joshua from the story of Moses in the Pentateuch. In addition, the focus of the divine speech on Joshua alone, as the one who must study Torah, also separates him from the people in terms of social function. Only he is required to study Torah for successful leadership, not the people.

The authority of Torah is grounded more *experientially* in the LXX. The LXX does not view the teaching of Moses as a single body of legislation. The phrase, "all the Torah," in v. 7 is absent and the Deity references the teachings of Moses in the plural, as a series of instructions that Joshua must recall from past experience with Moses, rather than through the study of a book. The LXX reads: "Do according to what my servant Moses commanded *you*. Do not turn from *them*" (v 7). Thus, the LXX weaves the story of Moses and Joshua together as a sequence of related events that Joshua must recall and claim in present circumstances. In this way, the memory of past experience with Moses undergirds the authority of the book of Torah. If the emphasis in the MT on "all the Torah" in the possession of Joshua alone creates a disjunction between the Pentateuch and the book of Joshua, then the literary effect of the LXX is just the reverse. It ties the book of Joshua more closely to the Pentateuch as a continuous history, in which Joshua must recall the individual commands of Yahweh and of Moses from past experience.[45] The result is that the LXX encourages a reading of Joshua 1 as a continuous history from the life of Moses through the leadership of Joshua—a Hexateuch if you will—as compared to the MT, where the time of Moses and the composition of Torah as a Pentateuch are more removed from the story of Joshua.

3.2. The Ending of Joshua

The endings of Joshua in the MT and the LXX are significantly different in content. We have seen that the MT presents a shorter text, which recounts the burials of Joshua, the bones of Joseph, and Eleazar, before closing with a positive portrayal of the Israelite people. The LXX features a longer ending with four burials—of Joshua, the bones of Joseph, Eleazar, and Phinehas; it also includes the motif of the flint knives in the burial notice of Joshua; and it concludes with the negative portrayal of the Israelite people. A study of the content accounts for some of the differences between the MT and the LXX, especially with regard to the flint knives. But when we broaden the lens to include the literary context of Joshua, the functions of the different "end forms" in the MT and the LXX snap into clearer focus.

In the previous section, we saw that the burials of Joshua and Eleazar punctuate the time period in salvation history, within which to read the MT version of Joshua. The emphasis of the MT is on the second generation of the Israelites who left Egypt. They represent the ideal of faithfulness as compared to the later generation, whose faithlessness is narrated in Judges. The focus

---

45. Van der Meer, *Formation and Reformulation*, 214–22.

on Joshua, Eleazar, and the generation of faithful Israelites suggests upon first reading that the book of Joshua is separated from Judges in the "end form" of the MT. But this is not the case. Joshua and Judges are linked into one composition in the MT through the repetition of the notices of Joshua's death and burial in Josh 24:28–31 and Judg 2:6–9, which forges a clear tie between the two books. Thus, although the book of Joshua is separated from the Pentateuch, it is associated with Judges in the MT.

The literary boundaries of the recountings of Joshua's death in Josh 24:28–31 and Judg 2:6–9 indicate, however, that the relationship between Joshua and Judges in the MT is limited. The repetition frames only the events pertaining to Joshua's generation, who are also described as being faithful to YHWH in Judg 2:7. The limited scope of the repetition *includes* the ending of Joshua (Josh 24:28–33) and the story of Joshua's generation in the opening section of Judges (Judg 1:1–2:9). It *excludes* the subsequent generation, who came to power after the death of Joshua's generation and "did not know YHWH or the work that he did for Israel" (Judg 2:10). In this way the content of the ending of Joshua in the MT corresponds to the literary context of the book of Joshua in the MT. Both reinforce the positive portrayal of Joshua's generation of Israelites. The literary relationship between the MT ending of Joshua and Judges ceases with Judg 2:10, where the events move beyond Joshua's generation with the rise of a new generation. The limited scope of the repetition suggests that, although the MT connects the books of Joshua and Judges, it also distinguishes the ideal vision of the Israelites during the lifetime of Joshua from the apostasy of the next generation, who are prominent in Judges. Thus the literary strategy of the MT emerges: the books of Joshua and Judges are related, even while the ideal portrait of Joshua and his generation remains separated, for the most part, from the subsequent story of the tribes in the book of Judges, who represent a later generation of unfaithfulness.

The final form of the LXX suggests a different literary relationship between Joshua and Judges. The basis for this conclusion is not the unique role of the flint knives in the "end form" of the LXX, but the expanded list of burials from three (Joshua, bones of Joseph, Eleazar) to four (Joshua, bones of Joseph, Eleazar, Phinehas) and the additional negative evaluation of the Israelites. J. M. Dines is certainly correct in concluding that the LXX additions to Joshua are intended to make "a deliberate link" to the book of Judges.[46] But the question remains, for what purpose? The question of purpose is important, since, as we have seen, the MT also relates the books of Joshua and Judges.

The key for interpreting the function of the LXX ending to Joshua is the extended timeline of its "end form," which expands the literary context of Joshua in two ways. First, the notice of Israel's unfaithfulness extends the con-

---

46. Jennifer M. Dines, *The Septuagint* (New York: T&T Clark, 2004), 16.

clusion of the book beyond the death of Joshua and his generation to include the apostasy of the next generation of Israelites (Judg 2:10–11) and their oppression by Eglon (Judg 3:12).[47] Second, the procession of the ark and the burial of Phinehas in Josh 24:33a LXX further expands the literary context of Joshua, since the only reference to Phinehas in Judges occurs at the end of the book, where Phinehas and the ark are also mentioned together during the story of intertribal warfare against Benjamin (Judg 20:28). In this way the content of the ending of Joshua in the LXX corresponds to the literary context of the book of Joshua in the LXX. Both downplay the separate idealization of Joshua and his generation, while also emphasizing the negative portrayal of the Israelites. The result of this literary strategy is that the context of Joshua in the LXX is inseparable from the more extended story of tribal unfaithfulness and disobedience that dominates in the larger literary design of the book of Judges, which also continues into the story of the monarchy in Samuel and Kings.

4. Editors as Authors in the Book of Joshua

The study of the beginning and ending of Joshua in the MT and the LXX provides insight into two related topics, which influence the identification of literary works that connect the Pentateuch and the Former Prophets. These are: the active role of editors in creating the final form of Joshua; and the relationship of content and literary context in the late editing of the book within the emerging MT and LXX canons.

4.1. The Final Form of Joshua in the MT and the LXX

The active role of editors is evident in the composition of the final form of Joshua. At the outset of this essay, I noted debate among contemporary literary and textual critics over the role of redactors or editors in the composition of the biblical books in general, including the book of Joshua. In literary criticism the dispute concerns the function of redactors in the formation of biblical texts, while in textual criticism the debate is over the role of

---

47. Rösel ("The Septuagint-Version of the Book of Joshua," 18–19) notes that the reference to Eglon ties the LXX version of the book of Joshua closer to the other historical books (Judges, Samuel, Kings) than the MT version. He speculates that the reason for the closer connection to Judges in the LXX is that the subsequent books are not yet translated. Thus the reference to Eglon is a preview of what is to come. This argument, based on the history and chronology of translation, is difficult to evaluate. Rösel's literary judgment, however, that the LXX of Joshua is tied more closely to the subsequent book of Judges than the MT, is certainly true, and it reinforces the emphasis throughout the LXX on the book of Joshua as historical narrative, as compared to the more prophetic focus of the MT.

the scribe in the production of the textual versions. In each case the issue is the same; namely, whether redactors or scribes simply preserve tradition (in the form of literary sources[48] or an Urtext),[49] or whether they function more creatively in contributing to the composition of texts.[50] The study of Joshua in the MT and the LXX indicates that scribes are not simply preservers of received tradition, but that they are actively involved in the late composition of the book. The introductions to Joshua in the MT and the LXX contain different portraits of Moses with distinct views of the authority of Torah, while the endings of the book also include separate motifs, such as the flint knives, and divergent views of the faithfulness of Israel. These differences suggest deliberate literary initiatives, with the result that the divergent final forms of

---

48. William H. Propp provides a recent example of this position in his Exodus commentary, where he views the redactor as a scribe, rather than an author: "His raw materials were already highly polished works of art, which he had but to transcribe" (*Exodus 1–18*, 52–53). The quotation indicates the assumption that sources are more or less completed literary compositions that redactors seek to preserve in fashioning the Pentateuch and portions of the Former Prophets.

49. Bruce K. Waltke ("How We Got the Hebrew Bible: The Text and Canon of the Old Testament," in *The Bible At Qumran: Text, Shape, and Interpretation* [ed. P. W. Flint; Studies in the Dead Sea Scrolls and Related Literature; Grand Rapids: Eerdmans, 2001], 27–50) represents the more tradition approach to textual criticism, concluding that the "aim of OT text criticism [is] that of recovering the original text that lies behind the Proto-MT recension" (42).

50. The traditional approach to textual criticism (see n. 49) has undergone change in two directions. One group of researchers focuses on the creativity of the LXX translator and thus maintains the priority of the MT text over the LXX. They do not, however, evaluate the differences in the LXX as instances of corruption, but as examples of where the translator sought to interpret the Hebrew for a Greek-speaking audience. Arie van der Kooij ("Perspectives on the Study of the Septuagint: Who are the Translators?" in *Perspectives in the Study of the Old Testament and Early Judaism: A Symposium in Honour of Adam S. van der Woude* on the Occasion of his 70th Birthday [ed. F. García Martinez and E. Noort; VTSup 73; Leiden: Brill, 1998], 214–29, esp. 228–29), for example, describes the Greek translator as a learned "scribe." For similar evaluations of the LXX translators see Bieberstein, *Josua—Jordan—Jericho*; van der Meer, *Formation and Reformulation*; Jacqueline Moatti-Fine, *Jésus (Josué): Traduction du texte grec de la Septante* (La Bible d'Alexandrie 6; Paris: Cerf, 1996); and Rösel, "The Septuagint-Version of the Book of Joshua," 5–23. Another group of interpreters focuses on the many additions in the MT in order to argue for the literary priority of the shorter LXX and its Hebrew *Vorlage* over the longer MT, thus reversing the classical position. See, for example, Holmes, *Joshua*; Orlinsky, "The Hebrew Vorlage," 187–95; Auld, *Joshua Retold*; A. Rofé, "Joshua 20: Historico-Literary Criticism Illustrated," in *Empirical Models for Biblical Criticism* (ed. J. H. Tigay; Philadelphia: University of Pennsylvania Press, 1985), 131–47); and Mazor, "The Origin and Evaluation of the Curse upon the Rebuilder of Jericho," 1–26. The Qumran texts have also influenced the reevaluation of the original model of textual criticism. See for example Orlinsky, "The Hebrew *Vorlage*," 187–95; E. Ulrich, "4QJosh[a]," 143–52; and Tov, *Textual Criticism*, 327.

Joshua represent the distinctive points of view or *Tendenzen* of the editors in the MT and the LXX. The contrasts support E. Ulrich's conclusion of textual pluriformity in the versions, which in turn reinforces the conclusion of T. Krüger noted earlier—that any redaction-critical study of composition based on the "given form" of a book or a literary work must reach beyond the traditional boundaries of literary criticism. It must also include the once separate field of textual criticism to identify the *Tendenz* of the late editors or authors.

4.2. The Literary Context of Joshua in the MT and the LXX Canons

The evidence of editorial influence in the MT and the LXX also indicates that literary context must be incorporated into the study of the final form of Joshua, since the late editing of the two versions is aimed at both content and context. The emphasis on "all the Torah" as the source of instruction in the opening divine command to Joshua not only signals the distinctive content of the MT, but it also functions contextually to separate the time of Joshua from Moses and the book of Joshua from the Pentateuch. The absence of this motif in the LXX, on the other hand, ties the book of Joshua more closely to the Pentateuch, since the instruction that Joshua requires for successful leadership must be recalled from his past experience with Moses rather than from the study of a separate book. We have seen that the interweaving of content and context also continues into the conclusion of Joshua, where the MT limits the relationship between Joshua and Judges in order to idealize Joshua and his generation over against the period of the judges, while the LXX downplays the idealization of Joshua's generation and ties the book more closely to Judges as a continuous story, in the same way as it merged the Pentateuch and Joshua into one history.

The combination of content and context in the late editing of Joshua indicates that the editors are not simply influencing the central themes of Joshua, but that they are also creating distinct literary works in the emerging MT and the LXX canons,[51] regardless of whether the book of Joshua may have been

---

51. The definition of canon has become a central topic of debate among contemporary interpreters. The traditional and more narrow definition of canon as an authoritative, closed set of books in a fixed form (e.g., Herbert E. Ryle, *The Canon of the Old Testament* [London: Macmillan, 1914], 93 et passim), has been expanded by recent interpreters who favor a broader understanding of canon as a process by which authoritative texts are used and collected over time (e.g., James A. Sanders, *Torah and Canon* [Philadelphia: Fortress, 1972], 56). The expanded definition has raised the question of whether the terms "canon" and "scripture"(or perhaps even a more descriptive term such as "foundational texts") must be distinguished in the study of the formation of authoritative literature (see, for example, Albert C. Sundberg, "Reexamining the Formation of the Old Testament Canon," *Int* 42 (1988): 78–82; and Margalit Finkelberg and Guy G. Stroumsa, "Introduction: Before the

transmitted and preserved on an individual scroll.[52] In the MT, the law of the Torah is separated from the story of Joshua. The two bodies of literature do not flow into each other as one continuous story of Israelite history. Rather, the pentateuchal literature, conceived as Torah, recounts the origin of the Israelite people and the revelation of law through Moses. The Mosaic age comes to a conclusion in the MT at the end of the Torah, while the book of Joshua begins the story of the influence of the Torah in human affairs. Whether the book of Joshua was intended to begin the section of the Prophets, as is its function in the fully developed MT canon, is not clear from the editing.[53] In

---

Western Canon," in *Homer, the Bible, and Beyond: Literary and Religions Canons in the Ancient World* [ed. M. Finkelberg and G. G. Stroumsa; Jerusalem Studies in Religion and Culture 2; Leiden: Brill, 2003], 1–8, esp. 5–7). In a recent review of the problems of definition, Eugene Ulrich ("The Notion and Definition of Canon," in *The Canon Debate* [ed. L. M. McDonald and J. A. Sanders; Boston: Hendrickson, 2002], 45–59 esp., 55–56) has sought to locate the poles of this debate in a definition of canon that includes, (1) books, although not necessarily the textual form of the books; (2) reflective judgment—hence a process of use; and (3) a closed list. The literature on the definition of canon and the comparison of "canon" to "scripture" in the Hebrew Bible (and at times also the New Testament) is extensive. See, among many others, Brevard S. Childs, *Introduction to the Old Testament as Scripture*. (Philadelphia: Fortress Press, 1979); Ellis, *The Old Testament in Early Christianity Canon and Interpretation in the Light of Modern Research*, 1991, 3–50; Steven B. Chapman, *The Law and the Prophets: A Study in Old Testament Canon Formation* (Tübingen: Mohr Siebeck, 2000); McDonald and Sanders, *The Canon Debate*. For definitions of canon in a comparative perspective see Finkelberg and Stroumsa, *Homer, the Bible, and Beyond*.

52. For discussion see Menahem Haran, "Book Scrolls in Pre-exilic Times," *JJS* 33 (1982): 161–73; idem, "Bible Scrolls in Eastern and Western Jewish Communities from Qumran to the High Middle Ages," *HUCA* 56 (1985): 21–62; Johann Maier, "Zur Frage des biblischen Kanons im Frühjudentum im Licht der Qumranfunde," in *Zum Problem des biblischen Kanons* (P. D. Hanson, U. Mauser, M. Saebo; ed. I. Baldermann, E. Dassmann, O. Fuchs; JBTh 3; Neukirchen-Vluyn: Neukirchener, 1988), 135–46, esp. 136; David M. Carr, "Canonization in the Context of Community," in *A Gift of God in Due Season: Essays on Scripture and Community in Honor of James A. Sanders* (ed. R. D. Weis and D. M. Carr; JSOTSup 225; Sheffield: Sheffield Academic Press, 1996), 22–64, esp. 41, 45–46; Ulrich, "Scrolls," 19–21; and Konrad Schmid, "Buchtechnische und sachliche Prolegomena zur Enneateuchfrage," in *Auf dem Weg zur Endgestalt von Genesis bis II Regum* (ed. M. Beck and U. Schorn; BZAW 370; Berlin: de Gruyter, 2006), 1–14.

53. Interpreters debate the history of the MT canon, especially the emergence of the tripartite canon. Important texts that may refer to an emerging tripartite division of the biblical books include, in the second century B.C.E.: Sirach 38:34–39:1; the prologue to the Greek translation by Ben Sira's grandson; 1 Macc 1:54–57; 2:50–60; 7:17; and 2 Macc 2:2–3; perhaps in the first century B.C.E.: 4QMMT (compare Eugene Ulrich, "The Non-attestation of a Tripartite Canon in 4QMMT," *CBQ* [2003]: 202–14); in the first century C.E.: Philo *Contempl.* 3.25–28; Josephus *C.Ap.* 1.37–43; and Luke 24:44. For discussion see Julio C. Trebolle Barrera, "Origins of a Tripartite Old Testament Canon," in McDonald and Sand-

the LXX, by contrast, the late editing of Joshua ties the book more closely to the preceding literature of the Pentateuch as a continuation of the history of Israel. Upon a first reading, this suggests a literary Hexateuch rather than the Pentateuch of the MT. But the downplaying of Joshua and his generation at the conclusion of the LXX version of the book indicates that the editors envision a larger literary work than the Hexateuch, continuing at least through Judges, even though its full extent cannot be identified on the basis of the editing of Joshua.[54]

The distinct literary context of Joshua in the MT and LXX canons is illustrated in the following diagram:

---

ers, *The Canon Debate*, 128-45. The books of the Torah and the Prophets were likely fixed at an earlier date than the tripartite structure. The list of famous men in Sirach 44–49 suggests that the Torah and the Prophets were established by the second century B.C.E., during the Hasmonean period. The fixing of the books of the Torah may go back as far as the early Persian period (so Ezra 9–10 and Neh 8–9) and the books of the (Former) Prophets (Joshua, Judges Samuel, Kings) to the late Persian period. Thus, the book of Joshua may have been incorporated within the emerging MT canon by the end of the Persian or in the early Hellenistic period. See Chapman (*The Law and the Prophets*, 241–79) for an argument favoring a canonical process in which the Torah and the Prophets emerge together, rather than the more traditional view of a sequence with the Torah preceding the Prophets. For discussion of the difficulty of discerning a set structure in the emerging canon see John Barton, *Oracles of God: Perceptions of Ancient Prophecy in Israel after the Exodus* (London: Darton, Longman & Todd, 1986), 83–86; and Carr, "Canonization in the Context of Community," 44–45.

54. The pre-Christian formation of the LXX is unclear (see J. Lust, "Septuagint and Canon," in *The Biblical Canons* [ed. J.-M. Auwers and H. J. de Jonge; BETL 163; Leuven: Leuven University Press and Peeters, 2003], 39–55). The Greek translation of the Torah likely occurred in the third century B.C.E., with the translation of the Prophets probably following a century later. Dines (*Septuagint*, 50) states that the gap of a century between the translation of the Torah and the Prophets is puzzling and may have been prompted by the political turmoil surrounding the Maccabean revolt. She writes: "Perhaps the need was felt for the old prophets to speak to a new generation." In any case, as noted above, the grandson of Ben Sira knows most of the books of the Prophets in their Greek form by the end of the second century. The organization of the LXX during this early period is also unclear, but what emerges over time is a different sequence to the books of the LXX from the MT. The LXX may have emerged as a four-part canon, which consisted of the Torah, Histories, Wisdom, and Prophets; or as a tripartite canon on the basis of literary genre: (1) legal and historical books; (2) poetic and sapiential books; and (3) prophetic books (see Tov, *Textual Criticism*, 13).

MT	LXX
Torah	*Pentateuch*
Genesis	Genesis
Exodus	Exodus
Leviticus	Leviticus
Numbers	Numbers
Deuteronomy	Deuteronomy
Prophets	*Histories*
Joshua	**Joshua**
Judges	Judges
	Ruth
Samuel	Regnorum 1-II (Samuel)
Kings	Regnorum III-IV (Kings)
Isaiah	Paralipomenon I-II (Chronicles)
Jeremiah	Ezra-Nehemiah
Ezekiel	Tobit
Book of the Twelve	Judith
	Esther
	Maccabees I-IV
Writings	*Poetical/Wisdom*
	Prophets

What is clear from our study of content and context is that late editing in both the MT and the LXX versions of Joshua creates an intertext, by which the book of Joshua is integrated editorially within an evolving collection of books.[55] And this insight brings this study full circle to the important role of Joshua in the identification of literary works throughout the modern period of interpretation. The study indicates that the ambiguity in the modern period over the appropriate context for interpreting Joshua is evident already in the earliest period of interpretation. We have seen, moreover, that the debate over literary context among the ancient editors goes beyond the simple juxtaposition of books in the early formation of the MT and the LXX canons and influences the very content of Joshua. The editors of the MT and the LXX have fashioned divergent final forms of Joshua with distinct horizons or conceptual profiles of its literary context. The result for the contemporary interpreter is

---

55. Gerald T. Sheppard (*The Future of the Bible: Beyond Liberalism and Literalism* [Toronto: The United Church Publishing, 1990], 29) writes of intertext as meaning that "the editors in the late stages of the formation of the biblical books registered their assumption that ... books belong together." Stephen B. Chapman ("How the Biblical Canon Began: Working Models and Open Questions," in Finkelberg and Stroumsa, *Homer, the Bible and Beyond*, 29–52 [38]) expands on Sheppard's definition, stating that an intertext is not as integrated as a single "'book,' but also not as random or diffuse ... (as) individual scrolls."

the inevitability of identifying distinct literary works within the two canons; whether the Pentateuch, conceived as Torah, in the MT; or something more like the Enneateuch in the LXX, by which I mean a continuous history from Genesis at least through Judges, but more likely through Kings, Chronicles, or even Maccabees.[56] Such interweaving of content and context in the MT and the LXX breaks down the once separate boundaries between literary and textual criticisms, for it requires the redaction critic to decide which final form of Joshua will be the starting point for interpreting the composition of the book and its function in relating the Pentateuch and the Former Prophets.

---

56. The term "Enneateuch" is rooted in the study of the MT canon, where it designates a collection of nine books from Genesis through Kings. I employ the term to designate a literary category in the LXX that exceeds the Pentateuch or the Hexateuch.

The Egyptian Bondage and Solomon's Forced Labor:

Literary Connections between Exodus 1–15 and 1 Kings 1–12?

Christoph Berner

Dedicated to
Prof. Dr. Dr. h.c. Hermann Spieckermann
on the occasion of his 60th birthday

1. Introduction

It is a well known fact that the accounts in Exod 1–15 and 1 Kgs 1–12 share a number of parallel motifs and narrative traits. According to 1 Kgs 5:27, Solomon conscripts forced labor out of all Israel in order to facilitate his building projects, just as Pharaoh had enslaved the Israelites and made them work on his construction sites (Exod 1:11–14). In both cases the building activities include the erection of store cities (Exod 1:11; 1 Kgs 9:19). Furthermore, when he increases the Israelites' burden (Exod 5), Pharaoh anticipates the actions of Solomon's heir Rehoboam, who in his imprudence takes similar measures against the northern tribes and thus forces them into segregation (1 Kgs 12:1–20). Under the leadership of Solomon's adversary Jeroboam, they turn their backs on the House of David, a development that is reminiscent of the Israelites' departure from Egypt with Moses. The two leaders, Moses and Jeroboam, even share a part of their early biography: both have to flee from the ruler who has imposed forced labor on the Israelites, and they may return only after his death to lead their people to freedom (Exod 2:11–23aα; 4:18–20; 1 Kgs 11:40–12:2).

The correspondences between the two accounts have found various explanations. According to Werner H. Schmidt, the passages adduced above from the Exodus narrative were originally part of the account of a Solomonic

Yahwist, whose description of Israel's situation in Egypt was influenced by the experience of Solomon's building activities.[1] A similar view has been put forward by Frank Crüsemann and Rainer Albertz,[2] but scholarly achievements of the past decades have ultimately shown that this view is no longer tenable. The Yahwistic source, if it existed at all, must be dated much later than the reign of Solomon, and the biblical account of this reign may not be taken at face value as a historical source. Any attempt to explain the parallels between Exod 1–15 and 1 Kgs 1–12 must therefore focus on the literary level and try to answer the question of which account was influenced by the other. Basically, the question seems to allow for two different answers, both of which have found supporters. While Walter Dietrich has argued that the Deuteronomistic account in 1 Kgs 1–12 was influenced by an older Exodus narrative,[3] Pekka Särkiö and John Van Seters have suggested just the opposite.[4]

However, a closer look reveals that neither of the two explanations can be correct, because the literary findings are much more complex. As recent studies have shown, the thematically corresponding accounts in Exod 5 and 1 Kgs 12:1–20 both represent rather late additions to their respective contexts, and the literary horizons of the remaining passages on the Egyptian bondage (esp. Exod 1:11) and Solomon's forced labor (1 Kgs 5:27–32; 9:15–24; 11:40–12:2)

---

1. See Werner H. Schmidt, *Exodus 1,1-6,30* (BKAT 2.1; Neukirchen-Vluyn: Neukirchener, 1988), 39.

2. See Frank Crüsemann, *Der Widerstand gegen das Königtum: Die antiköniglichen Texte des Alten Testaments und der Kampf um den frühen israelitischen Staat* (WMANT 49; Neukirchen-Vluyn: Neukirchener, 1978), 167–80; Rainer Albertz, *Religionsgeschichte Israels in alttestamentlicher Zeit* (2 vols.; GAT 8; Göttingen: Vandenhoeck & Ruprecht, 1992), 1:217–18; English translation: *A History of Israelite Religion in the Old Testament Period* (trans. J. Bowden; 2 vols.; OTL; Louisville: Westminster John Knox, 1994), 1:140–43. A similar stand is also taken by Jürgen Kegler, "Arbeitsorganisation und Arbeitskampfformen im Alten Testament," in *Mitarbeiter der Schöpfung: Bibel und Arbeitswelt* (ed. L. Schottroff et al.; Munich: Kaiser, 1983), 51–71.

3. See Walter Dietrich, "Das harte Joch (1 Kön 12,4): Fronarbeit in der Salomo-Überlieferung," *BN* 34 (1986): 7–16.

4. See Pekka Särkiö, *Exodus und Salomo: Erwägungen zur verdeckten Salomokritik anhand von Ex 1-2; 5; 14 und 32* (Schriften der Finnischen Exegetischen Gesellschaft 71; Göttingen: Vandenhoeck & Ruprecht, 1998), 165–73; John Van Seters, *The Life of Moses: The Yahwist as Historian in Exodus–Numbers* (Louisville: Westminster John Knox, 1994), 15–76. Likewise Robert B. Coote, *In Defense of Revolution: The Elohist History* (Minneapolis: Fortress, 1991), 71–75; Carlos A. Dreher, "Das tributäre Königtum in Israel unter Salomo," *EvT* 51 (1991): 49–60 (p. 59). See also Konrad Schmid, *Erzväter und Exodus: Untersuchungen zur doppelten Begründung der Ursprünge Israels innerhalb der Geschichtsbücher des Alten Testaments* (WMANT 81; Neukirchen-Vluyn: Neukirchener, 1999), 139–43. Schmid argues that the Exodus narrative was designed as the beginning of a larger literary composition comprising Exodus–1 Kings 12 which aimed at legitimizing the revolt of Jeroboam.

are debated as well.[5] As a result, the interpretation of the parallels between Exod 1–15 and 1 Kgs 1–12 has become a much greater challenge, because it can no longer be the task simply to decide which account has been composed on the basis of the other. Rather, one must now determine individually whether a particular Exodus text pertaining to the subject of servitude has been influenced by a passage in 1 Kings, or vice versa. The result may be that in one instance the Exodus narrative proves to be literarily dependent on the Deuteronomistic History, while in the next instance the situation is just the opposite. Moreover, once the relevant passages are considered individually within their respective redactional horizons, it may as well turn out that they have in fact developed independently and are not literarily connected with their putative enneateuchal parallels. In fact, many of these parallels may appear much weaker when the analysis is no longer based on an uncritical amalgamation of the extant textual material.

The following study newly assesses the question of literary connections between the Old Testament texts pertaining to the Egyptian bondage and Solomon's forced labor by discussing these texts on the basis of redaction-critical analysis. We will start with observations on the development of the motif of the Egyptian bondage (section 2), and then continue with a corresponding discussion of Solomon's forced labor (3). A final section (4) is devoted to the question of what can positively be said about literary connections between the texts previously discussed.

2. THE MOTIF OF THE EGYPTIAN BONDAGE AND ITS REDACTIONAL HORIZON IN THE EXODUS NARRATIVE

Within the last decades, the paradigm of the Documentary Hypothesis has been almost completely shattered. In contrast to the once widespread belief that the Tetrateuch (Genesis–Numbers) consists of the sources J, E and P, present scholarship finds its only remaining consensus in the distinction between Priestly and non-Priestly material. Furthermore, it has become increasingly clear that vast quantities of the non-Priestly material are in fact post-Priestly, which means that they presuppose (at least) the basic stratum of the Priestly Code (PG), be it an independent source or a redactional layer. Regardless of how the latter point is decided, there can be no doubt that the author of P was at least familiar with an existing pre-Priestly narrative thread. Thus, instead of the three sources of the Documentary Hypothesis, one can nowadays assume three basic stages of literary development within

---

5. See below.

the tetrateuchal narrative: pre-Priestly, Priestly, and post-Priestly.[6] In what follows, this model will serve as the interpretive framework for determining the redactional horizon of the bondage motif within the Exodus narrative.

2.1. The Absence of the Bondage Motif from the Earliest Pre-Priestly Stratum of the Exodus Narrative

Over the course of the long reception history of the Old Testament, the motif of the Egyptian bondage has gained such a prominent place that it is almost automatically taken as an authentic piece of tradition. It therefore comes as quite a surprise that there is no literary evidence to support this claim. The Exodus narrative in its earliest literary form lacks any explicit reference to the enslavement of the Israelites. The narrative begins with the account of Moses' birth and his growing up under the care of Pharaoh's daughter (Exod 2:1–10*), and it continues in Exod 2:11–15* with Moses' slaying of an Egyptian and flight to Midian.[7] The only reference to the Israelites' forced labor (Exod 2:11aβ: "and he [sc. Moses] saw their forced labor"— וירא בסבלתם) is a later addition, a fact that becomes clear from the repetition of the verb וירא ("and he saw") in Exod 2:11b.[8] Originally, Exod 2:11aαb mentioned only that Moses went out to his brothers and became a witness to how one of them was hit by an Egyptian. Without Exod 2:11aβ, the usual interpretation that the verse describes an overseer hitting a slave loses its only solid piece of textual evidence. Surely, the said situation could still be implied, but it is not explicitly stated and may therefore be counted only as one option among others. The only thing that can be known for certain is that the slavery framework was the option preferred by the author of Exod 2:11aβ, who explicitly introduced the motif of the Israelites' forced labor in order to specify the narrative setting for the first encounter between Moses and his people. We will come back to Exod 2:11aβ in our discussion of Exod 1:11–12.[9]

The next passage that provides information on the situation of the Israelites is the revelation scene situated at the burning bush (Exod 3).[10] Only a few verses of the chapter belong to the earliest pre-Priestly stratum of the Exodus narrative, where they followed directly upon Exod 2:15bβ₁ ("and he settled in

---

6. See Reinhard G. Kratz, *The Composition of the Narrative Books of the Old Testament* (trans. J. Bowden; London: T&T Clark, 2005), 225–29, 300–303.

7. See Christoph Levin, *Der Jahwist* (FRLANT 157; Göttingen: Vandenhoeck & Ruprecht, 1993), 317–25; Kratz, *The Composition of the Narrative Books*, 282.

8. See Levin, *Der Jahwist*, 322.

9. See below, section 2.2.

10. On the following see Christoph Berner, *Die Exoduserzählung: Das literarische Werden einer Ursprungslegende Israels* (FAT 73; Tübingen: Mohr Siebeck, 2010), 68–85.

the land of Midian"—(וישב בארץ מדין). In its reconstructed form the basic layer of Exod 3 reads as follows:

3:1*	Now Moses was keeping the flock of the priest of Midian. And he led the flock beyond the wilderness and came to the wasteland.	ומשה היה רעה את צאן כהן מדין וינהג את הצאן אחר המדבר ויבא חרבה
3:2b	And he looked, and behold, a bush was blazing, yet it was not consumed.	וירא והנה הסנה בער באש והסנה איננו אכל
3:3a	Then Moses said, "I must turn aside and look at this great sight."	ויאמר משה אסרה נא ואראה את המראה הגדל הזה
3:4a	When Yhwh saw that he had turned aside to see,	וירא יהוה כי סר לראות
3:5a	he said, "Come no closer!"	ויאמר אל תקרב הלם
3:6b	Then Moses hid his face, for he was afraid to look at the deity.	ויסתר משה פניו כי ירא מהביט אל האלהים
3:7aα	And Yhwh said, "I have surely observed the misery of my people who are in Egypt,	ויאמר יהוה ראה ראיתי את עני עמי אשר במצרים
3:8a	and I have come down to deliver them from the hand of the Egyptians and to bring them up out of that land to a good and broad land.	וארד להצילו מיד מצרים ולהעלתו מן הארץ ההוא אל ארץ טובה ורחבה
3:10*	Now go and bring forth my people out of Egypt."	ועתה לכה והוצא את עמי ממצרים

Again, the text is completely silent about the Israelites' forced labor. Certainly, Exod 3:7a mentions their "misery" (עֳנִי), but the term is not only quite vague, it is also not at all idiomatic in the context of slavery. The Old Testament never identifies the "miserable one" (עָנִי) with the slave, but uses the former term to denote a spectrum of phenomena related to social marginalization:

> In [Exod] 22:24 [עָנִי] is used to designate someone who socially is an underdog; one who possesses little or no land and so lacks a ready source of income; who has no power and influence and always runs the risk of falling victim to those who belong to the top social classes; with the foreigner (Lev. 19:10) and the widow and orphan (e.g., Isa. 10:2) he belongs to those who

are often without rights and the victim of social oppression (Isa. 3:14f.; 11:4; Amos 4:1; 5:12; Ps. 35:10); YHWH cares about them (22:22).[11]

When YHWH declares in Exod 3:7a that he has observed the misery of his people in Egypt, one should therefore not think of slaves, but rather of a marginalized group of Israelites in Egypt, the precise social status of which remains unclear. Despite the lack of sources it is nevertheless tempting to suggest a possible connection with fugitives from the Northern Kingdom who may have come to Egypt after the downfall of Samaria in 722 B.C.E. Circles of this kind do at least constitute a plausible background for the idea of the Exodus as an answer to the question of how Israel may continue without state and royal dynasty.

Be this as it may, it is at least safe to conclude that Exod 3:7a provides no positive evidence in favor of an enslavement of the Israelites in Egypt. The same applies to Exod 3:8aα, because YHWH's announcement that he is coming to deliver (נצל *hipʿil*) the Israelites from the hands of the Egyptians (מיד מצרים) is again not idiomatic for the liberation of slaves. In its present context, the phrase rather has military connotations[12] and already seems to anticipate the destruction of the Egyptian forces at the Sea of Reeds (Exod 14). At the very least, the account of this event did originally follow almost directly upon the revelation scene at the burning bush. The commissioning of Moses in Exod 3:10*, and the beginning of the account of the miracle at the sea (Exod 14:5a), were at first connected only by a set of short notes recounting the return of Moses (Exod 4:18*, 20aβ: "And Moses went and returned to the land of Egypt"-מצרים ארצה וישב משה וילך) and the first two stations of the Israelites' wanderings (Exod 12:37; 13:20, 21aα*).[13] Conversely, this means that the story of the Pharaoh increasing the burden of the Israelites (Exod 5), which has often been judged as an authentic piece of tradition, was not part of the earliest Exodus narrative. It will in fact prove to be a fairly late post-Priestly addition. That it cannot be original results from the simple observation that the burden of the Israelites has to exist before it can be increased. In other words, Exod 5 is dependent upon Exod 1:11–14, where the motif of the Israelites' forced labor is introduced and where it is further specified that one of their tasks was the making of bricks—hard labor which is then exacerbated in Exod 5. Such details are as alien to the earliest Exodus narrative as the motif of the Egyptian bondage itself.

---

11. Cornelis Houtman, *Exodus* (4 vols.; HCOT; Kampen: Kok, 1993–2002), 1:243.

12. Cf. e.g., Josh 9:26; Judg 6:9; 8:34; 9:17; 1 Sam 7:3, 14; 10:18; 12:10–11; 14:48; 17:37; 2 Kgs 17:39; 18:29, 33–35.

13. See Berner, *Die Exoduserzählung*, 430–34.

2.2. The Literary Origins of the Bondage Motif (Exod 1:11–14)

It is one of the few undisputed facts in pentateuchal criticism that Exod 1:13–14 does—at least in substance—belong to the original Priestly narrative (PG).[14] These two verses describe how the Egyptians made the lives of the Israelites bitter by imposing hard labor upon them (עבדה קשה). The motif is taken up again by the Priestly writer in Exod 2:23aβ; 6:5–9, which shows beyond doubt that the idea of the Egyptian bondage is firmly rooted within PG. However, the decisive question is whether the Priestly writer had already found the motif as part of a further elaborated version of the pre-Priestly exodus narrative, or whether he introduced it himself. The answer depends on the literary relationship between Exod 1:13–14 and the two preceding non-Priestly verses, Exod 1:11–12, which mention that the Israelites were enslaved by Egyptian taskmasters. Needless to say, this relationship cannot be established without considering the redactional history of the entire chapter, which will therefore be briefly sketched in the following.

Exodus 1 serves as a literary bridge between the end of the story of Joseph (Gen 50) and the beginning of the Exodus narrative (Exod 2), and it is impossible to reconstruct a basic layer that is independent of the preceding narrative sequence in the book of Genesis.[15] In fact, the basic layer of Exod 1 must be identical with the earliest literary hinge between the story of Joseph and the Exodus narrative. Quite recently there is a tendency to assume that this hinge was first established by PG and can be found in Exod 1:(1–5,) 7, 13–14.[16] As a result, the non-Priestly material in Exod 1:6, 8–12, 15–22, which was classically divided among the sources J and E, would now have to be attributed to a post-Priestly redactional phase. Although it is certainly true that there is little evidence for a Yahwistic source incorporating the stories of the patriarchs and the exodus into a coherent narrative, the possibility of a pre-Priestly redaction connecting the two formerly independent stories with each other

---

14. See e.g., Kratz, *The Composition of the Narrative Books*, 241.

15. See Kratz, *The Composition of the Narrative Books*, 279–95; Berner, *Die Exoduserzählung*, 10–48. Differently Jan Christian Gertz, *Tradition und Redaktion in der Exoduserzählung: Untersuchungen zur Endredaktion des Pentateuch* (FRLANT 186; Göttingen: Vandenhoeck & Ruprecht, 2000), 380–88. Gertz claims that Exod 1:11–12, 15–22* did belong to the earliest version of the exodus narrative, but he is forced to assume that its original beginning has not been preserved.

16. See Erhard Blum, "The Literary Connection between the Books of Genesis and Exodus and the End of the Book of Joshua," in *A Farewell to the Yahwist? The Composition of the Pentateuch in Recent European Interpretation* (ed. T. B. Dozeman and K. Schmid; SBLSymS; Atlanta: Society of Biblical Literature, 2006), 89–106; Jan Christian Gertz, "The Transition between the Books of Genesis and Exodus," in Dozeman and Schmid, *A Farewell to the Yahwist?* 73–87; Konrad Schmid, "The So-Called Yahwist and the Literary Gap between Genesis and Exodus," in Dozeman and Schmid, *A Farewell to the Yahwist?* 29–50.

should not be dismissed so easily. On the contrary, the literary evidence shows quite clearly that such a pre-Priestly connection must have existed, because the Priestly thread in the Joseph story suffers from serious gaps that are only filled by the non-Priestly narrative.[17] This evidence strongly indicates that PG is not a formerly independent source, but rather a redactional layer, an observation already made by Karl Heinrich Graf in 1867,[18] shortly before the Documentary Hypothesis started its triumphal procession in the wake of Julius Wellhausen.

The literary development of Exod 1 began with a short pre-Priestly hinge in Exod 1:6*, 8–9, 10*, 22 which connected Gen 50:21 and Exod 2:1.[19] After the death of Joseph a new Pharaoh arises who sees the Egyptians threatened by the immense proliferation of the Israelites and therefore orders that all of their male newborn children be thrown into the Nile. This command, devised as a narrative link to the exposure of Moses (Exod 2:1–10), would later trigger the story of Yhwh slaying the firstborn children of the Egyptians (Exod 12:29–33*) out of which the complex cycle of plagues would then gradually evolve.[20] It should be noted that the pre-Priestly author of Exod 12:29–33* was also responsible for a number of additions to Exod 3, which prepare for Moses' first appearance before Pharaoh (Exod 5:1–2*). Among these additions, Exod 3:9 is of crucial importance for our question, because the verse states that Yhwh has heard the cry (צעקה) of the Israelites[21] and has become aware of their oppression (לחץ) by the Egyptians. Like עני in Exod 3:7a, the term לחץ is also not idiomatic in the context of forced labor, but again rather designates the oppression of socially marginalized groups (cf. Exod 22:20; 23:9). Most likely, the author thought precisely of the measures taken by Pharaoh in Exod 1:22. The threats against the lives of their newborn sons cause the Israelites to cry out, and this cry makes Yhwh take action (cf.

---

17. See John Van Seters, "The Report of the Yahwist's Demise Has Been Greatly Exaggerated!" in Dozeman and Schmid, *A Farewell to the Yahwist?* 143–57 (esp. 147–50); Berner, *Die Exoduserzählung*, 11–17.

18. See Karl Heinrich Graf, "Die s.g. Grundschrift des Pentateuchs," *Archiv für wissenschaftliche Erforschung des Alten Testaments* 1 (1867): 466–77.

19. See Berner, *Die Exoduserzählung*, 17–26. Similarly Levin, *Der Jahwist*, 313–21; David M. Carr, "What is Required to Identify Pre-Priestly Narrative Connections Between Genesis and Exodus? Some General Reflections and Specific Cases," in Dozeman and Schmid, *A Farewell to the Yahwist?* 159–80 (esp. 167–75).

20. See Berner, *Die Exoduserzählung*, 430–448.

21. The mention of the Israelites' cry in Exod 3:7aα* (ואת צעקתם שמעתי) is part of the same redactional layer. That the cry was caused by "his taskmasters" (מפני נגשיו) already reflects a later development that is clearly indicated by the change from the plural to the singular. Together with Exod 3:7bβ, the phrase was added as a reference to the events described in Exod 5. Cf. below, 2.3.

Exod 22:22!). Moreover, this cry already anticipates the loud cry uttered by the Egyptians when they become aware that Yнwн has slain their firstborn children (Exod 12:30aβ).

Evidently, the author who created the story of the deaths of the Egyptian firstborn depicted the situation of the Israelites still very much in the same way as it was depicted in the earliest literary stratum of the exodus narrative. He shows no awareness of the motif of forced labor, wherefore it seems reasonable to conclude that he was not yet familiar with Exod 1:11–12. This brings us back to the place of the latter verses within the redactional history of Exod 1. In the first step, the basic layer (Exod 1:6*, 8–9, 10*, 22) was expanded with the story of the Hebrew midwives in Exod 1:15–21*. This story portrays an initial, unsuccessful attempt by Pharaoh to get rid of the newborn male children of the Israelites, and was primarily created as a side piece to the story of the commissioning of the Hebrew nurse in Exod 2:7–10aα. In stark contrast to the kind patronage of Pharaoh's daughter, who ensures the wellbeing of the foundling, her father shows his malignity and folly by attempting to make the Hebrew midwives an instrument in his evil plans.[22]

Both stories are of pre-Priestly origin, and the same also applies to Exod 1:11–12* which was inserted between Exod 1:10* and the beginning of the story of the midwives (Exod 1:15). Like Exod 1:15–21*, 22, these two verses focus on the proliferation of the Israelites, which the Egyptians now try to check by imposing on them forced labor (סבלות). By noting that despite these measures the Israelites continue to multiply and thus cause dread among the Egyptians (Exod 1:12), the author defines a new point of departure for the actions taken in Exod 1:15–21*, 22. The smooth transition between Exod 1:12 and 1:15 was only later interrupted by the Priestly writer who added Exod 1:13–14* and thus further accentuated the motif of Israel's forced labor, which he had already found in Exod 1:11–12*. The ultimate evidence for this development is provided by PG itself: in Exod 6:6 the writer first takes up the non-Priestly term סבלות from Exod 1:11, and then supplements it with the Priestly term עבדה from 1:13–14*. Exodus 6:6 thus precisely reproduces the sequence from Exod 1:11–14*—which can only mean that the Priestly writer deliberately refers to this passage on the Egyptian bondage, the second part of which (Exod 1:13–14*) he had created himself. Consequently, the first part (Exod 1:11–12*) must be of pre-Priestly origin.

A closer look at Exod 1:11–12 reveals clear traces of literary growth. Exod 1:11b, which provides detailed information on the building activities of the Israelites, interrupts the argument of the passage and must be judged a later

---

22. See Berner, *Die Exoduserzählung*, 27–44.

addition.[23] The original pre-Priestly text comprised only Exod 1:11a, 12, and read as follows:

| 1:11a | And they set work masters over them to oppress them with forced labor. | וישימו עליו שרי מסים למען ענתו בסבלתם |
| 1:12 | But the more they oppressed them, the more they multiplied and spread, so that they came to dread the Israelites. | וכאשר יענו אתו כן ירבה וכן יפרץ ויקצו מפני בני ישראל |

The pre-Priestly author of Exod 1:11a, 12 was the first to explicitly state that the Egyptians had enslaved the Israelites. He took up the phrase from Exod 3:7a mentioning the misery (עני) of the Israelites and further defined it by declaring that the Egyptians oppressed them (ענה) with forced labor (סבלות). This new interpretation he then integrated into the account of Moses' first encounter with his people: Exod 2:11aβ (וירא בסבלתם) relates how Moses becomes aware of his people's forced labor, just as Yнwн will declare in Exod 3:7a that he has become aware of the Israelites' misery (ראה ראיתי את עני עמי).

Whether the author had any clear idea of what precisely the forced labor involved remains unknown. That the Israelites built the store cities Pithom and Rameses (Exod 1:11b) is a piece of information that was supplied only later. It has left no further traces within the Exodus narrative and finds its most telling parallel in 1 Kgs 9:19 where the store cities of Solomon are mentioned. We will return later to the literary relationship between these two verses.[24]

The dread that befalls the Egyptians when they become aware that the Israelites continue to multiply despite the measures taken (Exod 1:12) forms the point of departure for the Priestly writer, who describes how the burden of the work is now intensified (Exod 1:13–14aα*):

| 1:13 | And the Egyptians made the Israelites serve with rigor | ויעבדו מצרים את בני ישראל בפרך |
| 1:14aα* | and they made their lives bitter with hard service. | וימררו את חייהם בעבדה קשה |

---

23. See Donald B. Redford, "Exodus I 11," *VT* 13 (1963): 401–18 (esp. 414–15); Levin, *Der Jahwist*, 314.

24. Cf. below, section 4.

Again, only these general remarks are original, while the idea that the service included work in mortar and brick (Exod 1:14aα$_{\text{fin}}$: ובחמר ובלבנים), as well as all kinds of field labor (Exod 1:14aβ: ובכל עבדה בשדה), is the result of later editorial work. Both specifications are only loosely connected to the preceding clause and are completely irrelevant for the remaining Priestly passages in the exodus narrative, where the details of the Israelites' hard work (עבדה) are never referred to again. Moreover, it can be shown that the details provided by Exod 1:14 are completely inspired by innerbiblical exegesis. The background for the specification in Exod 1:14aα$_{\text{fin}}$ is found in Gen 11:3, where the otherwise unattested combination of the terms "mortar" (חמר) and "brick" (לבנה) occurs again. The intertextual connection was triggered by the reasoning of Pharaoh in Exod 1:10* ("Come, let us deal wisely with them, lest they multiply"— הבה נתחכמה לו פן ירבה), which is strongly reminiscent of the plans devised by the generation of the tower of Babel (Gen 11:3aα: "Come, let us make bricks"—הבה נלבנה לבנים; Gen 11:4: "Come, let us build ourselves a city and a tower … lest we be scattered abroad upon the face of the whole earth"— הבה נבנה לנו עיר ומגדל … פן נפוץ על פני כל הארץ). By specifying that the Israelites were forced to work using the building materials of the Tower of Babel, the author of Exod 1:14aα$_{\text{fin}}$ tried to demonstrate that the hubris of the Egyptians was not inferior to that of the generation of the Tower.

An even later addition is found in Exod 1:14aβ, where it is specified that the Israelites were also forced to do all kinds of field labor. The roots of this idea lie not in the book of Genesis, but in the exodus narrative itself; namely, in the post-Priestly account of the plague of hail.[25] Exodus 9:21 recounts that some of Pharaoh's officials ignored Moses' warnings and left their servants (עבדים) in the fields (בשדה). Although it was originally implied that these servants were Egyptians, the motif of the Israelites' service (עבדה) also leaves room for the interpretation that they were Israelites. Precisely this interpretation has triggered the addition of Exod 1:14aβ, which explicitly includes field labor among the duties of the Israelite slaves. Exodus 1:14b, which ties the list of duties back to the general statement in Exod 1:13, is part of the same post-Priestly layer that gave these verses their final form. While the details provided by Exod 1:14aβb have found no further echo within the Exodus narrative and might therefore represent a very late addition, the older idea of the Israelites' work in mortar and brick (Exod 1:14aα$_{\text{fin}}$) inspired the story of Pharaoh increasing their burden (Exod 5) which will be treated in the following section.

---

25. On the post-Priestly origins of the plague see Levin, *Der Jahwist*, 337; Gertz, *Tradition und Redaktion*, 132–52.

2.3. The Increasing of the Burden: Bricks without Straw (Exod 5)

Exodus 5 recounts how the first appearance of Moses and Aaron at the Egyptian court ended in a complete failure. Pharaoh is not only totally unimpressed by their demand to go a three-days' journey into the desert to sacrifice to Yʜᴡʜ, but (rightly) suspects a pathetic excuse devised to obscure the Israelites' real plans. As a punishment, he orders that the taskmasters no longer give the people the straw to make bricks. Instead, the Israelites must now gather straw for themselves, although the required quantity of bricks is not reduced (Exod 5:6–9*). In its original form (Exod 5:6–13*, 22–23; 6:1), the story continued to tell how the Israelites were forced by their Egyptian task-masters to comply with the new terms (Exod 5:10–13*) whereupon Moses turns to Yʜᴡʜ with heavy accusations: not only had Yʜᴡʜ failed to fulfill his promise to save the Israelites, but their situation had become even worse (Exod 5:22–23). The story culminates with Yʜᴡʜ's reply in Exod 6:1, where he restates his intention to save the Israelites. The verse prepares for the older Priestly revelation scene that follows in Exod 6:2–7:7, which now reads like an explication of the announcement in Exod 6:1.

The main purpose of the story about the increasing of the burden is to solve a contradiction that had emerged during the post-Priestly development of the exodus narrative. Exodus 4:1–4, 6–8, 31a, represent a fairly late post-Priestly addition, which aims to show that Moses managed to make the people believe in his message of deliverance by working two miraculous actions. This faith of the people stands in sharp contrast to the disobedience with which they meet Moses' message in Exod 6:9 (PG). In order to explain this sudden change of behavior of the formerly faithful people the author of Exod 5:6–13*, 22–23; 6:1 has created a new situation by increasing the burden.[26] The faith of the people is thus heavily unsettled, and it becomes understandable that

---

26. Similarly Gertz, *Tradition und Redaktion*, 344, who is however mistaken when he claims that Exod 5:3–6:1 is a homogeneous literary unit created by the final redaction of the Pentateuch. The literary development of the passage is in fact much more complex. The basic literary stratum of Exod 5 is constituted by Exod 5:1–2*, two verses that are still pre-Priestly in origin and were once directly followed by the account of Yʜᴡʜ slaying the Egyptian firstborn in Exod 12:29–33*. In a next step, a sequence of three pre-Priestly plagues (Exod 7:14–8:28*) was inserted between Exod 5:2 and 12:29, whereupon the Priestly writer added the revelation scene in Exod 6:2–7:7*: this passage directly connects to Exod 5:2 as the point where it takes up the question of Yʜᴡʜ's identity; it establishes a new perspective on the three plagues following in Exod 7:14–8:28 by claming that it is in fact *Aaron* who is the spokesman before Pharaoh. Already in an advanced post-Priestly phase of development, the first encounter between Moses and Pharaoh (Exod 5:1–2*) was supplemented with Exod 5:3–4*, where the author of Exod 3:16–19a, 20; 8:4b, 21b–24a describes how Moses and the elders started the negotiations on the alleged sacrifice in the wilderness. Only after Exod 5 had reached this state of development was the basic stra-

they no longer want to listen to Moses, "because of their discouraged spirit and their hard work" (Exod 6:9bβγ PG), which in light of Exod 5:6–13* is now all the harder. An even later development is tangible in Exod 5:5, 14–21 where the tale gains the characteristic traits of the murmuring stories. In this context, the Israelite supervisors (שטרים) are introduced, in order to negotiate with Pharaoh and to blame Moses and Aaron after these negotiations have failed (Exod 5:20–21). Like these supervisors, the Egyptian taskmasters (נגשים), first mentioned by the author of Exod 5:6*, 10*, 13, should also be seen as scribal inventions which add to a late literary picture of the Egyptian bondage. The said taskmasters have finally also made their way to Exod 3, where a redactor claimed that they were responsible for the cry(ing) of the Israelites (Exod 3:7bα_fin: מפני נגשיו). He finished by stating that YHWH had also become aware of his people's pain (Exod 3:7bβ: כי ידעתי את מכאביו), a thought obviously inspired by Exod 5:14a, according to which the Israelite supervisors were hit.[27]

2.4. Conclusions

The motif of the Egyptian bondage is not a genuine part of the earliest literary strata of the exodus narrative,[28] which only mention the Israelites' misery (Exod 3:7a: עני) and their oppression by the Egyptians (Exod 3:9b: לחץ). Neither of these two terms is idiomatic in the context of forced labor; instead, they denote the ill treatment of socially marginalized groups. While the precise implications of the Israelites' misery remain obscure, their oppression is most likely to be identified with Pharaoh's order to kill all of their newborn sons (Exod 1:22). That the Israelites were enslaved by the Egyptians is a thought which is first explicitly expressed by the late pre-Priestly author of Exod 1:11a, 12; 2:11aβ, who introduces the term סבלות. This term is taken up and reinterpreted by the Priestly writer, who speaks of the hard labor (Exod 1:14aα*: עבדה קשה) which makes the Israelites' life bitter.[29] Interestingly, nei-

---

tum of the story of the increasing of the burden added. See Berner, *Die Exoduserzählung*, 438–48.

27. The idea that the Egyptians castigated their Israelite slaves is not expressed elsewhere in the exodus narrative.

28. See already Levin, *Der Jahwist*, 314; Kratz, *The Composition of the Narrative Books*, 280.

29. It should be noted that by introducing the term עבדה, the Priestly writer possibly alludes to the demand that the Israelites go out and serve (עבד) YHWH, a demand which is attested already in the pre-Priestly plagues (Exod 7:16*, 26; 8:16). Again, there is no textual evidence to support the claim that prior to the addition of PG the service of YHWH was meant to contrast the servitude in Egypt. Rather, the motif seems to be due to a literary connection between the Exodus und the revelation at mount Sinai which was first established in Exod 3:12aβγb. See Berner, *Die Exoduserzählung*, 68–85.

ther Exod 1:11a, 12, nor the Priestly passage in Exod 1:13–14*, specify any details of the forced labor. The building of the store cities (Exod 1:11b) is a later interpolation, and the same applies to the details mentioned in Exod 1:14aα$_{fin}$βb; both verses point to a post-Priestly background. The idea that the Israelites' service involved all kinds of field labor (Exod 1:14aβb) was inspired by the mention of the servants in the fields (Exod 9:21); while the older notion of the Israelites working in mortar and brick (Exod 1:14aα$_{fin}$) has been developed in light of Gen 11:3, where the same building materials are used to construct the Tower of Babel.

The brick motif was then further developed by the author of Exod 5:6–13*, 22–23; 6:1, who describes the increasing of the burden in order to explain why the Israelites reacted with disobedience (Exod 6:9 PG) after they at first had faithfully accepted the message of deliverance (Exod 4:31). Already in its final form, including the murmuring passages in Exod 5:5, 14–20, the story then gave rise to the short note in Exod 3:7bα$_{fin}$β, which mentions how the people suffered from the evil treatment of their supervisors. In sum, the picture of the Egyptian bondage as it is painted by the exodus narrative is neither original nor historically reliable. Rather, it developed as a multi-layered literary fiction which is primarily the result of the exegetical skill of learned scribes. Whether these scribes at least in some instances were inspired by the parallels in 1 Kgs 1–12 is a question which will be assessed in the course of the redaction-critical analysis of the literary evidence pertaining to Solomon's forced labor.

3. The Motif of Solomon's Forced Labor and Its Redactional Horizon in 1 Kings 1–12

Information on Solomon's forced labor is provided by various passages that do not add up to a coherent picture. According to 1 Kgs 5:27–32 Solomon conscripted forced labor (מס) out of all Israel, whereas 1 Kgs 9:15–23 claims that he conscripted only the descendants of the Canaanite population and made no slaves of the Israelites. In opposition to this, 1 Kgs 12:1–19 again assumes that Solomon had enslaved the Israelites—who, however, can no longer be identical with the inhabitants of the Davidic-Solomonic kingdom, but must be identified with the northern tribes about to withdraw. Evidently, a similar picture is also presupposed in 1 Kgs 11:26–28, where Jeroboam is said to have rebelled against Solomon, who had previously given him charge over the forced labor of the house of Joseph. The contradictory evidence clearly points to a complex redactional development which will be traced in this section.[30]

---

30. Concerning the complex text-critical issues pertaining to the account of 1 Kings it is presupposed here that the longer and more systematic version of the Septuagint is, as

3.1. The Conscription of Forced Labor (1 Kgs 5:27–32)

Martin Noth recognized that the passage in 1 Kgs 5:27–32 neither belongs to the earliest literary layer of the Deuteronomistic history (DtrH),[31] nor forms a coherent literary unit. The tensions are obvious. While 1 Kgs 5:27–28 recounts that a levy of thirty thousand men is sent to the Lebanon, 1 Kgs 5:29–31 quite abruptly introduces seventy thousand laborers and eighty thousand stone-cutters who are at work in the mountains and are ordered by Solomon to prepare the stones required to lay the foundations of the Temple. First Kings 5:32 concludes by stating that Solomon's and Hiram's builders, together with the Gebalites, did the stonecutting (בני שלמה ובני חירום והגבלים ויפסלו) and prepared *the timber* and the stone to build the Temple (ויכינו העצים והאבנים לבנות הבית), although Solomon's orders from the preceding verse in no way refer to woodwork. This peculiarity of 1 Kgs 5:32 offers the fundamental key to the redactional development of the entire passage, because the motif of preparing the timber proves to be original. It is indispensable for the syntax of the second part of 1 Kgs 5:32, which was designed as a transitory phrase between the passage on Solomon's forced labor (1 Kgs 5:27–32*) and 1 Kgs 6:1* (DtrH).[32] In contrast, all references to the preparation of stones can be easily subtracted from the verse, which originally knew nothing of this motif, introduced in 1 Kgs 5:29–30, but rather connected directly to 1 Kgs 5:27–28. More precisely, besides 1 Kgs 5:27 only the first two words of the following verse can be accepted as original, while the specifications of the mode of forced labor and the reflections on the role of Adoniram have to be judged

---

a rule, secondary compared to the Masoretic Text. See Percy S. F. van Keulen, *Two Versions of the Solomon Narrative: An Inquiry into the Relationship between MT 1 Kgs. 2–11 and LXX 3 Reg. 2–11* (VTSup 104; Leiden: Brill, 2005); Andrzej S. Turkanik, *Of Kings and Reigns: A Study of Translation Technique in the Gamma/Gamma Section of 3 Reigns (1 Kings)* (FAT 2/30; Tübingen: Mohr Siebeck, 2008). Cf. Adrian Schenker, *Älteste Textgeschichte der Königsbücher: Die hebräische Vorlage der ursprünglichen Septuaginta als älteste Textform der Königsbücher* (OBO 199; Fribourg: Universitätsverlag; Göttingen: Vandenhoeck & Ruprecht, 2004).

31. See Martin Noth, *Könige* (2 vols.; BKAT 9; Neukirchen-Vluyn: Neukirchener, 1964–1968), 1:92–94. Likewise, Ernst Würthwein, *Das Erste Buch der Könige: Kapitel 1–16* (ATD 11; Göttingen: Vandenhoeck & Ruprecht 1977), 1:56–57; Uwe Becker, "Die Reichsteilung nach I Reg 12," *ZAW* 112 (2000): 210–29 (esp. 222). Differently, see Dietrich, "Das harte Joch," 12; Pekka Särkiö, *Die Weisheit und Macht Salomos in der israelitischen Historiographie: Eine traditions- und redaktionskritische Untersuchung über 1 Kön 3–5 und 9–11* (Schriften der Finnischen Exegetischen Gesellschaft 60; Helsinki: Finnische Exegetische Gesellschaft; Göttingen: Vandenhoeck & Ruprecht, 1994), 92–99. According to Dietrich and Särkiö, 1 Kgs 5:27–32 is a genuine part of DtrH.

32. The end of 1 Kgs 5:32b ("to build the Temple"—לבנות הבית) prepares for 1 Kgs 6:1b ("he built the Temple for Yʜwʜ"—ויבן הבית ליהוה).

secondary.[33] Thus, in its earliest literary form the passage on the conscription of forced labor read as follows:

5:27	And King Solomon conscripted forced labor out of all Israel, and the levy numbered thirty thousand men.	ויעל המלך שלמה מס מכל ישראל ויהי המס שלשים אלף איש
5:28aα1	And he sent them to the Lebanon	וישלחם לבנונה
5:32b*	and they prepared the timber to build the house.	ויכינו העצים לבנות הבית

Thematically, the passage is closely connected to the preceding section on Hiram of Tyre providing the building material for the Temple (1 Kgs 5:15–26*). While 1 Kgs 5:20*, 22, 24 recount that Hiram ordered his workers to cut as much cedar and cypress timber as Solomon demanded, the author of 1 Kgs 5:27–32* takes up this notion and clarifies that the further preparation (כון *hip'il*) of this timber was a task entrusted to Israelites, who were sent to the Lebanon for precisely this reason. The author further implemented this new notion in 1 Kgs 5:20aα$_2$, by making Solomon announce that "my servants will join your servants" (ועבדי יהיו עם עבדיך). Although it is certainly true that the idea of Israelites joining the woodcutters in the Lebanon contradicts 1 Kgs 5:23a, according to which the timber is directly delivered to Solomon by Hiram's people, the contradiction need not be original: 1 Kgs 5:23a proves to be a secondary addition that separates the two parts of the agreement presented in 1 Kgs 5:22b ("I will fulfill all your needs in the matter of cedar and cyprus timber") and 1 Kgs 5:23b ("and you shall meet my needs by providing food for my household"). It is not unreasonable to assume that 1 Kgs 5:23b was supplemented by a later redactor to whom it seemed problematic that Israelite slaves were engaged in the preparations of the building material and who therefore tried to solve the problem by claiming that the timber had been delivered by Hiram's workers. The ideological perspective of the addition is reminiscent of 1 Kgs 9:15–23*, which will be discussed below.

---

33. 1 Kgs 5:28aα$_2$β interrupts the original verbal clause by specifying that the Israelite woodcutters used to work in shifts, so each of them had to do service for the king for one month out of every three. Obviously, the addition tries to extenuate the consequences of the forced labor through this ingenious invention of the wise Solomon. That Adoniram was set over the forced labor (1 Kgs 5:28b) represents an even later addition inspired by 1 Kgs 4:6b where the said person is listed among Solomon's officers; see Würthwein, *Das Erste Buch der Könige*, 51 n. 3. It is highly questionable whether this list is based on an ancient source. More likely, it is the product of learned scribes.

In contrast to later literary voices, the original stratum of 1 Kgs 5:27–32*
does not indicate that Solomon's conscription of forced labor out of Israel was
sensed as problematic. Quite to the contrary, the focus of the passage seems
to be that "all Israel" was actively involved in the erection of the Temple.[34]
That this was achieved through forced labor may have simply been judged
as a typical and therefore appropriate measure. On the whole, the text as it
stands hardly allows for the quite far-fetched conclusion that it was designed
to present Solomon as a despotic ruler responsible for a revival of the Egyptian bondage.[35] The term מס employed in 1 Kgs 5:27 does not belong to the
central vocabulary of the exodus narrative, where it occurs only once. Moreover, a comparison between Exod 1:11a and 1 Kgs 5:27–32* shows that besides
a loose terminological connection, the passages have nothing in common.
While Exod 1:11a notes that the Egyptians appointed taskmasters (שרי מסים)
to oppress (ענה) the Israelites with forced labor (סבלות), Solomon's measures
are presented entirely as an attempt to ensure the completion of the temple. In
light of these fundamental differences it is highly unlikely that 1 Kgs 5:27–32*
should have been purposefully modeled upon Exod 1:11a (or vice versa). Critical notions inspired by the exodus narrative are absent from 1 Kgs 5:27–32*.[36]

3.2. A Later Correction of the Picture of Solomon's Forced Labor (1 Kgs 9:15–23)

First Kings 9:15–23 gives the impression of an official document pertaining
to Solomon's building activities and has therefore been judged to be based on
a formerly independent source employed by the author of the Deuteronomistic history.[37] Yet a close look at the introductory phrase in 1 Kgs 9:15 shows
that this interpretation can hardly be correct. The verse states that "this was
the manner of the forced labor which King Solomon conscripted to build the
house of YHWH …" (וזה דבר המס אשר העלה המלך שלמה לבנות את בית יהוה)[38];
the phrasing clearly refers back to 1 Kgs 5:27–32*, where the subject of forced
labor is introduced with precisely the same wording. 1 Kings 9:15–23 therefore should be judged as a later addition devised to establish a clearer picture
of Solomon's forced labor. Part of the additional data provided is an extensive

---

34. Similarly Marvin A. Sweeney, *I & II Kings* (OTL; Louisville: Westminster John
Knox, 2007), 103. See also Dietrich, "Das harte Joch," 15.

35. So, e.g., Becker, "Die Reichsteilung," 222.

36. One should add that even in its final form the account in 1 Kgs 5:27–32 shows no
tendency to criticize Solomon's institution of forced labor.

37. See Noth, *Könige*, 218; Würthwein, *Das Erste Buch der Könige*, 109; Särkiö, *Die
Weisheit und Macht Salomos*, 109.

38. The Septuagint renders the term מס as προνομή ("spoil"). On the possible background of this secondary reading see van Keulen, *Two Versions of the Solomon Narrative*,
193–96.

list of building projects in 1 Kgs 9:15–19, although it is difficult to decide how much of this data belongs to the earliest literary layer. It is widely acknowledged that the note on the destruction of Gezer (1 Kgs 9:16–17aα) is a gloss[39], and it can furthermore be taken for granted that the list of different types of cities and buildings erected by Solomon (1 Kgs 9:19) must at least in part be judged as a secondary addition.[40]

Likewise, it would be rash to assume that all of the detailed specifications in 1 Kgs 9:15, 17aβ–18 are original. According to the superscription in 1 Kgs 9:15*, the passage is not about the buildings and cities erected by Solomon through forced labor, but deals with the conduct of this forced labor, as specified in 1 Kgs 9:20–22. While it is thus evident that the latter verses must have been an integral part of the passage from the very beginning,[41] it becomes all the more doubtful whether the long list which separates them from the superscription can be judged original. Although the question can not be pursued further in the present article, it seems likely that large parts of the list are secondary. This certainly also applies to 1 Kgs 9:23, which is only loosely connected to the preceding context and supplies additional information on (the number of) chief officers who were over Solomon's work (אלה שרי הנצבים אשר על המלאכה לשלמה). So far, the text remaining for the earliest literary layer of 1 Kgs 9:15–23 reads as follows:

9:15*	This was the manner of the forced labor which King Solomon conscripted to build the house of Yhwh [and …]:	וזה דבר המס אשר העלה המלך שלמה לבנות את בית יהוה [ו] ...
9:20	All the people who were left of the Amorites, the Hittites, the Perizzites, the Hivites, and the Jebusites, who were not of the people of Israel—	כל העם הנותר מן האמרי החתי הפרזי החוי והיבוסי אשר לא מבני ישראל המה
9:21	their descendants who were still left in the land, whom the Israelites were unable to destroy completely— these Solomon conscripted for slave labor, and so they are to this day.	בניהם אשר נתרו אחריהם בארץ אשר לא יכלו בני ישראל להחרימה ויעלם שלמה למס עבד עד היום הזה

---

39. See Würthwein, *Das Erste Buch der Könige*, 109; Särkiö, *Die Weisheit und Macht Salomos*, 134–36.

40. See the different reconstructions in James A. Montgomery, *A Critical and Exegetical Commentary on the Book of Kings* (ICC; Edinburgh: T&T Clark, 1951), 214; Noth, *Könige*, 215; Würthwein, *Das Erste Buch der Könige*, 109; Dietrich, "Das harte Joch," 11; Särkiö, *Die Weisheit und Macht Salomos*, 110.

41. See e.g., Noth, *Könige*, 216.

9:22	But of the Israelites Solomon made no slaves, for they were the soldiers, they were his slaves, his commanders, his captains, and the commanders of his chariotry and cavalry.	ומבני ישראל לא נתן שלמה עבד כי הם אנשי המלחמה ועבדיו ושריו ושלשיו ושרי רכבו ופרשיו

The main purpose of the passage is to correct the picture from 1 Kgs 5:27–32*, according to which Solomon conscripted forced labor from among the Israelites. This is explicitly rejected twice (1 Kgs 9:20, 22), and the author claims that only descendants of the Canaanite population were enslaved by Solomon. That the Canaanites had not been completely wiped out by the Israelites (1 Kgs 9:21a) is a late Dtr concept,[42] which is utilized here to postulate a different national identity for the slaves at Solomon's building sites. To enhance the contrast, 1 Kgs 9:22b states, in addition, that the Israelites instead of being subject to forced labor only held important offices. Strangely enough, the verse also mentions that they were Solomon's "slaves" (עבדיו), an obvious contradiction to the main point of the entire passage. Even if the idea should be that they were "only" his "servants,"[43] there remains a strong tension on linguistic grounds. What is more, this piece of information is also singular in content, because the remaining offices mentioned in 1 Kgs 9:22b do all designate high posts in Solomon's army. This provides additional evidence for the conclusion that the mention of the עבדים in 1 Kgs 9:22b is due to a later interpolation. Presumably, this interpolation results from the attempt to synchronize the list of offices with 1 Kgs 9:27b, according to which Solomon's "servants" (עבדי שלמה) joined the sailors of Hiram.[44]

Still, even without the mention of the עבדים in 1 Kgs 9:22b, the list is not without tension. It is conspicuous that the verse at first refers only in a general way to Solomon's commanders (ושריו) and then mentions specific military ranks, namely Solomon's captains (ושלשיו) and the *commanders* of his chariotry and cavalry (ושרי רכבו ופרשיו).[45] In short, one gets the impres-

---

42. See Becker, "Die Reichsteilung nach I Reg 12," 222. See also Mareike Rake, *'Juda wird aufsteigen!': Untersuchungen zum ersten Kapitel des Richterbuches* (BZAW 367; Berlin: de Gruyter, 2006).

43. Thus the LXX. The parallel in 2 Chr 8:9 omits the word, obviously for harmonistic reasons.

44. As an aside, it should be noted that 1 Kgs 9:27b is also not original to its direct context, but was interpolated between 1 Kgs 9:27a and 9:28a. Given the fact that this original layer antedates 1 Kgs 5:27–32*, the interpolation of 1 Kgs 9:27b could be due to the author of the latter verses or at least have been inspired by them.

45. The tension is smoothed over in 2 Chr 8:9b where it is no longer Solomon's commanders *and* captains (ושריו ושלשיו), but the commanders *of his* captains (שלשיו ושרי). Thus, the verse lists three different groups of commanders (שרים).

sion that these latter pieces of information reflect a secondary attempt to further specify the general reference to Solomon's commanders. Consequently, in its earliest literary form, 1 Kgs 9:22b would only have mentioned that the Israelites served as soldiers and commanders in Solomon's army (כי הם אנשי המלחמה ושריו). This hypothesis may be further corroborated when we include 1 Kgs 9:23 in our observations. The awkward syntax of the verse ("these [אלה] were the chief officers who were over Solomon's work: five hundred fifty, who had charge of the people who carried on the work") is best explained when the pronoun אלה is interpreted as a reference back to 1 Kgs 9:22 rather than as the beginning of a new thematic section. 1 Kings 9:23 was appended to the reconstructed basic layer of 1 Kgs 9:22b and provides a new interpretation of the tasks of Solomon's commanders (ושריו): "*they are the chief officers who were over Solomon's work*" (1 Kgs 9:23aα: אלה שרי הנצבים אשר על המלאכה לשלמה). The purpose of the addition is to show that the Israelites were not only spared the burden of Solomon's forced labor, but that they rather served as taskmasters of his Canaanite slaves, which in fact generates an even stronger contrast. The verse continues by stating that the said chief officers amounted to five hundred and fifty (1 Kgs 9:23aβ), but this piece of information is hardly original. Syntactically, it is only loosely connected with 1 Kgs 9:23aα, and 1 Kgs 9:23b testifies to the rather clumsy attempt of the redactor to integrate 1 Kgs 9:23aβ by creating a repetitive paraphrase of 1 Kgs 9:23aα. Thus, 1 Kgs 9:23aβb represents an even later redactional layer.[46]

We cannot conclude this section before briefly discussing one detail that is decisive for the main question pursued in this article: the store cities of Solomon in 1 Kgs 9:19. As noted above, it is questionable whether (and which) parts of the verse belong to the earliest literary layer of 1 Kgs 9:15–22. After the information provided in the previous verses, 1 Kgs 9:19 gives the impression of an appendix, explaining that Solomon had not only built the Temple (as well as his palace and various other specific buildings and cities), but that he had also erected certain types of cities (1 Kgs 9:19a) and had built whatever he had desired to build (1 Kgs 9:19b; cf. 1 Kgs 9:1b). As both parts of the verse interrupt the syntax of the earliest literary layer in 1 Kgs 9:15*, 20–22* and do not contribute to its message, it is most likely that neither is original. We need not determine whether 1 Kgs 9:19b represents an even later addition than 1 Kgs 9:19a, since this is of little interest for the main question pursued in this article. Of crucial importance, however, is the observation that the mention of the store cities (1 Kgs 9:19aα) has no further parallels in the Dtr account of Solomon's reign. In contrast to this, "the cities for the chariots" (ואת ערי הרכב)

---

46. Cf. below, n. 57.

and "the cities for the cavalry" (ואת ערי הפרשים) mentioned in 1 Kgs 9:19aβγ are closely linked with 1 Kgs 5:6–8; 10:26–29, which provide information on Solomon's mounted forces. It is easy to assume that the author of 1 Kgs 9:19aβγ was already familiar with 1 Kgs 10:26b, which notes that all mounted forces were stationed in "the cities for the chariots" (ערי הרכב). He transferred this piece of information to the list of building projects and by introducing the ערי הפרשים provided a proper place for the cavalry.

While it is easy to identify a literary background for 1 Kgs 9:19aβγ within the Dtr account of Solomon's reign, the store cities from 1 Kgs 9:19aα remain singular, even if one extends the scope to the entire Deuteronomistic History. Obviously, they represent a piece of information that was originally rooted in a different literary context and only secondarily transferred to 1 Kings, either by the author of 1 Kgs 9:19aβγ or by an even later hand. Interestingly, the store cities are well attested in the building accounts of 2 Chronicles, where they are mentioned twice in 2 Chr 8, the direct parallel to 1 Kgs 9.[47] As a result, the store cities in 1 Kgs 9:19aα might represent an addition inspired by 2 Chronicles.[48] Yet, there is also a second option, namely that 1 Kgs 9:19aα is literarily dependent on Exod 1:11b and reflects the attempt to establish a redactional link with the exodus narrative. The question which of the two options is preferable will be assessed in the final section of this article.[49]

3.3. The Forced Labor and the Segregation of the Northern Kingdom (1 Kgs 11:26–12:20)

When reading the text of 1 Kgs 11:26–12:20, one gets the impression that the secession of the northern kingdom was mainly the result of Solomon's forced labor. Jeroboam, who had previously been given charge over the forced labor of the house of Joseph (1 Kgs 11:27–28), is finally made king by the northern tribes after Solomon's successor Rehoboam foolishly rejects their plea for lessening the burden (1 Kgs 12:1–20). Yet, after the preceding sections of this article, it may not come as a surprise that neither of the two passages proves to be original. The secondary nature of the account of Rehoboam's folly becomes unmistakably clear from the fact that the respective verses (1 Kgs 12:1, 3–19) interrupt a more original narrative thread in 1 Kgs 12:2b, 20a. 1 Kings 12:20a shows no awareness of the motif of forced labor but simply states that the Israelites made Jeroboam king in the moment that they

---

47. Cf. 2 Chr 8:4, 6; 16:4; 17:12; 32:28. Apart from this, the Old Testament mentions store cities only in Exod 1:11b and 1 Kgs 9:19aα.

48. This has already been suggested by Montgomery, *A Critical and Exegetical Commentary on the Book of Kings*, 214.

49. Cf. below, section 4.

realized he had returned from Egypt. It is obvious that the verse must have originally connected directly to 1 Kgs 12:2b (LXX),[50] where the return of Jeroboam is narrated.[51]

The reason for Jeroboam's sojourn in Egypt is provided by 1 Kgs 11:40, which relates that he had to flee from Solomon, who sought to kill him. Why he did so becomes clear only from 1 Kgs 11:26, which recounts how Jeroboam rebelled against Solomon— who therefore quite naturally tries to get rid of his adversary. Evidently, 1 Kgs 11:26, 40 represent the original narrative thread, which was only later interrupted by the account of the prophet Ahijah (1 Kgs 11:29–39)[52] and the short section on Jeroboam's career as coordinator of the forced labor (1 Kgs 11:27–28). The latter two verses may therefore by no means be interpreted as part of a pre-Deuteronomistic source, but rather represent a redactional expansion that results from the way 1 Kgs 11:27a ("and these are the circumstances under which he rebelled against the king") takes up 1 Kgs 11:26b ("and he rebelled against the king"). With all later additions subtracted,[53] the earliest literary layer of the text (DtrH) reads as follows: [54]

---

50. In 1 Kgs 12:2b, the LXX ("and he returned from Egypt"—וישב ירבעם ממצרים) seems to have preserved the more original reading over the MT ("and he dwelt in Egypt"— וישב ירבעם במצרים). See Montgomery, *A Critical and Exegetical Commentary on the Book of Kings*, 249; Noth, *Könige*, 266–67; Würthwein, *Das Erste Buch der Könige*, 151. For a more detailed discussion of the text-critical issues involved, see Steven L. McKenzie, "The Source for Jeroboam's Role at Shechem (1 Kgs 11:43–12:3, 12, 20)," *JBL* 106 (1987): 297–300; Timothy M. Willis, "The Text of 1 Kings 11:43–12:3," *CBQ* 53 (1991): 37–44. Although McKenzie and Willis argue for a different reconstruction of the earliest version of 1 Kgs 12:2 that includes the reference to Jeroboam's dwelling in Egypt, both authors nevertheless agree that the verse must have originally referred to Jeroboam's return from Egypt as well. Basically, this model therefore allows for the same redaction-critical conclusions.

51. See Kratz, *The Composition of the Narrative Books*, 165; Becker, "Die Reichsteilung nach I Reg 12," 217–21.

52. The secondary nature of 1 Kgs 11:29–39 is widely acknowledged; see e.g., Montgomery, *A Critical and Exegetical Commentary on the Book of Kings*, 242; Noth, *Könige*, 258–62; Würthwein, *Das Erste Buch der Könige*, 143–44. Compared to 1 Kgs 12:1, 3–19* the account in 1 Kgs 11:29–39 represents an even later redactional layer because the prophecy of Ahijah is only referred to in 1 Kgs 12:15, which is clearly secondary to its direct context. One cannot escape the conclusion that 1 Kgs 11:29–39 and 1 Kgs 12:15 were written by one and the same person.

53. Minor additions that cannot be discussed in detail are the polemic reference to Jeroboam's mother in 1 Kgs 11:26, and the parenthesis in 1 Kgs12:2, according to which Jeroboam is still in Egypt. Finally, also the mention of the congregation (אל העדה) in 1 Kgs 12:20a must be judged as a secondary addition devised to adjust the verse to the situation in 1 Kgs 12:1, 3–19. See Becker, "Die Reichsteilung nach I Reg 12," 220.

54. The two verses in 11:41–42 contain concluding remarks on Solomon's reign that can be ignored for the purpose of the present study.

11:26*	Jeroboam son of Nebat, an Ephraimite of Zeredah, a servant of Solomon, rebelled against the king.	ירבעם בן נבט אפרתי מן הצרדה עבד לשלמה וירם יד במלך
11:40	And Solomon sought to kill Jeroboam; but Jeroboam fled to Egypt, to King Shishak of Egypt, and remained in Egypt until the death of Solomon.	ויבקש שלמה להמית את ירבעם ויקם ירבעם ויברח מצרים אל שישק מלך מצרים ויהי במצרים עד מות שלמה
[11:41–42]		
11:43	And Solomon slept with his ancestors and was buried in the city of his father David; and his son Rehoboam succeeded him.	וישכב שלמה עם אבתיו ויקבר בעיר דוד אביו וימלך רחבעם בנו תחתיו
12:2*	And Jeroboam son of Nebat who had fled from King Solomon heard of it, and Jeroboam returned from Egypt.	ויהי כשמע ירבעם בן נבט אשר ברח מפני המלך שלמה וישב ירבעם ממצרים
12:20a*	And when all Israel heard that Jeroboam had returned, they sent and called him and made him king over all Israel.	ויהי כשמע כל ישראל כי שב ירבעם וישלחו ויקראו אתו וימליכו אתו על כל ישראל

It is apparent that the earliest literary layer of 1 Kgs 11:26–12:20 is devoid of any specific parallels to the exodus narrative. That Jeroboam fled to Egypt because his life was threatened by Solomon (1 Kgs 11:40; 12:2*) is most likely a historically reliable piece of information[55] that hardly constitutes an exodus typology. The only comparable motif is Moses' flight to Midian, which is caused by Pharaoh's attempt to kill him (Exod 2:15), but a closer look at the texts quickly reveals that their differences outweigh their existing similarities. The reasons for the fugitive's conflict with the king are completely different, and the flight motif is realized in a diametrically opposed way. While Moses flees from the Egyptian king and settles in Midian, Jeroboam escapes from Solomon and comes to Egypt as a refuge. In sum, it is highly unlikely that one of the passages should have influenced the emergence of the other. Rather, they represent two originally independent pieces of Old Testa-

---

55. It remains, however, questionable whether the mention of Shishak must necessarily be original. The pertinent phrase (אל שישק מלך מצרים) is only loosely integrated into the syntactic structure of the clause and could represent a later gloss.

ment literature, each with its own distinct scope.[56]

The DtrH account was not only devoid of exodus typologies, it also offered quite a scant narrative by simply stating that "all Israel" had separated from Rehoboam and had made the returned rebel Jeroboam their king (1 Kgs 12:20a*). It is the author of 1 Kgs 12:1, 3–19* who first strives to explain why these things actually came to pass. According to him, it was all the fault of Solomon's heir Rehoboam, who had the opportunity to make the inhabitants of the northern kingdom his loyal subjects and instead achieved exactly the opposite when he rejected the request of the Israelites who had gathered at Shechem to confirm his kingship:

12:4	"Your father made our yoke heavy. Now therefore lighten the hard service of your father and his heavy yoke that he placed on us, and we will serve you."	אביך הקשה את עלנו ואתה עתה הקל מעבדת אביך הקשה ומעלו הכבד אשר נתן עלינו ונעבדך

While "the old men" (הזקנים) who had earlier attended Solomon strongly advised Rehoboam to meet the people's request (1 Kgs 12:6–8a), the counsel of "the young men" (הילדים) was quite different: they argued that instead of lightening the hard service, Rehoboam should rather increase it, in order to prove his superiority over his father (1 Kgs 12:8b–11). However, by following their council (1 Kgs 12:12–14), Rehoboam achieved exactly the opposite, as his apparently foolish decision sealed the fate of the united monarchy (1 Kgs 12:16).

The obvious attempt to contrast Rehoboam's folly with the wisdom of his father Solomon presupposes a picture of Solomon that was still alien to the earliest literary layers of the Deuteronomistic History. As was shown above, the same applies to the motif of forced labor first introduced in 1 Kgs 5:27–32*. The verses form another background required for the story in 1 Kgs 12:1, 3–19*, where they have been reinterpreted in the light of 1 Kgs 12:20a. Since the latter verse makes reference to the inhabitants of the northern kingdom as "all Israel," the author of 1 Kgs 12:1, 3–19* concluded that when Solomon

---

56. The widespread belief that the fates of Moses and Jeroboam are somehow linked on a literary level is to a large degree based on the observation that in 1 Kgs 12:28 Jeroboam makes reference to the exodus creed ("Here are your gods, O Israel, who brought you up out of the land of Egypt"; cf. Exod 20:2; Deut 5:6). However, the verse is neither a reliable piece of tradition nor part of the DtrH account, but rather reflects the attempt of a late Deuteronomist to portray the sin of Jeroboam as a violation of the first two commandments. See Kratz, *The Composition of the Narrative Books*, 162–63; Juha Pakkala, "Jeroboam without Bulls," *ZAW* 120 (2008): 501–25. Therefore, the evidence of 1 Kgs 12:28 proves to be irrelevant for our question.

had conscripted forced labor out of "all Israel" (1 Kgs 5:27) the measure had affected the same (northern) group, while the Judeans had been spared.[57] This reading of 1 Kgs 5:27, which was originally not implied, provided the perfect basis for a story explaining that Rehoboam became responsible for the segregation of the northern kingdom by increasing the hard service of "all Israel." Thus, in 1 Kgs 12:1, 3–19* the motif of Solomon's forced labor primarily serves as a means to an end, and one should be very cautious with any further conclusions that go beyond this scope. Although the text presents the forced labor as an actual problem, it would be misleading to conclude that it hereby aims to criticize Solomon, who, quite to the contrary, appears to be viewed as the wise father of a foolish son.

Although it has often been argued that Rehoboam's imprudent decision to increase the burden of the Israelites constitutes a strong parallel to Exod 5 and that the two texts must therefore be somehow dependent on each other, there is hardly any textual evidence to substantiate this claim.[58] Besides the uncontestable fact that both texts recount a similar incident, there are no distinct lexical parallels at all which might prove a literary dependency. While Exod 5:4–5 refers to the forced labor of the Israelites as סבלות the account in 1 Kgs 12:1, 3–19* is dominated by the term על ("yoke"),[59] which is not attested once in the entire Exodus narrative. The only clear terminological parallels between Exod 5 and 1 Kgs 12 exist in the use of the word עבדה ("work"; cf. Exod 5:9, 11; 1 Kgs 12:4) and in the employment of the verb כבד ("to be/make heavy"; cf. Exod 5:9; 1 Kgs 12:4, 10–11, 14), but even they are far too indistinct to establish a literary dependency. Only Exod 5:9 combines the two terms, whereas the author of 1 Kgs 12:1, 3–19* always uses the verb כבד with the noun על. In only one instance does this author refer to the increase of the "work" (עבדה); which he expresses, however, by employing a form of קשה

---

57. Despite this modification of the picture provided by 1 Kgs 5:27–32*, the author of 1 Kgs 12:1, 3–19* still contradicts 1 Kgs 9:15–22*, where the enslavement of Israelites is explicitly excluded. While it may be that he was not yet familiar with the latter passage, it is also conceivable that he either ignored or reinterpreted it. In the latter case he may have taken 1 Kgs 9:15–22* as evidence for his claim that the Judeans had been exempted from Solomon's forced labor.

One should note that the latter claim also seems to have influenced the number of five hundred fifty supervisors who were set over Solomon's forced labor according to 1 Kgs 9:23aβb. As in the case of the younger side parallel 1 Kgs 5:30 mentioning three thousand three hundred supervisors, the number can be divided by eleven, which implies that only the northern tribes were thought to have been involved in the institution of Solomon's forced labor. See Särkiö, *Die Weisheit und Macht Salomos*, 97.

58. See already Becker, "Die Reichsteilung nach I Reg 12," 223. Cf. Van Seters, *The Life of Moses*, 70–76; Särkiö, *Exodus und Salomo*, 69–77.

59. Cf. 1 Kgs 12:4, 9–11, 14 (par. 2 Chr 10:4, 9–11, 14).

hipʿil (1 Kgs 12:4). This does somehow recall the "heavy work" (עבדה קשה) of the Israelites in Exod 1:14* P, but even this parallel proves too weak to be taken as evidence for a literary dependency. In sum, it appears highly implausible that the author of 1 Kgs 12:1, 3–19* worked with a distinct *Vorlage* from the Exodus narrative, and there is no better evidence to assume that Exod 5 was modeled upon 1 Kgs 12 let alone to determine the reasons for this process. Both passages have developed independently.

What still remains to be discussed is the short passage in 1 Kgs 11:27–28 that has been redactionally appended to 1 Kgs 11:26 to provide information on the circumstances of Jeroboam's rebellion against Solomon.

11:27	And these are the circumstances under which he rebelled against the king: Solomon built the Millo, and closed up the gap in the wall of the city of his father David.	וזה הדבר אשר הרים יד במלך שלמה בנה את המלוא סגר את־פרץ עיר דוד אביו
11:28	And the man Jeroboam was very able, and when Solomon saw that the young man was industrious he gave him charge over all the forced labor of the house of Joseph.	והאיש ירבעם גבור חיל וירא שלמה את הנער כי עשה מלאכה הוא ויפקד אתו לכל סבל בית יוסף

Although the text does not provide information on the course of Jeroboam's rebellion, this hardly allows for the conclusion that the account of the rebellion has not been preserved.[60] Rather, it seems that the only purpose of the two verses is to clarify that Jeroboam had rebelled while holding an important position in Solomon's system of forced labor. He is responsible for coordinating the service of the "house of Joseph," which clearly refers to a group from the north and may most plausibly be taken as a designation of the northern kingdom here.[61] However, this piece of information provided by 1 Kgs 11:27–28 is plausible only in light of 1 Kgs 12:1, 3–19*, where the forced labor is introduced as the crucial factor which drives "all Israel" to secede from Rehoboam and to make Jeroboam their king. By mentioning that this Jeroboam had previously been responsible for Israel's forced labor,

---

60. So e.g., Julius Wellhausen, *Die Composition des Hexateuchs und der historischen Bücher des Alten Testaments* (4th ed.; Berlin: de Gruyter, 1963), 273; Montgomery, *A Critical and Exegetical Commentary on the Book of Kings*, 242; Würthwein, *Das Erste Buch der Könige*, 143; Simon J. DeVries, *1 Kings* (WBC 12; Waco: Word Books, 1985). But see also Noth, *Könige*, 256.

61. See Würthwein, *Das Erste Buch der Könige*, 143; Särkiö, *Die Weisheit und Macht Salomos*, 153 n. 417.

the author of 1 Kgs 11:27–28 further illuminates the background of the events that follow, and thus sharpens the profile of the entire narrative. Therefore, 1 Kgs 11:27–28 may hardly been taken as a historical source, but must rather be judged as a scribal creation devised in order to define more clearly the place of Jeroboam in the events described in 1 Kgs 12:1–20.[62] Literary connections between the two verses and the Exodus narrative again prove to be nonexistent. Although the term סבל used in 1 Kgs 11:28 to designate the forced labor is closely related to the word סבלות employed for the burdens of the Israelites (Exod 1:11; 2:11; 5:4–5; 6:6–7) this linguistic parallel is hardly sufficient to prove a literary dependency.

3.4. Conclusions

I was able to demonstrate that the motif of Solomon's forced labor was not part of the earliest literary layer of the Deuteronomistic History. Rather, it was first introduced in 1 Kgs 5:27, 28aα*, 32b*, where the conscription of forced labor is described as a measure of Solomon's to ensure that all Israel actively participates in the building of the Temple. Later, this picture was adjusted, in 1 Kgs 9:15*, 20–22a, 22bα*. The author of these supplementary verses found the enslavement of Israelites problematic and therefore claimed that Solomon had only conscripted forced labor from among the Canaanites. Still another approach is taken in 1 Kgs 12:1, 3–19*, a passage also dependent on 1 Kgs 5:27–32*. That Solomon conscripted forced labor out of "all Israel" (1 Kgs 5:27) is now reinterpreted as a reference to the enslavement of the inhabitants of the Northern Kingdom, and provides the background for explaining why they seceded. The reason given by the author of 1 Kgs 12:1, 3–19* is the folly of Rehoboam, who does not give in to the Israelites' request to lighten their hard service but instead increases it. The unclear role of Jeroboam in this new narrative setting finally gave rise to 1 Kgs 11:27–28, where it is clarified that Jeroboam had previously been given charge over the forced labor of the people he was supposed to lead into secession. With the exception of 1 Kgs 9:19aα, all of the passages discussed so far have developed within the literary horizon of 1 Kgs 1–12 and respond to issues inherent in the older redactional layers of the Deuteronomistic account. In contrast, the terminological links to the Exodus narrative have generally proven to be very weak. It therefore seems worth considering, in a final section, what can be positively said about literary connections between Exod 1–15 and 1 Kgs 1–12.

---

62. The same has already been cautiously suggested by Becker, "Die Reichsteilung nach 1 Reg 12," 221, n. 40.

4. Literary Connections between
Exodus 1–15 and 1 Kings 1–12

When the comparison between the passages on the Egyptian bondage and the texts dealing with Solomon's forced labor is based on redaction-critical analysis and the consideration of the distinct terminological parallels it soon becomes apparent that the literary evidence is much more complex than has widely been recognized. A uniform picture of the Egyptian bondage or of Solomon's forced labor does not exist, but we are rather dealing with variegated, sometimes contradictory, pictures that have developed gradually. Thus, the undifferentiated theory that the picture of the Egyptian bondage was painted with the colors of Solomon's forced labor (or vice versa) proves to be a scholarly myth. Actually, in light of the vague terminological parallels, there is not one single instance in which it may be demonstrated that one of the passages in Exodus and 1 Kings pertaining to the topic of servitude was composed in light of an enneateuchal intertext. The only distinct parallel is represented by two redactional notes mentioning the building of store cities (Exod 1:11b; 1 Kgs 9:19aα). As these store cities (ערי [ה]מסכנות) are elsewhere unattested in the entire Enneateuch it seems likely that the two verses are dependent upon one another.

The task of determining the direction of this dependency does, however, prove to be fairly difficult, since the store cities represent a singular detail in both Exod 1–15 and 1 Kgs 1–12. It has been argued above that there are basically two options towards accounting for 1 Kgs 9:19aα: either the verse is a post-Chronistic addition inspired by the building records in 2 Chronicles (esp. 2 Chr 8:4, 6), where the store cities are firmly rooted; or it was written against the background of Exod 1:11b in order to establish a typological connection to the Exodus narrative. In the first case, Exod 1:11b would in turn appear to be a very late intertextual link to 1 Kgs 9, while in the second case, its literary and historical origins would remain completely unclear.[63] Despite the fact that the latter consequence is hardly satisfactory, it seems nevertheless more likely that Exod 1:11b constitutes the *Vorlage* of 1 Kgs 9:19aα. While it is easy to conceive that a redactor who was familiar with the building of the store cities Pithom and Rameses in Exod 1:11b formulated the general state-

---

63. As Exod 1:11a, 12 are of pre-Priestly origin, Exod 1:11b could theoretically still represent a fairly old addition. However, the use of the term "store cities" with its strong parallels in 2 Chronicles, and the obviously fluid textual tradition of Exod 1:11b (LXX adds Heliopolis as a third store city), may just as well be taken as evidence for a late redactional horizon. That the names Pithom and Rameses hardly refer to cities erected by Ramesses II, but point to a much later period in the first millennium B.C.E. has been convincingly shown by Redford, "Exodus I 11," 416.

ment in 1 Kgs 9:19aα in order to demonstrate that Solomon's slaves used to construct the same types of cities, the alternative seems much less probable. It would imply that the author of Exod 1:11b picked one single item from the list of Solomon's building projects and, for no apparent reason, connected it with the names Pithom and Rameses. Thus, one should conclude that 1 Kgs 9:19aα is most likely dependent on Exod 1:11b and not vice versa.

Actually, even the cities for the chariots and the cities for the cavalry mentioned in 1 Kgs 9:19aβγ do carry an allusion to the Exodus narrative, although both items may certainly be explained against the background of 1 Kings alone. However, chariots (רכב) and cavalry (פרשים) are strongly reminiscent of Pharaoh's forces in Exod 14, and it is therefore not unreasonable to assume that 1 Kgs 9:19a was composed by a single author who had these intertextual references in mind. By referring to "all of Solomon's store cities" he implied that the king built a vast number of these cities, whereas Pharaoh had erected only two and (obviously) did not even possess cities for his mounted forces, as they are now claimed for Solomon. The same author may likewise be responsible for the short redactional note concluding 1 Kgs 9:22, according to which the Israelites were Solomon's captains and the commanders of his chariots and cavalry (ושלשיו ושרי רכבו ופרשיו). By employing vocabulary from Exod 14:6–9, the redactor apparently tried to demonstrate that the army of Solomon, who imported his horses and chariots from Egypt (1 Kgs 10:28–29), could in fact match that of Pharaoh in Exod 14.

Despite the fact that Solomon's close contacts to Egypt can be subjected to criticism elsewhere,[64] the king's portrayal in the additions to 1 Kgs 9 discussed above is hardly critical. Rather, the additions demonstrate that Solomon's power was superior to that of the king ruling Egypt at the time of the Exodus.[65] This study has shown that great caution is required when we attempt to interpret certain Pharaonic characteristics that the figure of Solomon has acquired over the time.[66] A redactional link connecting Solomon's reign to the situation

---

64. Cf. esp. Deut 17:16–17.

65. This does, of course, not exclude the possibility that the mention of Solomon's store cities in 1 Kgs 9:19aα could be sensed as problematic in later times. In fact, the omission of 1 Kgs 9:19aα in the Septuagint is most easily explained as an attempt to avoid the possible association of Solomon's building activities with the Egyptian bondage (Exod 1:11b). See van Keulen, *Two Versions of the Solomon Narrative*, 199.

66. One detail that should be mentioned in this context is the marriage between Solomon and Pharaoh's daughter (1 Kgs 3:1; 7:8; 9:16, 24; 11:1), which may represent an old piece of tradition, although it could as well be a late midrashic element inspired by the Exodus narrative (Exod 2). The same might also apply to the list of gifts in 1 Kgs 10:25 the first part of which is strangely reminiscent of the Israelites' booty (Exod 3:22; 12:35). In both cases, it can be excluded that the Exodus narrative has been influenced by the account in 1 Kings. See Berner, *Die Exoduserzählung*, 68–85, 99–102.

of the Exodus hardly needs to be an expression of subversive criticism, and can just as well represent an attempt to accentuate the literary bonds between two accounts that had independently developed a set of corresponding motifs and narrative traits. This gradual development of parallels between Exod 1–15 and 1 Kgs 1–12 must also be taken as the background of late texts such as the account of Hadad the Edomite in 1 Kgs 11:14–22,[67] which itself contains a couple of allusions to the exodus narrative.[68] As a detailed discussion of the passage is beyond the scope of this article, it may suffice to say that it represents a further example for a text in 1 Kgs 1–12 that is literarily dependent on the Exodus narrative. In contrast, the lack of Exodus texts inspired by a *Vorlage* in 1 Kings testifies to the fact that the establishment of explicit literary connections between Exod 1–15 and 1 Kgs 1–12 obviously followed a one-way street, leading from the Pentateuch to the Enneateuch.

---

67. See Erich Bosshard-Nepustil, "Hadad, der Edomiter: 1 Kön 11,14–22 zwischen literarischem Kontext und Verfassergegenwart," in: *Schriftauslegung in der Schrift* (ed. R.G. Kratz et al.; BZAW 300; Berlin: de Gruyter, 2000), 95–109. Bosshard-Nepustil convincingly shows that 1 Kgs 11:14–21 is a text from the Hellenistic period that reflects the increasing power of the Nabateans (Edom) and Ptolemaic rule over Egypt.

68. One should add that the account of Hadad the Edomite later influenced the alternative story of Jeroboam's rebellion as attested by the Septuagint (cf. 1 Kgs 12:24c–f); see Zippora Talshir, *The Alternative Story of the Division of the Kingdom: 3 Kingdoms 12:24 A–Z* (Jerusalem Biblical Studies 6; Jerusalem: Simor, 1993). Only at this later stage does the account of Jeroboam's flight to Egypt receive some explicit connections to the Exodus narrative that were still absent from the original version preserved by the Masoretic Text (1 Kgs 11:26*, 40).

"He Did What Was Right":
Criteria of Judgment and Deuteronomism in the Books of Kings[*]

Felipe Blanco Wißmann

1. "Judgment Texts" in the Books of Kings

There are distinctive "judgment texts" in the books of Kings that do not contribute to the development of the plot, but instead function within the narrative from a more distant point of view, evaluating the behavior of the king or the nation. Speeches are an important stylistic device in ancient Near Eastern and (even more) in Greek and Roman historiography; they characterize the protagonists and contribute to the continuity of the work.[1] In the books of Kings, speeches by prophets,[2] kings,[3] and YHWH[4] contribute to the judgment on the ruler (or the people). But the judgment formulas in the books of Kings also function to interrupt the narrative for the purpose of subdividing the text, while at the same time contributing to the continuity of the narrative. In this way, the judgment texts express the "historiosophy"[5] of

---

 * This paper is a very condensed summary of my doctoral dissertation (University of Zürich, 2007), published as Felipe Blanco Wißmann, *"Er tat das Rechte ..."*: Beurteilungskriterien und Deuteronomismus in 1Kön 12–2Kön 25 (ATANT 93; Zurich: Theologischer Verlag, 2008). I am grateful to Prof. Thomas B. Dozeman, who kindly revised an earlier draft of this paper.

1. See John Van Seters, *In Search of History: Historiography in the Ancient World and the Origins of Biblical History* (New Haven: Yale University Press, 1983), 37, 67, 125.

2. Cf. Blanco Wißmann, *"Er tat das Rechte ...,"* 187–204.

3. Cf. Blanco Wißmann, *"Er tat das Rechte ...,"* 175–87.

4. Cf. Blanco Wißmann, *"Er tat das Rechte ...,"* 204–11.

5. On the term "historiosophy" see Ziony Zevit, *The Religions of Ancient Israel. A Synthesis of Parallactic Approaches* (London: Continuum, 2001), 439–40.

the author/redactor.[6] In this paper, the distinct literary features of the judgment formulas in the books of Kings are investigated through a comparative study of parallels in Deuteronomy, in other books of the Hebrew Bible, and in ancient Near Eastern texts. The comparative study will provide the basis for critical evaluation of the hypothesis that the Deuteronomistic History is the appropriate literary context for interpreting the books of Kings. The paper will argue, instead, that the prophetic books are the more appropriate context for understanding the books of Kings.

2. The "Judgment Formulas"

The judgment formulas in the books of Kings have played a central role in the history of interpretation. Julius Wellhausen already saw the person who created the pattern of judgment notices on the different rulers as the actual author of the books of Kings.[7] Martin Noth described these notices as the framework of the Deuteronomistic Historian's account in this part of the Deuteronomistic History.[8] Since then, an analysis of these notices and especially of the theological judgments upon the kings of Israel[9] and Judah[10] has been a starting point for any work on the redaction history of the books of Kings and for any modification of the Deuteronomistic History hypothesis.[11]

---

6. In this paper, I use the terms "author" and "redactor" (of the books of Kings) synonymously, and in the sense of a working hypothesis, as a description of the person responsible for the notices concerning Judahite and Israelite kings in 1 Kgs 12–2 Kgs 25. Of course, this terminology is not without difficulties; see John Van Seters, "An Ironic Circle: Wellhausen and the Rise of Redaction Criticism," *ZAW* 115 (2003): 487–500; Blanco Wißmann, "*Er tat das Rechte . . . ,*" 28–30.

7. See Julius Wellhausen, *Die Composition des Hexateuchs und der historischen Bücher des Alten Testaments* (Berlin: de Gruyter, 1963), 297.

8. Cf. Martin Noth, *Überlieferungsgeschichtliche Studien: Die sammelnden und bearbeitenden Geschichtswerke im Alten Testament* (Halle: Niemeyer Verlag, 1943; 2d repr. ed., 1957; 3d repr. ed.: Darmstadt: Wissenschaftliche Buchgesellschaft, 1967), 73–74.

9. 1 Kgs 15:26, 34; 16:25–26, 30–31; 22:53; 2 Kgs 3:2–3; 10:29; 13:2, 11; 14:24; 15:9, 18, 24, 28; 17:2.

10. 1 Kgs 14:22; 15:3; 11, 14; 22:43–44; 2 Kgs 8:18, 27; 12:3–4; 14:3–4; 15:3–4, 34–35; 16:2–4; 18:3; 21:2–3, 20; 22:2; 23:32, 37; 24:9, 19.

11. On the history of research, cf. Thomas Römer, *The So-Called Deuteronomistic History: A Sociological, Historical and Literary Introduction* (London: T&T Clark, 2005), 13–43; Blanco Wißmann, "*Er tat das Rechte . . . ,*" 2–14.

2.1. Synchronisms

The constant connection of the history of Israel and Judah by means of the synchronic dating of the kings' reigns provides insight into the point of view of the author and his place in the history of biblical theology. The correlation of northern and southern kings locates the work of the author between the original book of Deuteronomy (which does not show any concern for "Israel" and "Judah" as states)[12] and the oldest parts of the book of Isaiah (with their purely Judean point of view; cf. Isa 7; 8:1–4),[13] on the one side, and the books of Chronicles on the other side (since in the latter text the concept of one "Israel" is embodied in the Judean kingdom).[14] There is yet no conception of an idealized, unified "Israel" in the judgment notices in the books of Kings,[15] although the synchronisms may be called a step in this direction. The most significant parallels to this perspective on "Israel" and "Judah" in the notices on the kings can be found in the book of Jeremiah.[16] The closest parallels in the literature of the ancient Near East are synchronisms in the Neo-Babylonian chronicles[17] and references to Babylonian *and* Assyrian history in Neo-Babylonian inscriptions that express a relationship between the two countries.[18]

---

12. The references to "Judah" as one of the tribes of Israel or as a region (Deut 33:7; 34:2) belong to secondary parts of the book, as do most of references to "Israel" (as a religious community). There might, however, have been references to "Israel" at the original beginning of Deuteronomy in Deut 4:45; 5:1; 6:4–5. Cf. Jan Christian Gertz, "Kompositorische Funktion und literarhistorischer Ort von Deuteronomium 1–3," in *Die deuteronomistischen Geschichtswerke: Redaktions- und religionsgeschichtliche Perspektiven zur "Deuteronomismus"-Diskussion in Tora und Vorderen Propheten* (ed. M. Witte et al.; BZAW 365; Berlin: Vandenhoeck & Ruprecht, 2006), 103–23, esp. 122–23.

13. Cf. Erich Bosshard-Nesputil, *Rezeptionen von Jesaja 1–39 im Zwölfprophetenbuch: Untersuchungen zur literarischen Verbindung von Prophetenbüchern in babylonischer und persischer Zeit* (OBO 154; Fribourg: Universitätsverlag; Göttingen: Vandenhoeck & Ruprecht, 1997), 251.

14. Cf. Reinhard Gregor Kratz, "Israel als Staat und als Volk," *ZTK* 97 (2000): 1–17.

15. Therefore, the Books of Kings cannot, as a whole, be described as a postexilic work representing a symbolic history of a culturally autonomous vision of "Israel," contra James Linville, "Rethinking the 'Exilic' Book of Kings," *JSOT* 75 (1997): 21–42, although there are additions in 1–2 Kings that express a later, more abstract conception of "Israel." Cf. 1 Kgs 8; 2 Kgs 17.

16. Cf., e.g., Jer 5:11; 11:14; 23:6; 30:1.

17. Cf. Chronicle 1 i 1, 9–10, 38; text: A. K. Grayson, *Assyrian and Babylonian Chronicles* (TCS 5; Locust Valley, N.Y.: Augustin, 1975), 70–74.

18. Cf. the Babylon Stela of Nabonidus; text: Hanspeter Schaudig, *Die Inschriften Nabonids von Babylon und Kyros' des Grossen, samt den in ihrem Umfeld entstandenen Tendenzschriften: Textausgabe und Grammatik* (AOAT 256; Münster: Ugarit-Verlag, 2001), 514–29. The so-called "Synchronistic History," however, offers only a limited parallel

2.2. "Good" and "Evil" in the Eyes of the Lord

Judging a king as "good" or "evil" (in relation to the will of the deities) is a typical feature of ancient Near Eastern royal ideology. Phoenician inscriptions provide some parallels, which show that, if similar inscriptions existed in Judah, a Judean redactor of the books of Kings could have been familiar with a traditional expression of judgment in the grammatical third person.[19] However, the particular way the reigns of different kings are presented and qualified in 1–2 Kings is without parallel among ancient Near Eastern texts with regard to form and continuity; only the Babylonian chronicles provide some limited parallels. The so-called "Weidner Chronicle" contains explicit judgments on rulers, using statements like: "Marduk looked upon him/her with joy."[20]

2.3. The "Fathers"

The motif of the "fathers" is used in the books of Kings and in the book of Deuteronomy in very different ways. A few times, the books of Kings speak about the patriarchs or the generation of the exodus as "fathers,"[21] but these references are probably later additions.[22] In the judgment formulas of the books of Kings, the term refers instead to the "ancestors" of the respective kings. Virtually all of these references are related to Judean, not Israelite kings.[23] Judean kings are compared to David or to one or more of their direct predecessors. These differences, however, do not point to multiple redactions. A king of Judah is normally compared to his direct predecessor, but not if he is judged differently; therefore, Asa, Ahaz, Hezekiah and Josiah are compared to their "father" David; Jehoram and Ahaz to "the kings of Israel"; and

---

with its repeated but imprecise expression "in the time of …." Cf. Grayson, *Chronicles*, 157–70.

19. For example, King Yahimilk is described in his inscription as "a righteous (ישר) king before the holy gods of Byblos," *KAI* (2002) 4:6–7. Cf. *KAI* (2002) 10:7–10.

20. "Weidner Chronicle," 44/48 (text: Grayson, *Chronicles*, 148).

21. On the question of whether "Deuteronomistic" references to "fathers" refer to the patriarchs or to the generation of the exodus cf. Thomas Römer, *Israels Väter: Untersuchungen zur Väterthematik im Deuteronomium und in der deuteronomistischen Tradition* (OBO 99; Fribourg: Universitätsverlag; Göttingen: Vandenhoeck & Ruprecht, 1990); Norbert Lohfink, *Die Väter Israels im Deuteronomium: Mit einer Stellungnahme von Thomas Römer* (OBO 111; Fribourg: Universitätsverlag; Göttingen: Vandenhoeck & Ruprecht, 1991).

22. Cf. 1 Kgs 14:15, 22; 18:31–36; 2 Kgs 13:23; 17:13–15, 34, 41; 21:8, 15, 22; 22:13.

23. But cf. 1 Kgs 15:26; 22:53; 2 Kgs 3:2; 15:9. On the motif of the "sin of Jeroboam" see below.

Josiah's sons Jehoahaz and Jehoiakim to "their fathers."[24] It is a reasonable assumption that the motif of the "fathers" is meant to underline the continuity of the dynasty of David in Judah and the dynastic changes in Israel; this usage of the motif is rooted in typical ancient Near Eastern royal ideology, and not in the book of Deuteronomy.

2.4. The bāmôt

The *bāmôt* are an important *leitmotif* in the books of Kings, above all in the judgment formulas of the kings of Judah. The word במה is often, but incorrectly, translated as "high place." But "*bāmôt*" is just a technical term for a sanctuary in or near an עיר[25] (therefore, it is appropriate to speak of a cult "in the *bāmôt*," not "on the *bāmôt*"). Phrases like "on every high hill and under every spreading tree" that seem to locate the *bāmôt* in a rural area are secondary additions.[26] Those rulers who support the cult of the *bāmôt* are evaluated negatively; those who do not, however, participate actively in this cult and accept it as a mere habit of the people (Asa, Jehoash, Amaziah, Azariah, and Jotham), or who—even better—take action against it (like Hezekiah and Josiah), are praised. The statements concerning the *bāmôt* are crucial to every discussion about the "Deuteronomistic" character of the books of Kings, because the judgments concerning the kings seem to be linked by this very motif to the Deuteronomistic concept of centralization of the cult. However, the redactor of the original books of Kings already found some texts about *bāmôt* in his sources (e.g., 1 Kgs 3*[27]; 2 Kgs 23*[28]), and integrated them into his work. The story of Sennacherib's siege of Jerusalem (2 Kgs 18–19*)

---

24. Cf. Erik Aurelius, *Zukunft jenseits des Gerichts: Eine redaktionsgeschichtliche Studie zum Enneateuch* (BZAW 319; Berlin: de Gruyter, 2003), 25; contra Helga Weippert, "Die 'deuteronomistischen' Beurteilungen der Könige von Israel und Juda und das Problem der Redaktion der Königebücher," *Bib* 53 (1972): 301–39, esp. 314–17, 331.

25. Cf. 1 Sam 9:5–6; 1 Kgs 12:32; 2 Kgs 17:9; 23:5, 8–9. Cf. Leonid Kogan and Serguei Tishchenko, "Lexicographic Notes on Hebrew *bamah*," *UF* 34 (2002): 319–52; Matthias Gleis, *Die Bamah* (BZAW 251; Berlin: de Gruyter, 1997), 44. The *bamah* that the Moabite king Mesha speaks of in his inscription is likewise a sanctuary in a city: it is located in Mesha's capital Dhiban; cf. Gleis, *Bamah*, 27–31.

26. 1 Kgs 14:23; 2 Kgs 16:4; 17:9–10. Cf. Aurelius, *Zukunft*, 55.

27. Cf. Gleis, *Bamah*, 94–95.

28. Cf. Christof Hardmeier, "König Joschija in der Klimax des DtrG (2Reg 22f.) und das vordtr Dokument einer Kultreform am Residenzort (23,4–15*)," in *Erzählte Geschichte: Beiträge zur narrativen Kultur im alten Israel* (ed. R. Lux; Biblisch-theologische Studien 40; Neukirchen-Vluyn: Neukirchener, 2000), 81–145; Martin Arneth, "Die antiassyrische Reform Josias von Juda: Überlegungen zur Komposition und Intention von 2 Reg 23,4–15," *ZABR* 7 (2001): 189–216.

was a source used by this redactor as well,[29] although the reference to the *bāmôt* in the speech of the Rab-shaqeh (2 Kgs 18:22) might be redaction-al.[30] Additionally, the redactor read in his source for 2 Kgs 23* that Josiah broke down *bāmôt* "at the entrance of the gate of Joshua" (2 Kgs 23:8b).[31] Obviously, the redactor tried to harmonize all of these different references to "*bāmôt*." His narrative related that the cult of the *bāmôt* was permitted in the time before the erection of the temple; that following this, the offerings made by the people at these cult places were a regrettable fact during the reigns of the following Judean kings; that the *bāmôt* were abolished by Hezekiah for the first time, and that they were definitively defiled and thus rendered unusable by Josiah (טמא *pi'el*; cf. 2 Kgs 23:8a).

No cult places called "*bāmôt*" are mentioned in the book of Deuteronomy,[32] and the typical wording of Deuteronomy's centralization law (במקום אשר יבחר יהוה; Deut 12:14, 18) is missing from the original books of Kings.[33] The closest parallels to this view of the *bāmôt* can be found in the Latter Prophets (cf., for example, Jer 7:31; 19:5; 32:35). The redactor of the books of Kings might have been familiar with at least some of the references to *bāmôt* in the Latter Prophets, like the announcements of the destruction of the *bāmôt* in Jer 17:3*, Hos 10:8*, and Amos 7:9*. Originally, these references in (earlier forms of) the prophetic books did not necessarily connote an accusation of the worship of other gods, but simply announced the end of the cultic life of Israel (or Judah), of which the *bāmôt* were a part. For the recipients of this prophetic tradition—including the redactor of the books of Kings—however, it was only a small step from these announcements of destruction to the opinion that the *bāmôt*, the sanctuaries of the ערים, were a

---

29. Cf. Brevard S. Childs, *Isaiah and the Assyrian Crisis* (SBT 2/3; London: SCM Press, 1967), 69–103; Nadav Na'aman, "Updating the Messages: Hezekiah's Second Prophetic Story (2 Kings 19.9b–35) and the Community of Babylonian Deportees," in *"Like a Bird in a Cage": The Invasion of Sennacherib in 701 BCE* (ed. L. L. Grabbe; JSOTSup 363; Sheffield: Sheffield Academic Press, 2003), 201–20.

30. Cf. Na'aman, "Updating," 218.

31. Cf. Arneth, "Reform," 198–99.

32. Deut 32:13; 33:29 have to be attributed to *bmt*, "body, back"; cf. Kogan and Tishchenko, "Lexicographic Notes," 330ff.

33. Descriptions of Jerusalem as Yhwh's chosen city are secondary additions in the Books of Kings: 1 Kgs 14:21; 2 Kgs 21:4, 7; and outside of the judgment formulas: 1 Kgs 8:16, 44, 48; 11:13, 32, 36. Cf. Reinhard G. Kratz, *Die Komposition der erzählenden Bücher des Alten Testaments: Grundwissen der Bibelkritik* (Uni-Taschenbücher 2157; Göttingen: Vandenhoeck & Ruprecht, 2000), 166; Konrad Schmid, "Das Deuteronomium innerhalb der 'deuteronomistischen Geschichtswerke' in Gen–2Kön," in *Das Deuteronomium zwischen Pentateuch und Deuteronomistischem Geschichtswerk* (ed. E. Otto and R. Achenbach; FRLANT 206; Göttingen: Vandenhoeck & Ruprecht, 2004), 193–211, esp. 204–5.

reason for the downfall of Judah. A comparable point of view is expressed in the Weidner Chronicle and on the "Cyrus Cylinder"[34]: Both texts are expressions of a typical Mesopotamian *Hauptstadttheologie*[35] (theology of the main city) and condemn certain kings for "duplicating" the sanctuary of Marduk in Babylon, i.e., favoring another city's sanctuary.

Although the judgment formulas in the books of Kings do not cite Deuteronomy's law of centralization, they are often considered expressions of the principle of cultic centralization.[36] There seems to be, however, a certain ambiguity in the conception of the *bāmôt* in the books of Kings:[37] To the author of Kings they are, of course, places where YHWH is worshipped (2 Kgs 18:22). However, when the author speaks about the abolishment of *bāmôt* (2 Kgs 18:4; 23:8; cf. 23:4–15), he speaks about cults of other gods in this context as well, and there is no reason to consider all these statements as secondary.[38] It is not possible to reconstruct a first edition of the books of Kings that did not contain any notion of the *bāmôt* as places where other gods were venerated.[39]

2.5. "Foreign" Gods

There are, as well, more explicit accusations concerning the worship of other gods in the books of Kings. Above all, it is the veneration of Baal that plays an important role for the evaluation of the kings (and the people). Some of these accusations were already part of the original books of Kings; they cannot be considered secondary additions because they are an indispensable element of the books' structure as expressed by the judgment formulas (cf. 1 Kgs 16:30–32; 22:53; 2 Kgs 3:2; 10:28; 11:18). Without the motif of the worship of Baal, there is no point in saying that, for example, Ahaziah "walked in the ways of his father and mother" (1 Kgs 22:53), or that Jehoram of Judah "walked in the ways of the kings of Israel, as the house of Ahab had done" (2 Kgs 8:18).

---

34. Cf. Weidner Chronicle, 56–61; text: Jean-Jacques Glassner, *Mesopotamian Chronicles* (SBLWAW 19; Atlanta: Society of Biblical Literature, 2004), 266; cf. ibid., 291 n. 10!; Cyrus Cylinder, 5–12; text: Schaudig, *Inschriften*, 551–52.

35. Cf. Stefan Maul, "Die altorientalische Hauptstadt—Abbild und Nabel der Welt," in *Die orientalische Stadt: Kontinuität, Wandel, Bruch* (ed. G. Wilhelm; Colloquien der Deutschen Orient-Gesellschaft 1; Saarbrücken: Saarbrücker Druckerei und Verlag, 1997), 109–24.

36. Cf. Aurelius, *Zukunft*, 211, Schmid, "Deuteronomium," 201–2.

37. Cf. Steven L. McKenzie, *The Trouble with Kings: The Composition of the Book of Kings in the Deuteronomistic History* (VTSup 42; Leiden: Brill, 1991), 120–22.

38. On 2 Kgs 18:4 cf. Aurelius, *Zukunft*, 16.

39. Contra Iain William Provan, *Hezekiah and the Books of Kings: A Contribution to the Debate about the Composition of the Deuteronomistic History* (BZAW 172; Berlin: de Gruyter, 1988), passim.

The worship of Baal, so important for the coherence of Kings, is never mentioned in the legal corpus of Deuteronomy,[40] and appears only once in Deuteronomy 4, a very late addition from Persian times (בעל פעור; Deut 4:3).[41] "Asherah" appears only in three exilic additions in Deuteronomy: The singular occurs in 16:21, while the late plural "Asherim," which functions as "a code-word for something cultically deviant,"[42] is mentioned in 7:5; 12:3. The veneration of Baal, however, is an important theme in the Latter Prophets, especially in the books of Hosea and Jeremiah. The statements about the worship of Baal in Kings presuppose the view of the cult of Baal as an historical phenomenon in Israel in the book of Jeremiah (cf. Jer 23:13–14), as well as the emphasis on this cult as *the* paradigm for the veneration of other gods in the later stages of the literary growth of that biblical book.[43] The development of special wording concerning the worship of Baal can even be observed in the book of Jeremiah: קטר לבעל *pi'el*, "burning incense to Baal." This phrase becomes a *terminus technicus* for the cultic offense. Then, in Jeremiah 44, קטר *pi'el*, without mentioning a deity, has become an equivalent for "venerating other gods." This use of קטר *pi'el* is present in the books of Kings from the beginning (without the preliminary stages visible in the book of Jeremiah) in the statements about the *bāmôt,* where "the people still sacrificed and burned incense" (e.g., 2 Kgs 15:4).[44]

To the redactor of the books of Kings, Baal is nothing but a foreign god, "imported" from Phoenicia together with King Ahab's wife. Other deities are encompassed by this view on the veneration of other gods as a foreign phenomenon, above all the goddess Asherah. But why are traditional elements of the religion of ancient Israel and Judah (like the *bāmôt,* Baal, and Asherah) understood as foreign cults in the books of Kings? A possible answer to this question may be the "openness" of preexilic religion; an openness to different names for and manifestations of a deity.[45] There is something like an intel-

---

40. "Baal" in Deut 15:2; 22:22; 24:4 does not refer to the deity. Cf. Deut 21:13; 24:1.

41. Cf. Römer, *Deuteronomistic History,* 124 with n. 30; Eckart Otto, *Das Deuteronomium im Pentateuch und Hexateuch: Studien zur Literaturgeschichte von Pentateuch und Hexateuch im Lichte des Deuteronomiumrahmens* (FAT 30; Tübingen: Mohr Siebeck, 2000), 167–75.

42. Nicholas Wyatt, "Asherah," *DDD* 2:99–105, esp. 103.

43. Cf. Jörg Jeremias, "Der Begriff 'Baal' im Hoseabuch und seine Wirkungsgeschichte (1994)," in *Hosea und Amos: Studien zu den Anfängen des Dodekapropheton* (ed. J. Jeremias; FAT 13; Tübingen: Mohr Siebeck, 1996), 86–103; idem, "Hoseas Einfluß auf das Jeremiabuch—ein traditionsgeschichtliches Problem (1994)," in Jeremias, *Hosea,* 122–41.

44. Cf. Jeremias, "Einfluß," 133; Hardmeier, "König," 126.

45. Cf. Manfred Weippert, "Synkretismus und Monotheismus: Religionsinterne Konfliktbewältigung im alten Israel," in *Kultur und Konflikt* (ed. J. Assmann and D. Harth; Edition Suhrkamp 1612; Frankfurt: Suhrkamp, 1990), 143–79.

lectual link between the multitude of cult places and the multitude of deities, even if they are all called "Yʜwʜ" (cf. the findings at Kuntillet Ajrud). [46] A hymn[47] of the Assyrian king Ashurbanipal to Ishtar of Nineveh and Ishtar of Arbela demonstrates how the actions of different manifestations of one deity could be imagined as "closely related, but slightly different in nuance."[48] The judgment formulas simply take this connection between the multitude of cult places and the multitude of deities seriously and take the condemnation of traditional elements of Judean (and Israelite) religion to its logical end.

This rigor distinguishes the books of Kings from the original book of Deuteronomy: The Urdeuteronomium demanded centralization of the worship of Yhwh, but this demand was not yet linked to the motif of the foreign gods. Much later, in the postexilic period, the prohibition of illegitimate, foreign cults was inserted into Deuteronomy 12.[49] In the original form of the books of Kings, however, the accusation of the lack of centralization and the accusation of the lack monolatry are already fused into one: the kings "did evil in the eyes of Yhwh," and even in the periods of the good Judean kings, the people's cult at the *bāmôt* continued. The connection of both accusations in the books of Kings hints at a later date than that of the Urdeuteronomium.

2.6. The "Sin of Jeroboam"

The "sin of Jeroboam" was defined by the polemical[50] text of 1 Kgs 12:26–30[51] in the original form of the books of Kings, and then repeated as a leitmotif in almost every judgment formula pertaining to the Israelite kings.[52] The motif of the "sin of Jeroboam" is the "Israelite" counterpart to the motif of

---

46. Cf. Zevit, *Religions*, 370-405.

47. Cf. Barbara Nevling Porter, "Ishtar of Ninineveh and her Collaborator, Ishtar of Arbela, in the Reign of Assurbanipal," *Iraq* 66 (2004): 41-44; text: Alasdair Livingstone, *Court Poetry and Literary Miscellanea* (SAA 3; Helsinki: Helsinki University Press, 1989), 10–13.

48. Nevling Porter, "Ishtar," 41.

49. Cf. Römer, *Deuteronomistic History*, 63–64, Timo Veijola, *Das fünfte Buch Mose: Deuteronomium Kapitel 1,1–16,17* (ATD 8,1; Göttingen: Vandenhoeck & Ruprecht, 2004), 274–77.

50. On the search for a non-polemical source of 1 Kgs 12 and for Jeroboam's historical religious policy, cf. Henrik Pfeiffer, *Das Heiligtum von Bethel im Spiegel des Hoseabuches* (FRLANT 183; Göttingen: Vandenhoeck & Ruprecht, 1999), 26–64.

51. 1 Kgs 12:31–33 is a secondary addition; cf. Ernst Würthwein, *Das erste Buch der Könige: Kapitel 1–16* (ATD 11.1; Göttingen: Vandenhoeck und Ruprecht, 1985), 165–66.

52. The exceptions are: Elah, Ahab, Shallum, and Hoshea. Cf. Francesca Stavrakopoulou, "The Blackballing of Manasseh," in *Good Kings and Bad Kings* (ed. L. L. Grabbe; LHB/OTS 393; London: T&T Clark International, 2005), 248–63, 252 with n. 8.

the *bāmôt*; both are expressed in a similar way, using a form of סור.[53] And just like the illegitimate cult taking place in the *bāmôt*, the "sin of Jeroboam" in the books of Kings should be interpreted both as breaching the principle of cultic centralization *and* as venerating foreign gods:[54] The text in 1 Kings 12 underscores the fact that Jeroboam chose two cultic places and made two calves, representing two gods (12:28).

Jeroboam is described in the books of Kings as a typical *Unheilsherrscher*[55] (a technical term sometimes translated as "calamitous ruler"). He commits the "sin of Jeroboam" and "makes Israel sin" (חטא *hipʿil*); i.e., he causes, in the context of a dynastic worldview,[56] subsequent punishment upon himself and upon the Israelite people. For, according to the books of Kings, the "sin of Jeroboam" is never abolished during the whole history of the Kingdom of Israel; the northern kingdom is doomed from the beginning of its existence. The motif of the "sin of Jeroboam" in the books of Kings presupposes the destruction of the northern kingdom and may presuppose the polemics against Jeroboam (II) in Hosea and Amos,[57] but it is older than its receptions[58] in Deuteronomy 9, and Exodus 32, and older than the extensive polemical texts against idolatry in "Deutero-Isaiah."[59] And, although Deuteronomy speaks of foreign peoples who teach (למד *piʿel*; cf. Deut 20:18) Israel to commit idolatry, it does not reflect the concept of a single person making a group of people sin (חטא *hipʿil*; but cf. Deut 24:4).

---

53. Cf., for example, 2 Kgs 10:31b, 13:2b, and 14:4.

54. Cf. Würthwein, *Könige I*, 164, Martin Noth, *Könige* (BKAT 9/1; Neukirchen-Vluyn: Neukirchener, 1968), 282–83.

55. On the *Unheilsherrscher* in Mesopotamian texts, cf. Hans-Gustav Güterbock, "Die historische Tradition und ihre literarische Gestaltung bei Babyloniern und Hethitern bis 1200. Erster Teil: Babylonier," *ZA* 42 (1934): 1–91; Carl D. Evans, "Naram-Sin and Jeroboam: The Archetypal *Unheilsherrscher* in Mesopotamian and Biblical Historiography," in *More Essays on the Comparative Method* (ed. W. W. Hallo et al.; Scripture in Context 2; Winona Lake: Eisenbrauns, 1983), 97–125.

56. Cf. Klaus Koch, "Gibt es ein Vergeltungsdogma im Alten Testament? (1955)," in *Um das Prinzip der Vergeltung in Religion und Recht des Alten Testaments* (ed. idem; WdF 125; Darmstadt: Wissenschaftliche Buchgesellschaft, 1972), 130–80.

57. Cf. Melanie Köhlmoos, *Bet-El—Erinnerungen an eine Stadt: Perspektiven der alttestamentlichen Bet-El-Überlieferung* (FAT 49; Tübingen: Mohr Siebeck, 2006), 153–79. Obviously, traditions about Jeroboam I and II were blended in the course of biblical literary history; cf. Christoph Levin, "Amos und Jerobeam I.," *VT* 45 (1995): 307–17.

58. See Konrad Schmid, *Erzväter und Exodus: Untersuchungen zur doppelten Begründung der Ursprünge Israels innerhalb der Geschichtsbücher des Alten Testaments* (WMANT 81; Neukirchen-Vluyn: Neukirchener, 1999), 142; Veijola, *Deuteronomium*, 226; Blanco Wißmann, *"Er tat das Rechte…,"* 120–21.

59. Cf., for example, Isa 44:9–20; 45:20.

In the books of Kings, the motif of the "sin of Jeroboam" is linked to a polemic against the sanctuary of Bethel. The rise of this sanctuary, which probably became "the one religious center authorized by the imperial authorities"[60] in the exilic period, is the likely historical background for this polemic. The priests of Marduk in Babylon faced comparable threats when Nabonidus favored Tayma over the main city's sanctuary. And texts from and about the time of Nabonidus like the "Verse Account" provide significant parallels to 1 Kings 12: the last king of Babylonia is described as an *Unheilsherrscher* in a similar polemical fashion.[61]

King Manasseh of Judah is blamed, in similar wording, for "making Judah sin" (החטיא *hipʿil*; see 2 Kgs 21:11, 16; cf. 21:17).[62] Just as in the case of Jeroboam, this wording in itself (regardless of the very explicit statements about Manasseh's guilt in 2 Kgs 23:26–27; 24:3–4, which are probably secondary additions)[63] already connotes a subsequent punishment of the sin committed by Manasseh (and the people of Judah); i.e., it seems that the motif of the "sin of Manasseh" presupposes the destruction of Judah.

2.7. The "Law"

There are few references to the Torah in the books of Kings. The report on the finding of the Torah was inserted (probably already in the postexilic period) into the text about the renovation of the temple and the reform of King Josiah in 2 Kgs 22–23,[64] with Jeremiah 36 and the report on Josiah's finding of the Torah, which were "written as two poles corresponding to each other."[65] While Josiah was praised in the original text of the books of Kings

---

60. Joseph Blenkinsopp, "The Judean Priesthood during the Neo-Babylonian and Achaemenid Periods: A Hypothetical Reconstruction," *CBQ* 60 (1998): 25–43, 34.

61. Cf. "Verse Account," II, 4–7, 11–12, 15 (text: Schaudig, *Inschriften*, 567).

62. While 21:11 is probably part of a later addition, the language and content of 21:16–17 fits the original Books of Kings very well. See Blanco Wißmann, *"Er tat das Rechte …,"* 161–72; contra Aurelius, *Zukunft*, 59 n. 167, who points out that Manasseh's sin could not have been mentioned in the "book of the annals of the kings of Judah." However, Aurelius's assessment might be a misconception of the character and value of the references to sources in the Books of Kings; see Nadav Naʾaman, "The Sources Available for the Author of the Book of Kings," in *Convegno Internazionale Recenti Tendenze nella Riccostruzione della Storia Antica d'Israele. Roma, 6-7 marzo 2003* (Contributi del Centro Linceo Interdisciplinare "Beniamino Segre"; Rom: Academia Nazionale dei Lincei, 2005), 105–20, 110; Blanco Wißmann, *"Er tat das Rechte …,"* 166–67.

63. Cf. Aurelius, *Zukunft*, 57–58, Ernst Würthwein, *Die Bücher der Könige. 1.Kön 17–2.Kön 25* (ATD 11.2; Göttingen: Vandenhoeck und Ruprecht, 1984), 468.

64. Cf. Christoph Levin, "Joschija im deuteronomistischen Geschichtswerk," *ZAW* 96 (1984): 351–71; Römer, *Deuteronomistic History*, 55–56.

65. Thomas Römer, "Transformations in Deuteronomistic and Biblical Historiography: On 'Book-Finding' and other Literary Strategies," *ZAW* 109 (1997): 1–11, 9.

because he took care of the temple in an exemplary way (Babylonian kings were evaluated positively for similar reasons in Neo-Babylonian texts), only this addition makes him an outstanding observer of the "Torah." This new understanding of Josiah is related to a concept of "Torah" similar to that of Deut 28:45–68: the "Torah" contains obligations of the covenant that have to be observed, and breaching them leads to the cursing of the violator.[66] Later, another addition (2 Kgs 23:25–27) defined the "Torah" as the "Torah of Moses."[67] The motif of the "Torah of Moses" is inserted several other times into the text of the books of Kings (1 Kgs 2:3;[68] 2 Kgs 14:6;[69] cf. 2 Kgs 21:8),[70] though perhaps by different hands. Another concept is expressed in the later references to the "Torah of YHWH" in 2 Kgs 10:31;[71] 17:13, 34, 37.[72] 2 Kings 17:13 claims that the prophets are interpreters of the Torah, a statement that can be found in such late texts as Deut 4:9–14[73] (cf. Deut 18:9–22). All of these references ignore the basic view of the first addition in 2 Kings 22 that the Torah was not "found again" until the reign of Josiah.

It is remarkable that in the original books of Kings the rulers were not judged in relation to any written law or loyalty oath: Provided that the *Urdeuteronomium* was a reception of the Neo-Assyrian loyalty oath tradition,[74] one would expect matching criteria of judgment in the judgment formulas of "Deuteronomistic" literature. The Assyrian annals prove that such a form of historiography was possible: they contain judgments on (foreign, non-Assyrian) kings in relation to the loyalty oath sworn to the Assyrian king.[75] But it was only in later Persian times that the concept of "the law" gained impor-

---

66. Cf. Otto, *Pentateuch*, 119 with n. 54, Reinhard Achenbach, "The Pentateuch, the Prophets, and the Torah in the 5th and 4th Century B.C.E.," in *Judah and the Judeans in the Fourth Century B.C.E* (ed. O. Lipschits et al.; Winona Lake: Eisenbrauns, 2007), 253–85, esp. 257.

67. See above n. 63.

68. Cf. Würthwein, *Könige I*, 20.

69. Cf. Würthwein, *Könige II*, 370.

70. Cf. Aurelius, *Zukunft*, 62–64, Percy S. F. van Keulen, *Manasseh Through The Eyes Of The Deuteronomists* (OTS 38; Leiden: Brill, 1996), 106.

71. Susanne Otto, *Jehu, Elia und Elisa: Die Erzählung von der Jehu-Revolution und die Komposition der Elia-Elisa-Erzählungen* (BWANT 152; Stuttgart: Kohlhammer, 2001), 53 with n. 142; Würthwein, *Könige II*, 343.

72. Cf. Würthwein, *Könige II*, 403.

73. Cf. Otto, *Pentateuch*, 167–75. On the late date of 2 Kgs 17:13 cf. Christl Maier, *Jeremia als Lehrer der Tora: Soziale Gebote des Deuteronomiums in Fortschreibungen des Jeremiabuches* (FRLANT 196; Göttingen: Vandenhoeck & Ruprecht, 2002), 149–50.

74. See below 3.1.

75. Cf. Ashurbanipal's annals (Rassam Cylinder): Col. VII, 82–85; VIII, 65–68; IX, 60–63; text: Maximilian Streck, *Assurbanipal und die letzten assyrischen Könige bis zum Untergang Niniveh's, II. Teil: Texte* (VAB 7.2; Leipzig: Hinrichs, 1916), 64, 70, 76.

tance throughout the ancient Near East:[76] the "Demotic Chronicle"[77] from Egypt provides closer parallels to the secondary identifications of the "Torah" in the books of Kings. It evaluates the pharaohs' behavior towards "the law" and was probably written in the third century B.C.E.

3. Conclusions

The parallels to the judgment formulas in the books of Kings among non-biblical and biblical texts provide insight into the historical setting of the original form of the books of Kings.

3.1. The Judgment Texts and Neo-Babylonian Literature

It was very probably in the Neo-Assyrian period that Judean scribes used elements of Assyrian royal ideology to create the *Urdeuteronomium*, which was intended to function in a subversive manner.[78] This specific cultural background of the *Urdeuteronomium* is not observable in the judgment formulas in the books of Kings,[79] although the Assyrian annals show that historiographical writing based on the criterion of "loyalty" was possible.

The books of Kings are dependent in both form and content, not only on Neo-Babylonian literature like chronicles, but also royal inscriptions (such as the Babylon Stela of Nabonidus or the Cyrus Cylinder) and other texts (e.g.,

---

76. On the problem of the so-called *Reichsautorisation* (imperial authorization) of texts like the Torah in Persian times cf. James W. Watts, ed., *Persia and Torah: The Theory of Imperial Authorization of the Pentateuch* (SBLSS 17; Atlanta: Society of Biblical Literature, 2001); Konrad Schmid, "Persische Reichsautorisation und Tora," *TRu* 71 (2006): 494–506.

77. Cf. Wilhelm Spiegelberg, *Die sogenannte Demotische Chronik des Pap. 215 der Bibliothèque Nationale zu Paris: Nebst den auf der Rückseite des Papyrus stehenden Texten* (Demotische Studien von Wilhelm Spiegelberg 7; Leipzig: Hinrichs 1914), 9–13.

78. See Moshe Weinfeld, *Deuteronomy and the Deuteronomic School* (Oxford: Oxford University Press, 1972); Eckart Otto, *Das Deuteronomium: Politische Theologie und Rechtsreform in Juda und Assyrien* (BZAW 284; Berlin: de Gruyter, 1999); Römer, *Deuteronomistic History*, 67–81. I consider the Neo-Assyrian cultural background of Deuteronomy to be a valid argument for a seventh-century dating of the book's original edition, although there is, of course, considerable evidence to the contrary. See Blanco Wißmann, *"Er tat das Rechte … ,"* 16–24.

79. Although traces of Assyrian cultural influence might be found in the source material of 1–2 Kgs; cf., for example, Arneth, "Reform," 208 (on 2 Kgs 23:4–15), and Victor Avigdor Hurowitz, *I Have Built you an Exalted House: Temple Building in the Bible in Light of Mesopotamian and Northwest Semitic Writings* (JSOTSup 115; Sheffield: JSOT Press, 1992) (on 1 Kgs 5–9).

254 PENTATEUCH, HEXATEUCH, OR ENNEATEUCH?

the "Verse account" of Nabonidus), all of which presuppose in different ways the idea of the uniqueness of Esagila. More precisely, it is likely that the books of Kings in their original form already presuppose the massive conflict during the time of Nabonidus over the special position of Esagila and Babylon: It is the literature from and about the reign of this king that shows the most significant parallels to the judgment texts of the books of Kings.

3.2. The Books of Kings, Deuteronomy, and the Principle of Monolatry

This comparative study also indicates that the traditional derivation of the judgment formulas in the books of Kings from Deuteronomy is questionable. There are no motifs connecting Deuteronomy and the original books of Kings. Such parallels can only be found in some texts in 1-2 Kings, which secondarily expand the perspective from the kings to the people, for example in 1 Kgs 14:22–24, 2 Kgs 21:7–9, and 2 Kgs 17:7–20. All these texts are interpolated; they employ the language of the Deuteronomistic stage of the book of Deuteronomy and introduce this perspective into the books of Kings. One could say that a "Deuteronomistic" perspective within the books of Kings is expressed in those texts that speak explicitly of the offences of the whole people (rather than implicitly, like the statements concerning the remnants of the cult in the *bāmôt*).

The explicit secondary accusations against the whole people in the books of Kings are regularly connected with allegations of venerating foreign gods. However, not every mention of gods other than YHWH in the books of Kings is secondary, and even the motifs of the *bāmôt* and the "sin of Jeroboam" are already connected to the principle of monolatry. A complete redaction-critical separation between the principle of the centralization of worship and the principle of monolatry is not possible, and the judgment formulas show that there is an intellectual link between the two principles.[80] It is true that explicit condemnation of the worship of other gods (mostly directed against the people) can be found only in secondary texts. But these explicit condemnations do not raise anything completely new, but only develop further the initial stages of these accusations as found in the original form of the books of Kings. It is noteworthy that even a Neo-Babylonian polemic against Nabonidus's religious policy could accuse the king of worshipping at the wrong place *and* the wrong "foreign" god.[81]

---

80. See Christian Frevel, "Wovon reden die Deuteronomisten? Anmerkungen zu religionsgeschichtlichem Gehalt, Fiktionalität und literarischen Funktionen deuteronomistischer Kultnotizen," in Witte et al., *Die deuteronomistischen Geschichtswerke*, 249–77, esp. 273, contra, for example, Aurelius, *Zukunft*, 211–12.

81. Cf. "Verse Account," I, 22–23 (text: Schaudig, *Inschriften*, 566): " … he had made

Apart from the explicit and secondary charges against worship of foreign gods, there is an even later criterion of evaluation within the books of Kings: the law. The passages that evaluate the kings (and the people) in relation to the Torah represent a later stage in the development of the books of Kings; they again presuppose a different cultural background, namely the later Persian period, when in the ancient Near East in general the concept of the "law" gained importance.

3.3. The Books of Kings and the "Deuteronomistic History"

The study of the history of the composition of the judgment formulas indicates that there is no reason to attribute a part of the evaluation of the kings in 1 Kgs 12–2 Kgs 25 to a prior, preexilic version of the books of Kings, as is often proposed in the model of a double redaction of the Deuteronomistic History.[82] The hypothetical two (or more) redactional stages of this model cannot be brought into connection with, on the one hand, the observations concerning the *bāmôt*, and on the other, the blending of the accusations concerning the lack of cultic centralization and the veneration of foreign gods, in the books of Kings. Biblical evidence and parallels from ancient Near Eastern literature show that the books of Kings already presuppose the destruction of Jerusalem (even though the redactor of the original form of the books of Kings used preexilic sources) and a Neo-Babylonian cultural background. There is no plausible time and place for an edition of the books of Kings during the times of either Hezekiah or Josiah, although the accounts of the reigns of these kings are culminating episodes in the narrative of the books of Kings. The global arguments for an original ending of the books of Kings in 2 Kgs 23 (or 2 Kgs 19) are not convincing. It is true that the narrative style becomes somewhat stinted and elliptical after the account of Josiah's reign, but the same is true for the presentation of the northern kingdom's last years (cf. 2 Kgs 15:8–31);[83] and although the judgments on Jehoahaz and Jehoiakim (2 Kgs 23:32, 37) contain very general statements about the "fathers," this does not imply an abrogation of Josiah's deeds: the text compares the deeds of

---

the image of a deity which nobody had ever seen in this country, he introduced it into the temple, he placed it on a pedestal."

82. Contra, for example, Frank Moore Cross, "The Themes of the Book of Kings and the Structure of the Deuteronomistic History," in *Canaanite Myth and Hebrew Epic* (Cambridge, Mass.: Harvard University Press, 1973), 274–89; Richard D. Nelson, *The Double Redaction of the Deuteronomistic History* (JSOTSup 18; Sheffield: JSOT Press, 1981); Provan, *Hezekiah*.

83. See Aurelius, *Zukunft*, 45; contra, for example, Erik Eynikel, *The Reform of King Josiah and the Composition of the Deuteronomistic History* (OTS 33; Leiden: Brill, 1996), 119.

each of these kings to "what his fathers had done"—i.e., the *evil* fathers, and *not* to "what all his fathers had done," including Josiah.[84] Furthermore, the claim that statements like "until this day"[85] are related to preexilic conditions and therefore point to a preexilic date for the books of Kings is untenable: these statements (which in any case function as a literary *topos*) either do not presuppose specific preexilic conditions, are part of the sources of 1–2 Kings, or are later additions.[86] And 2 Kgs 23 is not an original end, but a climax of the books of Kings, which underlines the defilement of the *bāmôt* (2 Kgs 23:8). This episode is intended to showcase Josiah as the king who did what every king should have done. The elliptical style of the subsequent chapters supports this showcasing.

There is no reason to believe that Deuteronomy was originally part of the same literary entity as the books of Kings. The question of where this entity might have begun is not easy to answer. However, a tentative solution is possible in the light of the findings of the present study. 1 Kings 12–2 Kings 25 originally belonged to a work that covered 1 Sam 1–2 Kgs 25, for the following reasons: first, the system of the judgment formulas of the kings reaches back to 1–2 Samuel (1 Sam 13:1; 2 Sam 2:10–11; 5:4–5); second, there is the frequent mention of David in 1–2 Kings; and, third, the motif of the *bāmôt* is yet another device of continuity in 1 Samuel–2 Kings (cf. 1 Sam 9). An additional support for this assumption of the original scope of this book is the observation that the judgment formulas in the book of Judges probably represent a later reception of those in the books of Kings.[87] It is also an important observation that, when one looks backward from 1 Kgs 12 to the preceding text, a fully valid beginning of the story is given only in 1 Sam 1:1. The research leads to the conclusion that the original form of the books of Kings was originally a part of 1 Samuel–2 Kings*.[88]

---

84. See Aurelius, *Zukunft*, 46–47; contra Gottfried Vanoni, "Beobachtungen zur deuteronomistischen Terminologie in 2 Kön 23,25–25,30," in *Das Deuteronomium: Entstehung, Gestalt und Botschaft* (ed. N. Lohfink; BETL 68; Leuven: Leuven University Press and Peeters, 1985), 357–62, esp. 359–60 with n. 24.

85. Cf. 1 Kgs 8:8; 9:13, 21; 10:12; 12:19; 2 Kgs 2:22; 8:22; 10:27; 14:7; 16:6; 17:23, 34, 41.

86. Contra Wellhausen, *Composition*, 298; and Jeffrey Geoghegan, *The Time, Place, and Purpose of the Deuteronomistic History: The Evidence of "Until This Day"* (BJS 347; Providence, R.I.: Brown University Press, 2006). See Martin Noth, "Zur Geschichtsauffassung des Deuteronomisten," in *Twenty-Second Congress of Orientalists: Vol. II. Communications* (ed. Z. V. Togan; Leiden: Brill, 1957), 558–66; and Blanco Wißmann, "Er tat das Rechte ...," 242–43.

87. See Schmid, *Erzväter*, 220, 235. Cf. Blanco Wißmann, "Er tat das Rechte ...," 50–53.

88. See Aurelius, *Zukunft*, 44, 207, Kratz, *Komposition*, 215–16. Cf. Provan, *Hezekiah*.

The research on the history of composition of the judgment formulas in the books of Kings raises the question of the validity of the hypothesis of a "Deuteronomistic History." The commonly accepted dating of the books of Kings in the middle of the sixth century B.C.E. (at least in German research) is confirmed by the results of the present study: the work of 1 Samuel–2 Kings* was written in the last years of the Neo-Babylonian empire, most likely in Babylon. But why should the literary work in 1 Sam 1–2 Kgs 25*, which did not form a literary continuity with the book of Deuteronomy and did not include the (in Noth's opinion) decisively Deuteronomistic text of 2 Kgs 17:7–20, be called Deuteronomistic? Of course, the evaluations of the kings and the original prophetic stories in the books of Kings share some basic concepts with the book of Deuteronomy: both writings emphasize the principle of the centralization of worship, and the exilic stages of both the book of Deuteronomy and the books of Kings feature the principle of monolatry. However, these similarities are quite general, and they are compelling only as long the differences in form and diction are neglected. In a similar way, the Neo-Babylonian texts (despite their formal differences) also share some basic ideas about kingship and the appropriate cult of Marduk.

Noth sought to prove that the Deuteronomistic Historian was a true author, whose work in Deuteronomy–2 Kings was obscured by later redactional processes. Without the book of Deuteronomy and without those texts, which Noth understood as the most significant examples of Deuteronomistic "reflection," there is no longer any place for an entity called the "Deuteronomistic History," although it might still be possible to describe the work of 1 Samuel–2 Kings* as "proto-Deuteronomistic,"[89] due to the very common, though abstract, similarities between the books of Kings and Deuteronomy. The books of Kings become "Deuteronomistic" in later times by means of additions that have their "starting point" in the book of Deuteronomy or, even later, in the whole Torah. By means of these revisions, the explicitly Deuteronomistic "reflection texts" like 2 Kgs 17:7–20 are inserted; the evaluations are expanded towards the whole people; the polemic against foreign gods is reinforced; and finally, the criterion of "law" is added to the books of Kings.

---

89. On this term, cf. A. Graeme Auld, "The Deuteronomists and the Former Prophets, or What Makes the Former Prophets Deuteronomistic?" in *Those Elusive Deuteronomists: The Phenomenon of Pan-Deuteronomism* (ed. L. S. Schearing and S. L. McKenzie; JSOTSup 268; Sheffield: Sheffield Academic Press, 1999), 116–26, esp. 122.

3.4. The Judgment Texts and the Prophets

The original edition of Kings already contained phrasing that is influenced by literary prophecy[90] and some accounts about prophets (like Elijah, Elisha, and Isaiah),[91] especially narratives about prophets interacting with kings. But there is a much deeper link between the books of Kings and literary prophecy: as this study has pointed out, similarities between the books of Kings and literary prophecy exist particularly in the perspectives on history and cult: for example, in the synchronistic perspective on the history of Israel *and* Judah; in the accusation of venerating Baal; and in the rejection of the *bāmôt* and the use of the phrase קטר *pi'el* as a *terminus technicus* for an illegitimate cult. This connection does not come as a surprise when history writing in the ancient Near East is taken into account: literature about divination was a starting point of historiography, be it omen literature in Mesopotamia[92] or early literary prophecy in Judah.[93] And just as the Babylonian chronicles belong to a self-consistent literary genre and do not cite omen texts but still show a link to omen literature in terms of their ideology and sociological background,[94] so also the books of Kings are linked in a similar way to prophetic books—especially to the book of Jeremiah,

90. Cf., for example, the *Botenformel* and the *Wortereignisformel*, e.g.,1 Kgs 16:1; 21:17, 28; 2 Kgs 1:6; 9:3, 6, 12; 19:6

91. Although the stories about Elijah and Elisha are, overall, from a redactional-critical perspective a secondary *sui generis* entity, some of these stories had already become part of the first edition of the books of Kings. See Otto, *Jehu*; Blanco Wißmann, "*Er tat das Rechte...*," 199–200.

92. See J. J. Finkelstein, "Mesopotamian Historiography," *Proceedings of the American Philosophical Society* 107 (1963): 461–72. Although Finkelstein might have been exaggerating the role of omen texts in the development of history writing (they are one starting point of history writing, but probably not the only one), critique of his proposal seems to be rooted in modern misconceptions of ancient Mesopotamian historiography; contra Van Seters, *Search*, 55–56, 77–79. See John Antony Brinkman, "The Babylonian Chronicle Revisited," in *Lingering Over Words* (ed. T. Abusch et al.; HSS 37; Altanta: Scholars Press, 1990), 73–104, esp. 73 with n. 2; Blanco Wißmann, "*Er tat das Rechte...*," 191–94.

93. See Christof Hardmeier, "Geschichtsdivinatorik und literatursoziologische Aspekte der Schriftprophetie am Beispiel von Jesaja 9–10," in *Die unwiderstehliche Wahrheit: Studien zur alttestamentlichen Prophetie. Festschrift für Arndt Meinhold* (ed. Rüdiger Lux and E.-J. Waschke; Arbeiten zur Bibel und ihrer Geschichte 23; Leipzig: Evangelische Verlagsanstalt, 2006), 129–51.

94. See Wilfred George Lambert, "Destiny and Divine Intervention in Babylon and Israel," *OTS* 17 (1972): 65–72, esp. 71. R. J. van der Spek argues "that chronicles, diaries, omens, astronomical, astrological, and other scholarly texts were written by the same persons"; see R. J. van der Spek, review of J.-J. Glassner, *Mesopotamian Chronicles*, *Review of Biblical Literature* (2005): 6 [Cited 27 May 2010]. Online: http://www.bookreviews.org/pdf/4467_4512.pdf. Blanco Wißmann, "*Er tat das Rechte...*," 201–4.

although this prophet is never mentioned in 1–2 Kings.[95] The author of the original books of Kings was a member of and had his first readers in circles of recipients of literary prophecy (probably in Babylon), particularly of the book of Jeremiah.[96] These circles, whose members were Judean upper-class *literati*,[97] were convinced that with the end of the Judean kingdom in 587 B.C.E. the announcements of judgment within the literary prophecy had been fulfilled. Therefore, with the rejection of the hypothesis of a "Deuteronomistic History" in Deuteronomy–2 Kings, the place of the books of Kings in the history of biblical theology should be the place that it had acquired already in the Jewish canonical tradition of the Tanak: among the prophets.[98]

---

95. On the problem of the so-called "Profetenschweigen" ("silencing of the prophets"), a term coined by Klaus Koch, "Das Profetenschweigen des deuteronomistischen Geschichtswerks," in *Die Botschaft und die Boten: Festschrift für Hans Walter Wolff zum 70. Geburtstag* (ed. J. Jeremias and L. Perlitt; Neukirchen-Vluyn: Neukirchener, 1981), 115–30, see Blanco Wißmann, "*Er tat das Rechte . . .*," 226–33.

96. See Hardmeier, "König Joschija," 115 with n. 115, 129ff, who speaks of "Komplementärbildungen" ("complementary compositions"), although he refers this description to a classic "DtrH" in Deuteronomy–2 Kings and to a Deuteronomistic form of the Book of Jeremiah.

97. On this sociological background see Jon L. Berquist, *Judaism in Persia's Shadow: A Social and Historical Approach* (Minneapolis: Fortress Press, 1995), 15–17; Römer, *Deuteronomistic History*, 116.

98. See Ernst Axel Knauf, "Kings among the Prophets," in *The Production of Prophecy: Constructing Prophecy and Prophets in Yehud* (ed. D. V. Edelman and E. Ben Zvi; BibleWorld; London: Equinox, 2009), 131–49.

BIBLIOGRAPHY

Abela, Anthony. "Is Genesis the Introduction of the Primary History?" Pages 397–406 in *Studies in the Book of Genesis: Literature, Redaction and History*. Edited by A. Wénin. BETL 155. Leuven: Leuven University Press and Peeters, 2001.

Achenbach, Reinhard. "Der Pentateuch, seine theokratischen Bearbeitungen und Josua–2 Könige." Pages 225–53 in *Les dernières rédactions du Pentateuque, de l'Hexateuque et de L'Ennéateuque*. Edited by T. Römer and K. Schmid. BETL 203. Leuven: Leuven University Press and Peeters, 2007.

———. *Die Vollendung der Tora: Studien zur Redaktionsgeschichte des Numeribuches im Kontext von Hexateuch und Pentateuch*. BZABR 3. Wiesbaden: Harrassowitz, 2003.

———. "Grundlinien redaktioneller Arbeit in der Sinai-Perikope." Pages 56–80 in *Das Deuteronomium zwischen Pentateuch und Deuteronomistischem Geschichtswerk*. Edited by R. Achenbach and E. Otto. FRLANT 206. Göttingen: Vandenhoeck & Ruprecht, 2004.

———. "Pentateuch, Hexateuch und Enneateuch: Eine Verhältnisbestimmung." *ZABR* 11 (2005): 122–54.

———. "The Pentateuch, the Prophets, and the Torah in the 5th and 4th Century B.C.E." Pages 253–85 in *Judah and the Judeans in the Fourth Century B.C.E.* Edited by O. Lipschits, G. N. Knoppers, and R. Albertz. Winona Lake: Eisenbrauns, 2007.

Albertz, Rainer. "Die Kanonische Anpassung des Josuabuches: Eine Neubewertung seiner sogenannten 'Priesterschriftlichen Texte.'" Pages 199–216 in *Les dernières rédactions du Pentateuque, de l'Hexateuque et de L'Ennéateuque*. Edited by T. Römer and K. Schmid. BETL 203. Leuven: Leuven University Press and Peeters, 2007.

———. "Exile as Purification: Reconstructing the 'Book of the Four.'" Pages 232–51 in *Thematic Threads in the Book of the Twelve*. Edited by P. L. Reddit and A. Schart. BZAW 325. Berlin: de Gruyter, 2003.

———. *A History of Israelite Religion in the Old Testament Period*. Translated by J. Bowden. 2 vols. OTL. London: SCM Press; Louisville: Westminster John Knox, 1994.

———. *Israel in Exile: The History and Literature of the Sixth Century B.C.E.* Translated by D. Green. SBL Studies in Biblical Literature 3. Atlanta: Society of Biblical Literature, 2003.

———. *Religionsgeschichte Israels in alttestamentlicher Zeit*. 2 vols. GAT 8. Göttingen: Vandenhoeck & Ruprecht, 1992.

Alt, Albrecht. "Josua." Pages 13–29 in *Werden und Wesen des Alten Testaments: Vorträge gehalten auf der internationalen Tagung alttestamentlicher Forscher zu Göttingen vom 4.–10, September 1935*. Edited by P. Volz, F. Stummer, and J. Hempel. BZAW 66. Berlin: Töpelmann, 1936.

Anbar, Moshé. *Josué et l'alliance de Sichem (Josué 24:1–28)*. BBET 25. Frankfurt: Lang, 1992.

Arneth, Martin. "Die antiassyrische Reform Josias von Juda: Überlegungen zur Komposition und Intention von 2 Reg 23,4–15." *ZABR* 7 (2001): 189–216.

Auld, A. Graeme. "Counting Sheep, Sins and Sour Grapes: The Primacy of the Primary History?" Pages 63–72 in *Sense and Sensitivity: Essays on Reading the Bible in Memory of Robert Carroll.* Edited by A. Hunter and P. R. Davies. JSOTSup 348. Sheffield: Sheffield Academic Press, 2002.

———. "The Deuteronomists and the Former Prophets, or What Makes the Former Prophets Deuteronomistic?" Pages 116–126 in *Those Elusive Deuteronomists: The Phenomenon of Pan-Deuteronomism.* Edited by L. S. Schearing and S. L. McKenzie. JSOTSup 268. Sheffield: Sheffield Academic Press, 1999.

———. *Joshua Retold: Synoptic Perspectives* OTS. Edinburgh: T&T Clark, 1998.

———. *Joshua, Moses and the Land: Tetrateuch–Pentateuch–Hexateuch in a Generation since 1938.* Edinburgh: T&T Clark, 1980.

———. "Judges 1 and History: A Reconsideration." *VT* 25 (1975): 261–85.

———. *Kings Without Privilege: David and Moses in the Story of the Bible's Kings.* Edinburgh: T&T Clark, 1994.

———. "Prophets through the Looking Glass: Between Writings and Moses." *JSOT* 27 (1983): 3–23.

———. *Samuel at the Threshold: Selected Works of Graeme Auld.* SOTSMS. Burlington, Vt.: Ashgate, 2004.

——— "Solomon at Gibeon: History Glimpsed." *ErIsr* 24 (1993): 1–7.

Aurelius, Erik. *Zukunft jenseits des Gerichts: Eine redaktionsgeschichtliche Studie zum Enneateuch.* BZAW 319. Berlin: de Gruyter, 2003.

Baden, Joel S. *J, E, and the Redaction of the Pentateuch.* FAT 68. Tübingen: Mohr Siebeck, 2009.

Barton, John. *Oracles of God: Perceptions of Ancient Prophecy in Israel after the Exodus.* London: Darton, Longman & Todd, 1986.

Baugh, Albert C. "Improvisation in the Middle English Romance." *Proceedings of the American Philosophical Society* 103 (1959): 418–54.

———. "The Middle English Romance: Some Questions of Creation, Presentation, and Preservation." *Speculum* 42 (1967): 1–31.

Becker, Uwe. "Die Reichsteilung nach I Reg 12." *ZAW* 112 (2000): 210–29.

———. "Endredaktionelle Kontextvernetzungen des Josua-Buches." Pages 139–61 in *Die deuteronomistischen Geschichtswerke: Redaktions- und religionsgeschichtliche Perspektiven zur „Deuteronomismus"-Diskussion in Tora und Vorderen Propheten.* Edited by M. Witte, K. Schmid, D. Prechel, and J. C. Gertz. BZAW 365. Berlin: de Gruyter, 2006.

———. *Richterzeit und Königtum.* BZAW 192. Berlin: de Gruyter, 1990.

Ben Zvi, Ehud. "Looking at the Primary (Hi)story and the Prophetic Books as Literary/ Theological Units Within the Frame of the Early Second Temple: Some Considerations." *SJOT* 12 (1998): 26–43.

Benzinger, Immanuel. *Die Bücher der Könige.* KHC 9. Freiburg: Mohr, 1899.

———. *Jahvist und Elohist in den Königsbüchern.* BWAT 2. Berlin: Kohlhammer, 1921.

Berner, Christoph. *Die Exoduserzählung: Das literarische Werden einer Ursprungslegende Israels.* FAT 73. Tübingen: Mohr Siebeck, 2010.

Berquist, Jon L. *Judaism in Persia's Shadow: A Social and Historical Approach.* Minneapolis: Fortress, 1995.

Biddle, Mark E. "Redaction Criticism, Old Testament." Pages 373–76 in vol. 1 of *Dictionary of Biblical Interpretation.* Edited by J. H. Hayes. 2 vols. Nashville: Abingdon. 1999.

Bieberstein, Klaus. *Josua–Jordan–Jericho: Archeologie, Geschichte und Theologie der Landnahme-erzählungen Josua 1–6*. OBO 143. Fribourg: Universitätsverlag; Göttingen: Vandenhoek & Ruprecht, 1995.

Blanco Wißmann, Felipe. *"Er tat das Rechte…": Beurteilungskriterien und Deuteronomismus in 1Kön 12–2Kön 25*. ATANT 93. Zurich: Theologischer Verlag, 2008.

Blenkinsopp, Joseph. "Deuteronomic Contribution to the Narrative in Genesis–Numbers: A Test Case." Pages 84–115 in *Those Elusive Deuteronomists: The Phenomenon of Pan-Deuteronomism*. Edited by L. S. Schearing and S. L. McKenzie. JSOTSup 268. Sheffield: Sheffield Academic Press, 1999.

———. "The Judean Priesthood during the Neo-Babylonian and Achaemenid Periods: A Hypothetical Reconstruction." *CBQ* 60 (1998): 25–43.

———. *The Pentateuch: An Introduction to the First Five Books of the Bible*. 1st ed. ABRL. New York: Doubleday, 1992; 2d ed. 2000.

———. "A Post-exilic Lay Source in Genesis 1–11." Pages 49–61 in *Abschied vom Jahwisten: Die Komposition des Hexateuch in der jüngsten Diskussion*. Edited by J. C. Gertz, K. Schmid, and M. Witte. BZAW 315. Berlin: de Gruyter, 2002.

———. *Sage, Priest, Prophet: Religious and Intellectual Leadership in Ancient Israel*. Louisville: Westminster John Knox, 1995.

———. "The Structure of P." *CBQ* 38 (1976): 275–92.

Blum, Erhard. "Beschneidung und Passa in Kanaan: Beobachtungen und Mutmaßungen zu Jos 5." Pages 292–322 in *Freiheit und Recht*. Edited by C. Hardmeier. Gütersloh: Kaiser, 2003.

———. "The Decalogue and the Composition History of the Pentateuch." in *The Pentateuch: International Perspectives on Current Research*. Edited by K. Schmid, T. B. Dozeman, and B. Schwartz. FAT. Tübingen: Mohr Siebeck, forthcoming.

———. "Der kompositionelle Knoten am Übergang von Josua zu Richter: Ein Entflectungsvorschlag." Pages 181–212 in *Deuteronomy and Deuteronomic Literature: Festschrift C. H. W. Brekelmans*. Edited by M. Vervenne and J. Lust. BETL 133. Leuven: Leuven University Press and Peeters, 1997.

———. *Die Komposition der Vätergeschichte*. WMANT 57. Neukirchen-Vluyn: Neukirchener, 1984.

———. "Die literarische Verbindung von Erzvätern und Exodus: Ein Gespräch mit neueren Endredaktionshypothesen." Pages 119–56 in *Abschied vom Jahwisten: Die Komposition des Hexateuch in der jüngsten Diskussion*. Edited by J. C. Gertz, K. Schmid, and M. Witte. BZAW 315. Berlin: de Gruyter, 2002.

———. "Esra, die Mosetora und die persische Politik." Pages 231–56 in *Religion und Religionskontakte im Zeitalter der Achämeniden*. Edited by R.G. Kratz. Veröffentlichungen der Wissenschaftlichen Gesellschaft für Theologie 22. Gütersloh: Gütersloher Verlagshaus, 2002.

———. "Gibt es die Endgestalt des Pentateuch?" Pages 46–57 in *Congress Volume: Leuven, 1989*. Edited by J. A. Emerton. VTSup 43. Leiden: Brill, 1991.

———. "The Literary Connection between the Books of Genesis and Exodus and the End of the Book of Joshua." Pages 89–106 in *A Farewell to the Yahwist? The Composition of the Pentateuch in Recent European Interpretation*. Edited by T. B. Dozeman and K. Schmid. SBLSymS 34. Atlanta: Society of Biblical Literature, 2006.

———. "Notwendigkeit und Grenzen historischer Exegese: Plädoyer für eine alttestamentliche Exegetik." Pages 11–40 in *Theologie und Exegese des Alten Testaments/der*

Hebräischen Bibel: Zwischenbilanz und Zukunftsperspektiven. Edited by B. Janowski. SBS 200. Stuttgart: Katholisches Bibelwerk, 2005.

———. "Pentateuch–Hexateuch–Enneateuch? Oder: Woran erkennt man ein literarisches Werk in der hebräischen Bibel?" Pages 375–404 in *Textgestalt und Komposition: Exegetische Beiträge zu Tora und Vordere Propheten.* Edited by W. Oswald. FAT 69. Tübingen: Mohr Siebeck, 2010.

———. "Pentateuch–Hexateuch–Enneateuch? Oder: Woran erkennt man ein literarisches Werk in der Hebräischen Bibel?" Pages 67–97 in *Les dernières rédactions du Pentateuque, de l'Hexateuque et de L'Ennéateuque.* Edited by T. Römer and K. Schmid. BETL 203. Leuven: Leuven University Press and Peeters, 2007.

———. *Studien zur Komposition des Pentateuch.* BZAW 189. Berlin: de Gruyter, 1990.

Boling, Robert G. *Joshua: A New Translation with Notes and Commentary.* AB 6. New York: Doubleday, 1982.

Boorer, Suzanne. "The Earth/Land ('*rts*) in the Priestly Material: The Preservation of the 'Good' Earth and the Promised Land of Canaan Throughout the Generations." *ABR* 49 (2001): 19–33.

———. "The Importance of a Diachronic Approach: the Case of Genesis–Kings." *CBQ* 51 (1989): 195–208.

———. "The 'Paradigmatic' and 'Historiographical' Nature of the Priestly Material as Key to its Interpretation." Pages 45–60 in *Seeing Signals, Reading Signs: The Art of Exegesis.* Edited by M. O'Brien and H. Wallace. London: T&T Clark, 2004.

———. *The Promise of the Land as Oath: A Key to the Formation of the Pentateuch.* BZAW 205. Berlin: de Gruyter, 1992.

Bosshard–Nepustil, Erich. "Hadad, der Edomiter: 1 Kön 11,14–22 zwischen literarischem Kontext und Verfassergegenwart." Pages 95–109 in *Schriftauslegung in der Schrift: Festschrift für Odil Hannes Steck zu seinem 65. Geburtstag.* Edited by R.G. Kratz, T. Krüger, and K. Schmid. BZAW 300. Berlin: de Gruyter, 2000.

———. *Rezeptionen von Jesaja 1–39 im Zwölfprophetenbuch: Untersuchungen zur literarischen Verbindung von Prophetenbüchern in babylonischer und persischer Zeit.* OBO 154. Fribourg: Universitätsverlag; Göttingen: Vandenhoeck & Ruprecht, 1997.

Braulik, Georg. "Das Deuteronomium und die Gedächtniskultur Israels: Redaktionsgeschichtliche Beobachtungen zur Verwendung von למד." Pages 9–31 in *Biblische Theologie und gesellschaftlicher Wandel.* Edited by G. Braulik, W. Gross, and S. McEvenue. Freiburg: Herder, 1993.

———. "'Weisheit' im Buch Deuteronomium." Pages 39–69 in *Weisheit ausserhalb der kanonischen Weisheitsschriften.* Edited by B. Janowski. Gütersloh: Kaiser and Gütersloher Verlaghaus, 1996.

Brekelmans, Chris "Joshua V 10–12: Another Approach." Pages 89–95 in *New Avenues in the Study of the Old Testament.* Edited by A. S. van der Woude. Leiden: Brill, 1989.

Brinkman, John Antony. "The Babylonian Chronicle Revisited." Pages 73–104 in *Lingering Over Words: FS William L. Moran.* Edited by T. Abusch, J. Huehnergard, and P. Steinkeller. HSS 37. Atlanta: Scholars Press, 1990.

Brockelmann, Carl. *Hebräische Syntax.* Neukirchen-Vluyn: Neukirchener, 1956; 2d.ed. 2004.

Brueggemann, Walter. "David and His Theologian." *CBQ* 30 (1968): 156–81.

———. "The Kerygma of the Priestly Writers." Pages 101–13, 159–67 in *The Vitality of Old Testament Traditions.* Edited by W. Brueggemann and H. W. Wolff. 2d ed. Atlanta: John Knox, 1982.

Budde, Karl. *Das Buch der Richter*. KHC 7. Freiburg: Mohr, 1897.

———. *Die Bücher Richter und Samuel: Ihre Quellen und ihr Aufbau*. Gießen: Ricker, 1890.

———. *Die Bücher Samuel*. KHC 8. Tübingen: Mohr, 1902.

Budde, Karl and Alfred Bertholet. *Geschichte der althebräischen Litteratur: Apokryphen und Pseudepigraphen*. Leipzig: Amelange, 1909.

Burney, Charles Fox. *The Book of Judges with Introduction and Notes*. London: Rivingtons, 1918.

Campbell, Antony F. "The Priestly Text: Redaction or Source?" Pages 32–47 in *Biblische Theologie und gesellschaftlicher Wandel: Für Norbert Lohfink SJ*. Edited by G. Braulik, W. Gross, and S. McEvenue. Freiburg: Herder, 1993.

Cancik, Hubert. *Grundzüge der hethitischen und alttestamentlichen Geschichtsschreibung*. Abhandlungen des Deutschen Palästinavereins. Wiesbaden: Harrassowitz, 1976.

Carr, David M. "Canonization in the Context of Community." Pages 22–64 in *A Gift of God in Due Season: Essays on Scripture and Community in Honor of James A. Sanders*. Edited by R. D. Weis and D. M Carr. JSOTSup 225. Sheffield: Sheffield Academic Press, 1996.

———. "Controversy and Convergence in Recent Studies of the Formation of the Pentateuch." *RelSRev* (1997): 22–31.

———. "Empirische Perspektiven auf das Deuteronomistische Geschichtswerk." Pages 1–17 in *Die deuteronomistischen Geschichtswerke: Redaktions- und religionsgeschichtliche Perspektiven zur „Deuteronomismus"-Diskussion in Tora und Vorderen Propheten*. Edited by M. Witte, K. Schmid, D. Prechel, and J. C. Gertz. BZAW 365. Berlin: de Gruyter, 2006.

———. *From D to Q: A Study of Early Jewish Interpretations of Solomon's Dream at Gibeon*. SBLMS 44. Atlanta: Scholars Press, 1991.

———. "Method in Determination of Direction of Dependence: An Empirical Test of Criteria Applied to Exodus 34,11–26 and its Parallels." Pages 107–140 in *Gottes Volk am Sinai: Untersuchungen zu Ex 32–34 und Dtn 9–10*. Edited by M. Köckert and E. Blum. Veröffentlichungen der wissenschaftlichen Gesellschaft für Theologie 18. Gütersloh: Kaiser and Gütersloher Verlaghaus, 2001.

———. "The Politics of Textual Subversion: A Diachronic Perspective on the Garden of Eden Story." *JBL* 112 (1993): 577–88.

———. *Reading the Fractures of Genesis: Historical and Literary Approaches*. Louisville: Westminster John Knox, 1996.

———. "What is Required to Identify Pre–Priestly Narrative Connections between Genesis and Exodus? Some General Reflections and Specific Cases." Pages 159–80 in *A Farewell to the Yahwist? The Composition of the Pentateuch in Recent European Interpretation*. Edited by T. B. Dozeman and K. Schmid. SBLSymS 34. Atlanta: Society of Biblical Literature, 2006.

———. *Writing on the Tablet of the Heart: Origins of Scripture and Literature*. New York: Oxford University Press, 2005.

Cassuto, Umberto. *From Adam to Noah: A Commentary on the Book of Genesis I–VI (Part One)*. Translated by I. Abrahams. Jerusalem: Hebrew University Magnes Press, 1961.

Chapman, Stephen B. "How the Biblical Canon Began: Working Models and Open Questions." Pages 29–51 in *Homer, the Bible and Beyond: Literary and Religious Canons in the Ancient World*. Edited by M. Finkelberg and G. G. Stroumsa. Jerusalem Studies in Religion and Culture 2. Leiden: Brill, 2003.

———. *The Law and the Prophets: A Study in Old Testament Canon Formation*. FAT 27. Tübingen: Mohr Siebeck, 2000.

Childs, Brevard S. *The Book of Exodus*. OTL. London: SCM Press, 1974.

———. "Deuteronomic Formulae of the Exodus Traditions." Pages 30–39 in *Hebräische Wortforschung: Festschrift zum 80. Geburtstag von Walter Baumgartner*. Edited by B. Hartmann. VTSup 16. Leiden: Brill, 1967.

———. *Introduction to the Old Testament as Scripture*. Philadelphia: Fortress, 1979.

———. *Isaiah and the Assyrian Crisis*. SBT 2/3. London: SCM Press, 1967.

Christian, Mark A. "Openness to the Other Inside and Outside of Numbers." Pages 579–608 in *The Books of Leviticus and Numbers*. Edited by T. Römer. BETL 215. Leuven: Leuven University Press and Peeters, 2008.

Clements, Ronald E., ed. *God and Temple: The Idea of the Divine in Ancient Israel*. London: SCM Press, 1965.

———. *Prophecy and Tradition*. Growing Points in Theology. Oxford: Blackwell, 1975.

———. "A Royal Privilege: Dining in the Presence of the Great King." Pages 49–66 in *Reflection and Refraction: Studies in Biblical Historiography in Honour of A. Graeme Auld*. Edited by R. Rezetko, T. H. Lim, and W. B. Aucker. VTSup 113. Leiden: Brill, 2007.

Clines, David J. A. "Theme in Genesis 1–11." *CBQ* 38 (1976): 483–507.

Coats, George W. *Genesis: With an Introduction to Narrative Literature*. FOTL 1. Grand Rapids: Eerdmans, 1983.

Coggins, Richard J. "Review of A. Graeme Auld, *Kings Without Privilege*." *Theology* 98 (1995): 383.

Collins, John J. *Introduction to the Hebrew Bible*. Minneapolis: Fortress, 2004.

Cooper, Jerrold. "Gilgamesh Dreams of Enkidu: The Evolution and Dilution of Narrative." Pages 39–44 in *Essays on the Ancient Near East in Memory of Jacob Joel Finkelstein*. Edited by M. Ellis. Hamden, Conn.: Archon, 1977.

Coote, Robert B. *In Defense of Revolution: The Elohist History*. Minneapolis: Fortress, 1991.

Cornill, Carl H. "Ein elohistischer Bericht über die Entstehung des israelitischen Königthums in I Samuelis 1–15 aufgezeigt." *Zeitschrift für kirchliche Wissenschaft und kirchliches Leben* 6 (1885): 113–41.

———. *Einleitung in das Alte Testament*. 3d and 4th ed. Grundriss der Theologischen Wissenschaft 2/1. Freiburg: Mohr, 1896.

———. "Noch einmal Sauls Königswahl und Verwerfung." *ZAW* 10 (1890): 96–109.

———. "Zur Quellenkritik der Bücher Samuelis." *Königsberger Studien* 1 (1887): 25–89.

Cortese, Enzo. *Josua 13–21: Ein priesterschriftlicher Abschnitt in deuteronomistischen Geschichtswerke*. OBO 94. Fribourg: Universitätsverlag; Göttingen: Vandenhoeck & Ruprecht, 1990.

Cross, Frank Moore. "The Priestly Tabernacle." Pages 40–67 in *Old Testament Issues*. Edited by S. Sandmel. London: SCM Press, 1968.

———. "The Themes of the Book of Kings and the Structure of the Deuteronomistic History (1968)." Pages 274–289 in idem, *Canaanite Myth and Hebrew Epic*. Cambridge, Mass.: Harvard University Press, 1973.

Cross, Frank Moore, Donald W. Parry, Eugene C. Ulrich, and Richard J. Saley, eds. *Qumran Cave 4, 12: 1–2 Samuel*. DJD 17. Oxford: Clarendon, 2005.

Crüsemann, Frank. "Autonomie und Sünde: Gen 4:7 und die 'jahwistische' Urgeschichte." Pages 60–77 in *Traditionen der Befreiung: Sozialgeschichtliche Bibelauslegungen*. Edited by W. Schottroff and W. Stegemann. Munich: Kaiser, 1980.

———. *Der Widerstand gegen das Königtum: Die antiköniglichen Texte des Alten Testaments und der Kampf um den frühen israelitischen Staat.* WMANT 49. Neukirchen-Vluyn: Neukirchener, 1978.

———. "Die Eigenständigkeit der Urgeschichte: Ein Beitrag zur Diskussion um den 'Jahwisten.'" Pages 11–30 in *Die Botschaft und die Boten: Festschrift für Hans Walter Wolff zum 70. Geburtstag.* Edited by J. Jeremias and L. Perlitt. Neukirchen-Vluyn: Neukirchener, 1981.

Davies, Graham I. "The Composition of the Book of Exodus: Reflections on the Theses of Erhard Blum." Pages 71–85 in *Texts, Temples, and Traditions: A Tribute to Menahem Haran.* Edited by M. V. Fox, V. A. Hurowitz, A. Hurvitz, M. L. Klein, B. I. Schwartz, and N. Shupak. Winona Lake: Eisenbrauns, 1996.

DeVries, Simon J. *1 Kings.* WBC 12. Waco, Tex.: Word Books, 1985.

Dietrich, Walter. "Das harte Joch (1 Kön 12,4): Fronarbeit in der Salomo-Überlieferung." *BN* 34 (1986): 7–16.

Dillmann, August. *Die Bücher Numeri, Deuteronomium und Josue.* Leipzig: Hirzel, 1886.

Dines, Jennifer M. *The Septuagint.* New York: T&T Clark, 2004.

Donner, Herbert. "Der Redaktor: Überlegungen zum vorkritischen Umgang mit der Heiligen Schrift." *Henoch* 2 (1980): 1–30.

Dozeman, Thomas B. "The Composition of Ex 32 within the Context of the Enneateuch." Pages 175–89 in *Auf dem Weg zur Endgestalt von Genesis bis II Regum.* Edited by M. Beck and U. Schorn. BZAW 370. Berlin: de Gruyter, 2006.

———. *God at War: Power in the Exodus Tradition.* New York: Oxford University Press, 1996.

Dozeman, Thomas B. and Konrad Schmid, eds. *A Farewell to the Yahwist? The Composition of the Pentateuch in Recent European Interpretation.* SBLSymS 34. Atlanta: Society of Biblical Literature, 2006.

Dreher, Carlos A. "Das tributäre Königtum in Israel unter Salomo." *EvT* 51 (1991): 49–60.

Eißfeldt, Otto. *Die Quellen des Richterbuches in synoptischer Anordnung ins Deutsche übertragen samt einer in Einleitung und Noten gegebenen Begründung.* Leipzig: Hinrichs, 1925.

———. *Einleitung in das Alte Testament, unter Einschluß der Apokryphen und Pseudepigraphen sowie der apokryphen und pseudepigraphenartigen Qumran-Schriften: Entstehungsgeschichte des Alten Testaments.* 3d ed. Neue theologische Grundrisse. Tübingen: Mohr, 1964.

———. *Hexateuch-Synopse: Die Erzählung der fünf Bücher Mose und des Buches Josua mit dem Anfange des Richterbuches in ihre vier Quellen zerlegt und in deutscher Übersetzung dargeboten samt einer in Einleitung und Anmerkungen gegebenen Begründung.* Leipzig: Hinrichs, 1922.

———. *The Old Testament: An Introduction.* Translated by P. R. Ackroyd. New York: Harper & Row, 1965.

Elliger, Karl. "Sinn und Ursprung der Priesterlichen Geschichtserzahlung." *ZTK* 49 (1952): 121–43.

Ellis, E. Earle. *The Old Testament in Early Christianity: Canon and Interpretation in the Light of Modern Research.* WUNT 54. Tübingen: Mohr, 1991.

Emerton, John A. "The Priestly Writer in Genesis." *JTS* 39 (1988): 381–400.

Emmrich, Martin. "The Temptation Narrative of Genesis 3:1–6: A Prelude to the Pentateuch and the History of Israel." *EvQ* 73 (2001): 3–20.

Evans, Carl D. "Naram-Sin and Jeroboam: The Archetypal *Unheilsherrscher* in Mesopotamian and Biblical Historiography." Pages 97–125 in *More Essays on the Comparative Method*. Edited by W. W. Hallo, J. C. Moyer, and L. Perdue. Scripture in Context 2. Winona Lake: Eisenbrauns, 1983.

Eynikel, Erik. *The Reform of King Josiah and the Composition of the Deuteronomistic History*. OtSt 33. Leiden: Brill, 1996.

Fewell, Danna Nolan and David M. Gunn. *Gender, Power, and Promise: The Subject of the Bible's First Story*. Nashville: Abingdon, 1993.

Finkelberg, Margalit and Guy G. Stroumsa. "Introduction: Before the Western Canon." Pages 1–8 in *Homer, the Bible, and Beyond: Literary and Religions Canons in the Ancient World*. Edited by M. Finkelberg and G. G. Stroumsa. Jerusalem Studies in Religion and Culture 2. Leiden: Brill, 2003.

Finkelstein, J.J. "Mesopotamian Historiography." *Proceedings of the American Philosophical Society* 107 (1963): 461–72.

Fishbane, Michael. "Varia Deuteronomica." *ZAW* 84 (1972): 349–52.

Fohrer, Georg. *Einleitung in das Alte Testament*. 10th ed. Heidelberg: Quelle & Meyer, 1965.

———. *Überlieferung und Geschichte des Exodus*. BZAW 91. Berlin: de Gruyter, 1964.

Franz, Matthias. *Der barmherzige und gnädige Gott: Die Gnadenrede vom Sinai (Exodus 34,6-7) und ihre Parallelen im Alten Testament und seiner Umwelt*. Stuttgart: Kohlhammer, 2003.

Freedman, David N. "The Law and the Prophets." Pages 250–65 in *Congress Volume: Bonn, 1962*. Edited by G. W. Anderson. VTSup 9. Leiden: Brill, 1963.

———. "Pentateuch." Pages 711–27 in vol. 3 of *Interpreter's Dictionary of the Bible*. Edited by George Buttrick. 4 vols. Nashville: Abingdon. 1962.

———. *The Unity of the Hebrew Bible*. Ann Arbor: University of Michigan Press, 1993.

Freedman, David N. and Jeffrey C. Geoghegan. "Martin Noth: Retrospect and Prospect." Pages 129–52 in *The History of Israel's Traditions: The Heritage of Martin Noth*. Edited by S. L. McKenzie and M. P. Graham. JSOTSup 182. Sheffield: Sheffield Academic Press, 1994.

Freedman, David N. and Brian Kelly. "Who Redacted the Primary History?" Pages 39–47 in *Sefer Moshe: The Moshe Weinfeld Jubilee Volume. Studies in the Bible and the Ancient Near East, Qumran, and Post-Biblical Judaism*. Edited by C. Cohen, A. Hurvitz, and S. M. Paul. Winona Lake: Eisenbrauns, 2004.

Fretheim, Terence E. "The Priestly Document: Anti-Temple?" *VT* 18 (1968): 313–29.

Frevel, Christian. "Wovon reden die Deuteronomisten? Anmerkungen zu religionsgeschichtlichem Gehalt, Fiktionalität und literarischen Funktionen deuteronomistischer Kultnotizen." Pages 249–277 in *Die deuteronomistischen Geschichtswerke: Redaktions- und religionsgeschichtliche Perspektiven zur „Deuteronomismus"-Diskussion in Tora und Vorderen Propheten*. Edited by M. Witte, K. Schmid, D. Prechel, and J. C. Gertz. BZAW 365. Berlin: de Gruyter, 2006.

Friedman, Richard E. "Tabernacle." Pages 292–300 in vol. 6 of *Anchor Bible Dictionary*. Edited by D. N. Freedman. 6 vols. New York: Doubleday. 1992.

Fritz, Volkmar. *Das Buch Josua*. Tübingen: Mohr (Siebeck), 1994.

———. "Das Geschichtsverstandnis der Priesterschrift." *ZTK* 84 (1987): 426–39.

Frolov, Serge. "Evil-Merodach and the Deuteronomists: The Sociohistorical Setting of Dtr in the Light of 2 Kgs 25,27–30." *Bib* 88 (2007): 174–90.

Geoghegan, Jeffrey C. *The Time, Place, and Purpose of the Deuteronomistic History: The Evidence of "Until This Day".* BJS 347. Providence, R.I.: Brown Judaic Studies, 2006.

Gertz, Jan Christian. "Beobachtungen zu Komposition und Redaktion in Ex 32–34." Pages 88–106 in *Gottes Volk am Sinai: Untersuchungen zu Ex 32–34 und Dtn 9–10.* Edited by M. Köckert and E. Blum. Veröffentlichungen der Wissenschaftlichen Gesellschaft für Theologie 18. Gütersloh: Gütersloher Verlagshaus, 2001.

————. "Die Stellung des kleinen geschichtlichen Credos in der Redaktionsgeschichte von Deuteronomium und Pentateuch." Pages 30–45 in *Liebe und Gebot: Studien zum Deuteronomium.* Edited by R. G. Kratz and H. Spieckermann. FRLANT 190. Göttingen: Vandenhoeck & Ruprecht, 2000.

————, ed. *Grundinformation Altes Testament: Eine Einführung in Literatur, Religion und Geschichte des Alten Testaments.* Uni-Taschenbücher 2745. Göttingen: Vandenhoeck & Ruprecht, 2006.

————. "Kompositorische Funktion und literarhistorischer Ort von Deuteronomium 1–3." Pages 103–123 in *Die deuteronomistischen Geschichtswerke: Redaktions- und religionsgeschichtliche Perspektiven zur „Deuteronomismus"-Diskussion in Tora und Vorderen Propheten.* Edited by M. Witte, K. Schmid, D. Prechel, and J. C. Gertz. BZAW 365. Berlin: de Gruyter, 2006.

————. *Tradition und Redaktion in der Exoduserzählung: Untersuchungen zur Endredaktion des Pentateuch.* FRLANT 186. Göttingen: Vandenhoeck & Ruprecht, 2000.

————. "The Transition between the Books of Genesis and Exodus." Pages 73–87 in *A Farewell to the Yahwist? The Composition of the Pentateuch in Recent European Interpretation.* Edited by T. B. Dozeman and K. Schmid. SBLSymS 34. Atlanta: Society of Biblical Literature, 2006.

————. "Von Adam zu Enosch: Überlegungen zur Entstehungsgeschichte von Gen 2–4." Pages 215–36 in *Gott und Mensch im Dialog: Festschrift für Otto Kaiser zum 80. Geburtstag.* Edited by M. Witte. 2 vols. Vol. 1. BZAW 345. Berlin: de Gruyter, 2004.

Gertz, Jan Christian, Konrad Schmid, and Markus Witte, eds. *Abschied vom Jahwisten: Die Komposition des Hexateuch in der jüngsten Diskussion.* BZAW 315. Berlin: de Gruyter, 2002.

Gesche, Petra. *Schulunterricht in Babylonien im ersten Jahrtausend v. Chr.* AOAT 275. Münster: Ugarit-Verlag, 2001.

Gese, Hartmut. "Die ältere Simsonüberlieferung (Richter c. 14–15)." *ZTK* 82 (1985): 261–80.

Gevaryahu, Hayyim M. J. "A Set of Remarks about Scribes and Books in Biblical Times." *Beth Miqra* 43 (1990): 368–74 [in Hebrew].

Glassner, Jean-Jacques. *Mesopotamian Chronicles.* SBLWAW 19. Atlanta: Society of Biblical Literature, 2004.

Gleis, Matthias. *Die Bamah.* BZAW 251. Berlin: de Gruyter, 1997.

Gosse, Bernard. "L' inclusion de l'ensemble Genèse–II Rois, entre la perte du jardin d'Eden et celle de Jérusalem." *ZAW* 114 (2002): 189–211.

Graf, Karl Heinrich. "Die s.g. Grundschrift des Pentateuchs." *Archiv für wissenschaftliche Erforschung des Alten Testaments* 1 (1867): 466–77.

Grayson, A. Kirk. *Assyrian and Babylonian Chronicles.* TCS 5. Locust Valley, N.Y.: Augustin, 1975.

————. "History and Historians of the Ancient Near East: Assyria and Babylonia." *Or* 49 (1980): 140–94.

Gressmann, Hugo. *Die Anfänge Israels (von 2. Mosis bis Richter und Ruth).* Schriften des Alten Testaments 1/2. Göttingen: Vandenhoeck & Ruprecht, 1914.

Groß, Walter. *Richter*. HTKAT. Freiburg: Herder, 2009.

———. *Zukunft für Israel: Alttestamentliche Bundeskonzepte und die aktuelle Debatte um den Neuen Bund*. SBS 176. Stuttgart: Katholisches Bibelwerk, 1998.

Gunkel, Hermann. *Genesis*. Translated by M. E. Biddle. Macon, Ga.: Mercer University Press, 1997.

Güterbock, Hans-Gustav. "Die historische Tradition und ihre literarische Gestaltung bei Babyloniern und Hethitern bis 1200. Erster Teil: Babylonier." *ZA* 42 (1934): 1–91.

Habel, Norman. "Geophany: The Earth Story in Genesis 1." Pages 34–48 in *The Earth Story in Genesis*. Edited by N. Habel and S. Wurst. Sheffield: Sheffield Academic Press, 2000.

Hahn, Joachim. *Das "Goldene Kalb": Die Jahwe-Verehrung bei Stierbildern in der Geschichte Israels*. Europäische Hochschulschriften 23/154. Frankfurt: Lang, 1981.

Haran, Menahem. "Bible Scrolls in Eastern and Western Jewish Communities from Qumran to the High Middle Ages." *HUCA* 56 (1985): 21–62.

———. "Book Scrolls in Pre-exilic Times." *JJS* 33 (1982): 161–73.

———. "Book-Size and the Device of Catch-Lines in the Biblical Canon." *JJS* 36 (1985): 1–11.

———. "Book-Size and the Thematic Cycles in the Pentateuch." Pages 165–76 in *Die Hebräische Bibel und ihre zweifache Nachgeschichte: Festschrift für Rolf Rendtorff zum 65. Geburtstag*. Edited by E. Blum, C. Macholz, and E. W. Stegemann. Neukirchen-Vluyn: Neukirchener, 1990.

———. "Shiloh and Jerusalem: The Origin of the Priestly Tradition in the Pentateuch." *JBL* 81 (1962): 14–24.

Hardmeier, Christof. "Geschichtsdivinatorik und literatursoziologische Aspekte der Schriftprophetie am Beispiel von Jesaja 9–10." Pages 129–151 in *Die unwiderstehliche Wahrheit: Studien zur alttestamentlichen Prophetie. Festschrift für Arndt Meinhold*. Edited by R. Lux and E.-J. Waschke. Arbeiten zur Bibel und ihrer Geschichte 23. Leipzig: Evangelische Verlagsanstalt, 2006.

———. "König Joschija in der Klimax des DtrG (2Reg 22f.) und das vordtr Dokument einer Kultreform am Residenzort (23,4–15*)." Pages 81–145 in *Erzählte Geschichte: Beiträge zur narrativen Kultur im alten Israel*. Edited by R. Lux. Biblisch–theologische Studien 40. Neukirchen-Vluyn: Neukirchener, 2000.

Harvey, John E. *Retelling the Torah: The Deuteronomistic Historian's Use of Tetrateuchal Narratives*. London: T&T Clark, 2004.

Hauser, Alan J. "Linguistic and Thematic Links between Genesis 4:1–16 and Genesis 2–3." *JETS* 23 (1980): 297–305.

Heckl, Raik. *Moses Vermächtnis: Kohärenz, literarische Intention und Funktion von Dtn 1–3*. Arbeiten zur Bibel und ihrer Geschichte 9. Leipzig: Evangelische Verlagsanstalt, 2004.

Hertog, Cornelis G. den. "Jos 5,4–6 in der griechischen Übersetzung." *ZAW* 104 (1992): 601–6.

Hill, John. "'Your Exile Will Be Long': The Book of Jeremiah and the Unended Exile." Pages 149–61 in *Reading the Book of Jeremiah: A Search for Coherence*. Edited by M. Kessler. Winona Lake: Eisenbrauns, 2004.

Holmes, Samuel. *Joshua: The Hebrew and Greek Texts*. Cambridge: Cambridge University Press, 1914.

Hölscher, Gustav. "Das Buch der Könige, seine Quellen und seine Redaktion." Pages 158–213 in *Eucharistērion: Studien zur Religion und Literatur des Alten und Neuen*

Testaments. Hermann Gunkel zum 60. Geburtstag. Edited by H. Schmid. 2 vols. Vol. 1. FRLANT 36. Göttingen: Vandenhoeck & Ruprecht, 1923.

———. *Geschichte der israelitischen und jüdischen Religion.* Gießen: Töpelmann, 1922.

———. *Geschichtsschreibung in Israel: Untersuchungen zum Jahwisten und Elohisten.* Skrifter utgivna av [K.] Humanistika Vetenskapssamfundet i Lund 50. Lund: Gleerup, 1952.

Holzinger, Heinrich. *Exodus.* KHC 11. Tübingen: Mohr, 1900.

Houtman, Cornelis. *Exodus.* HCOT. Kampen: Kok, 1993–2002.

Hughes, Jeremy. *Secrets of the Times: Myth and History in Biblical Chronology.* JSOTSup 66. Sheffield: Sheffield Academic Press, 1990.

Hurowitz, Victor Avigdor. *I Have Built You an Exalted House: Temple Building in the Bible in Light of Mesopotamian and Northwest Semitic Writings.* JSOTSup 115. Sheffield: Sheffield Academic Press, 1992.

Jacob, Benno. *The Second Book of the Bible: Exodus.* Translated by W. Jacob. Hoboken, N.J.: Ktav, 1992.

Japhet, Sara. *1 and 2 Chronicles.* OTL. Louisville: Westminster John Knox, 1993.

———. *The Ideology of the Book of Chronicles and Its Place in Biblical Thought.* Translated by A. Barber. Frankfurt: Lang, 1989.

Jenni, Ernst. "Zwei Jahrzehnte Forschung an den Büchern Josua bis Könige." *TRu* 27 (1961): 1–32, 97–146.

Jensen, Philip P. *Graded Holiness: A Key to the Priestly Conception of the World.* JSOTSup 106. Sheffield: Sheffield Academic Press, 1992.

Jeremias, Jörg. "Der Begriff 'Baal' im Hoseabuch und seine Wirkungsgeschichte (1994)." Pages 86–103 in idem, *Hosea und Amos: Studien zu den Anfängen des Dodekapropheton.* FAT 13. Tübingen: Mohr (Siebeck), 1996.

———. "Hoseas Einfluß auf das Jeremiabuch—Ein traditionsgeschichtliches Problem (1994)." Pages 122–41 in idem, *Hosea und Amos: Studien zu den Anfängen des Dodekapropheton.* FAT 13. Tübingen: Mohr (Siebeck), 1996.

Johnstone, William. "Recounting the Tetrateuch." Pages 209–34 in *Covenant As Context: Essays in Honour of E. W. Nicholson.* Edited by A. D. H. Mayes and R. B. Salters. Oxford: Oxford University Press, 2003.

Kaestli, Jean-Daniel. "La formation et la structure du canon biblique: Que peut apporter l'étude de la Septante?" Pages 99–113 in *The Canon of Scripture in Jewish and Christian Tradition—Le canon des Écritures dans les traditions juive et chrétienne.* Edited by P. S. Alexander and J.-D. Kaestli. Publications de l'institut romand des sciences bibliques 4. Prahins: Zèbre, 2007.

Kalimi, Isaac. *The Reshaping of Ancient Israelite History in Chronicles.* Winona Lake: Eisenbrauns, 2005.

Kegler, Jürgen. "Arbeitsorganisation und Arbeitskampfformen im Alten Testament." Pages 51–71 in *Mitarbeiter der Schöpfung: Bibel und Arbeitswelt.* Edited by L. Schottroff and W. Schottroff. Munich: Kaiser, 1983.

Keulen, Percy S. F. van. *Manasseh Through the Eyes of the Deuteronomists.* OTS 38. Leiden: Brill, 1996.

———. *Two Versions of the Solomon Narrative: An Inquiry into the Relationship between MT 1 Kgs. 2–11 and LXX 3 Reg. 2–11.* VTSup 104. Leiden: Brill, 2005.

Kissling, Paul J. *Reliable Characters in the Primary History: Profiles of Moses, Joshua, Elijah and Elisha.* JSOTSup 224. Sheffield: Sheffield Academic Press, 1996.

Kittel, Rudolf. "Die pentateuchischen Urkunden in den Büchern Richter und Samuel." *TSK* 65 (1892): 44–71.

Klein, Ralph W. *1 Chronicles: A Commentary*. Hermeneia. Minneapolis: Fortress, 2006.

———. "The Message of P." Pages 57–66 in *Die Botschaft und die Boten: Festschrift für Hans Walter Wolff zum 70. Geburtstag*. Edited by J. Jeremias and L. Perlitt. Neukirchen-Vluyn: Neukirchener, 1981.

Knauf, Ernst Axel. "1–2 Rois." Pages 302–11 in *Introduction à l'Ancien Testament*. Edited by T. Römer, J.-D. Macchi, and C. Nihan. MdB 49. Geneva: Labor et Fides, 2004.

———. "Buchschlüsse in Josua." Pages 217–24 in *Les dernières rédactions du Pentateuque, de l'Hexateuque et de L'Ennéateuque*. Edited by T. Römer and K. Schmid. BETL 203. Leuven: Leuven University Press and Peeters, 2007.

———. *Josua*. ZBK 6. Zurich: Theologischer Verlag, 2008.

———. "Kings among the Prophets." Pages 131–49 in *The Production of Prophecy: Constructing Prophecy and Prophets in Yehud*. Edited by D. V. Edelman and E. Ben Zvi. London and Oakville, Conn.: Equinox, 2009.

Knierim, Rolf. "Criticism of Literary Features: Form, Tradition, and Redaction." Pages 123–66 in *The Hebrew Bible and Its Modern Interpreters*. Edited by D. A. Knight and G. M. Tucker. Philadelphia: Fortress, 1985.

Knoppers, Gary. "Review of A. Graeme Auld, *Kings Without Privilege*." *ATJ* 27 (1995): 118–21.

Koch, Klaus. "Das Profetenschweigen des deuteronomistischen Geschichtswerks." Pages 115–130 in *Die Botschaft und die Boten: Festschrift für Hans Walter Wolff zum 70. Geburtstag*. Edited by J. Jeremias and L. Perlitt. Neukirchen-Vluyn: Neukirchener Verlag, 1981.

———. "Gibt es ein Vergeltungsdogma im Alten Testament? (1955)." Pages 130–80 in *Um das Prinzip der Vergeltung in Religion und Recht des Alten Testaments*. Edited by K. Koch. WdF 125. Darmstadt: Wissenschaftliche Buchgesellschaft, 1972.

Köckert, Matthias. *Vätergott und Väterverheißungen: Eine Auseinandersetzung mit Albrecht Alt und seinen Erben*. FRLANT 142. Göttingen: Vandenhoeck & Ruprecht, 1988.

Kogan, Leonid and Serguei Tishchenko. "Lexicographic Notes on Hebrew *bamah*." *UF* 34 (2002): 319–52.

Köhlmoos, Melanie. *Bet-El-Erinnerungen an eine Stadt: Perspektiven der alttestamentlichen Bet-El-Überlieferung*. FAT 49. Tübingen: Mohr Siebeck, 2006.

Konkel, Michael. *Sünde und Vergebung: Eine Rekonstruktion der Redaktionsgeschichte der hinteren Sinaiperikope (Exodus 32–34) vor dem Hintergrund aktueller Pentateuchmodelle*. FAT 58. Tübingen: Mohr Siebeck, 2008.

Kooij, Arie van der. "Perspectives on the Study of the Septuagint: Who are the Translators?" Pages 214–29 in *Perspectives in the Study of the Old Testament and Early Judaism: A Symposium in Honour of Adam S. van der Woude on the Occasion of his 70th Birthday*. Edited by F. García Martínez and E. Noort. VTSup 73. Leiden: Brill, 1998.

Krašovec, Jože. "Punishment and Mercy in the Primeval History (Gen 1–11)." *ETL* 70 (1994): 5–33.

Kratz, Reinhard G. *The Composition of the Narrative Books of the Old Testament*. Translated by J. Bowden. London: T&T Clark; New York: Continuum, 2005.

Kratz, Reinhard G. "Der literarische Ort des Deuteronomiums." Pages 101–20 in *Liebe und Gebot: Studien zum Deuteronomium*. Edited by R. G. Kratz and H. Spieckermann. FRLANT 190. Göttingen: Vandenhoeck & Ruprecht, 2000.

———. "Der vor- und der nachpriesterschriftliche Hexateuch." Pages 295–323 in *Abschied vom Jahwisten: Die Komposition des Hexateuch in der jüngsten Diskussion*. Edited by J. C. Gertz, K. Schmid, and M. Witte. BZAW 315. Berlin: de Gruyter, 2002.

———. *Die Komposition der erzählenden Bücher des Alten Testaments: Grundwissen der Bibelkritik*. Uni-Taschenbücher 2157. Göttingen: Vandenhoeck & Ruprecht, 2000.

———. "Israel als Staat und als Volk." *ZTK* 97 (2000): 1–17.

Krüger, Thomas. "Anmerkungen zur Frage nach den Redaktionen der Grossen Erzählwerke im Alten Testament." Pages 47–66 in *Les dernières rédactions du Pentateuque, de l'Hexateuque et de L'Ennéateuque*. Edited by T. Römer and K. Schmid. BETL 203. Leuven: Leuven University Press and Peeters, 2007.

Kuenen, Abraham. *An Historico-Critical Inquiry into the Origin and Composition of the Hexateuch: Vol. 1*. Translated by P. H. Wicksteed. London: Macmillan, 1886 (Dutch original 1861; 2d ed. 1885).

Lambert, Wilfred George. "Destiny and Divine Intervention in Babylon and Israel." *OtSt* 17 (1972): 65–72.

Lemaire, André. "Towards a Redactional History of the Book of Kings." Pages 446–61 in *Reconsidering Israel and Judah: Recent Studies on the Deuteronomistic History*. Edited by G. N. Knoppers and J. G. McConville. Winona Lake: Eisenbrauns, 2000.

Lemke, Werner E. "The Synoptic Problem in the Chronicler's History." *HTR* 58 (1965): 349–63.

———. "Synoptic Studies in the Chronicler's History." Ph.D. diss., Harvard University, 1963.

Levenson, Jon D. "The Last Four Verses in Kings." *JBL* 103 (1984): 353–61.

Levin, Christoph. "Abraham erwirbt seine Grablege (Genesis 23)." Pages 96–113 in *"Gerechtigkeit und Recht zu üben" (Gen 18, 19)*. Edited by R. Achenbach and M. Arneth. BZABR 13. Wiesbaden: Harrassowitz, 2009.

———. "Amos und Jerobeam I." *VT* 45 (1995): 307–17.

———. "Das System der zwölf Stämme Israels." Pages 111–23 in idem, *Fortschreibungen: Gesammelte Studien zum Alten Testament*. BZAW 316. Berlin: de Gruyter, 2003.

———. *Der Jahwist*. FRLANT 157. Göttingen: Vandenhoeck & Ruprecht, 1993.

———. "Die Frömmigkeit der Könige von Israel und Juda." Pages 129–68 in *Houses Full of All Good Things*. Edited by J. Pakkala and M. Nissinen. Publications of the Finnish Exegetical Society 95. Helsinki: Finnish Exegetical Society; Göttingen: Vandenhoeck & Ruprecht, 2008.

———. "Die Redaktion R^JP in der Urgeschichte." Pages 15–34 in *Auf dem Weg zur Endgestalt von Genesis bis II Regum*. Edited by M. Beck and U. Schorn. BZAW 370. Berlin: de Gruyter, 2006.

———. *Die Verheißung des neuen Bundes*. FRLANT 137. Göttingen: Vandenhoeck & Ruprecht, 1985.

———. "Joschija im deuteronomistischen Geschichtswerk." *ZAW* 96 (1984): 351–71.

———. "The Yahwist and the Redactional Link between Genesis and Exodus." Pages 131–41 in *A Farewell to the Yahwist? The Composition of the Pentateuch in Recent European Interpretation*. Edited by T. B. Dozeman and K. Schmid. SBLSymS 34. Atlanta: Society of Biblical Literature, 2006.

———. "The Yahwist: The Earliest Editor in the Pentateuch." *JBL* 126 (2007): 209–30.

Levinson, Bernard M. *"The Right Chorale": Studies in Biblical Law and Interpretation*. FAT 54. Tübingen: Mohr Siebeck, 2008.

Licht, Jacob. *Testing in the Hebrew Scriptures and in Post-Biblical Judaism*. Jerusalem: The Hebrew University Magnes Press, 1973 [in Hebrew].

Linville, James. "Rethinking the 'Exilic' Book of Kings." *JSOT* 75 (1997): 21–42.

Livingstone, Alasdair. *Court Poetry and Literary Miscellanea.* SAA 3. Helsinki: Helsinki University Press, 1989.

Lohfink, Norbert. "Darstellungskunst und Theologie in Dtn 1,6–3,29." *Bib* 41 (1960): 105–34.

———. "Deuteronomium 9,1–10,11 und Exodus 32–34: Zu Endtextstruktur, Intertextualität, Schichtung und Abhängigkeiten." Pages 41–87 in *Gottes Volk am Sinai: Untersuchungen zu Ex 32–34 und Dtn 9–10.* Edited by M. Köckert and E. Blum. Veröffentlichungen der wissenschaftlichen Gesellschaft für Theologie 18. Gütersloh: Gütersloher Verlagshaus, 2001.

———. "Die deuteronomistische Darstellung des Übergangs der Führung Israels von Moses auf Josue: Ein Beitrag zur alttestamentlichen Theologie des Amtes." *Schol* 37 (1962): 32–44.

———. *Die Väter Israels im Deuteronomium: Mit einer Stellungnahme von Thomas Römer.* OBO 111. Fribourg: Universitätsverlag; Göttingen: Vandenhoeck & Ruprecht, 1991.

———. "Kerygmata des Deuteronomistischen Geschichtswerks." Pages 87–100 in *Die Botschaft und die Boten: Festschrift für Hans Walter Wolff zum 70. Geburtstag.* Edited by J. Jeremias and L. Perlitt. Neukirchen-Vluyn: Neukirchener, 1981.

———. "The Priestly Narrative and History." Pages 136–72 in idem, *The Theology of the Pentateuch: Themes of the Priestly Narrative and Deuteronomy.* Translated by L. M. Maloney. Edinburgh: T&T Clark; Minneapolis: Fortress, 1994.

———. "The Strata of the Pentateuch and the Question of War." Pages 173–226 in idem, *The Theology of the Pentateuch: Themes of the Priestly Narrative and Deuteronomy.* Translated by L. M. Maloney. Edinburgh: T&T Clark; Minneapolis: Fortress, 1994.

———. *Studien zum Deuteronomium und zur deuteronomistischen Literatur II.* SBAB 12. Stuttgart: Katholisches Bibelwerk, 1991.

Longstaff, Thomas R. W. *Evidence of Conflation in Mark? A Study in the Synoptic Problem.* SBLDS 28. Missoula, Mont.: Scholars Press, 1977.

López, Felix García. "Deut 34, Dtr History and the Pentateuch." Pages 47–61 in *Studies in Deuteronomy: In Honour of C. J. Labuschagne on the Occasion of his 65th Birthday.* Edited by F. García Martínez, A. Hilhorst, J. T. A. G. M. van Ruiten, and A. S. van der Woude. VTSup 53. Leiden: Brill, 1994.

Lust, Johan. "Septuagint and Canon." Pages 39–55 in *The Biblical Canons.* Edited by J.-M. Auwers and H. J. de Jonge. BETL 163. Leuven: Leuven University Press and Peeters, 2003.

Maier, Christl. *Jeremia als Lehrer der Tora: Soziale Gebote des Deuteronomiums in Fortschreibungen des Jeremiabuches.* FRLANT 196. Göttingen: Vandenhoeck & Ruprecht, 2002.

Maier, Johann. "Zur Frage des biblischen Kanons im Frühjudentum im Licht der Qumranfunde." Pages 135–46 in *Zum Problem des biblischen Kanons.* Edited by I. Baldermann, E. Dassmann, and O. Fuchs. JBTh 3. Neukirchen-Vluyn: Neukirchener, 1988.

Mandell, Sara. "Primary History as a Social Construct of a Privileged Class." Pages 21–35 in *Concepts of Class in Ancient Israel.* Edited by M. R. Sneed. Atlanta: Scholars Press, 1999.

Mandell, Sara and David N. Freedman. *The Relationship between Herodotus' History and Primary History.* SFSHJ 60. Atlanta: Scholars Press, 1993.

Margolis, Max L. *The Book of Joshua in Greek.* 5 vols. Paris: Guethner, 1931–36.

Maul, Stefan. "Die altorientalische Hauptstadt-Abbild und Nabel der Welt." Pages 109–24 in *Die orientalische Stadt: Kontinuität, Wandel, Bruch*. Edited by G. Wilhelm. Colloquien der Deutschen Orient-Gesellschaft 1. Saarbrücken: Saarbrücker Druckerei und Verlag, 1997.

Mazor, Lea. "A Nomistic Reworking of the Jericho Conquest Narrative Reflected in LXX to Joshua 6:1–20." *Textus* 18 (1995): 47–62.

———. "The Origin and Evolution of the Curse upon the Rebuilder of Jericho—A Contribution of Textual Criticism to Biblical Historiography." *Textus* 14 (1988): 1–26.

———. "The Septuagint Translation of the Book of Joshua: Abstract of Thesis Submitted for the Degree Doctor of Philosophy to the Senate of the Hebrew University, Jerusalem." *BIOSCS* 27 (1994): 29–38.

McDonald, L. M. and J. A. Sanders, eds. *The Canon Debate*. Boston: Hendrickson, 2002.

McEvenue, Sean. *The Narrative Style of the Priestly Writer*. Rome: Biblical Institute, 1971.

McKane, William. *A Critical and Exegetical Commentary on Jeremiah*. 2 vols. ICC. Edinburgh: T&T Clark, 1986–1996.

McKenzie, Steven L. "The Chronicler as Redactor." Pages 70–90 in *The Chronicler as Author: Studies in Text and Texture*. Edited by M. P. Graham and S. L. McKenzie. JSOTSup 263. Sheffield: Sheffield Academic Press, 1999.

———. *The Chronicler's Use of the Deuteronomistic History*. HSM 33. Atlanta: Scholars Press, 1984.

———. "The Source for Jeroboam's Role at Shechem (1 Kgs 11:43–12:3, 12, 20)." *JBL* 106 (1987): 297–300.

———. *The Trouble with Kings: The Composition of the Book of Kings in the Deuteronomistic History*. VTSup 42. Leiden: Brill, 1991.

Meer, Michaël N. van der. *Formation and Reformulations: The Redaction of the Book of Joshua in the Light of the Oldest Textual Witnesses*. VTSup 102. Leiden: Brill, 2004.

———. "Textual Criticism and Literary Criticism in Joshua 1:7 (MT and LXX)." Pages 355–71 in *X Congress of the International Organization for Septuagint and Cognate Studies, Oslo, 1998*. Edited by B. A. Taylor. SBLSCS 51. Atlanta: Scholars Press, 2001.

Metso, Sarianna. *The Textual Development of the Qumran Community Rule*. STDJ 21. Leiden: Brill, 1997.

Mettinger, Trygge N. D. *The Dethronement of Sabbaoth: Studies in the Shem and Kabod Theologies*. ConBOT 18. Lund: Gleerup, 1982.

———. *The Eden Narrative: A Literary and Religio-historical Study of Gen 2–3*. Winona Lake: Eisenbrauns, 2001.

Meyer, Eduard. "Kritik der Berichte über die Eroberung Palästinas." *ZAW* 1 (1881): 117–46.

Moatti–Fine, Jacqueline. *Jésus (Josué): Traduction du texte grec de la Septante*. La Bible d'Alexandrie 6. Paris: Cerf, 1996.

Montgomery, James A. *A Critical and Exegetical Commentary on the Book of Kings*. ICC. Edinburgh: T&T Clark, 1951.

Moore, George F. *A Critical and Exegetical Commentary on Judges*. ICC. Edinburgh: T&T Clark, 1895.

———. "Tatian's *Diatessaron* and the Analysis of the Pentateuch." Pages 243–56 in *Empirical Models for Biblical Criticism*. Edited by J. H. Tigay. Philadelphia: University of Pennsylvania Press, 1985.

Mowinckel, Sigmund. *Tetrateuch–Pentateuch–Hexateuch: Die Berichte über die Landnahme in den drei altisraelitischen Geschichtswerken*. BZAW 90. Berlin: Töpelmann, 1964.

Müller, Reinhard. *Königtum und Gottesherrschaft*. FAT 2/3. Tübingen: Mohr Siebeck, 2004.

Na'aman, Nadav. "The Sources Available for the Author of the Book of Kings." Pages 105–20 in *Convegno Internazionale Recenti Tendenze nella Riccostruzione della Storia Antica d'Israele: Roma, 6–7 marzo 2003*. Contributi del Centro Linceo Interdisciplinare "Beniamino Segre". Rome: Academia Nazionale del Lincei, 2005.

———. "Updating the Messages: Hezekiah's Second Prophetic Story (2 Kings 19.9b–35) and the Community of Babylonian Deportees." Pages 201–20 in *"Like a Bird in a Cage": The Invasion of Sennacherib in 701 BCE*. Edited by L. L. Grabbe. JSOTSup 363. Sheffield: Sheffield Academic Press, 2003.

Nelson, Richard D. *The Double Redaction of the Deuteronomistic History*. JSOTSup 18. Sheffield: JSOT Press, 1981.

———. *Joshua: A Commentary*. Louisville: Westminster John Knox, 1997.

Nicholson, Ernest W. "P as an Originally Independent Source in the Pentateuch." *IBS* 10 (1988): 192–206.

Niditch, Susan. *Oral World and Written Word: Ancient Israelite Literature*. Library of Ancient Israel. Louisville: Westminster John Knox, 1996.

Nihan, Christophe. *From Priestly Torah to Pentateuch: A Study in the Composition of the Book of Leviticus*. FAT 2/25. Tübingen: Mohr Siebeck, 2007.

Nogalski, James D. *Literary Precursors to the Book of the Twelve*. BZAW 217. Berlin: de Gruyter, 1993.

Noort, Edward. *Das Buch Josua: Forschungsgeschichte und Problemfelder*. EdF 292. Darmstadt: Wissenschaftliche Buchgesellschaft, 1998.

Noth, Martin. *The Chronicler's History* Translated by H. G. Williamson. JSOTSup 50. Sheffield: Sheffield Academic Press, 1987. Translation of *Überlieferungsgeschichtliche Studien, Teil 2*. 2d ed. Halle: Niemeyer, 1957.

———. *Das Buch Josua*. HAT 1/7. Tübingen: Mohr, 1938; 2d ed. 1953; 3d (unrevised) ed. 1971.

———. "Das formgeschichtliche Problem des Hexateuchs (1938)." Pages 9–86 in idem, *Gesammelte Studien zum Alten Testament*. TB 8. Munich: Kaiser, 1958.

———. *The Deuteronomistic History*. Translated by J. Doull and J. Barton. JSOTSup 15. Sheffield: Sheffield Academic Press, 1981; 2d ed. 1991. Translation of pages 1–110 of *Überlieferungsgeschichtliche Studien: Die sammelnden und bearbeitenden Geschichtswerke im Alten Testament*. 2d ed. Halle: Niemeyer, 1957.

———. *Die Welt des Alten Testaments: Einführung in die Grenzgebiete der alttestamentlichen Wissenschaft*. 4th ed. Berlin: Töpelmann, 1962.

———. *Exodus: A Commentary* Translated by J. Bowden. OTL. London: SCM Press, 1962.

———. *A History of Pentateuchal Traditions*. Translated by B. W. Anderson. Englewood Cliffs, N.J.: Prentice Hall, 1972. Translation of *Überlieferungsgeschichte des Pentateuch*. 2d ed. Stuttgart: Kohlhammer, 1948. Reprint edition: Scholars Press Reprint 5. Atlanta: Scholars Press, 1981.

———. *Könige*. 2 vols. BKAT 9. Neukirchen-Vluyn: Neukirchener, 1964–1968.

———. *Leviticus: A Commentary*. Translated by J. E. Anderson. OTL. Philadelphia: Westminster, 1965.

———. *Numbers: A Commentary*. Translated by J. Martin. OTL. London: SCM Press, 1968.

———. *Überlieferungsgeschichtliche Studien: Die sammelnden und bearbeitenden Geschichtswerke im Alten Testament*. Halle: Niemayer, 1943; 2d repr. ed., 1957; 3d repr. ed.: Darmstadt: Wissenschaftliche Buchgesellschaft, 1967.

———. "Zur Geschichtsauffassung des Deuteronomisten." Pages 558–566 in *Proceedings of the Twenty-Second Congress of Orientalists, Held in Istanbul, September 15th to 22nd, 1951, Vol. 2: Communications.* Edited by Zeki Velidi Togan. Leiden: Brill, 1957.

Olmstead, Albert Ten Eyck. *Assyrian Historiography: A Source Study.* Columbia, Mo.: University of Missouri Press, 1916.

Olson, Dennis T. *Deuteronomy and the Death of Moses: A Theological Reading.* OBT. Minneapolis: Fortress, 1994.

Orlinsky, Harry M. "The Hebrew *Vorlage* of the Septuagint of the Book of Joshua." Pages 187–95 in *Congress Volume: Rome, 1968.* Edited by G. W. Anderson. VTSup 17. Leiden: Brill, 1969.

Otto, Eckart. *Das Deuteronomium im Pentateuch und Hexateuch: Studien zur Literaturgeschichte von Pentateuch und Hexateuch im Lichte des Deuteronomiumrahmens.* FAT 30. Tübingen: Mohr Siebeck, 2000.

———. *Das Deuteronomium: Politische Theologie und Rechtsreform in Juda und Assyrien.* BZAW 284. Berlin: de Gruyter, 1999.

———. "Die nachpriesterschriftliche Pentateuchredaktion im Buch Exodus." Pages 196–222 in *Studies in the Book of Exodus: Redaction–Reception–Interpretation.* Edited by M. Vervenne. BETL 126. Leuven: Leuven University Press and Peeters, 1996.

———. "Die Paradieserzählung Genesis 2–3: Eine nachpriesterschriftliche Lehrerzählung in ihrem religionshistorischen Kontext." Pages 167–192 in *"Jedes Ding hat seine Zeit . . .": Studien zur israelitischen und altorientalischen Weisheit: Diethelm Michel zum 65. Geburtstag.* Edited by A. A. Diesel, E. Otto, and R. G. Lehmann. BZAW 241. Berlin: de Gruyter, 1996.

———. "Forschungen zur Priesterschrift." *TRu* 62 (1997): 1–50.

———. "The Pentateuch in Synchronical and Diachronical Perspectives: Protorabbinical Scribal Erudition Mediating Between Deuteronomy and the Priestly Code." Pages 14–35 in *Das Deuteronomium zwischen Pentateuch und Deuteronomistischem Geschichtswerk.* Edited by E. Otto and R. Achenbach. FRLANT 206. Göttingen: Vandenhoeck & Ruprecht, 2004.

Otto, Susanne. *Jehu, Elia und Elisa: Die Erzählung von der Jehu–Revolution und die Komposition der Elia-Elisa-Erzählungen.* BWANT 152. Stuttgart: Kohlhammer, 2001.

Pakkala, Juha. "Jeroboam without Bulls." *ZAW* 120 (2008): 501–25.

———. "Zedekiah's Fate and the Dynastic Succession." *JBL* 125 (2006): 443–52.

Parry, Milman. "Studies in the Epic Technique of Oral Verse-Making, I: Homer and Homeric Style." *Harvard Studies in Classical Philology* 41 (1930): 73–147.

Peckham, Brian. "The Significance of the Book of Joshua in Noth's Theory of the Deuteronomistic History." Pages 213–34 in *The History of Israel's Traditions: The Heritage of Martin Noth.* Edited by S. McKenzie and M. Graham. JSOTSup 182. Sheffield: Sheffield Academic Press, 1994.

Perlitt, Lothar. *Deuteronomium.* BKAT 5. Neukirchen-Vluyn: Neukirchener, 1990.

———. "Deuteronomium 1–3 im Streit der Methoden." Pages 149–63 in *Das Deuteronomium: Entstehung, Gestalt, und Botschaft.* Edited by N. Lohfink. BETL 68. Leuven: Leuven University Press and Peeters, 1985.

———. "Priesterschrift im Deuteronomium?" *ZAW* 100 Supplement (1988): 65–88.

Person, Raymond F. "The Ancient Israelite Scribe as Performer." *JBL* 117 (1998): 601–9.

Peters, Norbert. *Unsere Bibel: Die Lebensquellen der Heiligen Schrift.* Paderborn: Bonifacius, 1929.

Petersen, J. E. "Priestly Materials in Josh 13–22: A Return to the Hexateuch?" *HAR* 4 (1980): 131–46.

Pfeiffer, Henrik. *Das Heiligtum von Bethel im Spiegel des Hoseabuches.* FRLANT 183. Göttingen: Vandenhoeck & Ruprecht, 1999.

Pola, Thomas. *Die ursprüngliche Priesterschrift: Beobachtungen zur Literarkritik und Traditionsgeschichte von PG.* WMANT 70. Neukirchen-Vluyn: Neukirchener, 1995.

Popper, Julio. *Der biblische Bericht über die Stiftshütte: Ein Beitrag zur Geschichte der Composition und Diaskeue des Pentateuch.* Leipzig: Hunger, 1862.

Porter, Barbara Nevling. "Ishtar of Niniveh and her Collaborator, Ishtar of Arbela, in the Reign of Assurbanipal." *Iraq* 66 (2004): 41–44.

Propp, William H. C. *Exodus 1–18: A New Translation with Introduction and Commentary.* AB 2A. New York: Doubleday, 1999.

Provan, Iain William. *Hezekiah and the Books of Kings: A Contribution to the Debate about the Composition of the Deuteronomistic History.* BZAW 172. Berlin: de Gruyter, 1988.

Pury, Albert de. "The Jacob Story and the Beginning of the Formation of the Pentateuch." Pages 51–72 in *A Farewell to the Yahwist? The Composition of the Pentateuch in Recent European Interpretation.* Edited by T. B. Dozeman and K. Schmid. SBLSymS 34. Atlanta: Society of Biblical Literature, 2006.

Rad, Gerhard von. *Das erste Buch Mose: Genesis.* ATD 2/4. Göttingen: Vandenhoeck & Ruprecht, 1976 (original 1949).

———. "Das formgeschichtliche Problem des Hexateuchs (1938)." Pages 9–86 in idem, *Gesammelte Studien zum Alten Testament.* TB 8. Munich: Kaiser, 1958.

———. "The Form-Critical Problem of the Hexateuch." Pages 1–78 in idem, *The Problem of the Hexateuch and Other Essays.* Translated by E. W. Trueman Dicken. Edinburgh: Oliver & Boyd, 1966; repr. London: SCM Press, 1984; essay reprinted as pages 1–58 in *From Genesis to Chronicles: Explorations in Old Testament Theology.* Edited by K. C. Hanson. Minneapolis: Augsburg Fortress, 2005.

———. "Hexateuch oder Pentateuch?" *VF* 1–2 (1947–1948): 52–56.

———. *Old Testament Theology, Vol. 1: The Theology of Israel's Historical Traditions.* Translated by D. M. G. Stalker. New York: Harper, 1962.

———. "The Promised Land and Yahweh's Land in the Hexateuch." Pages 79–93 in idem, *The Problem of the Hexateuch and Other Essays.* Translated by E. W. Trueman Dicken. Edinburgh: Oliver & Boyd, 1966; repr. London: SCM Press, 1984.

———. "The Tent and the Ark." Pages 103–24 in idem, *The Problem of the Hexateuch and Other Essays.* Translated by E. W. Trueman Dicken. Edinburgh: Oliver & Boyd, 1966; repr. London: SCM Press, 1984.

Rake, Mareike. *"Juda wird aufsteigen!" Untersuchungen zum ersten Kapitel des Richterbuches.* BZAW 367. Berlin: de Gruyter, 2006.

Redford, Donald B. "Exodus I 11." *VT* 13 (1963): 401–18.

Rendtorff, Rolf. *The Problem of the Process of Transmission in the Pentateuch.* Translated by J. J. Scullion. JSOTSup 89. Sheffield: Sheffield Academic Press, 1990. Translation of *Das überlieferungsgeschichtliche Problem des Pentateuch.* BZAW 147. Berlin: de Gruyter, 1977).

Rezetko, Robert. *Source and Revision in the Narratives of David's Transfer of the Ark: Text, Language, and Story in 1 Samuel 6 and 1 Chronicles 13, 15–16.* Library of Hebrew Bible/Old Testament Studies 470. New York: T&T Clark, 2007.

Richter, Wolfgang. "Beobachtungen zur theologischen Systembildung in der alttestamentlichen Literatur anhand des 'Kleinen geschichtlichen Credo." Pages 1:175–212 in *Wahrheit und Verkündigung: Michael Schmaus zum 70. Geburtstag*. Edited by L. Scheffczyk, W. Dettloff, and R. Heinzmann. 2 vols. Vol. 1. Paderborn: Schöningh, 1967.

Ringgren, Helmer. "Oral and Written Transmission in the Old Testament: Some Observations." *Studia Theologica* 3 (1949): 34–59.

Rofé, Alexander. "The Editing of the Book of Joshua in the Light of 4QJosh[a]." Pages 73–80 in *New Qumran Texts and Studies: Proceedings of the First Meeting of the International Organization for Qumran Studies, Paris 1992*. Edited by G. J. Brooke. STDJ 15. Leiden: Brill, 1994.

———. "The End of the Book of Joshua according to the Septuagint." *Henoch* 4 (1982): 17–36.

———. "Joshua 20: Historico-Literary Criticism Illustrated." Pages 131–47 in *Empirical Models for Biblical Criticism*. Edited by J. H. Tigay. Philadelphia: University of Pennsylvania Press, 1985.

———. "The Nomistic Correction in Biblical Manuscripts and its Occurrence in 4QSam[a]." *RevQ* 14 (1989): 247–54.

———. "The Piety of the Torah-Disciples at the Winding-Up of the Hebrew Bible: Josh 1:8; Ps 1:2; Isa 59:21." Pages 78–85 in *Bibel in jüdischer und christlicher Tradition: Festschrift für Johann Maier zum 60. Geburtstag*. Edited by H. Merklein, K. Müller, and G. Stemberger. BBB 88. Bonn: Hahn, 1993.

Römer, Thomas. "Das doppelte Ende des Josuabuches: Einige Anmerkungen zur aktuellen Diskussion um 'deuteronomistisches Geschichtswerk' und 'Hexateuch.'" *ZAW* 118 (2006): 523–48.

———. "The Form-Critical Problem of the So-Called Deuteronomistic History." Pages 240–52 in *The Changing Face of Form Criticism for the Twenty-First Century*. Edited by M. A. Sweeney and E. Ben Zvi. Grand Rapids: Eerdmans, 2003.

———. *Israels Väter: Untersuchungen zur Väterthematik im Deuteronomium und in der deuteronomistischen Tradition*. OBO 99. Fribourg: Universitätsverlag; Göttingen: Vandenhoeck & Ruprecht, 1990.

———. *The So-Called Deuteronomistic History: A Sociological, Historical and Literary Introduction*. London: T&T Clark, 2005. Paperback edition: New York: Continuum, 2007.

———. "Transformations in Deuteronomistic and Biblical Historiography: On 'Book-Finding' and Other Literary Strategies." *ZAW* 109 (1997): 1–11.

Römer, Thomas and Konrad Schmid. "Introduction: Pentateuque, Hexateuque, Ennéateuque: Exposé du problème." Pages 1–7 in *Les dernières rédactions du Pentateuque, de l'Hexateuque et de l'Ennéateuque*. Edited by T. Römer and K. Schmid. BETL 203. Leuven: Leuven University Press and Peeters, 2007.

Römer, Thomas C. and Marc Z. Brettler. "Deuteronomy 34 and the Case for a Persian Hexateuch." *JBL* 119 (2000): 401–19.

Römer, Thomas C. and Christophe Nihan. "Une source commune aux récits de rois et chroniques? À propos d'un ouvrage récent d'A. G. Auld." *ETR* 79 (1999): 415–22.

Römer, Thomas and Konrad Schmid, eds. *Les dernières rédactions du Pentateuque, de l'Hexateuque et de l'Ennéateuque*. BETL 203. Leuven: Leuven University Press and Peeters, 2007.

Rose, Martin. *Jahwist und Deuteronomist: Untersuchungen zu den Berührungspunkten beider Literaturwerke*. ATANT 67. Zurich: Theologischer Verlag, 1981.

———. "The Septuagint-Version of the Book of Joshua." *SJOT* 16 (2002): 5–23.

Rost, Leonhard. *The Succession to the Throne of David*. Translated by M. D. Rutter and D. M. Gunn. Sheffield: Almond Press, 1982.

Ryle, Herbert E. *The Canon of the Old Testament*. London: Macmillan, 1914.

Sacchi, Paolo. "Le Pentateuque, le Deutéronomiste et Spinoza." Pages 276–88 in *Congress Volume: Paris, 1992*. Edited by J. A. Emerton. Leiden: Brill, 1995.

Sanders, James A. *Torah and Canon*. Philadelphia: Fortress, 1972.

Särkiö, Pekka. *Die Weisheit und Macht Salomos in der israelitischen Historiographie: Eine traditions- und redaktionskritische Untersuchung über 1 Kön 3–5 und 9–11*. Schriften der Finnischen Exegetischen Gesellschaft 60. Helsinki: Finnische Exegetische Gesellschaft; Göttingen: Vandenhoeck & Ruprecht, 1994.

———. *Exodus und Salomo: Erwägungen zur verdeckten Salomokritik anhand von Ex 1–2; 5; 14 und 32*. Schriften der Finnischen Exegetischen Gesellschaft 71. Helsinki: Finnische Exegetische Gesellschaft; Göttingen: Vandenhoeck & Ruprecht, 1998.

Schäfer-Lichtenberger, Christa. *Joshua und Salomo: Eine Studie zu Autorität und Legitimität des Nachfolgers im Alten Testament*. VTSup 58. Leiden: Brill, 1995.

Schaudig, Hanspeter. *Die Inschriften Nabonids von Babylon und Kyros' des Grossen, samt den in ihrem Umfeld entstandenen Tendenzschriften: Textausgabe und Grammatik*. AOAT 256. Münster: Ugarit-Verlag, 2001.

Schenker, Adrian. *Älteste Textgeschichte der Königsbücher: Die hebräische Vorlage der ursprünglichen Septuaginta als älteste Textform der Königsbücher*. OBO 199. Fribourg: Universitätsverlag; Göttingen: Vandenhoeck & Ruprecht, 2004.

Schipper, Jeremy. "'Significant Resonances' With Mephiboshet in 2 Kings 25:27–30: A Response to Donald F. Murray." *JBL* 124 (2005): 521–29.

Schmid, Hans Heinrich. *Der sogenannte Jahwist: Beobachtungen und Fragen zur Pentateuchforschung*. Zurich: Theologischer Verlag, 1976.

Schmid, Konrad. "Buchtechnische und sachliche Prolegomena zur Enneateuchfrage." Pages 1–14 in *Auf dem Weg zur Endgestalt von Genesis bis II Regum*. Edited by M. Beck and U. Schorn. BZAW 370. Berlin: de Gruyter, 2006.

———. "Das Deuteronomium innerhalb der 'deuteronomistischen Geschichtswerke' in Gen–2 Kön." Pages 193–211 in *Das Deuteronomium zwischen Pentateuch und Deuteronomistischem Geschichtswerk*. Edited by E. Otto and R. Achenbach. FRLANT 206. Göttingen: Vandenhoeck & Ruprecht, 2004.

———. "Der Pentateuchredaktor: Beobachtungen zum theologischen Profil des Toraschlusses in Dtn 34." Pages 183–97 in *Les dernières rédactions du Pentateuque, de l'Hexateuque et de l'Ennéateuque*. Edited by T. Römer and K. Schmid. BETL 203. Leuven: Leuven University Press and Peeters, 2007.

———. "Die Unteilbarkeit der Weisheit: Überlegungen zur sogenannten Paradieserzählung Gen 2f. und ihrer theologischen Tendenz." *ZAW* 114 (2002): 21–39.

———. *Erzväter und Exodus: Untersuchungen zur doppelten Begründung der Ursprünge Israels innerhalb der Geschichtsbücher des Alten Testaments*. WMANT 81. Neukirchen-Vluyn: Neukirchener, 1999.

———. *Literaturgeschichte des Alten Testaments: Eine Einführung*. Darmstadt: Wissenschaftliche Buchgesellschaft, 2008.

———. "Persische Reichsautorisation und Tora." *TRu* 71 (2006): 494–506.

———. "The So-Called Yahwist and the Literary Gap Between Genesis and Exodus." Pages 29–50 in *A Farewell to the Yahwist? The Composition of the Pentateuch in Recent European Interpretation*. Edited by T. B. Dozeman and K. Schmid. SBLSymS 34. Atlanta: Society of Biblical Literature, 2006.

———. "Une grande historiographie allant de Genèse à 2 Rois a-t-elle un jour existé?" Pages 35–45 in *Les dernières rédactions du Pentateuque, de l'Hexateuque et de L'Ennéateuque.* Edited by T. Römer and K. Schmid. BETL 203. Leuven: Leuven University Press and Peeters, 2007.

Schmidt, Ludwig. *Studien zur Priesterschrift.* BZAW 214. Berlin: de Gruyter, 1993.

Schmidt, Werner H. *Exodus 1,1–6,30.* BKAT 2.1. Neukirchen-Vluyn: Neukirchener, 1988.

Schmitt, Hans-Christoph. *Arbeitsbuch zum Alten Testament: Grundzüge der Geschichte Israels und der alttestamentlichen Schriften.* Uni-Taschenbücher 2146. Göttingen: Vandenhoeck & Ruprecht, 2005.

———. "Das sogenannte jahwistische Privilegrecht in Ex 34,10–28 als Komposition der spätdeuteronomistischen Endredaktion des Pentateuch." Pages 157–71 in *Abschied vom Jahwisten: Die Komposition des Hexateuch in der jüngsten Diskussion.* Edited by J. C. Gertz, K. Schmid, and M. Witte. BZAW 315. Berlin: de Gruyter, 2002.

———. "Das spätdeuteronomistische Geschichtswerk Gen i–2 Regum xxv und seine theologische Intention." Pages 261–79 in *Congress Volume: Cambridge, 1995.* Edited by J. A. Emerton. VTSup 66. Leiden: Brill, 1997. Reprinted as: Pages 277–94 in idem, *Theologie in Prophetie und Pentateuch: Gesammelte Aufsätze.* Edited by U. Schorn and M. Büttner. BZAW 310. Berlin: de Gruyter, 2001.

———. "Das spätdeuteronomistische Geschichtswerk Gen I–2Regum XXV und seine theologische Intention." Pages 277–94 in idem, *Theologie in Prophetie und Pentateuch: Gesammelte Schriften.* Edited by U. Schorn and M. Büttner. BZAW 310. Berlin: de Gruyter, 2001.

———. "Die Erzählung vom Goldenen Kalb Ex. 32 und das Deuteronomistische Geschichtswerk." Pages 311–25 in idem, *Theologie in Prophetie und Pentateuch: Gesammelte Schriften.* Edited by U. Schorn and M. Büttner. BZAW 310. Berlin: de Gruyter, 2001.

———. "Die Josephsgeschichte und das Deuteronomistische Geschichtswerk: Genesis 38 und 48–50." Pages 295–308 in idem, *Theologie in Prophetie und Pentateuch: Gesammelte Schriften.* Edited by U. Schorn and M. Büttner. BZAW 310. Berlin: de Gruyter, 2001.

———. "Die Suche nach der Identität des Jahweglaubens im nachexilischen Israel." Pages 255–76 in idem, *Theologie in Prophetie und Pentateuch: Gesammelte Schriften.* Edited by U. Schorn and M. Büttner. BZAW 310. Berlin: de Gruyter, 2001.

———. "Dtn 34 als Verbindungsstück zwischen Tetrateuch und Deuteronomistischen Geschichtswerk." Pages 180–92 in *Das Deuteronomium zwischen Pentateuch und Deuteronomistischem Geschichtswerk.* Edited by E. Otto and R. Achenbach. FRLANT 206. Göttingen: Vandenhoeck & Ruprecht, 2004.

Schneider, Wolfgang. "Und es begab sich . . .: Anfänge von Erzählungen im Biblischen Hebräisch." *BN* 70 (1993): 62–87.

Schüle, Andreas. "Made in the 'Image of God': The Concepts of Divine Images in Gen 1–3." *ZAW* 117 (2005): 1–20.

Sellin, Ernst. *Einleitung in das Alte Testament.* 5th ed. Evang.-Theologische Bibliothek. Leipzig: Quelle & Meyer, 1929.

Sheppard, Gerald T. *The Future of the Bible: Beyond Liberalism and Literalism.* Toronto: The United Church Publishing, 1990.

Simpson, Cuthbert A. *Composition of the Book of Judges.* Oxford: Blackwell, 1957.

Sisam, Kenneth. "Notes on Old English Poetry: On the Authority of Old English Poetical Manuscripts." *Review of English Studies* 22 (1946): 257–268.

Smend, Rudolf. "Das Gesetz und die Völker: Ein Beitrag zur deuteronomistischen Redaktionsgeschichte." Pages 494–509 in *Probleme biblischer Theologie: Gerhard von Rad zum 70. Geburtstag*. Edited by H. W. Wolff. Munich: Kaiser, 1971.

———. *Deutsche Alttestamentler in drei Jahrhunderten*. Göttingen: Vandenhoeck & Ruprecht, 1989.

———. *Die Entstehung des Alten Testaments*. ThW 1. Stuttgart: Kohlhammer, 1978.

———. "Nachruf auf Martin Noth." Pages 137–65 in *Gesammelte Studien zum Alten Testament 2*. Edited by H. W. Wolff. TB 39. Munich: Kaiser, 1969.

Smend, Rudolf (Sr.). "JE in den geschichtlichen Büchern des AT." *ZAW* 39 (1921): 181–217.

Soggin, J. Alberto. *Joshua: A Commentary*. OTL. Philadelphia: Westminster, 1972.

Sonnet, Jean-Pierre. *The Book Within the Book: Writing in Deuteronomy*. Biblical Interpretation Series 14. Leiden: Brill, 1997.

Spek, R. J. van der. "Review of J.-J. Glassner, *Mesopotamian Chronicles*." *RBL* 9 (2005): Online: http://www.bookreviews.org/pdf/4467_4512.pdf [Cited 27 May 2010].

Spiegelberg, Wilhelm. *Die sogenannte Demotische Chronik des Pap. 215 der Bibliothèque Nationale zu Paris: Nebst den auf der Rückseite des Papyrus stehenden Texten*. Demotische Studien von Wilhelm Spiegelberg 7. Leipzig: Hinrichs, 1914.

Spina, Frank A. "The 'Ground' for Cain's Rejection (Gen 4): *'adāmāh* in the context of Gen 1–11." *ZAW* 104 (1992): 319–32.

Spinoza, Baruch de. *A Theologico-Political Treatise*. Edited by J. Israel. Cambridge Texts in the History of Philosophy. Cambridge: Cambridge University Press, 2007. Original (1670): *Opera I: Tractatus theologico-politicus*. Edited by G. Gawlik and F. Niewöhner. Darmstadt: Wissenschaftliche Buchgesellschaft, 1979.

Staerk, Willy. *Die Entstehung des Alten Testaments*. Sammlung Göschen 272. Leipzig: Göschen, 1905.

Stavrakopoulou, Francesca. "The Blackballing of Manasseh." Pages 248–63 in *Good Kings and Bad Kings*. Edited by L. L. Grabbe. LHB/OTS 393. London: T&T Clark International, 2005.

Steuernagel, Carl. *Das Buch Josua*. 2d ed. HKAT I/3/2. Göttingen: Vandenhoeck & Ruprecht, 1923.

Stipp, Hermann-Josef. *Das masoretische und alexandrinische Sondergut des Jeremiabuches: Textgeschichtlicher Rang, Eigenarten, Triebkräfte*. OBO 136. Fribourg: Universitätsverlag; Göttingen: Vandenhoeck & Ruprecht, 1994.

———. *Jeremia, der Tempel, und die Aristokratie: Die patrizische (schafanidische) Redaktion des Jeremiabuches*. Waltrop: Spenner, 2000.

Streck, Maximilian. *Assurbanipal und die letzten assyrischen Könige bis zum Untergang Niniveh's, II. Teil: Texte*. VAB 7.2. Leipzig: Hinrichs, 1916.

Sundberg, Albert C. "Reexamining the Formation of the Old Testament Canon." *Int* 42 (1988): 78–82.

Sweeney, Marvin A. *I & II Kings*. OTL. Louisville: Westminster John Knox, 2007.

Tadmor, Hayyim. "Autobiographical Apology in the Royal Assyrian Literature." Pages 36–57 in *History, Historiography, and Interpretation: Studies in Biblical and Cuneiform Languages*. Edited by H. Tadmor and M. Weinfeld. Jerusalem: The Hebrew University Magnes Press, 1984.

Talmon, Shemaryahu. "The Textual Study of the Bible—A New Outlook." Pages 321–400 in *Qumran and the History of the Biblical Text*. Edited by F. M. Cross and S. Talmon. Cambridge, Mass.: Harvard University Press, 1975.

Talshir, Zipora. *The Alternative Story of the Division of the Kingdom: 3 Kingdoms 12:24 A–Z*. Jerusalem Biblical Studies 6. Jerusalem: Simor, 1993.

———. "The Reign of Solomon in the Making: Pseudo-Connections Between 3 Kingdoms and Chronicles." *VT* 50 (2000): 233–49.

Talstra, Eep. *Solomon's Prayer: Synchrony and Diachrony in the Composition of I Kings 8, 14–61*. CBET 3. Kampen: Kok Pharos, 1993.

Tertel, Hans Jürgen. *Text and Transmission: An Empirical Model for the Literary Development of Old Testament Narratives*. BZAW 221. Berlin: de Gruyter, 1994.

Tigay, Jeffrey H. "Conflation as a Redactional Technique." Pages 61–83 in *Empirical Models for Biblical Criticism*. Edited by J. H. Tigay. Philadelphia: University of Pennsylvania Press, 1985.

Tigay, Jeffrey H., ed. *Empirical Models for Biblical Criticism*. Philadelphia: University of Pennsylvania Press, 1985.

———. *The Evolution of the Gilgamesh Epic*. Philadelphia: University of Pennsylvania Press, 1982.

Toorn, Karel van der. *Scribal Culture and the Making of the Hebrew Bible*. Cambridge, Mass.: Harvard University Press, 2007.

Tov, Emanuel. "Copying of a Biblical Scroll." *JRH* 26 (2002): 189–209.

———. *The Greek and Hebrew Bible: Collected Essays on the Septuagint*. VTSup 72. Leiden: Brill, 1999.

———. "The Literary History of the Book of Jeremiah in Light of Its Textual History." Pages 215–37 in *Empirical Models for Biblical Criticism*. Edited by J. H. Tigay. Philadelphia: University of Pennsylvania Press, 1985.

———. *Scribal Practices and Approaches Reflected in the Texts Found in the Judean Desert*. STDJ 54. Leiden: Brill, 2004.

———. *Textual Criticism of the Hebrew Bible*. 2d ed. Minneapolis: Fortress, 2001.

———. "The Writing of Early Scrolls: Implications for the Literary Analysis of Hebrew Scripture." *DSD* 13 (2006): 339–347.

Trebolle Barrera, Julio C. "Origins of a Tripartite Old Testament Canon." Pages 128–45 in *The Canon Debate*. Edited by L. M. McDonald and J. A. Sanders. Boston: Hendrickson, 2002.

Turkanik, Andrzej S. *Of Kings and Reigns: A Study of Translation Technique in the Gamma/Gamma Section of 3 Reigns (1 Kings)*. FAT 2/30. Tübingen: Mohr Siebeck, 2008.

Ulrich, Eugene. "4QJosh[a]." Pages 143–52 in *Qumran Cave 4.IX: Deuteronomy, Joshua, Judges, Kings*. Edited by E. Ulrich, F. M. Cross, S. W. Crawford, J. A. Duncan, P. W. Skehan, E. Tov, and J. C. Trebolle Barrera. DJD 14. Oxford: Clarendon, 1995.

———. "4QJoshua[a] and Joshua's First Altar in the Promised Land." Pages 89–104 in *New Qumran Texts and Studies: Proceedings of the First Meeting of the International Organization for Qumran Studies, Paris 1992*. Edited by G. J. Brooke and F. García Martínez. Leiden: Brill, 1994.

———. "The Canonical Process, Textual Criticism, and Latter Stages in the Composition of the Bible." Pages 267–91 in *Sha'arei Talmon: Studies in the Bible, Qumran, and the Ancient Near East Presented to Shemaryahu Talmon*. Edited by M. Fishbane, E. Tov, and W. W. Fields. Winona Lake: Eisenbrauns, 1992.

———. *The Dead Sea Scrolls and the Origins of the Bible*. Studies in the Dead Sea Scrolls and Related Literature. Grand Rapids: Eerdmans, 1999.

———. "Double Literary Editions of Biblical Narratives and Reflections on Determining the Form to be Translated." Pages 101–16 in *Perspectives on the Hebrew Bible: Essays in*

Honor of Walter J. Harrelson. Edited by J. L. Crenshaw. Macon, Ga.: Mercer University Press, 1988.

———. "Multiple Literary Editions: Reflections Toward a Theory of the History of the Biblical Text." Pages 78–105 in *Current Research and Technological Developments on the Dead Sea Scrolls: Conference on the Texts from the Judean Desert, Jerusalem, 30 April 1995.* Edited by D. W. Parry and S. D. Ricks. STDJ 20. Leiden: Brill, 1996.

———. "The Non-attestation of a Tripartite Canon in 4QMMT." *CBQ* 65 (2003): 202–14.

———. "The Notion and Definition of Canon." Pages 45–59 in *The Canon Debate.* Edited by L. M. McDonald and J. A. Sanders. Boston: Hendrickson, 2002.

———. "Pluriformity in the Biblical Text, Text Groups, and Questions of Canon." Pages 23–41 in *The Madrid Qumran Congress: Proceedings of the International Congress on the Dead Sea Scrolls, Madrid 18–21 March, 1991.* Edited by J. Trebolle Barrera and L. Vegas Montaner. STDJ 11. Leiden: Brill, 1992.

———. *The Qumran Text of Samuel and Josephus.* HSM 19. Missoula, Mont.: Scholars Press, 1978.

Van Seters, John. *Abraham in History and Tradition.* New Haven: Yale University Press, 1975.

———. *The Edited Bible: The Curious History of the "Editor" in Biblical Criticism.* Winona Lake: Eisenbrauns, 2006.

———. *In Search of History: History in the Ancient World and the Origin of Biblical History.* New Haven: Yale University Press, 1983.

———. "An Ironic Circle: Wellhausen and the Rise of Redaction Criticism." *ZAW* 115 (2003): 487–500.

———. *The Life of Moses: The Yahwist as Historian in Exodus–Numbers.* Louisville: Westminster John Knox; Kampen: Kok Pharos, 1994.

———. *The Pentateuch: A Social Science Commentary.* Trajectories. Sheffield: Sheffield Academic Press, 1999.

———. *Prologue to History: The Yahwist as Historian in Genesis.* Louisville: Westminster John Knox; Zurich: Theologischer Verlag, 1992.

———. "The Report of the Yahwist's Demise Has Been Greatly Exaggerated!" Pages 143–57 in *A Farewell to the Yahwist? The Composition of the Pentateuch in Recent European Interpretation.* Edited by T. B. Dozeman and K. Schmid. SBLSymS 34. Atlanta: Society of Biblical Literature, 2006.

Vanoni, Gottfried. "Beobachtungen zur deuteronomistischen Terminologie in 2 Kön 23,25–25,30." Pages 357–362 in *Das Deuteronomium: Entstehung, Gestalt und Botschaft.* Edited by N. Lohfink. BETL 68. Leuven: Leuven University Press and Peeters, 1985.

Vaux, Roland de. *Ancient Israel: Its Life and Institutions.* London: Darton, Longman & Todd, 1961.

Veijola, Timo. *Das fünfte Buch Mose: Deuteronomium Kapitel 1,1–16,17.* ATD 8.1. Göttingen: Vandenhoeck & Ruprecht, 2004.

Veijola, Timo. *Königtum in der Beurteilung der deuteronomistischen Historiographie.* AASF 198. Helsinki: Suomalainen Tiedeakatemia, 1977.

Veldhuis, Niek. *Elementary Education at Nippur: The Lists of Trees and Wooden Objects.* Groningen: Styx, 1997.

Vermeylen, Jacques. "L'affaire de veau d'or (Ex 32–34): Une clé pour la 'question deuteronomiste'?" *ZAW* 97 (1985): 1–23.

Wagenaar, Jan A. "The Cessation of the Manna: Editorial Frames for the Wilderness Wandering in Ex 16,35 and Josh 5,10–12." *ZAW* 112 (2000): 192–209.

Waltke, Bruce K. "How We Got the Hebrew Bible: The Text and Canon of the Old Testament." Pages 27–50 in *The Bible At Qumran: Text, Shape, and Interpretation.* Edited by P. W. Flint. Studies in the Dead Sea Scrolls and Related Literature. Grand Rapids: Eerdmans, 2001.

Watts, James W., ed. *Persia and Torah: The Theory of Imperial Authorization of the Pentateuch.* SBLSymS 17. Atlanta: Society of Biblical Literature, 2001.

Weimar, Peter. "Das Goldene Kalb: Redaktionsgeschichtliche Erwägungen zu Ex 32." *BN* 38–39 (1987): 117–60.

———. "Struktur und Composition der priesterschriftlichen Geschichtsdarstellung." *BN* 23 (1984): 81–134; 24 (1985): 138–62.

Weinfeld, Moshe. *Deuteronomy and the Deuteronomic School.* Oxford: Oxford University Press, 1972.

Weippert, Helga. "Die 'deuteronomistischen' Beurteilungen der Könige von Israel und Juda und das Problem der Redaktion der Königebücher." *Bib* 53 (1972): 301–39.

Weippert, Manfred. "Fragen des israelitischen Geschichtsbewusstseins." *VT* 23 (1973): 415–42.

———. "Synkretismus und Monotheismus: Religionsinterne Konfliktbewältigung im alten Israel." Pages 143–79 in *Kultur und Konflikt.* Edited by J. Assmann and D. Harth. Frankfurt: Suhrkamp, 1990.

Weiss, Meir. *The Bible From Within: The Method of Total Interpretation.* Jerusalem: The Hebrew University Magnes Press, 1984. Hebrew original: 1962.

Weiss, Raphael. "Chiasm in the Bible." Pages 259–73 in *Studies in the Text and Language of the Bible.* Edited by R. Weiss. Jerusalem: The Hebrew University Magnes Press, 1981.

Wellhausen, Julius. *Die Composition des Hexateuchs.* 4th ed. Berlin: de Gruyter, 1963; originally published 1876–1878; 2d ed. 1889; 3d ed. 1899.

———. *Prolegomena to the History of Israel.* Translated by J. S. Black and A. Menzies. Edinburgh: Black, 1885.

Werf, Hendrik van der. *The Chansons of the Troubadours and Trouvères: A Study of the Melodies and their Relation to the Poems.* Utrecht: Oosthoek, 1972.

Wesselius, Jan-Wim. "The Functions of Lists in Primary History." Pages 83–89 in *"Basel und Bibel": Collected Communications to the XVIIth Congress of the International Organization for the Study of the Old Testament, 2001.* Edited by M. Augustin and H. M. Niemann. BEATAJ 51. Frankfurt: Lang, 2004.

———. *The Origin of the History of Israel: Herodotus's Histories as Blueprint for the First Books of the Bible.* JSOTSup 345. Sheffield: Sheffield Academic Press, 2002.

Westermann, Claus. *Genesis 1–11: A Commentary.* Translated by J. J. Scullion. Minneapolis: Augsburg, 1984.

Wette, Wilhelm Martin L. de. *Beiträge zur Einleitung in das Alte Testament.* 2 vols. Halle: Schimmelpfenning, 1806–1807.

Willi, Thomas. *Die Chronik als Auslegung: Untersuchungen zur literarischen Gestaltung der historischen Überlieferung Israels.* FRLANT 106. Göttingen: Vandenhoeck & Ruprecht, 1972.

Williamson, Hugh. "The Death of Josiah and the Continuing Development of the Deuteronomic History." *VT* 26 (1982): 351–61.

———. "Reliving the Death of Josiah: A Reply to C. T. Begg." *VT* 37 (1987): 9–15.

———. "A Response to A. Graeme Auld." *JSOT* 8 (1983): 36–37.

———. "Review of A. Graeme Auld, *Kings Without Privilege.*" *VT* 46 (1996): 553–55.

Willis, Timothy M. "The Text of 1 Kings 11:43–12:3." *CBQ* 53 (1991): 37–44.

Witte, Markus. *Die biblische Urgeschichte: Redaktions- und theologiegeschichtliche Beobachtungen zu Genesis 1:1–11:26*. BZAW 265. Berlin: de Gruyter, 1998.

——. "Die Gebeine Josefs." Pages 139–56 in *Auf dem Weg zur Endgestalt von Genesis bis II Regum*. Edited by M. Beck and U. Schorn. BZAW 370. Berlin: de Gruyter, 2006.

——. "Wie Simson in den Kanon kam–Redaktionsgeschichtliche Beobachtungen zu Jdc 13–16." *ZAW* 112 (2000): 526–49.

Witte, Markus, Konrad Schmid, Doris Prechel, and Jan Christian Gertz, eds. *Die deuteronomistischen Geschichtswerke: Redaktions- und religionsgeschichtliche Perspektiven zur „Deuteronomismus"-Diskussion in Tora und Vorderen Propheten*. BZAW 365. Berlin: de Gruyter, 2006.

Woudstra, Marten H. *The Book of Joshua*. NICOT. Grand Rapids: Eerdmans, 1981.

Würthwein, Ernst. *Das erste Buch der Könige: Kapitel 1–16*. ATD 11.1. Göttingen: Vandenhoeck & Ruprecht, 1985.

——. *Die Bücher der Könige: 1.Kön 17–2.Kön 25*. ATD 11.2. Göttingen: Vandenhoeck & Ruprecht, 1984.

——. "Erwägungen zum sog. deuteronomistischen Geschichtswerk: Eine Skizze." Pages 1–11 in *Studien zum Deuteronomistischen Geschichtswerk* Edited by E. Würthwein. BZAW 227. Berlin: de Gruyter, 1994.

Wyatt, Nicholas. "Asherah." Pages 99–105 of *Dictionary of Deities and Demons in the Bible*. Edited by K. van der Toorn, B. Becking, and P. W. van der Horst. Leiden: Brill. 1999.

——. "Interpreting the Creation and Fall Story in Genesis 2–3." *ZAW* 93 (1981): 10–21.

Wyckoff, Chris. "Have We Come Full Circle Yet? Closure, Psycholinguistics, and Problems of Recognition with the *Inclusio*." *JSOT* 30 (2006): 475–505.

Zenger, Erich, ed. *Einleitung in das Alte Testament*. 7th ed. Kohlhammer Studienbücher Theologie 1/1. Stuttgart: Kohlhammer, 2008; 5th ed. 2004.

——. "Theorien über die Entstehung des Pentateuch im Wandel der Forschung." Pages 74–123 in *Einleitung in das Alte Testament*. Edited by E. Zenger. 7th ed. Kohlhammer Studienbücher Theologie 1/1. Stuttgart: Kohlhammer, 2008.

Zevit, Ziony. *The Religions of Ancient Israel: A Synthesis of Parallactic Approaches*. London: Continuum, 2001.

Contributor List

Christoph Berner
  Georg-August-Universität Göttingen, Germany

Erhard Blum
  Eberhard Karls Universität Tübingen, Germany

Suzanne Boorer
  Murdoch University, Australia

David M. Carr
  Union Theological Seminary, New York, NY

Thomas B. Dozeman
  United Theological Seminary, Dayton, OH

Cynthia Edenburg
  The Open University, Israel

Michael Konkel
  Lehrstuhl fuer Altes Testament, Germany

Christoph Levin
  Ludwig-Maximilians-Universitaet Muenchen, Germany

Thomas C. Römer
  Université de Lausanne, Switzerland

Konrad Schmid
  Universität Zürich, Switzerland

Felipe Blanco Wißmann
  Nieder-Roden, Germany

INDEX OF MODERN AUTHORS

Index of Ancient Sources

1 Kings

1	132, 135
1-2	133
1-12	5, 7, 211, 212, 213, 224, 237, 238, 240
2:3	90, 252
3	245
3:1	239
3:2-15	90, 94, 95
3:4b	77
3:5	78
3:5a	77
3:8	77, 78
3:16-28	84
4:6b	226
4:6b-7	86
5	211
5-9	253
5:6-8	231
5:7-8	86
5:15-26	226
5:20	226
5:20aa	226
5:22	226
5:22b	226
5:23a	226
5:23b	226
5:24	226
5:27	211, 225, 226, 227, 235, 237
5:27-28	86, 225
5:27-32	212, 224, 225, 227, 229, 234, 235, 237
5:28aa	237
5:28aa1	226
5:28aa2β	226
5:28b	226
5:29-30	225
5:30	235
5:29-31	225

5:32	225
5:32b	225, 226, 237
5:9-14	84
6-8	42
6:1	39
6:4-18	84
6:25-27	84
6:28-32	84
6:34-7:12	84
7:8	239
8	24, 28, 90, 243
8:1-11	48
8:5b	78
8:8	256
8:9	88, 90, 177, 182
8:16	88, 90, 246
8:21	88, 90
8:18	134
8:27	134
8:32	51
8:33-34	183
8:43	51
8:44	246
8:48	246
8:51	90
8:53	90
8:56	90
8:56	90
9	231, 238, 239
9-10	38
9:1b	230
9:13	256
9:15	227, 228, 230, 237
9:15-19	228
9:15-22	230, 235
9:15-23	224, 226, 227, 228
9:15-24	212
9:16	239
9:16-17aa	228

1 Chronicles

2 CHRONICLES

1:1-13	94, 95
1:6	77
1:7a	77
1:9	77, 78
5:10	88, 90
6:5	88, 90
7:22	88
8	231
8:4	231, 238
8:6	231, 238
8:9	229
8:9b	229
10:4	86, 235
10:9-11	235
10:14	235
10:15	86
11	88, 90
16:4	231
17:12	231
25:4	88
32:28	231
33:8	88
34:15, 20	88
34:15, 18, 21, 24	88
34:30-31	88

EZRA

9-10	207

NEHEMIAH

8:1	142
8-9	207

JOB

1:1	136
31:40b	58

PSALMS

18	133
27	161
32:5	160
34:15	161
37:3	161
72:20	58
78	42
80	42
95	42
105	42
106	42
114	42
136	42

PROVERBS

25:1	58

ISAIAH

1:1	26
1:7	36
1:8-9	37
3:14f	216
7	243
7:11	60
8:1-4	243
10:2	215
11:4	216
29:15	60
36-39	36
44:9-20	250
45:20	250

JEREMIAH

5:11	243
7:22-28	53, 181
7:31	246

CPSIA information can be obtained at www.ICGtesting.com
Printed in the USA
LVOW101139270112

265829LV00002B/20/P